Diane Caryl Slifer Scott

FLIVVERIN' WITH YOU

The True Story of a Great Love

in Letters

BLUE BLAZE BOOKS™

Copyright © 2014 by Diane Caryl Slifer Scott

All rights reserved. This book or any portion thereof may not be reproduced or used in any manner whatsoever without the express written permission of the publisher except for the use of brief quotations in a book review.

First Printing 2014

ISBN 978-0-9913288-0-2

Blue Blaze Books
Newark, DE 19711

BlueBlazeBooks.com

"And I think, how I miss you two. I was used to turning to you. It was heaven. Always to have you two to turn to in despair, in joy. There you were: strong, funny. Two rocks. What you did for me — wow! What luck, to be born out of love and to live in an atmosphere of warmth and interest."

— Katharine Hepburn

Dedicated with love

to Ken and Caryl Slifer's grandchildren
Ellen, Wendy, Kevin, Tim, and Lisa

Introduction

In the late summer of 1923, between his freshman and sophomore years at Bucknell University, 17-year-old Kenneth Slifer of Woodbury, New Jersey, set out for a camping trip with his older friend and high school YMCA leader, Roy Clement. They were heading for Niagara Falls – 500 miles away – in Clem's flivver, more than likely a black Model T Ford.

The campers had planned a stop in Buffalo, New York – not far from the falls – to visit Rolland Dutton, one of Ken's fraternity brothers (later also his roommate). When they arrived at the Dutton home, the travelers were welcomed by Rolland (rhymes with Holland) and his family – his parents, the Rev. E. Herbert and Mabel B. Dutton . . . and his younger sister Caryl, who may have sparked more than a casual interest in Ken a few months earlier by visiting the old Susquehanna River town of Lewisburg, Pennsylvania, to attend her brother's freshman House Party weekend at Bucknell.

The travelers eagerly accepted an invitation to stay at the Duttons' for dinner. For the rest of his life, Ken enjoyed recalling Clem's pronouncement, delivered while the young men were washing up before their meal: "Slifer, you're in love!"

Ken and Clem drove no farther and returned to New Jersey a few days later.

Ken and his hosts were not total strangers. When the nineteenth century rounded into the twentieth, Herbert Dutton and Mabel Batten were students at Bucknell, as were Ken's parents, Rob Slifer and Edna Shires. Family lore holds that the two families once had a picnic together near the Slifers' home in New Jersey, when all the children were small. But there were no other get-togethers until their two sons became college classmates.

Ken, Caryl, and Rolland at Crystal Beach on Lake Erie, September 1923

Both Caryl and Ken were born in 1905 and finished high school in 1922. But because keeping two children in college at once on a Baptist minister's salary was going to be difficult at best for her father, Caryl postponed further education after graduating from Buffalo's Masten Park High School in order to work for a year before entering Bucknell in the fall of 1923. Over the next four years, Caryl held a variety of jobs in Lewisburg – tutoring, working for professors, giving typing lessons, even hairdressing – and during the final two years, she was head waitress in the women's dining room.

Although Ken was known throughout his life for beautiful messages of appreciation, which he composed at every opportunity, no letters exist from the summer of 1923. Once Caryl arrived at Bucknell, however, a tentative correspondence began, even though she and Ken, having just turned 18 (in June and September, respectively), lived only a few blocks apart on the campus. Gradually their love grew, and letters became ever more frequent. Following Ken's graduation in 1926, they wrote to each other nearly every day – sometimes twice in a single day – until their wedding on September 4, 1928. Most of their letters traveled back and forth between Woodbury and Buffalo, but the young lovers also wrote faithfully from anywhere they might be traveling.

The first communication that survives from their five years of correspondence was postmarked in Lewisburg on October 8, 1923, and addressed to:

Miss Caryl Dutton
Taylor St.
Town

Throughout the 1920s, within the jurisdiction of any given post office, no further geographical designation was needed beyond the street address, and "Town" was sufficient to indicate Lewisburg. First-class postage was 2¢, a cost that remained unchanged for decades. (During my own college years at Bucknell in the 1950s, a letter required only 3¢.) Long-distance telephone calls, however, were prohibitively expensive and were not even considered. For emergencies, a hand-delivered telegram usually sufficed. And even they required careful planning, because the sender was charged by the word, and the messenger boy expected a tip.

Ken's first envelope to Caryl, as was often the case during the early years of their correspondence, boasts one of his meticulous drawings, designed to impress the recipient. Later, the frequency of his epistles would make that labor-intensive effort impossible. One of Ken's work-your-way-through-college businesses was selling beautifully decorated envelopes to fellow students, at 25¢ each, for letters to special people. No two illustrations were ever quite identical, and he constantly devised new designs. Ken's larger productions included paintings on students' yellow rain slickers, as well as posters, banners, and placards advertising campus events. Friends entering Ken's dorm room were instructed to walk carefully — some sort of artwork was always spread out on the floor or hanging to dry.

Both Ken and Caryl mentioned saving every single letter, but many are now missing. Those that remain, along with a number of inexplicably empty envelopes, had, over many years and moves, been jumbled into a small cardboard box. In 1987, my daughter Wendy helped the Slifers sort through a lifetime of belongings to prepare for their move to the farm in Salem, New Jersey, that my husband, Vic Scott, and I called home for many years. During those weeks of downsizing, Wendy was entrusted by her grandmother with that precious box.

Sometime during the Slifers' marriage, Ken artistically arranged a selection of Caryl's favorite decorated envelopes in a large frame. His letters were still inside. Caryl promised Wendy that treasure would pass to her as well. I'm grateful for Wendy's willingness to dismantle such a family keepsake in order to make the record that follows as complete as possible.

I have a poignant memory from September 1991. After 63 years of marriage, Caryl was dying in our home while Ken grieved helplessly. Two Hospice nurses, changing shifts, stood before the large framed fan of envelopes hanging in the living room of my parents' upstairs apartment. I overheard the departing nurse explaining Ken's artwork to the nurse who had just arrived. With awe in her voice, she said, "Just look at all these beautiful love letters he wrote her!"

In addition to painting envelopes, Ken often added drawings to illustrate his letters. Sometimes he printed in increasingly large letters to add emphasis, or he appended marginal notes, using astonishingly minuscule lettering.

When Vic and I retired from New Jersey to North Carolina in 1999, I planned to spend perhaps one summer organizing and reading my parents' courtship letters and taking lots of notes. I wanted to learn more about my wonderful mother and dad during their teenage years, long before I was born. And I hoped to write something about those extraordinary people to pass on to their grandchildren.

The task I expected to complete in a few months has taken thirteen years. Along the way, I came across the quotation that graces the epigraph page in the front of this book; written with her parents in mind, it is from Academy Award-winning actress Katharine Hepburn, who died in 2003 at the age of 96. I have since read her words again and again. They motivated me to continue.

Simply chronologizing this material took months. Few letters are dated, except by the postmarks on the envelopes. Dates largely were unnecessary in the 1920s because envelopes were hand stamped with the name of the city and state from which they were sent; the month, day, and year; and the time of day (with the time reset every half hour). The Slifers' twice-a-day mail deliveries usually required two days or less in transit, so headings on the letters simply say "late Sunday night" or "Tuesday afternoon." There was just one mail delivery on Saturdays – and around Christmas, sometimes another on Sundays.

When I found a postmark to be blurry – or worse yet, if the envelope itself was missing – only lengthy study of a letter's contents, and later comparison with others, made it possible to assign a reasonably accurate date. I also had to maintain a running list of what the calendar date might be for "Wednesday morning," which seemed to be the spring of 1925 – or perhaps it was 1926.

I learned to handle the letters cautiously. Since they rarely show calendar dates, I dared not separate any from their postmarked envelopes. And because they are now nearly a century old, I've had to slide them in and out with infinite care. Stationery is whatever paper those young people had at hand; some sheets are flimsy, fragile, and yellowed. Often, simply unfolding meant reaching for more mending tape.

I had no idea their letters were so long. If you write to your love nearly every day – occasionally twice a day, sometimes one letter in the afternoon and another that same evening – how much is there to say? A lot, I learned. And they often filled a minimum of two pages, usually three or four – or more. Whenever I could set aside a chunk of time, I rarely was able to complete note-taking on more than three letters. Nor had I an inkling how many yellowed and crumbling envelopes had been crammed into that small box. Despite months of disappointing time gaps, almost exactly four hundred letters survive from the Slifers' five-year courtship.

Because this account could have become impossibly long, I spent hours making difficult editorial choices as to how much I could cut out and still convey this compelling story.

Penmanship is good – Ken's is truly beautiful and precise – but the ink has faded. After their respective graduations in 1926 and 1927, Ken and Caryl held office jobs, which accounts for the times they used a typewriter. Although they agreed that "a typewriter is an awfully cold instrument" for love letters and preferred to avoid it, fortunately for me, those letters remain fairly clear.

Occasionally, I altered punctuation for clarity; but often when I typed in the Slifers' spellings – impeccable in the 1920s, but sometimes no longer used – my computer insisted they were incorrect. Some spellings vary: I found counselor, counsellor, and councillor, and decided to keep them all. Eventually, a box appeared on my screen:

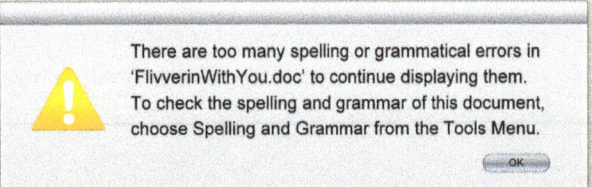

Following that announcement, a great variety of words the Slifers used, like "s'pose" and "thot," stopped being automatically underlined in red.

The scope and use of their vocabularies, especially considering their ages, is impressive; I had to reach for the dictionary to check on "benignantly," "chirography," and "osculation." But English keeps changing. Words and expressions Ken and Caryl liked — "splendid" is a favorite, along with "wholesouled," "whelming," and "a prince of a chap" — now sound quaint. Sometimes they misspelled to be silly — Ken liked to call Caryl's hometown "Boofalo" and both frequently began sentences with "Yes'm" or "No'm." Both writers condensed words to save time (thoroly, brot, tho). So words that appear to be typos may just be the writers' idiosyncrasies.

One thing I had not anticipated was the overwhelming emotion I experienced when reading the private thoughts of my parents as teenagers in love. I found myself becoming an intimate part of the lives of those dear folks. I yearned to make comments and to ask questions. Sometimes I wanted to cheer. I couldn't wait to see what would happen next — and was keenly disappointed from time to time on discovering that the next few letters had disappeared.

Whenever I completed a few hours of time-travel with those young people I so loved, it was hard to return home. Events in my 21st century life often caused interruptions for months at a time, and the work was exhausting. All the while, however, I remained grateful that email — ephemeral by nature — was not available in their day. Given their penchant for constant communication, I am sure they would have embraced it, and the legacy of their correspondence would have been the poorer for it.

Along the way, I learned fascinating trivia about life in the 1920s. For instance, when flivvering, a trip that featured nine flat tires and included hand-pumping one four times was not unusual. In 1923, many radio stations signed off at midnight, "when the radio men say their last words." Neither the Slifer nor the Dutton family had yet bought a radio. When Caryl and her father shared a cross-country train trip in 1925, she enjoyed her first meal in a dining car: "Of course, the prices were awfully high, but we managed to get a respectable breakfast for 50¢ apiece." Doctors and dentists made house calls. In 1927, a suitable gift for Caryl's hope chest was "a cute little apron and dusting cap to match." And, in 1928, Ken's overnight stay in a hospital, which included minor surgery and four meals, was $5. He had expected to pay at least $15!

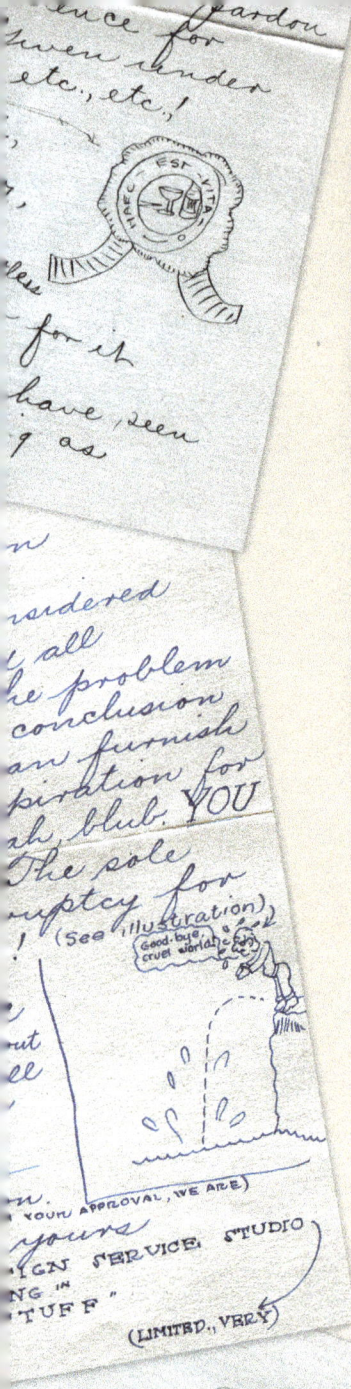

Caryl and her mother, Mabel, "supervise" while Rolland works on their flivver.

Caryl and Ken were married in Buffalo on Tuesday evening, September 4, 1928. Caryl became a bride at 23, and Ken turned 23 on September 19. Saturday weddings were not traditional then, since most people worked a five-and-a-half- or six-day week. The bride and groom had decided against holding their ceremony on Monday, September 3, because several relatives and close friends would be unavailable on Labor Day

Hoping to arrive in Buffalo on Sunday night, September 2, Ken spent the last day of August frantically writing ads he had to finish at the Philadelphia advertising agency N. W. Ayer & Son before he could depart. His two-week vacation, for their wedding and honeymoon, was to begin on Saturday. He planned to leave Woodbury early on the morning of September 1 – in the flivver borrowed from his friend Clem – to drive more than 450 miles to Buffalo, some of the way over poorly maintained roads where flat tires and breakdowns were common. With luck, it would be only a two-day trip.

Introduction • xi

Ken arrived in time for the wedding, which was just one of the special moments in what was to become a lifelong love affair with Caryl. But their union signalled the end of the almost daily correspondence.

In May 2008, I finished making notes on the last courtship letter. Written five days before the wedding, Ken's letter was addressed to Caryl at the Woodward Avenue address in Buffalo where he had sent hundreds of letters over the years. Undated as usual, this last letter was written "Thursday evening," in Woodbury. It was postmarked at 11:30 the next morning, August 31, 1928, in Philadelphia, before being routed northward to Buffalo.

Writing on his final Thursday evening as a bachelor, Ken said, "This is probably going to be the last letter I'll write you for a long long time. I wish I could make it so loving and eloquent that you'd treasure it always."

That wish was granted.

(At home, walk in)

Dear Ken,

You surely did perform well, and I am very grateful to you for your trouble in getting the ___ for me. Of course I shall not inqu___ into the tricks of your trade. I a___ much pleased to have anott___ to decorate my memor___ the means by whic___ It is surely ___ famil___

___hy is a nice girl
___ncer, but ___ (again).
___sn't Miss Caryl
___ofalo, by any means!
___ear in Paris and her
___ow skirt we managed
___ing well enough together
___ stood this time ___
___ch better
___ by appr___

MISS CARYL DUTTO[N]
TAYLOR ST.
TOWN

Mis___
3___
___odward Ave.
Buffalo, N.Y

1923

At age 11, on the sudden death of his beloved father, Rob Slifer, Ken assumed a serious Man-of-the-House attitude toward his mother and little sister Roberta ("Bobby"); thus, early on he exhibited personal independence and maturity. The verdict pronounced in Buffalo by Ken's friend Clem couldn't have been more right. Ken had fallen head-over-heels for Caryl. His feelings may have been reciprocated, but Caryl, the daughter of a preacher and a little sister herself, generally deferred to her parents' conservative views on young folks' relationships. Ken and Caryl, both active in their respective Baptist churches, may have had some correspondence the summer before she arrived at Bucknell. But even later, as letters became more frequent, each was instructed not to write too often. More than once a week was seen as too often!

Over time, those restrictions gradually were relaxed. But despite Ken's increasingly romantic outpouring, it took Caryl two years to acknowledge frankly in her epistles a love that had been growing inside her for a very long time . . . and to apologize to Ken for her reticence.

When Caryl entered Bucknell in the fall of 1923, she boarded with "Aunt Jennie" Phillips, a close college friend of her mother's, to save money during her first two years. Dr. Llewellyn Phillips, Jennie's late husband, had been a Bucknell professor, and not long after his death, Jennie began teaching English at Bucknell. Their Taylor Street home was right on campus. From something Caryl once said, the couple seemingly had no children. Jennie probably was doing her best to fulfill what she saw as an obligation to Mabel Dutton, but to Ken and Caryl she represented nothing less than an omnipresent ogre, enforcing impossible rules to prevent their enjoying any social life. Ken's letters often refer to her as "The Missus." Twenty years later, during my childhood, the mere mention of Aunt Jennie's name elicited rolling of the eyes.

To the Lady of the House or Whom it May Concern, from SLIFER'S SPEEDY SIGN SERVICE STUDIO (LIMITED, VERY) SPECIALIZING IN SNAPPY STUFF

Monday, October 8, 1923, Lewisburg to Lewisburg

Exact dates on letters were rare, but at some later time, in a tiny penciled notation, Caryl added "Oct. 8" to this first surviving communication. Addressed to Caryl at "Taylor St., Town," it is not really a letter, but it is a wonderful example of charming, early Ken-style fun and flippancy.

Ken's plan to call on Caryl on "Saturday, Oct. 13, about 2:30 o'clock" is buried in a paragraph of circumlocution. A line drawing in the margin shows Ken diving off a cliff into the sea saying "Good-bye, cruel world!" should she turn him down. He adds a note apologizing for his "sudden spasm," and tells Caryl there's really only one sentence that matters.

We are left to hope they did have a visit on Saturday afternoon.

Wednesday, November 14, 1923 Lewisburg to Lewisburg

The heading of Ken's second letter to Caryl shows both time (11:45 p.m.) and date (almost Nov. 15) – again rare – and Ken's Old Main residence: 10 East Wing. Ken, his roommate, Dick Horter, of Collingswood, New Jersey, and later Rolland Dutton, shared that address during their years at Bucknell. It became such a home away from home that long afterward, whenever they returned to the campus for reunions, they liked to visit the room and get acquainted with its occupants. Ten East Wing also was home base for Ken's artistic endeavors and for Rolland's endless practical jokes on other students. Some of those pranks famously backfired, but from all reports, Rolland usually found a way to exact revenge.

Friday, November 30, 1923
Wilkes-Barre, Pa., to Lewisburg

Caryl describes spending Thanksgiving weekend, Wednesday to Sunday, with Aunt Jennie and Jennie's friends and relatives in the Wilkes-Barre area. Caryl "feasted lavishly on turkey" and enjoyed a movie and a drive in the country, but it is clear she would prefer to be back at Bucknell by Saturday to attend a dance with Ken and to see her brother.

Dear Caryl,

This hasty, hectic missive is intended primarily to use this envelope which I painted for you. But à propos (notice how carefully I am introducing the French which you have painstakingly taught me) your brother has conjured up some dire duty to prevent a hike on Saturday! I hereby offer my humble escort as a poor alternative. If this is too much of an imposition, don't hesitate to turn me down hard, though I shudder at the mere thought of my martyrdom if you do so.

Foolishly, feverishly, faithfully,
flippantly, etc.,
Ken

Dear Ken,

I am just as sorry as I can be that we can't get back in time to accept your invitation for Saturday night, but it would lessen our stay here by a day, and to Aunt Jennie and these folks that seems like a good deal of time. I hate to miss the dance, for I know you will have lots of fun. Thank you for the invitation anyway.

If you didn't know before that Rolland is twenty tomorrow, don't tell him I informed you, as I might lose his brotherly love. Since I won't be there to perform the deed myself, please give him a good spanking for me. Be sure 'n make 'em hard ones! He needs it.

Tell him we hope that if he is asked to sing Sunday he won't until night, for we want to hear him. Then, too, I can help him practice Sunday afternoon.

Sincerely yours,
Caryl

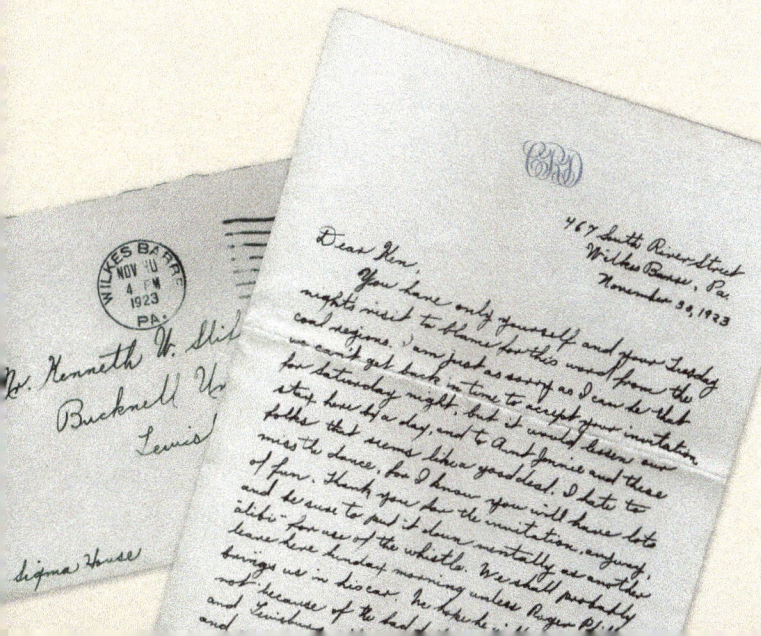

Sunday afternoon, December 16, 1923, Woodbury, N.J., to Buffalo, N.Y.

Ken and Caryl traveled to their respective homes for Christmas vacation. Caryl took a train Friday night, missing her Pi Beta Phi sorority's Christmas dance, but she arranged a date for Ken with one of her friends. Before Ken left Bucknell, he obtained an extra dance program to send to Caryl, in order to write her name on each line as his wished-for partner for every dance. Ken's trip home began early Saturday morning – train to Philadelphia, subway to the Delaware River, ferry across, and finally another train to Woodbury.

This letter also contains the first reference to "Attie," an African-American woman whose given name was Eliza Harris. Like Caryl's mother, Mabel Batten Dutton, Attie grew up in Salem County, New Jersey. She was 12 when she began working for the Batten family, around 1901, when Mabel married Herbert Dutton and left the family farm in Auburn, New Jersey, for Troy, New York, where Herbert had his first pastorate. For the rest of her life, Attie was a loved and indispensable part of the Dutton household. I was first introduced to Attie in 1934 when I was but six months old. I remember her kindness during childhood visits with my grandparents. She may have been lonely at times, but wherever the Duttons lived, they made sure she had return trips to New Jersey to visit her family.

Attie holding Diane at six months, 1934

Dear Caryl,

Not one program, but two, grace this fair white envelope! It was a dandy dance and I enjoyed it, but ~~~. Our friend Dorothy is a nice girl and a fair dancer, but ~~~ (again). And then she isn't Miss Caryl Dutton, of Boofalo, by any means! Despite her year in Paris and her very narrow skirt we managed to get along well enough together, but ~~~. At any rate, it was much better than the movies, and I thoroly appreciate your efforts in my behalf that made it possible. I hope the programs may help to alleviate any disappointment you my have experienced.

Thus far I have done my duty and attended all the church services today. Whether my spasm of religious fervor will continue, I can't say. As soon as I showed myself inside the door I was asked to be "Sir Percival" in a pageant based on "The Holy Grail." It seems that no one else wanted that part, and they left it for me – hence I'm almost afraid to go to church again. But I guess the matter will blow over before I come home again. Once before I was Ham, son of Noah, and I have never quite recovered.

Give my regards to the rest of the family, including "Attie."

As ever,
Ken

Sunday, December 23, 1923, Buffalo to Woodbury

Dear Ken,

I am grateful to you for your trouble in getting the programs for me. I am pleased to have another fair lady to decorate my memory book. It is surely a lovely picture. The whole family are still admiring her.

I am glad that you enjoyed the dance. No "but ~~~s" allowed or accepted. I certainly did hate to miss all the fun. I had rather a shock on reaching Buffalo. The Barbers and Mother and Father were there to meet me, but Mother was so sick she could hardly stand. Dr. Barber rushed her home as quickly as possible and worked over her for three hours before she could get any relief or breathe with comfort. It was the worst attack of asthma she has had, and we were much worried, but she was better the next day.

Since Mother has been so sick, she has had no time to get anything for Xmas, and I had to spend two whole days pushing and shoving my way thru the awful crowds downtown, trying to secure gifts for family and friends. It was quite a task. But Xmas will mean a lot more than ever before to me, because of my own share in hunting for the gifts.

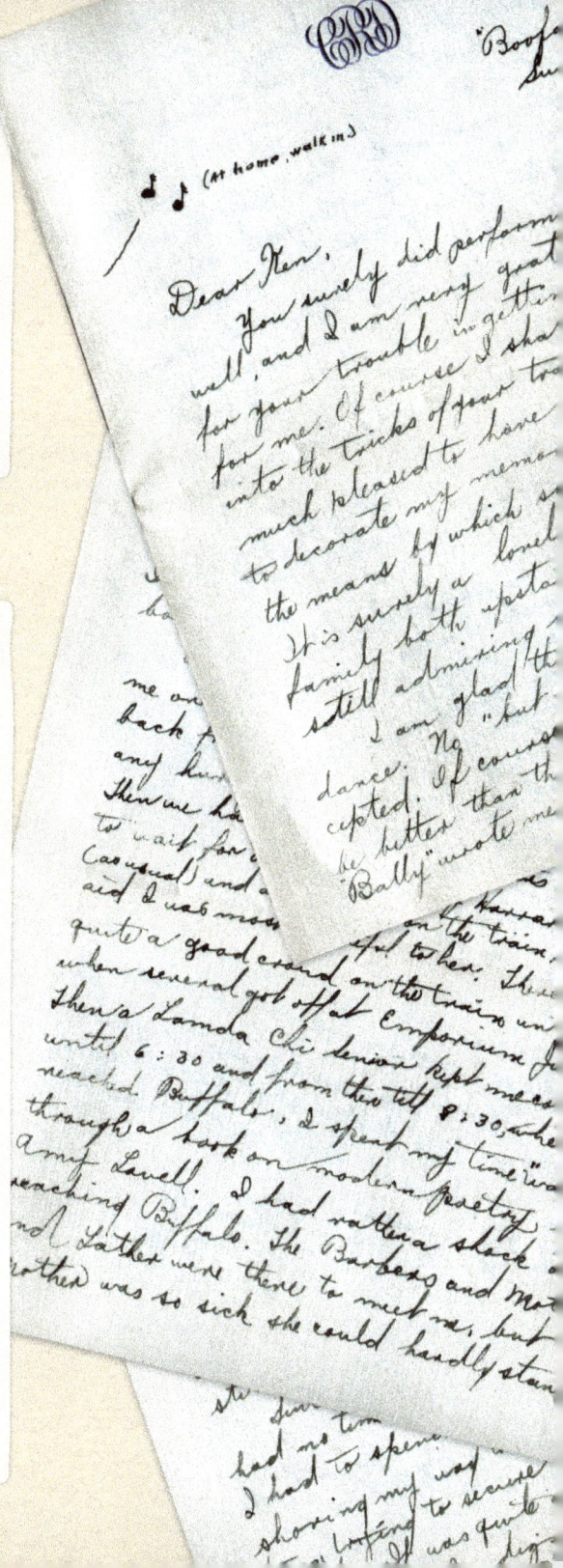

I had somewhat the same luck as you on going to church. I also was asked to take part in a play. I was so astonished. I stammered an acceptance, but the family made me back out, on plea of needing a rest. But talk about rest! Last night I had three invitations to dinner and about eight to evening affairs. Even my seeming mathematical ease didn't help me on this problem.

Today it is snowing great large flakes. Every bush and tree is loaded with white, and all outdoors is a lovely fairyland.

Please remember me to your Mother. My best wishes for a merry, merry Xmas.

Sincerely,
Caryl

Tuesday evening, December 25, 1923, Woodbury to Buffalo

Ken writes Caryl on "Xmas to be exact" in reply to a letter he received from her on Christmas Day – a regular delivery day in the 1920s. To launch this giddy missive, Ken creates a cartoon of the Delta Sigma fraternity crest, accompanied by the words, "He [the knight atop the crest, drawn with a red and swollen nose] positively has not been imbibing spiritous liquers."

Dear Caryl,

I must confess that I was worried by a whole week's absence of Buffalo correspondence, kicking myself both mentally and physically, wondering what the deuce I had done to merit such a long silence. I was all set to write a formal apology when your missive arrived this morning to end my mournful musings. Had it not been for Chance and the Fates, you might now be reading a stilted, stiff, and utterly conventional apology, instead of this foolish and nonsensical note. Be that as it may,

I, K. W. Slifer, being imbued with Yuletide spirits, do hereby grant you gracious pardon and commutation of sentence. Given under my hand and seal etc., etc.!

You really should have seen little Kenneth performing as Sir Percival, one of Kink Arthur's loyal, lengthy, lusty knights. I was clad in a gleaming coat of mail (slightly tarnished and lacking a few postage stamps), with a red cloak (full of moth holes) and a tin sword rattling playfully against my shins. Thus bedecked, I strode thru the halls of Camelot, ever and anon, clanking my head against the "rafters" of its spacious (?) banquet chamber. Enough, gazooks, of this idle mockery! Ods Bodkins, I shall hie me hence forthwith!

Yes, thank you, I had a very merry Christmas. Was out with a mob of Caryllers on Xmas Eve. In fact, I was muchly moved to Caryl!

Clem bought his lot and has plans for his house ready. He is including everything I ever wanted in a house, except a studio – sleeping-porch, big fireplace, and best of all – shower bawths!

I am afraid I can't match your lengthy list of engagements. And if I were anywhere near Boofalo there would have been 9 dates on a certain evening instead of a mere, paltry 8!

I have succeeded in completing a cover for the next "Belle Hop" [a humor magazine published by Bucknell students].

When are you heading back to Lewisburg? I'll do my darndest to meet the train. I expect to go back on New Year's Day, myself.

Foolishly & flippantly,
Ken

Between the lines of these six letters, something special had started to happen.

1924

As the year begins, Caryl, a freshman, and Ken, a sophomore, are back at Bucknell after the Christmas break. Both are 18.

Thursday, February 14, 1924
Lewisburg to Lewisburg

On Valentine's Day, Ken sends a decorated envelope, sealed with a painted heart. Tucked inside is his calling card, on which he had written: "Please realize that the modesty of my offering is due entirely to your lectures on extravagance!!!"

Thursday morning, February 28, 1924
Lewisburg to Lewisburg

The salutation in this letter is the first suggestion of a bolder approach — for which Ken will be "reproved." Nevertheless, he addresses Caryl with increasing affection and amazing inventiveness.

> Caryl, dear,
>
> Throwing convention and formality to the winds, I humbly beg, beseech, and entreat you to bestow upon me the inexpressibly delightful pleasure of accompanying or escorting your charming self to that highly elaborate and pretentious social function — termed in local parlance — "The Junior Prom," on Friday, the twenty-first of March, 1924. I am anxiously awaiting your gracious permission, and thus timorously and timidly trying to test your tractability, time, and temper (alliteration is one of my grammatical bad habits, of which there are many).
>
> Foolishly and flippantly,
> Ken

Friday, February 29, 1924
Lewisburg to Lewisburg

> Dear Ken,
>
> I must primarily reprove you for your deviation from "Houghton Mifflin's" laws of etiquette in reversing the word order of the salutation! However I shall consider forgiving you.
>
> Without extraordinary difficulty, I "caught the drift" of your elaborate and unique method of invitation, and "mille fois" do I thank you for your thot of me, yet I fear my conclusive answer will be disappointingly negative. In view of the large expense involved, and a partial consideration for my Father's and Mother's wishes, I am influenced to refuse the pleasure of an evening which I know I should greatly enjoy.
>
> Sincerely and gratefully yours,
> Caryl

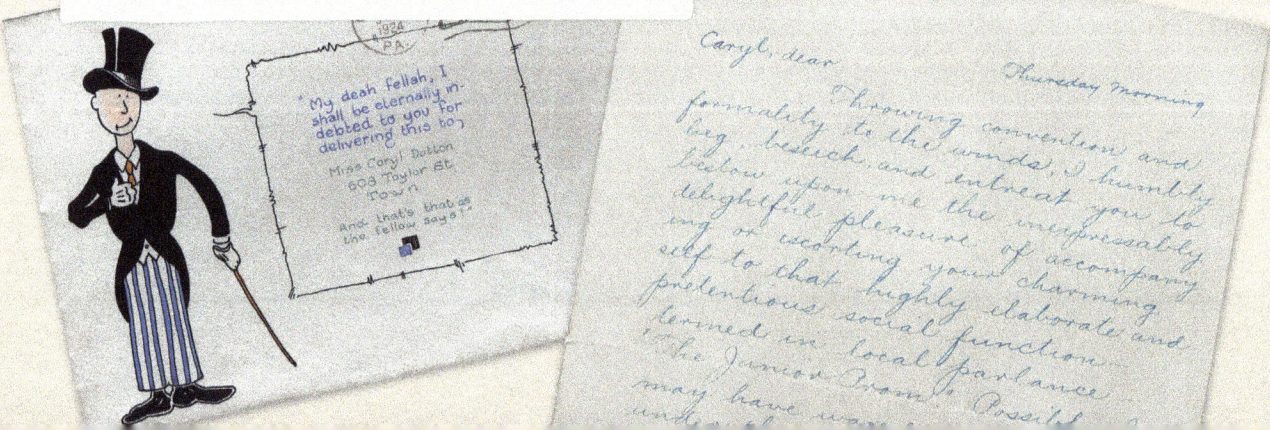

Wednesday morning, March 12, 1924
Lewisburg to Lewisburg

The entire front page of this foldover stationery shows the side view of a rotund man, striding forth. Chastened for the "Caryl, dear" greeting in his previous letter, Ken omits a salutation for the "Wednesday morning" letter inside. There is also evidence that Caryl feels constrained by her landlady in Lewisburg, as well as by her parents in Buffalo.

> Having been once reproved for deviation in salutation, my better judgment warns me against repetition. Instinct on the other hand advises me ——— ? At any rate I have been a hermit for so long that my resolution is beginning to weaken. It has been three whole days! Earnestly hoping that has been long enough for Mrs. Phillips to notice my exemplary conduct, I am
>
> A Temporarily Model Young Man

Wednesday, March 19, 1924
Lewisburg to Lewisburg

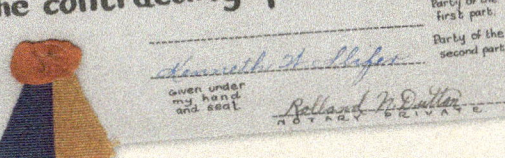

Thursday, April 17, 1924, Buffalo to Woodbury

Caryl and Ken have returned to their respective homes for Easter vacation. She sends Ken a small, beautifully engraved Easter card, the verse carefully chosen, and signed simply "Caryl."

Friday morning, April 18, 1924, Woodbury to Buffalo

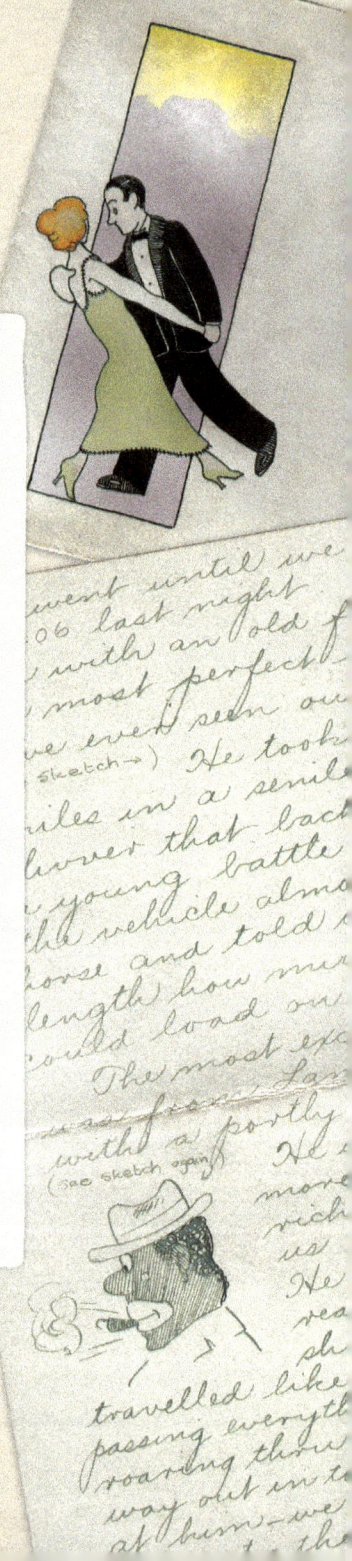

Caryl, dear,

The record of my adventures since the smoke of your train vanished in the distance is something like this . . .

Played tennis for the balance of the day, and sobbed myself sadly to sleep that night.

Wednesday morning I managed to slide thru my two classes. Then Rolland and I called on Prof. "Docky" Stewart to recite for him the mere 120 bones in the codfish – including the anterior gygapothysis, the coracoid, the parietal, the palatine, the super-occipital, and a few more. I knocked him for a row with a 9, while your brother dragged down a 7.

Once more I passed the afternoon slamming an inoffensive white sphere around the court. After a scanty supper I hied me off to bed, while Rolland "tripped the light fantastic."

I fell out of bed at 6 A.M. on Thursday morning to find a cold dismal rain drenching the campus. By the time I had succeeded in awakening the social butterfly (your brother), it had momentarily abated, and we started across the river bridge, hitchhiking to N.J., at precisely 7:30.

We walked perhaps 20 miles in all, with one stretch of 10 miles. It rained off and on nearly all day, but every time the moisture began to descend upon us, we got a lift that carried us thru it, and so it went until we reached Woodbury at 8:06 last night.

Our funniest "hop" was with an old farmer who was the most perfect "hecker" type I have ever seen outside the movies. He took us five miles in a senile, decrepit flivver that backfired like a young battle. He drove the vehicle almost like a horse, and told us at great length how much hay he could load on the thing at one time.

The most exciting lap we covered was from Lancaster into Phila. with a portly gentleman of color. He was a gentleman, too – more so than some of the rich whites who sped by us as we trudged along. He also drove one of the reasons why Henry Ford should be president. He traveled like a veritable demon, passing everything on the road and roaring thru city traffic as if he were way out in the country.

F. F.,
Ken

Monday, April 21, 1924, Buffalo to Woodbury

Dear Ken,

Just to save myself from a severe lecture from His Royal Highness, the Artist, I shall attempt some script with which you say you have hardly had a chance to become familiar!

Mother and the dress-maker are trying to sew in the growing dusk, and every two minutes or so the machine needle becomes unthreaded, and I must dash to their rescue. The folks have all been laughing over your account of experiences along the way home.

I spent parts of two days writing my final on "Coeducation." Thanks to your assistance and points on the subject, I had no trouble in finding twelve to fifteen hundred words about it.

"F. F." myself,
Caryl

Monday, May 5, 1924
Lewisburg to Lewisburg

Caryl receives an engraved invitation from Ken to the Demies' Annual Spring House Party Weekend, a three-day gala, May 8–10.

Tucked inside the envelope is Ken's calling card; underneath he has lettered **Harry F. Bradley pro tem**. Ken will be attending a convention at Allegheny College that weekend and has entrusted his friend Harry Bradley to escort Caryl to dances, picnics, or whatever social events Delta Sigma has planned.

Thursday, May 8, 1924, Lewisburg to Allegheny College, Meadville, Pennsylvania

Ken and his friend Paul Reiman are attending a Phi Delta Theta convention to request national affiliation for their local Bucknell fraternity, Delta Sigma. Members were known as "Demies," after their role model, the Greek orator Demosthenes. For nearly a century, their annual Demie Play (often a farce or parody written, directed, and performed by the brothers) has remained an important event on Bucknell's calendar, and is the university's longest-running tradition.

The Delta Sigma ("Demie") fraternity house (now Hulley House), where Ken socialized, took his meals, and got his mail, across St. George Street from the women's dorms.[1]

Dear Ken,

Thank you so much for sending the pictures so promptly for approval. I don't think they are so bad, but one might have been better if you hadn't frowned so fiercely at the camera man! The one of the stadium work is wonderfully clear. [The multi-purpose Christy Mathewson-Memorial Stadium, built in 1924 and renovated in 1989, is named in honor of Mathewson, a Bucknell student who became a Major League Baseball pitching great. He was one of the first five inducted into the National Baseball Hall of Fame, along with Babe Ruth, Ty Cobb, Honus Wagner, and Walter Johnson.]

Friday, May 9, 1924
Meadville to Lewisburg

Poor Rolland has been storming around here deploring the fates which made it rain today, when he had a date with girlfriend Mary to play tennis!

You haven't the slightest idea how hard I'm wishing for your success, and knowing the sort of representatives the Demies have sent, I am decidedly optimistic.

Yours,
Caryl

P. S. Wish you were going to be here for tonight, but thank you ever so much for making it possible for me to go. [Caryl refers to the Thursday evening festivities of the Demies' three-day house party, to which she had received the engraved invitation a few days earlier.]

Dear Caryl,

Observe, please, that I am restraining my impulses and remaining strictly formal in salutation, per your admonitions, but oh, the things I'd like to write! Our ride to Pittsburgh was quite comfortable, despite the heat, but the dirt and soot! Ugh! Next morning we continued on our way to Meadville, sloshing down to the station thru the rain.

Bucknell Memorial Stadium under construction, spring 1924.[1]

This morning we appeared before the convention, made our speeches, answered questions and presented the petitions. (Rutgers and West Virginia are also petitioning here.) Everyone was thoroly "sold," and they expected to vote immediately after dinner. At the last minute the Penn delegate blew in. The province president decided to hold off until tomorrow morning. If the Penn man had not come in I would have left immediately, caught the midnight train out of Pittsburgh, and been in Lewisburg on Saturday morning in lots of time for the dance. Dawgone the luck!!!

You limited salutations, but not farewells, hence I am Devotedly,
Ken

Wednesday, June 18, 1924
Eagles Mere Park, Pennsylvania, to
Lewisburg, forwarded to Woodbury

The first of two letters from The Forest Inn in Eagles Mere Park is headed simply "Hollywood, 9:45 P.M." Caryl has just arrived, with ten other Bucknell women. The gathering is a YWCA conference — which only becomes evident from a reference in an August letter.

Dear Ken,

We have been down by the lake, gazing at the full moon, and its tinting effect on the floating clouds. I think we are all still sane, but if my words are peculiar, blame it on a state of being moon-struck.

Thank you so much for helping me to the station and Post Office. We made fine train connections. We have a cottage ("Hollywood" by name) all to ourselves, and it is just great — large, and roomy, and comfortable. I brot your picture along and set it up on the bureau to see what would happen. It certainly did create a commotion. A man in the house, and no chaperone!

Sincerely,
Caryl

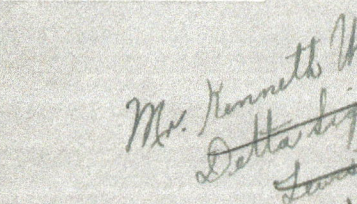

Saturday, June 21, 1924, Eagles Mere Park to Woodbury

Dear Ken,

I shocked the whole crowd today (or rather made them all jealous) by getting three letters! One of them was from home, and the folks seem to prefer coming up here Thursday night. Won't that be great? I know they'll just love this place, and I want them to see what good times we are having all together in one cottage. We can "bunk" Mother with us, and I will try to get rooms for Father and Dut.

I'm certainly grateful to you for use of the bathing cap. Mine finally arrived 2 or 3 days after I came. I've been in 3 times already and the water is fine. There's a fairly good diving board, and a better high dive. I was in at 6:30 A.M. yesterday but was too lazy this morning and slept right thru rising bell, and everything else – except breakfast, of course. It's a wonder I slept at all, or that any of us did, for late last night, we were all parked down here in the cottage living room feasting on cheese, olive, ham, and lettuce sandwiches, and all kinds of pop. Of course, I didn't indulge in the latter.

I am awfully glad you missed me. If nothing happens, and of course it won't, it will be less than a week before I make my acquaintance with your famous city [Caryl and her parents have planned a brief visit to Woodbury], and renew my acquaintance with Lizzie [the Slifers' Ford] and her Master. Change it to friendship for the latter.

Sincerely,
Caryl

Tuesday, June 24, 1924, Woodbury to Eagles Mere Park

Ken has just returned home for the summer. He doesn't hitchhike from Bucknell this trip — his mother and sister have driven to Lewisburg to visit Slifer relatives and pick him up. Ken writes in a tone a bit more bold. The stationery he often uses bears the engraved Delta Sigma crest.

Lady mine,

I have been vigorously swinging a sickle in the wilderness that used to be our lawn, consequently my hand is shaking so that I can hardly write or draw.

Dr. Hill spoke at Commencement. Having read his speech in the original manuscript for the Commencement News, I knew better than to go. Nearly two hours in length and read in a drowsy monotone – most of the audience wanted to sleep but couldn't because the benches were so hard!

Mother, Bobby, Lizzie, and I left Lewisburg and Bucknell early Thursday morning. We rolled right along and reached Philadelphia in 6 hours and 35 minutes actual traveling time. We lost an hour really, by leaving on standard time and reaching Phila. on daylight-saving time!

I commenced my tennis career at the Country Club but haven't yet paid my dues, which by a special summer concession are only $30.00! Playing in such fast company ought to be worth the cost in improving my game. At present I'm accumulating blisters on my lily-white hands that will seriously hamper my tennis technique, if I possess any such thing.

I went to the Senior Prom at Trenton Normal School on Saturday night. NEVER AGAIN! The dance was nice enough BUT ~~~ you weren't there! I felt as if my 90-mile drive were all for nothing, and I've learned my lesson now! Never again do I go to any dance without you! Once more, I swear it! [Followed by @*!#&*$=! and other symbols, labeled "business of swearing."]

I have only seen Clem once since reaching home. Of course he and the Missus [Clem's fiancée Becky, often called "Bec" or "Mrs. Clem"] are deep in the throes of preparation for their wedding. We expect to have a rehearsal this week, so that I, as best man, don't drop the ring or otherwise distinguish myself. Rehearsal tho, can't keep me from sneezing.

I had planned an original drawing for your birthday on the 26th, but I won't have time to do it justice before then. Therefore this letter must needs convey my best and sincerest wishes for a happy 19th birthday.

As ever,
Ken

Wednesday evening, July 2, 1924, Buffalo to Woodbury

Caryl, Rolland, and their parents have just returned to Buffalo after a long weekend with a one-night stopover at the Slifers'. Caryl misaddresses her letter, postmarked July 3, to Woodbury, New York; on July 4, that Post Office correctly forwards it to Woodbury, New Jersey.

Dear Ken,

Mother says that she has written to your Mother, thanking her for all the good times we had at your home. But I had such a wonderful time myself, I just have to put in my meager, inexpressive thanks to Bobby and your Mother and to you, the main instigator of the invitation. I appreciate your trusting spirit in turning over to me your room with all its valuables.

We made good time going thru Camden and Phily and were in Narberth in less than an hour. It was rather aggravating to have been in Woodbury only a day, and then be less than 20 miles away for another whole day. Finally, next morning we were delayed for two hours or so for fixing soft tires and didn't get started until 2:30.

We got to Lewisburg about 7:00. R. and Father slept in his room in E. College, and Mother and I in my room at Aunt Jennie's. Goodness! I left it in fairly good shape, ready to enter next fall, but Aunt Jennie decided it needed a thorough cleaning, and now it's a wreck! Things are piled up everywhere, all mixed up, and all my pretty trimmings torn down and boxed up. About the only things she left up were three or four dance programs. We finally reached home Tuesday night about 8:30, weary and hungry.

I started right in this morning to earn my daily bread, attempting to bring order out of the chaos of Father's mail at the office, and attend to telephone and visitors at the same time. My office hours aren't fair. We left the office tonight at 6:15! Talk about an 8-hour day! [Caryl's father was not currently serving in a pastorate. From 1919 to 1931, he was the executive of the Buffalo Baptist Union, which encompassed all the area's Baptist churches, including many that were non-English-speaking.]

Please, Ken, don't feel that you must put a painting on every envelope you send me. I just love all of them, but I appreciate the letter just as much if it hasn't a drawing, and I know they take an awful lot of time that you ought to be spending on something more important.

Sincerely,
Caryl

Friday, July 4, 1924, Woodbury to Buffalo

Ken's letter, dated simply "Bobby's Birthday" – she turns 13 – is long, full of tiny marginal notes, and illustrated with snapshots. Ken's late father, Rob Slifer, was an excellent photographer and Ken often makes use of his father's darkroom in their cellar. One picture shows Ken seated on the ground with binoculars, "Sweeping the horizon for Buffalo." An arrow drawn across the page ends at a charming photo of Caryl, captioned, "Who wouldn't sweep the horizon?" On page 4, Ken, in coat and tie, is emerging from a cave carrying a log. Caption: "G-r-r-r-r! I'm a bold, bad cave man looking for a mate."

Beauteous Damsel:

  It's been only five days since you rolled away from Horace Street, but already I'm commencing to expire from utter boredom, ennui and kindred diseases. There was one delightful reminder of your all-too-brief stay in my room. A subtle fragrance clung to everything. Here I am, writing romantic slush like the cheapest of novelists!

  Wednesday we went out to Willow Grove Park, just outside Philadelphia, to hear Sousa and his band – the best in the world. It is a big amusement park, and he plays there all summer. It was part of Bobby's birthday celebration, and, doggone it, I kept right on wishing you were along! Bobby and I "did" everything, at least as long as our funds lasted.

  Little Kenneth must address the assembled Sunday School on Sunday July 6th upon the subject "Christian Citizenship." Fancy that! Wonder if they know how long it is till I'll be a citizen! [At 18, Ken will not be able to vote for nearly two and a half years.]

Your foolish, flippant, faithful
Ken

Sunday, July 6, 1924, Woodbury to Buffalo

Ken's letter begins with "an ominous and portentous warning." He scolds Caryl for a "heinous offense." On another page, he pastes a snapshot of Caryl's brother, captioned "Come, all ye sinners here below! – The Young Salesman." Rolland is standing on the front walk at the Slifers' home in Woodbury. Destined to follow his father into the Baptist ministry, Rolland has a summer job selling bibles door-to-door. Ken gives his future brother-in-law a halo, wings, and a harp in his right hand.

O-maiden-fair-with-midnight tresses:

It was really a very, very serious crime, and one that must never happen again! NO, NEVER, NEVER, NEVER, NEVER!!!!! You addressed my valuable letter to Woodbury, New York! It went there (wherever the deuce it is), and arrived a whole day late, just barely saving me from dire death and destruction!

I appreciate your motive in offering to excuse me from decorating envelopes. You are your unselfish and gracious self in sparing me for "more important things," but don't you realize that so long as I have time, there's nothing more important to me than doing things for you that give you pleasure? I'm enclosing all the pictures that were good. Get your brother started on taking a 12-film pack of yourself – please.

I made my funny address (funny in the sense of peculiar) in Sunday School this morning and escaped without any scars of conflict. Probably they were all too near sleep to throw hymnals!

Your poor, penniless, penurious, pen-and-pencil pusher,
Ken

Wednesday, July 9, 1924, Buffalo to Woodbury

Dear Ken,

You had me all scared and nervous by your scathing denunciation in your "note." My hands shook so, I could hardly read it! I'm sorry if I kept you waiting by my slip of address. But don't you know that was a compliment? Anything good enough to be classed in New York State is pretty nice, you know!

Your new trend of salutations is certainly amusing to say the least. I couldn't possibly scold you for them, except on grounds of their excessive extremeness and absurdity, but I won't . Thank you for the illustrations and enclosed additions. You certainly are clever in ideas and arrangements.

I'm glad you spoke in church Sunday. I should love to have heard you. I know it was good! I speak next Sunday in Lafayette Ave. church. Six of us college folks, by request, are using the evening service to urge young folks to go to college. My topic: "Why Should the Christian Girl Go to College?" I'm just scared to pieces at the thot of getting up on the platform of that big church and talking to a large audience. I have spent some time preparing my speech – the family's reputation is at stake!

Mary landed in for 5 minutes a few nights ago & set Rolland's heart a-throbbin'! Poor boy! Three nights a week he comes home, pounces on his awaiting letter, & vanishes. He says tell you the Bible business is all right. Working only 3 or 4 days part time, he's sold $40 worth, making about $17 for himself.

Fourth of July we had lots of fun going to the beach along lake Erie where we went the Sat. you were here. You can imagine the memories I had! [Caryl details a trip with three families in three cars. There was swimming, baseball, and quoits on the beach, which Caryl and her partner won. Then all moved to a friend's nearby cottage being painted by Rolland – another of his summer jobs.] On a great big long table we spread out our food and feasted. Barbers and Hillings had brot loads of fireworks, and we got home about 2:30 A.M.!

Yours sincerely,
Caryl

Sunday, July 13, 1924, Woodbury to Buffalo

Eight pages long, this is an especially memorable letter – the envelope alone is stunning. Ken, who continues to paint envelopes to sell in the next semester, makes a pun in a marginal note: "Please tell me if any of the 'guilt' rubs off the envelope."

Lovely, lively, lithesome, laughsome, learned lady:

(Pardon for a moment, while I wipe off the perspiration occasioned by the above mouthful of inspiration! Some of these days, when both –spirations fail me, I'll lapse into more natural forms of expression and require another scolding. Be gentle and forgiving, please, remembering that I am only human and very, very fond of a certain fair damsel!)

I am glad the Lafayette Ave. church is to have the pleasure of hearing you speak. I'm wishing you all kinds of luck tonight, but if there's anything to mental telepathy, you won't need this letter to tell you so.

I wish you could see our place now – the Slifer estate, I mean. It looks 50% better than when you were here, for I've been working every day. Everything is trimmed up and painted, and there isn't a weed in the garden! One day isn't nearly enough for you to learn to appreciate South Jersey. Lizzie is yearning for the hand of her new mistress on the wheel. I have a hard time keeping her from heading toward Boofalo! It's all the harder because I must first restrain myself!

Bobby has had a bad attack of poison ivy on her face and hands, so that she can't write and can hardly eat anything but milk thru a tube. She vows she'll write as soon as she is physically capable.

I've been playing tennis every afternoon or evening. I stand in 7th place on the ladder, having beaten the former occupant 6-2, 6-2. I defeated the third man, 6-4, 9-7. Yesterday in the West

Jersey Tennis League tournament, six clubs entered the five events. Woodbury captured two first places – and the tournament.

Tomorrow I have an appointment with Mr. Robey at one of his several banks, concerning advertising work for him. I have plenty of drawing to do – "L'Agenda" [the Bucknell yearbook], "Belle Hop," envelopes for Miss Dutton, etc., but I get so much fun out of it all that I feel like a lazy loafer.

Clem and Mrs. Clem came around last evening, and there ensued an interesting adventure. (They'll be in their new house in a week. I stuck my card under the door the other evening, so as to be their first caller.)

For some weeks past, the papers have been full of advance propaganda for a "mammoth" Ku Klux Klan Klonvocation at Alcyon Park in Pitman [near Woodbury] on Saturday, July 12. According to the papers, there would be "thousands" of Klansmen and Kamelias (feminine of Klansman) at the Park for a big holiday. I don't know how matters stand in your section, but around here the Klan is a vital issue – everyone takes sides pro or anti-Klan. Most of its supporters are the ignorant, uneducated type of farmer or laborer – attracted largely by the mystery and secrecy of its methods. I'm completely convinced, after considerable study, the Klan is rotten to the core. Clem is even more rabid in his opposition. We make it a point to attend all their demonstrations, in order that we may argue more intelligently against them. I hadn't intended going to Pitman, but Clem and Bec called and took me along in their flivver.

We arrived just before the "gigantic" parade started. There was a great crowd of people in the park – mostly sweating, shouting, surging curiosity-seekers. The parade formed within the enclosure that surrounds the race track, and we waited outside the big gates. As we stood there talking, one of the white-robed figures took my

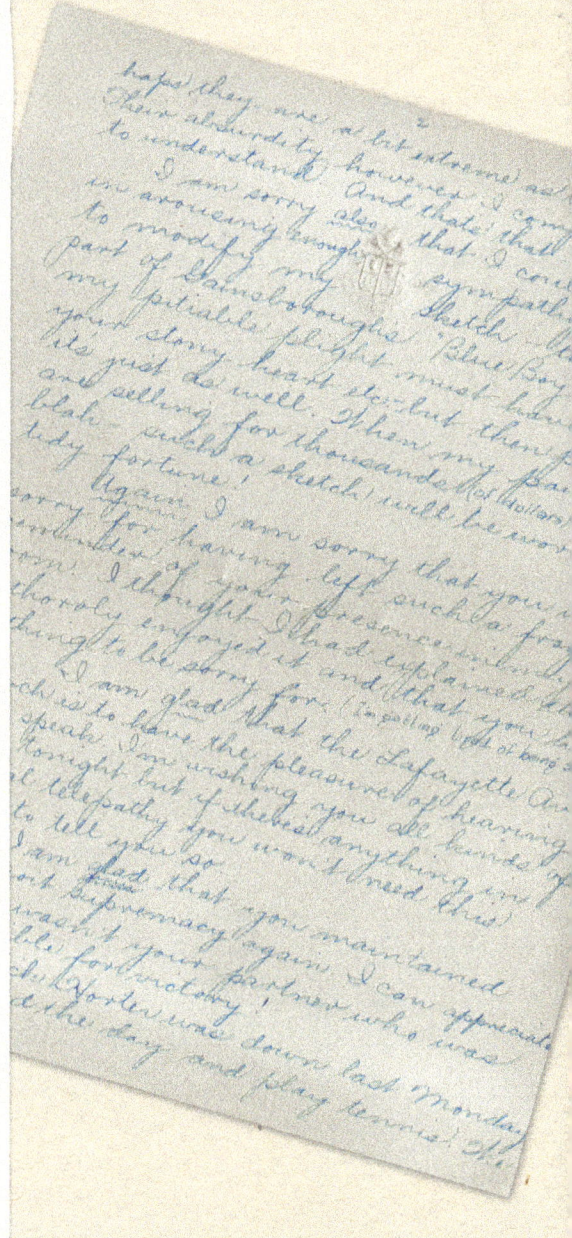

arm and drew me aside. (This will interest Rolland.) I had visions of being shot at sunrise on the next rainy day, and all that sort of thing. The apparition shook my hand and said, "Do you know me?" I stared into the slits that were his eyes and, trying to place his voice, finally ventured, "It's Warren, isn't it?" And so it proved to be – the Phi Delt from Syracuse who persuaded Rolland to sell Bibles. Since he was outside the state, he ventured to raise his hood as he talked with us.

Finally the "mammoth" parade straggled out of the gates, led by the mysterious "Colonel J.," who is a professional agitator, clad in gold stripes, red cape, and a clanking sword. They were all sizes and ages, from scrawny kids in short trousers to old farmers and plumbers, whose thin gray locks and leathery necks minus collar and tie could be glimpsed thru the side of the hood as it divided over the shoulders. Occasionally one of the "Noble Citizens of the Invisible Empire" would raise his hood to expectorate tobacco juice or toss away a cigarette stub. They loudly proclaim excessive patriotism, but none were ever in the Army or even the Boy Scouts, judging from the way they marched and obeyed commands.

To check on the newspaper stories, we three separated and carefully counted the marchers. By actual count, the "thousands" in the parade consisted of 317 men, women, and children, including every soul.

Following the parade, they returned to the race track to stage a big demonstration and initiation. Now comes the fun! There is a big grandstand at one side in which the "aliens" were supposed to sit, where they could see a little bit and hear nothing. In front of that is a half-mile track, and in the center of the oval speedway the ceremonies were to transpire.

We three, keeping in the shadows, climbed the low fence and got inside the sacred circle just before they threw a cordon of white-shrouded pickets around to keep out strangers. There were a few civilians among the hooded Knights – Klansmen not in regalia – and we mingled freely with the Klan, acting as if we owned the place. So self-assured were we that no one questioned us. (Out at Darby, Pa., two policemen who approached a Klan meeting were shot and killed. Thinking of that gave us rather a thrill.)

They initiated some 200 candidates on one side of the field – men – and about 40 women in another part of the enclosure. We watched the men being put thru, standing in the very front of the surrounding Klansmen and directly behind the group of Kleagles and High Umpty-Umps. Suffice it to say we heard and saw everything – the long solemn oaths and all the ritualistic rigamarole. They finished (having collected $10 plunks per man) by burning two big fiery crosses at least 30'–40' high. As the affair ended, Clem and I rashly decided to see how far we could go. Clem's crazy that way anyhow!

Says I (loudly), "I must say, I prefer pajamas to these old-fashioned night shirts!" (That drew a sharp stare from the Grand Kleagle. They didn't dream that any stranger could be so near.)

Says Clem (more loudly), "They get candidates in mobs like this – that's how they tried to get me!"

A whispered consultation among the Imperial Council.

Says Clem (very loudly), "Hurray for the Pope!"

By now the red capes, swords, and gold lace had their heads together. Then three of them stalked over to us. The leader hissed to Clem, "Have you the password?"

Says Clem, "Certainly not!"

Says K. K. K., "How did you get in?"

Clem came back, "Just walked in!"

The chief Mucha-much responded, "You can just beat it out as fast as you can then!" Then turning to me he asked again, "Have you the password?" in blood-and-thunder tones.

Says little Kenneth, "Applesauce!" (It was the first word that entered my head. Wonder what a psychology prof would say?)

Then the Exalted Cyclops blew a whistle and a little hunchback orderly came running. "Take these three aliens to the gate and see that they go out!" barked the spectre sovereign.

"Well," Clem says, "it is late, so we might as well go."

Off we started, strolling arm in arm, the hunchback hard on our heels. We took our time and stopped to look at the fireworks and everything else. Finally our guard, growing agitated, blew a whistle and five big Klansmen came up, one on either side, and three behind us. One of them snapped, "Step lively, buddy," but Clem airily replied, "Keep your night shirt on, we're not hurrying for anybody!"

At the gate, Clem turned and, not at all abashed, thanked them effusively for the pleasure of their company and the honor (?) of their escort, finally wishing them a good night. They stood there, dumfounded at such impudence, and staring after us as we mixed with the crowd and sauntered away. We might have fared worse if Bec hadn't been along – at least more violent ejection.

It was a very interesting evening, and we reached home about 1 A.M. Sorry that space does not permit better punctuation and explanation. Will give you all the details sometime.

I am still feeling sorry for myself because Buffalo is 475 miles away! I am –

A temporary bachelor,
Ken

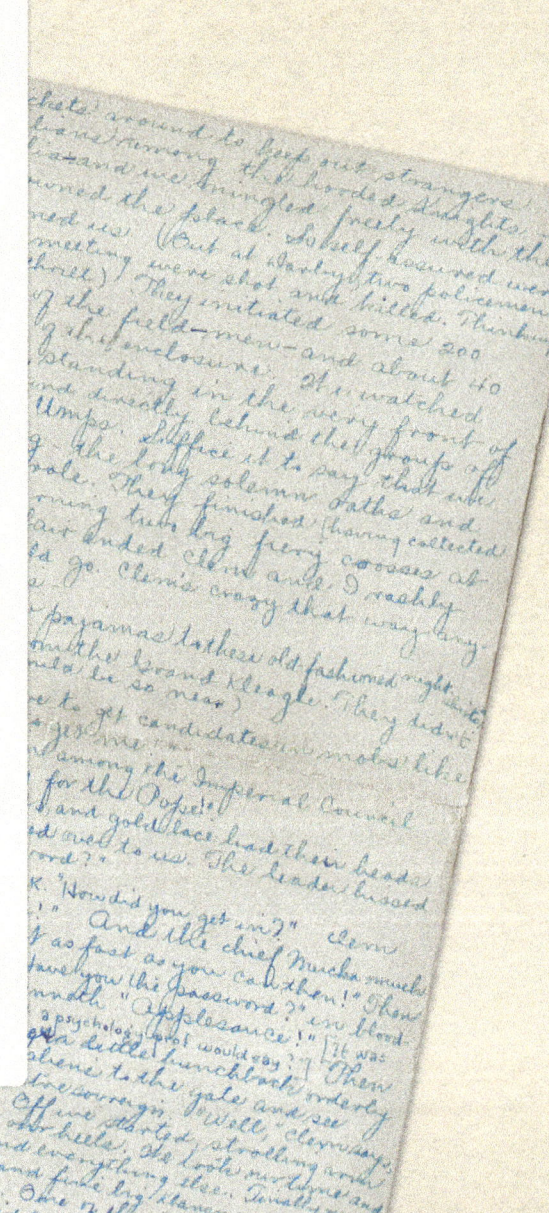

Tuesday and Wednesday, July 15 and 16, 1924, Buffalo to Woodbury

Dear Accomplished Artist, (There! That's a little different, anyway!)

It's awfully late, but I've turned the clock around so I can't see the time. Tomorrow night I'm going away and will not have time to write. You know I have spoken of Vera Herrick, the girl who was to come down next year. She has been refused admittance, and I'm so sorry and disappointed about it. I was looking forward so much to having her there. It is to her house that I am going, but I won't enjoy talking over college to her as I did at Xmas when I was trying to persuade her to come.

I am sure the "Slifer estate" looks excellent, but I couldn't find fault with anything when I was there. You haven't any idea how much I appreciate South Jersey – for several reasons, one in particular.

Saturday we all went out to Hamburg to a young people's picnic. The main events were two baseball games. They were lots of fun. I pitched on one team, but in spite of me we won 18-8.

The salutation of this letter is absolutely necessary after receiving such a letter as your last one with its coveted picture. My words are inexpressive, but it surely is just beautiful! As far as I can see, not a bit of the gilt has rubbed off. Don't tell me you haven't enough talent to do art work!

Your description of your attendance at the spooky spree is certainly interesting. I read it to the folks and they thought so, too. They expressed concern for your welfare on such daring deeds.

I am at the office and will be fired if I don't get to work. In case of any troubles (but financial – we're poor as church mice in this office), apply to business address: Buffalo Baptist Union, 409 Crosby Building, Buffalo, N.Y.

Yours,
Caryl

Sunday afternoon, July 20, 1924, Woodbury to Buffalo

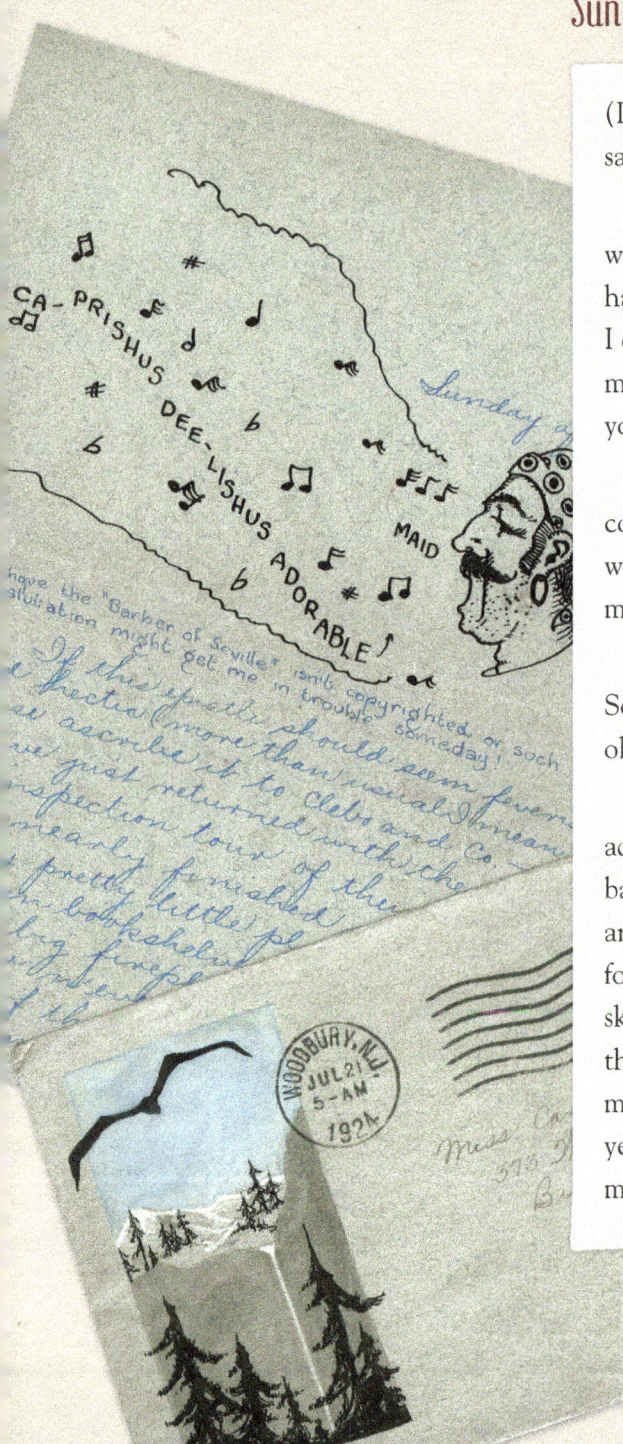

(I hope the "Barber of Seville" isn't copyrighted, or such a salutation might get me in trouble someday!)

The postman deserves a Congressional Medal of Honor this week. He brought me your delightful letter a whole mail before I had dared expect it. Trying to hit upon a suitable reward for him, I decided that one of your smiles would be as much as any mortal man could want. Consequently, if you'll send me two or three in your spare time, I'll try to see that he gets one of them.

Judging from the program that you sent, the Lafayette congregation must have wished fervently that the students would supplant the sermon on every Sunday night. I wish I might have heard you!

Little Kenneth is teaching a Teacher Training Class in the Sunday School for the next three weeks. Fawncy that! They are all of them older than I am, with the possible exception of some of the girls.

The best piece of news (to me) is this – my first venture into advertising was a huge success. Mr. Robey told me that two of his banks were going to issue a monthly bulletin (House Organs they are called technically) and offered me the opportunity of trying for it. I submitted a dummy booklet, together with my ideas and sketches, in competition with a professional agency, and came thru. I had to appear before an august Board of Directors in a big mahoganied room and "sell my stuff." The details are tentative yet, but I will produce it monthly for at least a year, and it will mean several hundred dollars to me. They are printing at least

10,000 copies per issue. I have fooled around a lot with small jobs at school etc., but this is my first real venture, and I'm quite elated over it – for which you will please pardon me. Thanx.

Your
Ruminating, Ruinating Romeo

P.S. A most portentous threat – you have never scolded me for the "Complimentary Close" to my letters. Someday I'm going to break loose. Be gentle.

Thursday, July 24, 1924, Buffalo to Woodbury

Dear Ken,

You can have all the smiles you want, but I'm afraid you'll have to come after them yourself. I appreciate your high valuation of them – just tell the mailman that it's pay enough for him to be entrusted with starting one of your works of art on its journey!

To keep the owner from being sent to court for unlawful parking, I had to sit in a "Flivver" the other day and be prepared to drive off, in case orders to do so were given me by the policeman. I was thankful for your very careful and enjoyable "tutorage" as to Lizzie's whims and caprices, but fortunately I didn't have to use my knowledge. The man came for his car before any trouble arose. Rolland went to Bradford to spend last weekend. I suppose it was two whole days of bliss! But the poor boy took our old Dodge (Father refused to let him wreck the new one), and had eleven tires to change during the course of his trip. Every time he moved, he had either a puncture or a blowout. But with his angelic spirit he bore it all in martyred silence.

He left Mary's at 3:30 Monday afternoon, and arrived in Buffalo 3:30 Tuesday morning! The doors were all locked, and he had to climb in a cellar window over the coal bin to get upstairs. But thru it all he triumphantly carried a new big picture of Mary that she gave him. He can't say things nice enough for her family and the wonderful time they gave him, in spite of the tire troubles.

In Dr. Tullis's Council of Churches office, I have to handle all sorts of people now, particularly a big bundle of female importance who introduces herself condescendingly as Mrs. Frank Williams, chairman of the – oh, I don't know what, something to do with the League of Women Voters. Aren't some of these political women awful! She expects everyone to do her bidding. She smiled so benignantly on me yesterday, because I climbed up on chairs and pasted posters all over the office for her. This is about the fourth time I've been interrupted. Please don't mind the scribbling, for I'm on a trolley car, and it jerks all over the track. A man came in the office and sent me way out on an hour's ride, to take a box of all-day suckers to a bunch of children who are eagerly awaiting them – even if the day is almost gone.

The funniest things have been happening to me. This morning, waiting for the trolley, thinking how late I was going to be, a man offered me a ride downtown in his big Haynes. He looked sort of safe, so in I got, and he took me right to the office door! Even tho I worked all last summer and took the trolley every morning, it was the first time anyone offered me a ride. Later, in the Western Union waiting for a check to be receipted, a man offered me a piece of gum! Now, can you imagine! Do I honestly look like the gum-chewing kind? Last of all, at the bank, a young man accosted me, tipped his hat, called me by name, and asked if I was working there! I haven't the slightest idea who he is, tho I think I remember somebody like him in High School. Life is certainly getting very exciting and unusual all of a sudden.

Please accept my very best congratulations on your business success. That sounds terribly formal, but I'm really awfully glad that you won out. Didn't I say all along that you deserved it?

Sincerely,
Caryl

P.S. Oh, I forgot all about thanking you for your beautiful country scene, which brot with it a cool breeze on a sweltering day. And the musical salutation was so original and clever. "Complimentary Closes" will get a reprimand too, if necessary!

Sunday afternoon, July 27, 1924, Woodbury to Buffalo

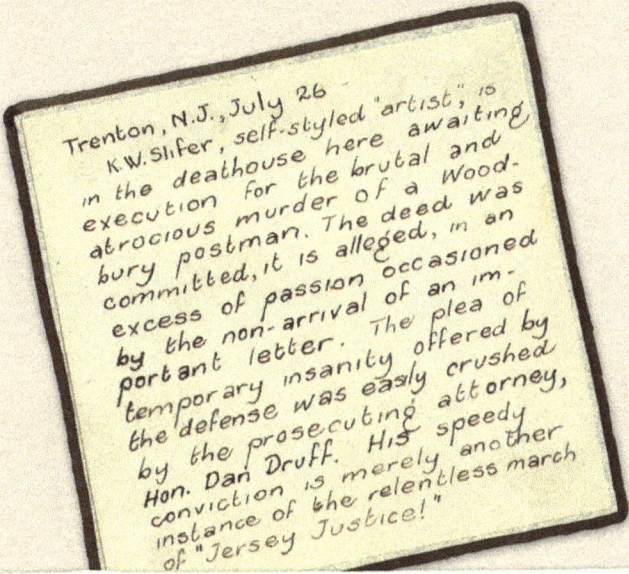

"Trenton, N.J., July 26. K.W. Slifer, self-styled "artist," is in the deathouse here awaiting execution for the brutal and atrocious murder of a Woodbury postman. The deed was committed, it is alleged, in an excess of passion occasioned by the non-arrival of an important letter. The plea of temporary insanity offered by the defense was easily crushed by the prosecuting attorney, Hon. Dan Druff. His speedy conviction is merely another instance of the relentless march of "Jersey Justice!""

Dear Caryl,

Not even my knowledge that your mother was sick and that you expected a lot of company prevented my obituary, above, from appearing in all the important Eastern papers, not even excluding the Woodbury Daily Times. However, I understood the circumstances, and waited as patiently(?) as I could.

This morning little Kenneth had his first real contact with the science of Pedagogy. I've taught before, but never anything so exacting as Teacher Training. Being worried as to the outcome, I hoped the class would fail to appear, since this is the vacation period. Worse than that! I stalked up to my allotted section to find seven young ladies awaiting me! Just as the opening exercises ended and we began the lesson, one lone male came straggling in to keep me company and save me from utter disaster. Whew! What an ordeal it was! Somehow, I struggled thru it. I shudder to contemplate the future and what it may bring forth!

While you were dashing around frantically Thursday, I was designing the best envelope I've made yet, for next week's letter. At least it is the most artistic. I hope you'll like it. I thoroly enjoyed your description of Rolland's difficulties "Hunting Big Game in Bradford." Despite punctures and blowouts, he is more fortunate than I in being near his lady-love! How is he succeeding in purveying bibles? Do you s'pose he's going to amass $600? What did he think of my encounter with Warren at the KKK rally?

Bobby went to YMCA camp yesterday for a week. Mother and I drove her down in the "Lizzie." She says she'll write you from there – if she has time! In my case, there's no question of "time" – I'm your Perspired, inspired ink-slinger,

Ken

Wednesday, July 30, 1924, Buffalo to Woodbury

Mr. Slifer:

I'm awfully anxious to see the new envelope for next week. I don't know how to thank you for your fancy decorations each week, nor to tell you how much I like them, so I just won't try.

Imagine, please. Mary's been restricted by her mother to only 2 letters a week instead of 3. R. is bearing up bravely under the strain, but will survive by reading each of her letters 15 instead of 10 times.

This new Ku Klux letter is clever as can be. Clem wrote it, didn't he? Sounds like him. Thank you . . . am sending it back, judging you wanted me to. [That letter, by an unnamed writer, did not survive. But Ken's reply also mentions it.]

Three questions:

1. Nocturnal encounter with Warren – R. grunted an expressive "Huh," and spoke no more.

2. Purchasing of Bibles – action suspended at present while painting houses, wiring houses, building verandas, writing letters, etc.

3. Amassing of $600 – not very hopeful for him. Very for you! He may make it, but not in Bible selling.

Get your suitcase packed to come in style. [This is the first indication Ken will visit Caryl this summer.] R. plans to have Mary here at the same time and make a foursome to enjoy Boofalo. Does that suit your Royal Highness, or would you rather have "Dut" more to yourself?

Here's a smile for you (not the postman), to counteract the frown caused in compiling the first page.

Yours in a smiling mood,

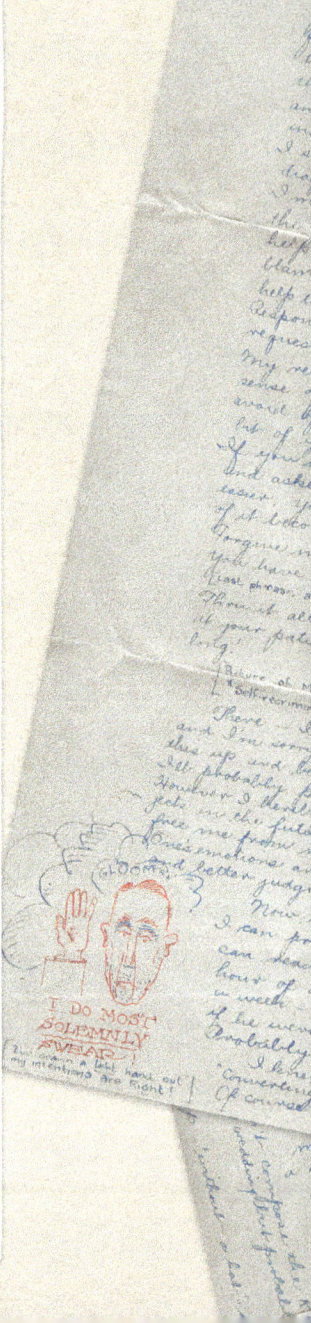

Sunday afternoon, August 3, 1924, Woodbury to Buffalo

Dear Caryl:

I must confess I do enjoy the facile flow of censure from your ready pen, but its very fluency is its own undoing. I must disclaim all responsibility for my "crimes," shifting the guilt to your shoulders. Why? Simply this – how can I help loving you? It isn't my fault, is it? You are to blame by just being you!

You know how I feel toward you, but when reminders of it become offensive, of course I'll eliminate such features. Forgive me, please, perhaps I've written too freely again. I hereby swear to shun all such subjects in the future, or until you see fit to free me from my oath. One's emotions are apt to confuse one's intellect (?) and better judgment – with disastrous results!

(Picture of me, kicking myself vigorously – "Self-recrimination is good for the soul" . . . Epictetus)

(I've drawn a left hand, but my intentions are Right!)

The summer to me thus far, without exaggeration, has been just a series of Fridays – when your letters come. The time in between is just one long interminable wait until the next Friday. When the 4th of July fell on Friday with no mail delivery, I would cheerfully have helped to shoot all the Signers of the Declaration! I usually take up my position as per sketch, in an upper window, watching and waiting for the postman. Wan and haggard, as I croak "letter, letter, let—ter," I resemble nothing so much as a ship-wrecked mariner, starving and parched with thirst, straining for the first glimpse of life-giving land.

My vacation, tho long and monotonous (excluding Fridays), is wonderfully inexpensive. I have carried the same 8 cents in my pocket for the last two weeks! I shan't have any money to get new clothes – or even alter old ones as you are doing.

Clem didn't compose the K.K.K. letter. It took some patient sleuthing to discover that Ned Carpenter, editor of the Gloucester County Democrat, composed the thing.

Penitently penning a passionate plea for patient, pondered pardon,
Ken

Wednesday morning, August 6, 1924, Buffalo to Woodbury

Dear Ken,

I don't wonder that my reproof sounded to you insincere. Most of it was, as you could tell by the foolish vocabulary drill, an exaggeration. But the underlying thot was sincere, as you know. You mustn't think expressions of your feelings are "offensive." They aren't, but are better omitted. I'm sorry I'm to blame, but, anyway, you have not only a "bit of friendship," but my deepest friendship. You must think I'm terribly inconsistent. Well, I don't blame you, but that's just plain, unexplainable me!

The fancy young lady is surely artistic, but, depraved tho my taste may be, I like the scenes you have sent me better. Is this a suggested model for me to follow? Bobbing is easy, but the color might be a bit more difficult!

Rolland put a whole new porch floor on the downstairs veranda and just today left for Fredonia to start in on selling Bibles again. I guess Paul has been making fine money, but R. hasn't spent more than a week at it. Off to my day's labor again! Attie says lunch is ready and getting hot. (It's ice cream.)

Yours sincerely,
Caryl

Sunday afternoon, August 10, 1924
Woodbury to Keuka Park, New York

Dear Caryl.

First of all, I must hasten to correct a seeming illusion on your part. No, the young lady of last week was not a model for you to follow, emphatically NO! (My drawing models for you would be like "painting the lily and perfuming the rose"!) Rather, she was a horrible example of what not to be. In fact, I imagine that your family was deeply disapproving, as they should be!

That envelope was the opening gun in my "Concentrated Campaign against Cutting or Curtailing Caryl's Copious Curls." The second round is appended this week. Such stern measures were rendered imperative by the unseemly levity with which you regard this sacred subject – a levity that has deeply grieved and injured my sensitive nature!

Clem and Bec moved into their "Connubial Cottage" and are happy, with that newly-wed "pride of possession."

Wednesday evening Gert dropped in, and we decided to serenade Clem and Bec. ["Gert" is Ken's lifelong friend, Walter Hunter, whose nickname came from a 1920s movie, "Getting Gertie's Garter."] We scurried around town in his Jordan, picking up friends & acquaintances with "gypping" qualifications. We met the DeHart brothers in their big Velie, and added them to our string. I painted a big sign, JUST MARRIED, and annexed a cannon-cracker that had been kicking around the house. Then with horns, whistles and dishpans we descended upon the unsuspecting couple. We put them on display in separate cars, and with our sign in front, horns blowing and an announcer shrieking forth their name, we toured the center part of town. Finally, the riotous paraders returned to the "Cottage" and produced ice cream and cake, to which Bec added grape juice and pretzels for a real feed.

"Old Sol" sent a terrific heat wave our way this last week. On Wednesday the thermometer reached 106 degrees. Friday, however, brot a little relief. That evening I moved up another notch in the tennis ranking – acquiring fifth place by defeating its former occupant 3-6, 6-3, 6-2.

Ned and Gert Hunter were here after dinner with vague plans for a two-week "pollutin' party" in Ned's Packard, starting this Saturday or Sunday, wherefore your letter may be a little irregular next week.

Mother seems to think my coming to Buffalo would be an unnecessary strain on your Mother. Her reasoning that we'll have a school year together anyway doesn't impress me as a strong argument!

As usual, I am your
Watchful, Waiting Ken

Wednesday p.m., August 13, 1924
Keuka College, Keuka Park to Woodbury

Dear Ken,

Please don't shoot me too hard with your ferocious "guns" for the "campaign," because I'm innocent and blameless. I have not the slightest desire to acquire short hair. That has passed, and has left me happy and contented with my long hair (not curls).

No, my family wasn't disapproving of your picture – just amused. I was just joking about the "model," but I'm glad you seriously denounce it.

Your Mother doesn't really disapprove of your coming to Buffalo, does she? Our "quartet" would be broken up, for I am quite sure Mary is coming. With Attie here, I don't think there will be a strain on Mother. Would a letter to your Mother help?

This is a mighty interesting Conference, even tho most of the girls here are younger than I am. Every minute is packed full, and every spare minute, I play tennis. I played my first tournament game today, and it was a "love" set. But I was just playing with a little girl who hadn't had much practice.

I refrain from reading this over. You'll be the victim!

Yours,
Caryl

P. S. For want of an expressive vocabulary (I've used up all my adjectives) – I'm crazy about the drawing. My estimation of your ability increases!!!

Friday evening and Saturday morning, August 15 and 16, 1924, Woodbury to Buffalo

Lady, mine,

I venture, tomorrow, "into the great open spaces – where men are men," and all that rot. In other words (interruption to answer the phone. Clem called "to kiss me good-bye"), Ned, Gert, Pete and I hit the trail for Montreal, Quebec and all way stations – hiking by Packard. Outward bound, we strike up thru New England and into Canada by way of Portland, Maine, returning thru New York State and the Adirondacks.

I'm glad your longing for "curtailed curls" has subsided, for I might have run out of campaign literature at an awkward moment. A barber downtown has a regular "scalp line" strung across his big

window. There are locks of every shade and length – a striking display that never fails to attract attention.

Monday I saw the cashier of my two patron banks. More luck! My original plans for a bulletin are being expanded into a small paper – Little Kenneth acting as editor with two paid assistants! I made up the "dummy" this week, and submitted it for an OK. Real work commences when I return from the trip.

Saturday morning (early):

Granted our weather was a trifle warm last week but, on Thursday, I played five hard sets of singles and followed that up with nine holes of "golluf." Oh yes, I'm taking up ye ancient Scottish game in order to trim Rolland when I come to Buffalo. Besides, one must be in the social swim, n'est-ce pas?

I didn't mean to alarm you unduly by saying Mother didn't approve of our projected plans. She merely suggested it was unnecessary and would involve added expense, but she wouldn't go so far as to forbid me. Moreover, if I should hike, the question of expense would be largely removed.

My recital of our party on the first page sounds like a gang of desperadoes, but let me hasten to assure you that we are all would-be gentlemen, college men (Penn, Lafayette, B.U.), and that there is slight danger of my associates debasing me!

Hastily,
Ken

Wednesday, August 20, 1924, Oak Ledge Farm, Silver Creek, New York, to Woodbury

Dear Ken – (Wandering Wayfarer),

You must be having a wonderful trip. Be sure you take in particularly the wonders of New York State (!) and especially my favorites – the Adirondacks.

Everything at Keuka was as lovely as could be. Our room was on the Lake side, and we enjoyed so much the beautiful view thru the two immense windows in our room. We had full moon while we were there, and every night it came up like a big ball of glowing fire, making a shining path of light across the water, almost to the foot of our window. I went into the swimming contest, but didn't make any first places, tho I had to do two different exhibition dives.

We came to Silver Creek yesterday afternoon, and will be here for two weeks, resting and recuperating. Nothing to do but write letters, eat, sleep, and swim – which is a lot after all, isn't it?

I just got a round robin letter from the "Y" cabinet with 8 letters enclosed. They are full of plans for the best-ever year in the Y. Now I must write to my "little sister" and two other freshmen whose names they have sent me.

Sincerely,
Caryl

P. S. You shouldn't have taken time to decorate the envelope, tho I thank you just loads for it. In the first breath with which my family greeted me Monday, they announced that a letter was awaiting me, and in the second breath clamored to see the one you sent me at Keuka!

Labor Day, Monday, September 1, 1924, Woodbury to Buffalo

Bestest Lady,

"Labor" Day doesn't mean a thing to me, for it's anything but labor to retail the grand and glorious tidings! Little Kenneth will join you in Buffalo on Wednesday, Sept. 10th – whence the extraordinary exhilaration on my part. Money is scarce, and I'll have to hike – but I'll get there just the same.

You can't realize how much the mere thought of your charming companionship means to me, nor how I've had to scheme to realize it. It took me most of Sunday afternoon to tactfully and diplomatically persuade Mother that the climate in Buffalo was necessary to my well-being and health. I may come, but must finance the expedition myself – a tough proposition.

We had a splendid trip home after our visit with you at Silver Creek, camped on Lake Seneca that evening, and after viewing the sights next morning continued on to Lewisburg. We drove out to the stadium at once, and I got a real thrill at my first sight of the huge structure. It is near enough finished to play in. Practice starts tomorrow. I saw Burns [Burns Drum, a Slifer cousin close to Ken's age], and called on Mrs. Phillips to ingratiate myself for the extension of privileges this year!

Au revoir,
Ken

Completed Bucknell Memorial Stadium, fall 1924.[1]

Friday, September 5, 1924 Buffalo to Woodbury, forwarded back to Buffalo

Caryl hopes to catch Ken with a note before he leaves. This time, next-day delivery doesn't work, and Ken won't read this letter (written and postmarked September 5), until he gets to Buffalo. The second postmark is Monday, September 8. Apparently delivered to Woodbury the morning of the 8th after Ken has departed, the envelope was readdressed by Ken's mother, and picked up by the postman that afternoon.

Dear Ken,

Please excuse me for this hasty, brief note, but even so, I'm afraid you may not get it before you go. We just got home last night at midnight, and your letter was awaiting me here. Oh! I'm so glad you can come.

I shall be eagerly watching for your arrival. This is really mild in comparison to what I feel, but one dare not put in words (if possible!) one's thots. I have lots to do too, and will be rushed every minute for a few days. I hope you have good luck for your trip. Wish I could show my gratitude to your Mother for letting you come! We're going to have a grand old time! I'll try to write you more at Lewisburg.

Hurriedly,
Caryl

Friday and Saturday, September 5 and 6, 1924, Buffalo to Lewisburg

Dear Ken,

This seems funny – to be writing two letters to you in one day, but you may not have gotten my other one, and if I don't write soon you won't get this at Lewisburg. I hardly know what I said this morning, for Mother was standing in the doorway waiting while I wrote the note so that we could go downtown.

It is such a relief to be home again. Country life is all right for a change, but the city is best.

                    Saturday

I have had the grandest news – that is – next "grand and glorious" to news of your coming! Vera Herrick, the girl whom I wanted so much at Bucknell and who was told she could not enter, has had word that there is room for her. Tonight she is coming over for dinner, and we are going to talk over plans and such. We're going to choir rehearsal tonight, just to try out our lungs!

I have to go out now. Good luck and early arrival!

Yours,
Caryl

Friday, September 19, 1924, Lewisburg to Lewisburg

This is a small card, with a cheerful painted illustration, four-line message, signed simply "Caryl." No more communications survive until Bucknell's Christmas vacation, when Caryl and Ken, now both 19, are in the middle of their sophomore and junior years, respectively.

Thursday, December 18, 1924, 10:27 p.m. Lewisburg to Buffalo

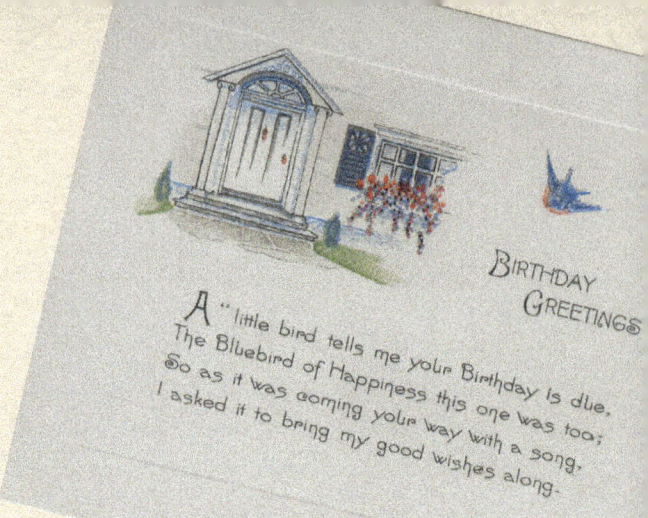

Lady-love, (The same day that witnessed "Paradise Lost")

Old man Tempus has just been crawling along, since I departed from you at the train station so suddenly this momentous afternoon. The last time you saw me I was moving like this but ever since then I have been ambling listlessly and hopelessly like this.

Probably some of my next epistles will be written in pencil, for I'm used to a drawing pen like this, and don't care for a fountain pen. Do you mind?

I mailed your laundry-case as soon as we reached Lewisburg. Here's hoping it isn't too long on the way. Under separate enclosure I'm sending you a Demie "Trumpet." They were scheduled to appear in August, and the Shamokin printer just got them out this week!

Accept herewith my present promise not to present you a present for Christmas, but ~~~ . . .

Give my regards to the rest of the family, but keep the great bulk of them for your own charming self.

Good night and sweet dreams,
Ken

Saturday morning, December 20, 1924, Buffalo to Woodbury

Caryl, who always regrets her own inability to decorate letters, fastens this envelope with a circle of red sealing wax.

Dear Ken,

I must still use the same old salutation, but you don't mind, do you? I can't write clever ones, and I mustn't use any other kind!

I was scared when I saw the train starting at Milton, and was so afraid it would be going too fast for you to jump off without being hurt. I hope you didn't get hurt! Your picture of your flying leap is so funny. (I don't dare share the humor with anyone else, because of the salutation just above! But I don't mind. I can enjoy it all by myself, and more than anybody else would, anyway.)

We had a lovely trip, in spite of the dreariness outside and personal thoughts of Lewisburg(!). Bobby Dilworth had his chess set with him, and soon as we got seats opposite, he started the laborious work of teaching me to play. I couldn't win a game without more practice, but it served nicely to pass the time.

Vera and I got quite excited when we reached Olean, for the rain turned to sleet, and the ground became more and more glassy as we neared Buffalo. Everything here is just sheeted with ice, and you can imagine the effect of a cold sunlight on it all this morning. The temperature is only 10 above! As soon as my laundry bag comes, I'm going skating out in the street.

Oh! Yes, we have a piano! It was a surprise, and it's a wonderful-toned one, even if it is old-fashioned in appearance. So we're going to have some good sings.

Your
"Lady C."

Monday evening, December 22, 1924, Woodbury to Buffalo

My own dear Caryl,

Our poor postman's ears must have blazed all day today – for I was cussing and discussing him with myself most of the time. Here's how!

I had an appointment out at the bank with Mr. Robey before noon today. Since our mail usually arrives about 9 o'clock, I sat me down to await your letter, which I knew would be along today. As patiently as possible!! * ¢ ~ # – @ * ! I gazed up the street until 10:30, narrowly avoiding a stiff neck in consequence – but no postman! I finally had to drive off, frettin' and fumin' and fussin', with an achin' heart and downcast mien, etc., etc.

I found a most delightful epistle awaiting me when I hurried back this evening – it having arrived a few minutes after I left, of course! (They always do!)

I drove the flivver up to Camden today, and parked it in the Ferry plaza. Of course, it had to stand there in the bitter cold. When I was ready to depart this evening, the starter gave a few spasmodic barks, and then died – dead! The illustration herewith represents the next 15 minutes!

The crank, never having been used, was stiff and well-nigh immovable. I finally got Lizzie to coughing, and got home alright, but the intense muscular strain for those few minutes affected my arm so much that it still trembles when I try to write or draw.

Lady, mine: I have acquired two new and unusual possessions – a hat and a cold in the head. At one side you will notice a picture of both (on me).

You will please observe the graceful lines of the hat, and how shamelessly it shows my face. Imbued with Xmas spirit, I came out from under my old bonnet, resolving to hand the world a few laughs by baring my features to the common gaze. The cold probably resulted from faulty ventilation in the new skypiece, but Mother has a different theory. We spent last evening at Clem's Cottage before the fireplace, chewing the rag and downing a Welsh "rabbit." The fire bell rang, and Clem and I dashed out without hats or coats. Whence Ma sez, "I told you so." Worst of all, she's probably right!

Saturday, Bobby and I wended our way to the busy me-tro-po-lis. We were a-shopping bound, and did we shop? Yes'm, furiously! Having last Christmas bought a suit to match my sox, I was now faced with the problem of finding sox to match my suit! Accordingly, I drifted into Wanamaker's "London Shop." Displayed on a shapely dummy I saw some sox. Sez I to the clerk, "How much?" Sez he to me, casual-like, "$12.00!" My reaction is painfully pictured at the right!

We continued to search the city, and finally located some that would answer the purpose, for a mere $8. They are a green-blue heather, with very modest orange and gray checks. They harmonize beautifully with everything – except my pocketbook. The trademark even harmonizes with the color – for it says "Made in Ireland"!

I am leaving here Christmas Night about midnight, and traveling all night, to meet Charlie and Bob next day. [Ken and his fraternity brothers will apply for Delta Sigma's inclusion in Phi Delta Theta.] I don't know what my address will be in Cleveland. I'll wire you at once if we should be successful.

Tell Rolland that I think I've doped out a plan that will enable us to room together next year. At least it should work.

S'getting late, Lady, and near my bedtime. The Season's Greetings from all of us to all of you, and for yourself, remember that I'm a'lovin' of you all the time.

Just
Ken

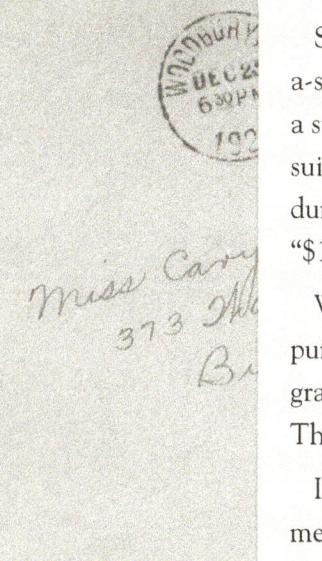

Tuesday, December 23, 1924, Buffalo to Woodbury, forwarded December 27 to Cleveland

A Christmas card is forwarded by Ken's mother to The Cleveland, Rooms 1082-1084, Cleveland, Ohio. The tiny 3" by 4" Christmas card is illustrated with a cozy fireplace scene and simply signed Caryl, in her minute script. Then, at the end of the card's six-line rhyme, she seconds the sentiment with her familiar "Yes'm."

Thursday, December 25, 1924, from Ken to Caryl in Buffalo

Verses to Lady C.
By the Poet-Laureate of Patagonia
(Irresponsible and Irrepressible)

1. You ask me, dear, how much I love you.
Thus may my fancy find
An answer to your mind:
"Past count, as there are stars above you."

2. "If all the leaves on all the trees
I should count o'er,
Yet would I love more
Than all the waves on all the seas."

3. "How many blades of grass?" I ask.
"How many honey bees
Hummed through the centuries?"
And still you spurn me at my task.

4. "Tell me how many roses
have bloomed red
From the first one fair
To this in your hair?
How many butterflies are born?" I said.

5. "How many raindrops are in a shower?
How many sands
On the ocean strands?
More than this is past my power."

6. Thereat you smiled, and tossed your head.
"Vast is my love
As the height above."
"Ah, 'tis not enough," you said.

7. "Then, love," I said, "this will I do:
Unbind these tresses
Which thy cheek caresses,
And I shall sum my love for you."

8. Therewith, the rippling torrents rushed
Adown each cheek.
I could not speak,
And watching, thine own speech was hushed.

9. Then I began to count each raven thread,
An eternal task,
But you did ask!
"'Twill last our lives," you said.

Saturday, December 27, 1924, Buffalo to #1080, The Cleveland, Cleveland, Ohio

My dear Ken,

I just got your special delivery letter this morning. Thank you so much for your note. You will have a grand time in that big Statler hotel – that is, if you don't have to spend all your time, day and night, "conventioning."

The folks in the state are after Father with all their powers of persuasion to get him to take the State secretaryship of the Federation of Churches. That would mean living in Rochester, or more probably in Syracuse. But I don't know what Father will do. I sort of hope he accepts.

Monday morning Rolland is going to have his tonsils out. He thinks the loss of these will turn him into a Caruso – or, at least, that's what he thinks, judging from his ardent pleas to lose them!

Oh! I must tell you about our nicest Xmas present. And that's a Victrola – a console – and we're all so glad to have it. Father had said he would give R. on his 21st birthday [December 1] a radio or a Victrola. The latter was his choice. We have a "junior" floor lamp for the davenport, and now our living room is complete, I think. Come see it, won't you, pl-e-e-e-se?

Talk about your white Xmas! Since that first night when rain turned to sleet, it has been snowing almost constantly. I have the same kiddish desire that I had to roll in the piles of leaves on the Campus, and I'd like to bundle up and roll in the banks of soft, fluffy snow.

Yours with my best wishes,
Caryl

Monday, December 29, 1924, Buffalo to Lewisburg, marked "Do not forward"

Dear Ken,

I'm at the hospital to visit Rolland, but he doesn't appreciate my effort, for he's sound asleep – or was. Now he's having some attention by the nurse. When I first came, I was almost frightened. The room was dark, and R. looked like a sheet-wrapped ghost lying on the bed. The Dr. said beside removing his tonsils, he extracted something from his nose and thinks these actions will help him both breathing and singing.

A Pi Phi called me on the phone and invited me to a Pi Phi tea on Saturday. The only trouble is that they're going to play bridge, and neither Vera nor I play, but perhaps they'll do something else.

Too bad you had trouble with your car, but that is a common complaint these cold days. Ours is laid up in a garage, being torn to pieces, & Father is getting a bill of $55! Isn't that awful. Poor Father feels like "cussin'" himself, I guess.

Oh! I just love your house on the hilltop. It is a beautiful scene, and I agree with you in that it is artistic. You make me want to climb the winding path till I can look over the other side of the hill, then go in, explore the little house, and sit by its fireside with that great big yellow moon peeking in the windows.

Your poem is a dear, and thank you so much for your efforts for me. But that deserves an awful "lecture," don't you think? But I'm afraid I need the lecture and not you, because I've let you do most everything – even when my conscience bothered me. I'm mos' awfully afraid that your Mother wouldn't approve at all, if she knew the salutations you use, and the things you've told me. She wouldn't think nearly as much of me, if she knew I had let you do it at all. I misbehave all the time, in spite of your constant "Be good," and don't use the self-control I should. I confess to you that I have a sense of guilt. But I guess my troubles at Aunt Jennie's made me turn to you more than ever for sympathy, and you gave it so wonderfully. I apologize, and promise to behave myself. Do you s'pose I can? I don't want to!

Well – 'bye till next time,
Caryl

Tuesday, December 30, 1924, Buffalo to the Demie House, Lewisburg

Caryl's final communication of the year is another tiny card. The front is embossed with a black and gold wall clock with pendulum, set at a minute before midnight. She writes on the back.

Dear Ken,

Please pardon my not writing before, but I honestly haven't had a minute since I got your letter. Hope to make explanations and apologies when I see you. Please reserve judgment till then.

In reply to your question, I expect to arrive in Milton Wednesday on the 3:45. Rolland may come then, too, if he decides he can afford to cut Biology. Otherwise he will leave Tuesday night.

In haste,
Caryl

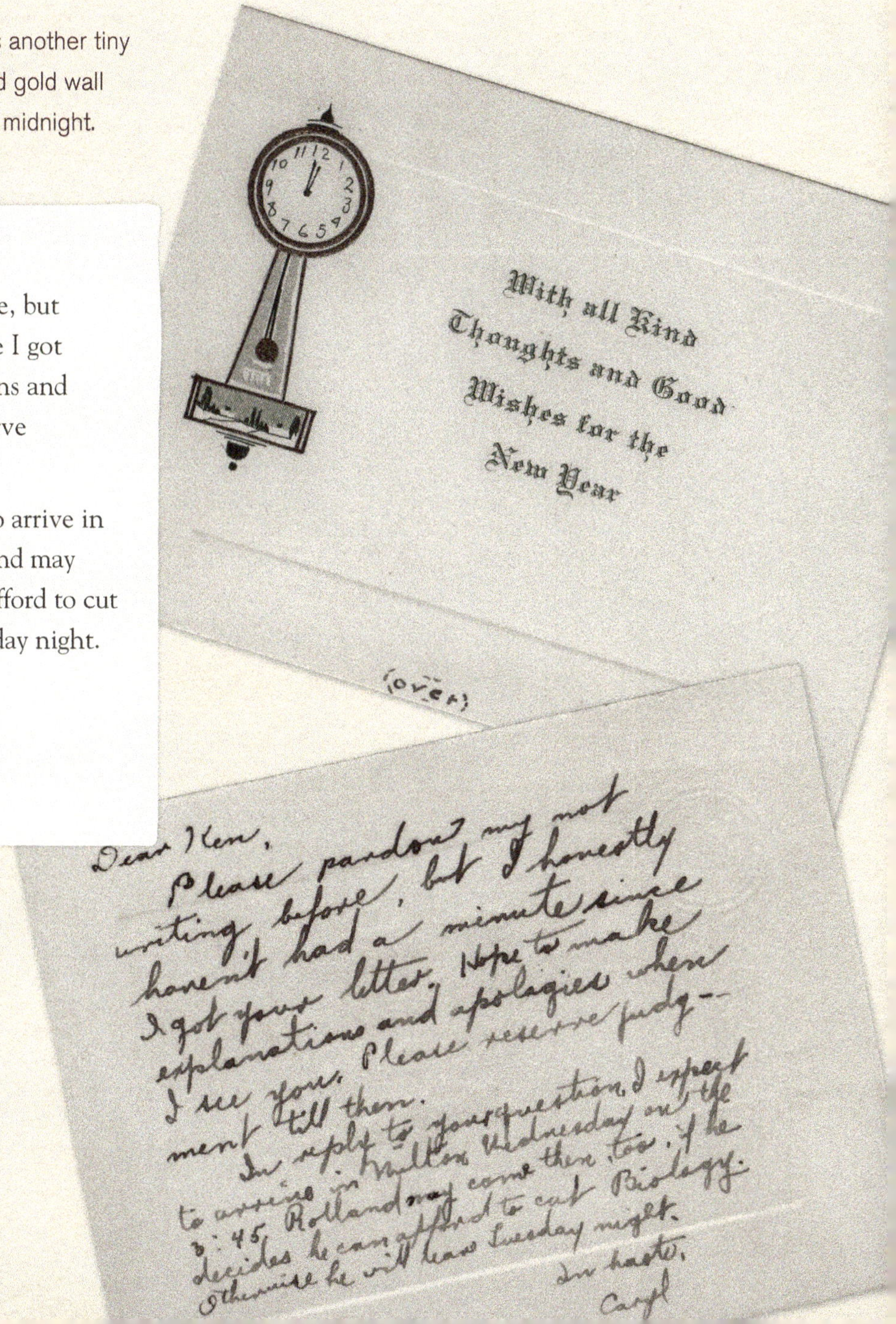

LELAND HOTEL
Kamloops, B.C.
Clear Junction, N. Y.
LET'S GO! CITIZENS MILITARY TRAINING CAMPS
SAN FRANCISCO, CALIF. JUN 25 12-M 1925
RETURN IN 10 DAYS TO
The Continental Hotel
127 ELLIS ST AT POWELL
Say Fellah!
Please
MISS
EVANSTO
% CONFERENCE HEADQ
INTERDENOMINATIONAL
CHRISTMAS GREETINGS!
I know that love
After 3 days, return to
CAMP KANUKA,
LAKE CLEAR JUNCTION, N. Y.
FOR
MISS CARYL R. DUTTON
373 WOODWARD AVE.
BUFFALO
N.Y.
UNITED STATES POSTAGE
2 CENTS
AUG
1925

As the year begins, Caryl, a sophomore, and Ken, a junior, are both 19.

Thursday evening, January 1, 1925
Buffalo to Lewisburg

Dear Ken,

You were so good to take time from your busy work to let me know how things were going at the Convention. It is a shame you didn't make it, after all your work and time and strength spent on it. I think you had the odds against you, tho, with so many chapters already in Pennsylvania. At any rate, you've put Delta Sigma "on the map."

This morning I waxed ambitious and went skating. It was lots of fun and thrilling, but the ice was full of big cracks, and it was awfully cold. We had to go in every few minutes to get warm.

Tonight, as is our custom, we ate New Year's dinner with our doctor and family at one of the hotels. A wonderful turkey dinner, and I did full justice to it.

Rolland came home Tuesday morning, and has been enjoying invalid attention ever since. He is improving fast and hopes to go Sunday to visit Mary. Au revoir – hoping to see you Monday.

Yours,
Caryl

There are no letters between January and the beginning of Easter vacation in April. But the closing of Caryl's letter and the first letter from Ken in April suggest lots has been happening.

Tuesday evening, April 7, 1925
Lewisburg to Buffalo

My dearest Lady,

Little Kenneth set his inventive genius to percolating this morning, and as a result I carried my wastebasket to chapel and employed it most successfully, to receive the chapel attendance cards that showered in from all directions. Next week I'm going to shut my eyes and add pencils, shoestrings, and chewing gum as a sideline.

This afternoon, funeral services were held for Dr. Harris [Bucknell President Emeritus John Howard Harris, Ph.D., LL.D]. The faculty and students assembled in front of the Sem and lined both sides of St. George Street, from the bridge to the corner. As the funeral cortège passed, the faculty fell into line behind, followed by the girls and men in a double column. There were some 300–400 students in attendance – by my rough estimate. The procession moved slowly to the cemetery. There were simple, brief services, "Taps" was blown, and it was all over – a dignified and eloquent tribute to his memory. [Founded by a group of Baptists in 1846, Bucknell first opened college courses to women in the Female Seminary in 1883. Seminary, shortened to "Sem," came to mean the women's dormitory quadrangle – its inhabitants: "Sem gems."]

Confessions again – I've been to the Sem twice since you left, lady mine! You see, Rolland and I are checking our baggage to Phila., and we finally succeeded in obtaining tickets. I packed my suitcase hurriedly, and it was not overfull – but then Rolland added a typewriter and six books! It feels like a trunk, and tho it's new, I doubt if it will stand the strain, because we had to force it shut. I'm afraid it's a Dutton trait to always travel with an over-abundance of luggage ('scuse).

It's nice, dear lady, to be able to write you in this way – fully, freely – exactly as I think, without worrying too much about "propriety" and giving offense. My only hope is that you can find it in your heart to answer in the same spirit.

Lots of love for your own charming self,
Ken

P. S. Miss Carey allowed Sem girls till 10 P.M. Thurs., all day Sat., and till midnight that night, at the Demie house party! Ye Gawds, who'd a thunk it!

Thursday, April 9, 1925, Buffalo to Woodbury

My own dear Ken,

We had a wonderful time on our trip home. The lugs on the back wheel gave trouble every 5 or 10 miles, so finally we stopped at a garage and changed the rim for the spare rim and tire on the back. We'd gone only 10 miles when that tire blew out, so we had to change. We stopped at twelve to eat lunch in a beautiful, quarry-shaped, grassy place on the side of a mountain. The old flivver certainly did its best, and that was very creditable! With several stops to tighten the lugs and change two tires, we reached Rochester about 8. Of course, I couldn't shut my eyes and imagine I was riding in a Pierce Arrow, or a Willys Knight(!), but I'll have to admit, for your benefit at least, that the Flivver is a pretty good car.

Too bad R. had to keep up the family reputation in regard to luggage, tho I'll have you know my suitcase was only half full, coming home! I'm sorry for your suitcase, & also for my typewriter. Goodness knows what will be left of it after being thrown around by those trainmen.

Shall I go to the Sem, now that I can come to the House Party? Only two more months at Aunt Jennie's.

I thot you might like to know that my spring hat has a funny thing on the side like my winter one, so you'll have to continue to sit on my left. This one is stiff, and can't be tucked up!!

We expect to have a wonderful trip over the weekend. Father has to preach in Bradford, so he is going to take Mother and me with him, by train, tho by auto if it is a nice day. We are going to be "real swell," and stop at the hotel overnight. Wonder if I'll know how to behave?

Mother seems to be feeling well, much brighter than at Christmas time. I hope she can now build up for her June trip.

My love to you,
Caryl

Caryl's parents plan to travel to Seattle in June for the Northern Baptist Convention.

Tuesday, April 14, 1925, Buffalo to Lewisburg

Dear Ken,

I have the dressmaker today to help me make a new dress – orange and blue, but not school colors. Hope you'll like it. I have been working furiously to put up hems, take tucks, and slightly alter most of my old dresses. It's an awful job, but it has to be done before I get back.

I went to the osteopath yesterday with Mother, and he twisted me all up, and joyously cracked my bones. He said he always sends his patients home in baskets, and he intended to do a thorough job on me!

Hope to see you soon. Just got your letter. It's a dear, lovely one.

Lovingly,
Caryl

Ken's "dear, lovely" letter is missing, along with many more. We get no more news until a "penny postcard" (that rate lasted for decades) from Caryl two months later, with no salutation. From this note we learn that, at the last moment, it is Caryl who accompanies her father on the long-planned trip to the West Coast and the Northern Baptist Convention in Seattle, rather than her mother, who remains unwell.

Saturday, June 13, 1925, Buffalo to Lewisburg

Haven't time to write now, for we are in the station waiting for the train. Shall write you lengthily there. First stop is Rialto, Cal., Thurs. noon, where we shall stay at least five days. Address me there (as often as you like) c/o Mr. Beecher Crandall.

"L"

[Caryl is not yet able to write "Love" openly, on a post card. Instead, she closes with an "L" for Lady.]

10 p.m., Saturday, June 13, 1925, Chicago to Woodbury

Dear Ken,

The journey to Buffalo was passed safely, with the aid of your detective stories, which I stole, trusting in your good nature; and Mr. Stickle was there in his car to meet me. Friday morning I washed my hair, went downtown to get it curled, buy a pair of shoes, and, of course, get a Chinese dinner. The rest of the day I sorted, sewed, and packed, until my trunk came, and I unpacked it as hastily as possible, considering the way things were thrown in!

We left this morning at 8:30, and arrived here in Chicago at 8:30 P.M., but if we get good reservations, we'll go straight thru to Denver Mon. noon, change there for Salt Lake City, where we'll spend a day, and arrive in San Bernardino Thurs. A.M. Our friend Mr. Crandall will take us to Rialto, where we'll stay from 5 days to a week. Address me at Rialto, Cal., c/o Mr. Beecher Crandall, and you can't write me too many letters.

I suppose the dance is going on now. I'm not sorry to miss it – only the date with you, dear, and that awful, awful much.

Lovingly,
C

Tuesday, June 16, 1925, Denver to Woodbury
Two letters enclosed, written en route

LETTER #1

Sunday

Dear,

The temptation is too strong to use this clever little writing desk in the Observation Car. It's funny trying to write when the desk comes up to meet you for one letter and then mischievously eludes your pen on the next letter.

Well, my first night in the sleeper is successfully passed. Father and I both had to take upper berths, so I had the funny experience of trying to undress and dress while sitting up in bed. It's a risky job, too, to safely descend that ladder. Father is lazy, and is still asleep, I guess. All of it isn't such a novelty to him.

This being Sunday, it seems as tho we ought to go to church, but I don't see how we can, since we'll be on this train till tomorrow morning. It's a beautiful day, tho, & the sun on the rails is almost blinding.

I wish I could be in Lewisburg for just a little while, with a moon, a highway, and you in your car. Wouldn't that be great? You ought to be here, to sit on the observation platform with me.

I wonder how A. Jennie is getting along, and whether she was sorry to have me leave her so suddenly. It's a happy thot that I don't have to go back there, and that next time I go to school, I'll be with all the rest of the girls.

If we have time, I want a bath in Great Salt Lake. That would be a good place for you, for you wouldn't be afraid of sinking below the surface.

I see telegram blanks here. I'd like to send you one. But probably it wouldn't be a sendable message. Just supposin' it might consist mainly of three words.

Missin' you awful,
C

LETTER #2
Monday

Ken, dear,

After I wrote the crazy letter enclosed for your amusement, Father came out in the Observation Car & informed me that because I hadn't reset my watch, I'd gotten up at 5:30 instead of 7:30. Now, wasn't that dumb! And here I'd been thinking Father was so lazy!

We went to the diner for breakfast, and such fun as it was for me. It was my first experience in a dining car, and I thoroughly enjoyed it. Of course, the prices were awfully high, but we managed to get a very respectable breakfast for 50¢ apiece.

The rest of the day we spent enjoying the luxury of the Pullman Car. About 2:30 I fell asleep. Next thing I knew, Father was awakening me to tell me we were in Omaha, Nebraska, & would stay there for an hour. We decided to get our suppers there, even tho it was only 4:00, so in a cafeteria we pushed down some eatables. We encouraged an acute attack of indigestion by racing madly down the street toward the station. However, I felt nearer heat prostration, for it was blazing hot, but we made the train with 5–10 minutes to spare.

We sat out on the observation platform last night until 10 o'clock, watching a beautiful play of lightning all over the sky, & arose this morning to get off at Denver at 7:30. We didn't want to miss the Rockies by sleeping, so we got off here at Salida to spend the night; tomorrow at 6:45, we take a narrow gauge railway which takes all day to cover the same distance the larger train covers in 3–4 hours, for the little train can go thru narrow gorges impossible for the larger road.

The train stopped in Pueblo for us to get a little lunch, & here is where the beautiful scenery begins. For the rest of the time till 5:00, we went thru the narrow gorge of the Arkansas River, a marvelous opening between two precipitous, rocky cliffs rising on either side. The stream is like a wide mt. torrent, something like the rapids of Niagara. At one place we had to go over a hanging bridge, for there was no place on the bank for the train to go.

Father has been writing a letter, too (also to "The One"), and has finished, so I must stop too, for 6:00 will come all too early tomorrow.

My love to you,
Caryl

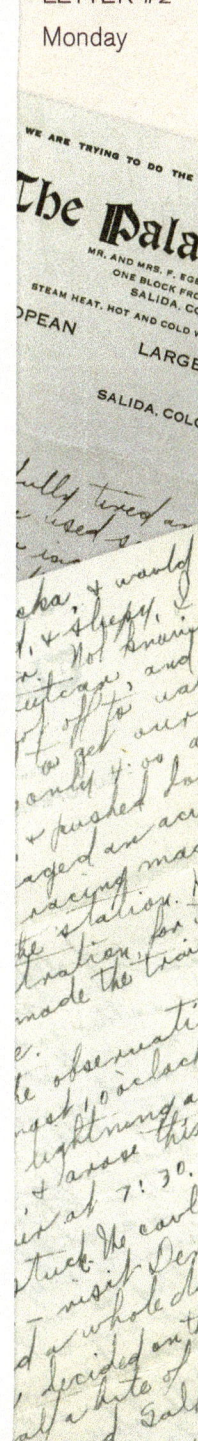

There is no letter at Rialto; in fact, Caryl's trip involves forwarding mail in several directions.

Tuesday, June 16, 1925, Lewisburg to Rialto, California, forwarded June 20 to San Francisco, then June 23 to Baptist City Mission Society, Los Angeles

In this letter, Ken describes hitchhiking home to Woodbury to "reune with the folks" and visit some friends ("One highlight on the way home: I was stung by a bee!"), then driving back to Lewisburg the next day with his mother and sister to complete a set of posters for which he is to be paid $6 and to enjoy commencement weekend activities on campus. Rolland's girlfriend Mary Schilling is to graduate.

My own dear Lady,   1 A.M. after Symposium

Only five days since I said goodbye to you! – and it seems like an eternity already! Your absence is harder to bear since it was so unexpected – tho I don't mean I begrudge you your glorious trip. 'Scuse me for cryin' the blues! You know the reason – that age-old phrase, "I love you."

The church was packed on Sunday, for both the Baccalaureate Sermon and the Oratorio. Sam Simonton (Delta Sigma ex-'25) is back for Symposium in his West Point uniform, setting the girls' hearts aflutter. Brass buttons surely make a difference. People who scarcely knew him before fall all over him now.

The picture on the envelope depicts little Kenneth in his newest outfit. I bought a pair of white duck "sailor pants" with 24-inch cuffs. I purchased also a vivid red flannel tie (they are the "stuff" just now), and with a blue coat the effect is much as I have shown you. You might be tempted to disown me if you saw me, tho I hope not.

You will have another pin to wear next year, dear. I have just been bid to Theta Alpha Phi, national honorary dramatic fraternity. Initiation is to be held early in the fall.

My regards to your Dad, and my love to your own sweet self.

Ever and always,
Your Ken x ———— x

Wednesday evening, June 17, 1925
Lewisburg to Rialto, forwarded June 22
to Baptist City Mission Society, Los Angeles

My dearest Lady,

I'm writing this by the dim and flickering light of an oil lamp set atop the marble surface of a high old-fashioned bureau. I'm all packed for the summer and spending the night at Grandmother's with the folks. We're leaving for Woodbury early in the morning. [Ken's grandmother, Charity Slifer, lived near Lewisburg with her daughter, his Aunt Clara, a nurse who also was a Bucknell graduate. Charity and Clara had lived with Rob Slifer and his family in their big house in Woodbury until Rob's untimely death in 1917, at age 42. Edna was forced to sell that home and move the family to a smaller one some blocks away. Charity's other children then purchased a small property for her and Clara in Montandon, Pa., two miles east of Lewisburg. Bedfast in her later years, Charity died in 1926.]

It's only two days since I wrote you, dear, but it seems like an age, because so much has happened, and because I've spent so much time thinking about you, my love is increasing, as rapidly as you travel West, in order to bridge the greater gap between us.

Carl Geiger, Delta Sigma '15, a professor at Peddie [prep school for boys in Hightstown, N.J.], and three other Peddie profs conduct a summer camp for boys on Lake Clear in the Adirondacks. They give summer school make-up work in conjunction with the regular camping activities. He came back for Commencement and went to Prof. Benny Griffiths, asking him to recommend a student as a tutor in 1st and 2nd year French, and because of my chalk-talking and tennis, asked me to take it. Benny's comment to him had been that tutoring would do me good, because I wasn't working hard enough in French! Carl did not want to accept my refusal and said I would earn $5 to $10 a day.

Rolland pulled another funny stunt yesterday. Since he had two cars and only one set of license plates, he has been perplexed by the problem of getting both home. About six last night he came dashing up to me with a proposition of driving the old Maxwell to Bradford – traveling most of the night and bumming back today. I didn't see how I could go, with my family here and all my packing to do.

He was slightly peeved, but he took Bill White, and I painted a sign for them and loaned them a pennant. About 7:30 P.M. they started off – without saying a word to Mary! It was my pleasant duty to inform her about it, and I had some trouble making her believe that Rolland had left on the eve of her graduation. They got back about 11 A.M. today. They tried to tell us they had hiked it, which is a physical impossibility, for it took 7 hours to cover the distance in the Willys-Knight! As it was, he saw the last part of Commencement, and the awarding of prizes. Rolland won the Junior Oratory Prize. Mary won the prize for the highest standing in Psychology and Ethics.

Good Night, Lady dear, and great gobs of love,
Ken   x ——— x

Saturday morning, June 20, 1925, Long Beach, California, to Woodbury

Dear Ken,

My, it seems like an age since I left home, and yet it's not much more than a week. I must think back to Monday night in Salida, Col. Well, as I told you, we left early next morning on the narrow gauge road. And oh, what a trip it was.

It was wonderful to be on top of those mts. and look down into the valleys, tracing our curved route all the way up. Finally we got to what they call the top of the world, up among the snow peaks. We got out, made snow balls, & had a snow battle – all this while the people at the foot of the mt. were sweltering. Then we started to descend – by the same kind of a figure-8 track. Finally we got into a canyon – the greatest thing I ever saw. Those rocky mts. with their jagged, peculiarly shaped peaks & edges, rose on either side of the narrow torrent to a height of 1,000 feet. The river itself was a rushing mass of waters.

At 8:30 Wed. morning we pulled into Salt Lake City and found a sight-seeing bus that showed us the city. Honestly, that was the craziest trip. I laughed & laughed, for the driver, a student at Utah Univ., made one wise-crack after another. I wrote them down, & I'll tell you them sometime, tho of course they're not so funny afterward. After this trip we went into the Morman tabernacle and heard an organ recital. I was interested to learn more about the Mormans & their history. We had dinner in a beautiful place. The West has the East beaten "all hollow" for eating places. Our train left at 2:30.

We got off at last at San Bernardino, but no friends greeted us, and after inquiries, Rialto seemed almost impossible to reach, but after lunch, we were strolling down the street, and ran right into our friends. A man & his wife, members of our church in Glens Falls [New York], live about 4 miles outside of Rialto, with the desert across the road. There is only the Edison Electric Power house and two dear little houses on this plot of ground which, thru irrigation, is made very beautiful.

After supper we walked out thru the desert land with its sage brush & cactus, & came back in no time to green grass and every evidence of fertile soil. As we came from the power station, it seemed so funny to be passing thru large groves of trees, and see oranges, lemons, grapefruits, and walnuts – palm trees growing everywhere. The houses look cropped off, most only one story high with flat roofs, funny little arches & curved doorways, outside stairways, and great big windows that look so different to us.

Yesterday we packed up and drove 60 miles to Long Beach, where Mr. Crandall's brother lives. He is a contractor and has a beautiful home on the edge of the ocean (I have at last seen the Pacific, so Balboa & I now have a "fellow-feelin'"). Tho over 20 miles from Los Angeles, we will make it our headquarters, for it is so restful, & if we want a swim, we dive off the edge of the wall in front of the house.

Today we shall see Los Angeles & Pasadena. Monday I'm going to see Hollywood! Isn't that exciting?

Well, I have carried this around all day, writing it in snatches when we stopped at various times. It's the only way to write, tho, when on a sight-seeing trip.

Yours,
Caryl

June 20, 1925, Woodbury to Rialto, forwarded June 25 to Seattle, Washington

Honey Girl,

Your wish as to the flivver and the moon drew a fervent and heartfelt echo from me. You can't know how dull life was in Lewisburg after you'd gone. Your brother and Dick Horter were away – most of the Demies had departed – and I spent the bulk of my time longing for you.

I could console myself only by thinking of the glorious experience that is yours. Of course we'll do it together someday, dear, when I sell my $50,000 picture, etc. I love to dream dreams and build air castles, for you always figure in them, Lady mine. You are a natural inspiration to sweet and beautiful thoughts. I'm just overflowin' with love for you, and can't restrain myself.

When I reached Grandma's Wednesday evening, she kissed me twice and murmured, "One's for Caryl." Wherefore I am transmitting it as faithfully as I can, across three thousand miles! x (Add an infinite number of my own.) (x = the unknown quantity.)

Thus far, after refusing my tutoring offer (haw-haw), I have no definite summer job. Work is scarce around here, but I hope to land something.

Goodbye, dear girl, and remember that there's three thousand miles of love between.

Devotedly,
Your Ken x

Wednesday evening, June 24, 1925
San Francisco to Woodbury

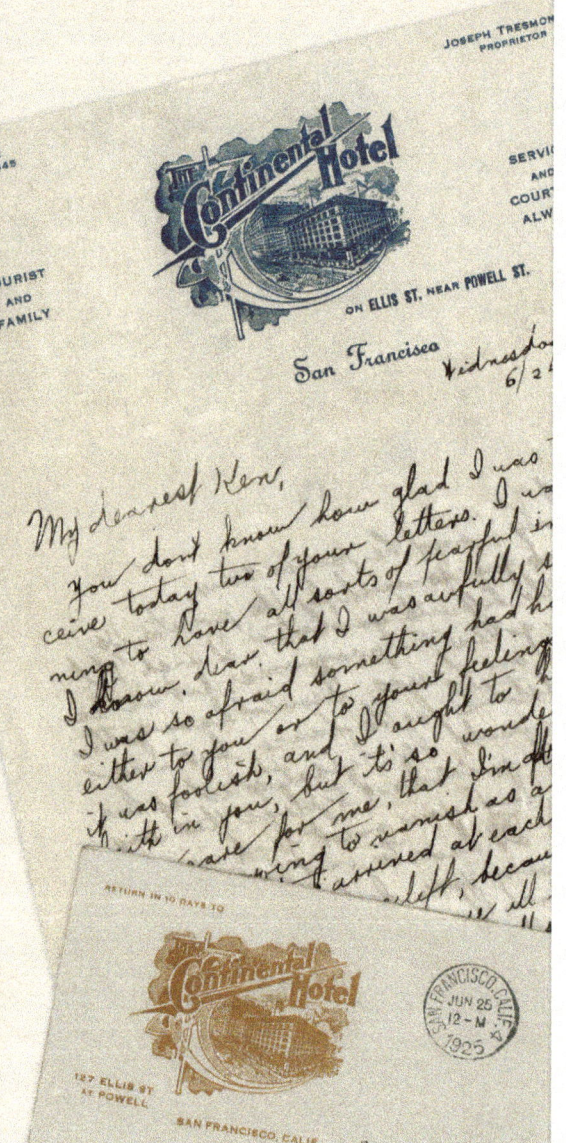

My dearest Ken,

You don't know how glad I was to receive today two of your letters. I guess the letters arrived at each place only a few hours after we left, because you ought to see them now! They are all marked up, front and back, in pen & ink, with all sorts of remailing addresses. Two whole weeks with no word from a loved one is an awfully long time.

I am glad you had so lucky a trip home and back. It's too bad the bee had to sting you, but you see, she was looking for "honey," and she found him! How "funny" you must look in your new outfit! I'll have to wait to see you in it before I disown you, but I have a little idea in the back of my head that it would take more than that to make me do so.

Today we went out to Golden Gate State Park and to the ocean beach. This afternoon we saw the Leland Stanford Univ. and went up to U.C. Berkeley. Tomorrow we will take a 7-hour tour down the coast to the Muir Wood, where the great redwood trees are. I saw Hollywood, but not much that was exciting – the outside of the Pickford-Fairbanks studios. On the beach, we saw a picture being taken, but that too is a dry and monotonous process, with little of interest for the onlooker.

I'm longing for your company every minute, dear, and wishing, oh so much that you were here to enjoy these things with me, and make them twice as enjoyable.

Love to your dear self,
Caryl

June 26, 1925, Woodbury to Northern Baptist Convention, Seattle

My dearest Lady,

　Your third lovely letter came late this afternoon, and I'm hastening to answer it at once, as I should, since it is your birthday. At present rates you may not have received your birthday card, altho I sent that six days ahead. In any case, I entrust again to Uncle Sam bushels of love and good wishes, to the dearest, sweetest girl I know, on this, her twentieth birthday! On second thought, I'll let Balboa's ship, on the envelope, bear them up to your very door! Uncle Sam is overburdened, anyhow.

　Dear, if you could only know how I've missed you and longed for you! My waking thoughts centre entirely about a certain good-looking head-waitress-to-be, and I even dream of her. x I love you, Caryl mine, deeply. Reverently, and with all my heart and soul, I love you.

　Since my last letter my summer position has found itself for me. Another letter from Carl Geiger insisted they need me, stressed the advantages involved, and pointed out I could have four weeks at home, two before and after the camp season. I'm to act as councillor, tutor in French I and II, chalk-talker and krayon kracker, director of dramatics, and sign-painter at Camp Kanuka, Lake Clear, N. Y.!

It's an exclusive affair for 40 boys charged $250 apiece, with tutoring extra at $2 an hour per student. They have tennis courts, ball diamonds, a gym, cabins and cottages, electricity, and running water. They pay all expenses and $2 per hour tutoring time. Carl said I should clear $150 to $300 – quite enough for me with such a delightful summer included. Work is not to be had around here, and most of my friends are envious of my opportunity.

A special car attached to the "Adirondack Express" leaves New York at 7 P.M. on July 6. I am to look after the boys on the way up. My conscience is clear, since I warned them about my French, and once refused. I'll struggle thru it somehow. Next week I'll drive to Lewisburg to get my easel, chalk, smock, etc.

Have been playing tennis regularly, with varying success. Wednesday last I was given a pass to the semifinal round of the Intercollegiate Singles Championship at the historic and exclusive Merion Cricket Club, Philadelphia. I spent the day mingling (but not too much!) with the best society, in that picturesque setting. There is a great rambling club house – and a veritable maze of tennis courts, all of grass. I saw 8 men – the cream of all American colleges – display a brand of tennis that was scintillating to say the least.

I spent two days this week working on my Memory Books, and now have them nearly up to date. [Ken created four scrapbooks – one for each of his college years at Bucknell – with photos, news clippings, and announcements, as well as drama and dance programs, adding his own drawings and captions.]

Bobby went deep-sea fishing today with friends – got sea-sick and sunburnt, and two big fish!

Your own
Ken

Sunday evening, June 28, 1925, Woodbury to Northern Baptist Convention, Seattle

Dear,

Bec and Clem held a big dinner today for the bridal party, to celebrate the completion of their first year of married life. Bec is a genius in the kitchen, and we had a sumptuous feed! I told them I remembered the date not because they had been married – that didn't matter – but because you had been here! All of which elicited a sofa pillow from Clem's direction!

Bobby has just begged to have her love included. Did you notice that the birthday card she sent she had painted herself?

I know of nothing else to tell you except the old three word story.

Lovingly and longingly,
Ken X

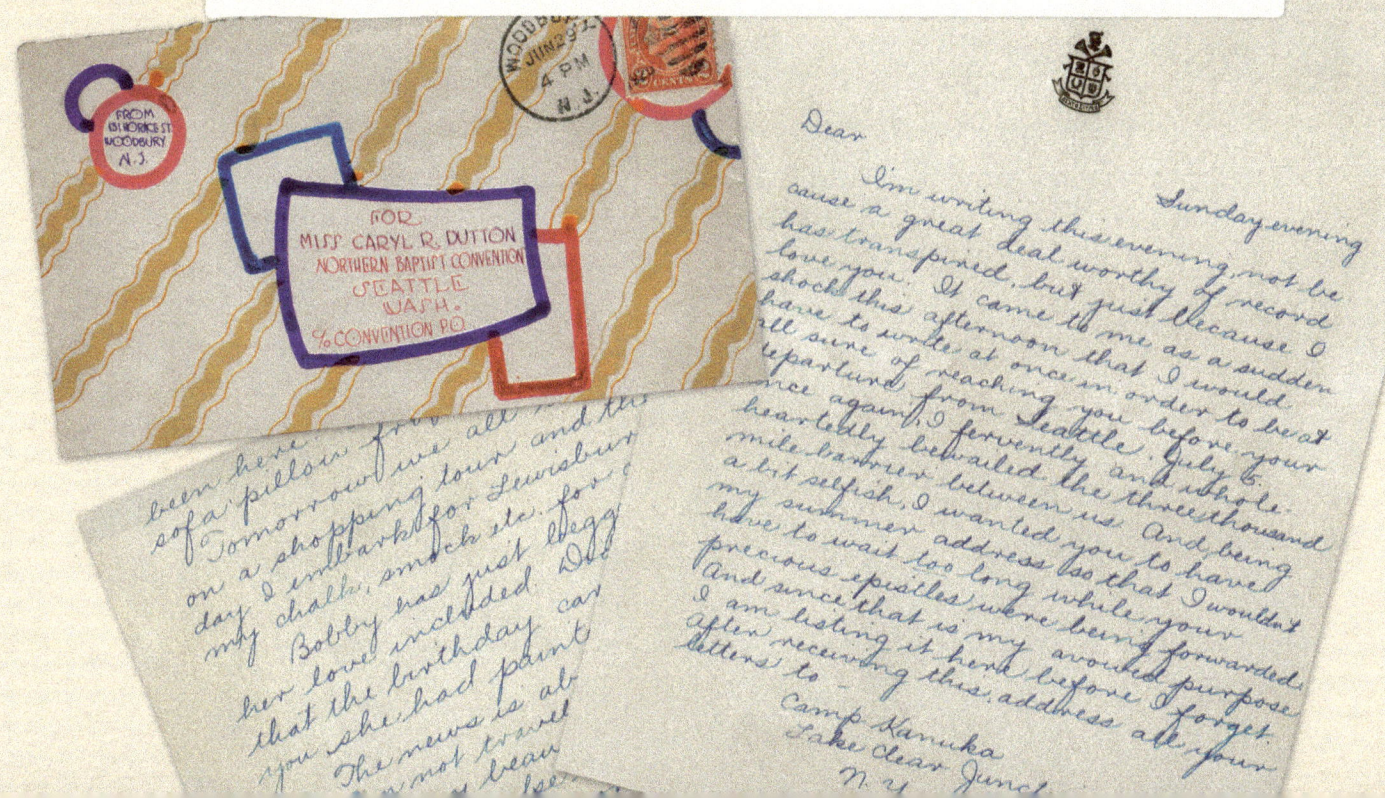

July 9, 1925, Camp Kanuka, Lake Clear Junction, New York to Buffalo:
Two letters and the card from Ken's birthday gift to Caryl are enclosed.

LETTER #1, Sunday

My darling Lady,

After reading your letter forty 'leven times – the fullest, freest expression of your love you have yet ventured to set on paper – I was hung'ring so for you. My fervent hope is that Time will build for us a sublime and lofty Faith that shall withstand petty doubts and misgivings. That sounds rather grandiloquent, honey girl, but all the sincerity I possess lies back of it. I've loved you so intensely and so long that I'm likely to spout "melodrammer" most any time.

Monday last, the Slifer family invaded Philly en masse for a wearing, weary round of shopping. Nothing tires me so quickly as trailing the womenfolks thru a lot of feminine departments – ribbons, notions, cretonne, lingerie, hosiery, kitchenware, etc., ad infinitum. Let's you and me agree to do all our shopping in Sears Roebuck's catalogue!

Tuesday at 5:30 A.M., Kenneth, "Duke" Chadwick [Ken's neighbor], and Lizzie embarked for Bisontown [Lewisburg, in the Buffalo Valley; Bucknell's mascot is the bison]. We reached there early in the afternoon, and I spent a considerable part of the day rescuing things I wanted from 10 East Wing, and painfully opening boxes I had laboriously nailed shut two weeks before.

Thursday I played tennis and did odd jobs around the house. Bobby found out that President Coolidge's birthday was the same as hers, July Fourth, so she sent him a pretty card, just for fun. I decorated the envelope for her very carefully, and he ought at least to look at it. Saturday we celebrated Bobby's fourteenth birthday. I gave her a curling iron, for she had asked for one "like Caryl's." She idolizes you, Lady mine, and highly approves of her brother's taste in femininity.

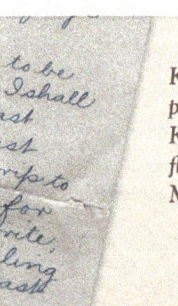

Ken made a marginal note beside his self-portrait in minute but perfect lettering with this message: Personal pen picture of little Kenneth, clad in his new collegiate white-gold glasses and sombre flannel tie, engaged in the highly enjoyable business of welcoming Miss Caryl Dutton back from her globe-trotting.

Tomorrow I am to meet one of the directors at Princeton J'ct'n. (He describes himself as a fat man accompanied by 3 kids – I know I shall like him.) We journey on to New York and spend the afternoon meeting boys and reassuring fond mommas and poppas. At 7:10 we embark on a special car attached to the Adirondack-Montreal sleeper and reach Lake Clear next morning.

Lots and lots of LOVE (End of Part One – Continued in our next.)

Flivver, parked behind hedge, at Ivy-covered East Wing of Old Main at Bucknell University.[1]

LETTER #2,
Wednesday

Dear,

This must of necessity be penned fast and furiously, for having just tucked my four Little Scorpions to bed I have only a half hour till I'm supposed to turn in myself. "I came, I saw, and I'm throwing a good bluff at conquering," describes my introduction to Camp Kanuka.

On Monday, I spent 5 hours in Grand Central Station, sent early arrivals to the movies to keep them amused, & restrained latecomers from going, so they wouldn't miss the train. I assured fond mammas we wouldn't be rough with Jack or Willie – "He's so sensitive and high strung" – at the same time assented to poppas' whispered pleas to "Toughen him up a bit." After a noisy trip in a non-sleeping sleeper with 25 "boys" (all ages and sizes, 9–21 years – mostly wealthy, a couple of millionaires' sons), we piled off at Lake Clear Junction, and after being driven to camp, set about the acclimation process. We sleep in little "bungalows" that jut out into the lake on pilings. They have diminutive front porches, each open but screened on all four sides. Four boys and a councillor sleep in each.

I was assigned four of the smallest "Kanukites" (9–11 years). They thought they were giving me a ticklish proposition, but we're getting along famously. The first day I painted crazy signs – each fellow's nickname with a cartoon of him – and tacked them over the bunks. That made a hit with the kids, and I've had no trouble at all. A thumbnail sketch of my "hopefuls" follows.

1. Dick Haggarty – son of a wealthy New York Irishman, and very clever with his fists.
2. Robert E. Lee ("General" of course) – slight and frail, mostly tortoise-shell glasses, has an impressive collection of knives, axes, etc.
3. Walton Geiger – nephew of Carl Geiger (Delta Sigma '15), big brown eyes and very intelligent, a mechanical genius. Talks learnedly of radio and things beyond my ken (no pun intended).
4. Freddy Blanchard – millionaire's son, but a lovable, good-natured little towhead.

Began my teaching career today with 3 + ½ classes. My schedule runs like this:

8:45 – French I R (remedial), "bonehead" French, 1 student

9:45 – French II A (advanced), 2 students, one a brilliant Spaniard

10:45 – French II B (repeat), 2 flunkers

11:45 – Elementary French, ½ hour, 1 student

Ken's birthday gift to Caryl awaits her upon return from travels. A lamp "for the room next year - a beacon light of love and faith."

That schedule nets me $33 a week; a chap from a town near here will enter one of the existing classes, jumping my pay to $42 per week. Board and room are free, and my money is all clear, with little chance to spend it. As for the French, I make a grammar assignment, then study it hard myself! The translation gives me no trouble, except that I have to know every word.

Time was up ten minutes ago, dear, and I must hie me to my downy cot (5 blankets), where I can watch the moon, listen to the lapping of the waves, and dream of you. Good night, darling Lady mine, and sweet dreams wherever you are now, and a welcome home and happy birthday when you finally read this scrawl.

Ken x

Friday, July 10, 1925, North Bay and Fort William, Canada, to Camp Kanuka

My own Ken,

We are speeding Eastward on the Canadian Pacific and arrive in Fort William tomorrow morning. From there we take the boat thru Lake Superior, the upper part of Huron, to Georgian Bay, landing at Port McNicoll Monday afternoon; from there to Toronto and home at last. No use in mailing this till we get to Fort William, for we are traveling as fast as mail could.

I had no idea that Bobby painted the card herself. It is lovely work. Ken, I shall be hopelessly lost in such an artistic family!

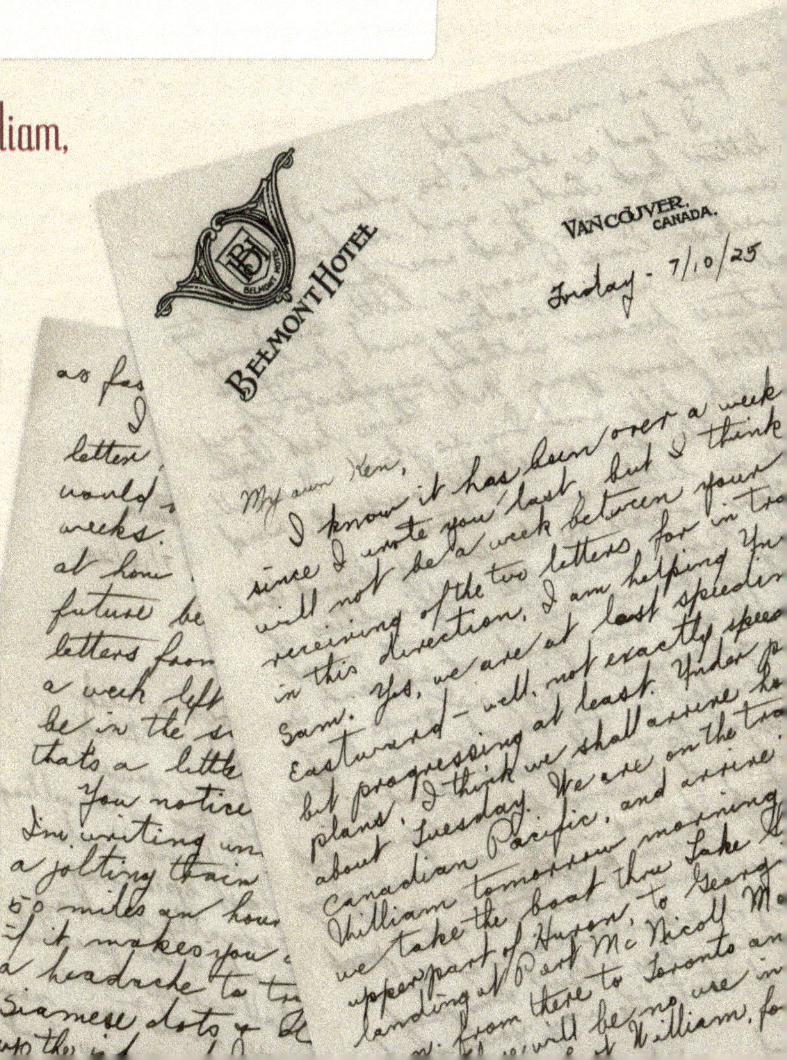

The days have been very full since I wrote you last. All day Thursday we had a big Baptist fight. The old denomination almost split, and oh, how tense were those meetings. I sat thru the whole thing, from 8:30 a.m. to 10:00 p.m., with only time out to eat. You who like debating would certainly have found those sessions very interesting. I simply marvelled at the way those men could get up there without previous notice and plead eloquently for their side.

It was great, but painful too, to see some of these great men forgetting their Christianity enough to bitterly fight over technicalities. And then it was fine to see others disregarding their own convictions and desires in order to keep peace among all.

One of the two big fights was caused by some fundamentalists who tried to unseat the delegates from the Park Avenue Bap. Ch. (our old church in N. Y.), because of the radical stand which the church has taken in backing up Harry Fosdick's plans. [Known today as the Riverside Church, this congregation is affiliated jointly with the American Baptist Churches USA (called the Northern Baptist Convention in 1925) and the United Church of Christ.] My, how thankful we were not to be in that church now, for the names of Dr. & Mrs. Woelfkin and Mr. & Mrs. Carter (the man in Father's place) were brot up again and again, and the whole convention fought for or against them for a whole morning.

I never saw such a display of parliamentary procedure as that masterly Conv. President handled. Never for a minute did he lose control of the affairs, and he always knew what to do. I think he must have learned the rules of order by heart. We finally won out by leaving the delegates seated in the convention, and the Conv. adjourned to meet again in the afternoon and fight some more.

This time it was the fundamentalists again, who presented a resolution to call home all missionaries who wouldn't affirm belief in the fundamentals, and replace them by other workers. Another wonderful debate followed, lasting all afternoon, and finally the resolution was voted down and discarded. When the vote was at last taken, we all sank back, weak and worn out by the strain.

Defeated twice, the fundamentalists made another attack on the Park Avenue Church Friday morning, and everyone feared another awful struggle, but with a plea for peace, the author of the resolution got up and took out the most cutting parts of the resolution, and then with an almost unanimous vote taken immediately, it was passed, for without those cutting statements, it was a wise measure. When the people saw how the vote was, while they were still standing, all with one accord sang "Praise God From Whom All Blessings Flow." It was a great moment, and one I shall never forget.

Thursday night I went to the Bucknell banquet. Dr. & Mrs. Hunt [Bucknell president

Rev. Emery William Hunt and his wife Elizabeth Olney Hunt] were there, and I met lots of other Bucknellians.

Saturday afternoon, Mr. Shank, last year's Conv. pres., invited the whole Conv. out to his home there in Seattle, assuring us that he had plenty of room! And he surely did! It was a garden party on his beautiful lawn, which slopes down behind the house in beautiful green velvet terraces with all sorts of flower beds and arbors, shady nooks with big easy chairs, and umbrella-shaded tea tables. They served us with grape juice and little cakes, and I met a Pi Phi! She was lovely, too. I had a hard time recognizing her pin, for instead of the pearls I'm used to seeing, she had three great big diamonds! She has a very good-looking son, too (!), but of course I didn't care anything about him. I care too much for a certain other good-looking son!

Sunday morning we heard Dr. Abernethy of Wash., D.C. [Dr. William S. Abernethy, pastor of Calvary Baptist Church, the founding church of the Northern Baptist Convention] and after dinner took several street-car rides all over the city.

Early Monday morning we packed up and boarded the steamboat for Vancouver, B.C. We should have liked to stay at the Canadian Pacific Hotel, but they wanted $7 apiece for the privilege of sleeping there, so we contented ourselves with the Belmont, which was very pleasant.

The trip thru the Canadian Rockies is magnificent. To get it all in by daylight, we got off at Kamloops, B.C., "did" the town, and went to bed early. Two sleepy Duttons crawled out of bed Wed. at 5 A.M. and hurriedly dressed for the 5:40 train. On the back of these trains they carry an open observation car that has neither sides nor top; it's the only thing for mt. country. Despite the soot and flying cinders, we stayed out there all day and "drank in" the gorgeous scenery.

We got to Lake Louise about 8 o'clock. This place is called the gem of all America, comparable to the most beautiful glacier lakes of Switzerland. The Can. Pac. has a palatial hotel on the edge of the lake, but the prices were palatial too, so we stayed at the Y.W.

Thursday morning we started up the mt. to Mirror Lake and Lake Agnes, almost at the foot of the glacier, then on up to what they call the "Beehive," a lookout 7500 ft. in elevation. Our hotel was about 5700 ft. A severe climb (3½ hours) but oh! the view!

Hope you're having a great time. When I get home, I'm going to make a beeline for the mail! C.

Sunday, July 12, 1925, Sault Saint Marie, Ontario, Canada, to Camp Kanuka

Dear Ken,

The Rotary Club of Sault Ste. Marie is coming down to the boat to take all passengers, who so desire, to church. Isn't that great of them? This is the loveliest boat, and I'm having a perfectly wonderful time. The meals are all full course, served in the height of style, and I have a ravenous appetite. And beside regular meals, we have tea served in the tea garden on the deck. We have wonderful staterooms too, with the cleverest little fixtures and funny things.

I hope you are taking my orders about resting! Remember, you said the "senior partner" was boss! Love to the French tutor,

C. [Caryl turned 20 on June 26; Ken will not be 20 until September 19.]

Tuesday evening, July 14, 1925, Buffalo to Camp Kanuka

My dearest,

Home at last, and glad to be here. But it was best of all to receive your own dear welcome. I read it over and over, along with those repeated three words I can never hear too often, and I was so glad that at last you can speak your heart freely without my feeling any need of restraining you. Until this spring, I must have had heavy bolted doors on my feelings, for I have never before missed you half as much as I do this summer. I'll tell you all about it, when we're close enough to talk. I'll try to hold it in till then, and not let my wishes and longings run away with me.

I am writing by the light of the loveliest lamp I have ever had! I needed one, and love this kind best of all. I love it too because it's your gift, and because part of it is your own workmanship. The seal is so pretty, and such a clever idea. Thank you, dear, ever and ever so much. It will be a beacon light of love and faith between you and me, and next year as you pass by in the evenings, I hope you will see its light shining down from my window with a constant message for you.

Your description of the camp is so interesting! You used a great deal of strategy when you won those boys' hearts by your drawings. They're four lucky boys. You're succeeding with your French, too! I knew you knew a lot more about the language than you used to pretend, when we did it together.

So you don't like to go shopping with the ladies. I don't blame you. I won't promise to do my shopping in Sears Roebuck's catalogue, but you won't ever need to go with me, for I like to be alone when I shop. I can get twice as much done. We might meet someplace for lunch, tho. Don't you think that'd be fun?

We got in the old home town at 8:30 safe and sound, and climbed into our faithful "Willy," and home we flew. Wasn't it funny we left June 13 and returned July 13, and for all that it wasn't an unlucky trip!

I'm sure no girl ever had a dearer boy than you, my own Ken.

Your "Lady"

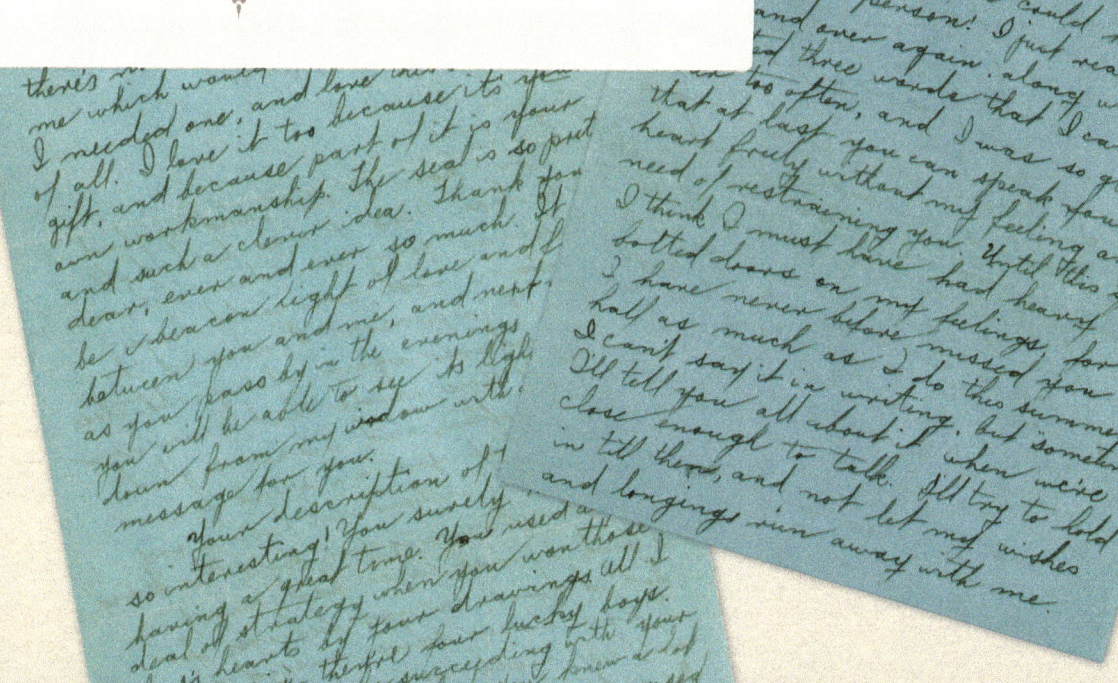

Friday afternoon, July 17, 1925, Camp Kanuka to Buffalo

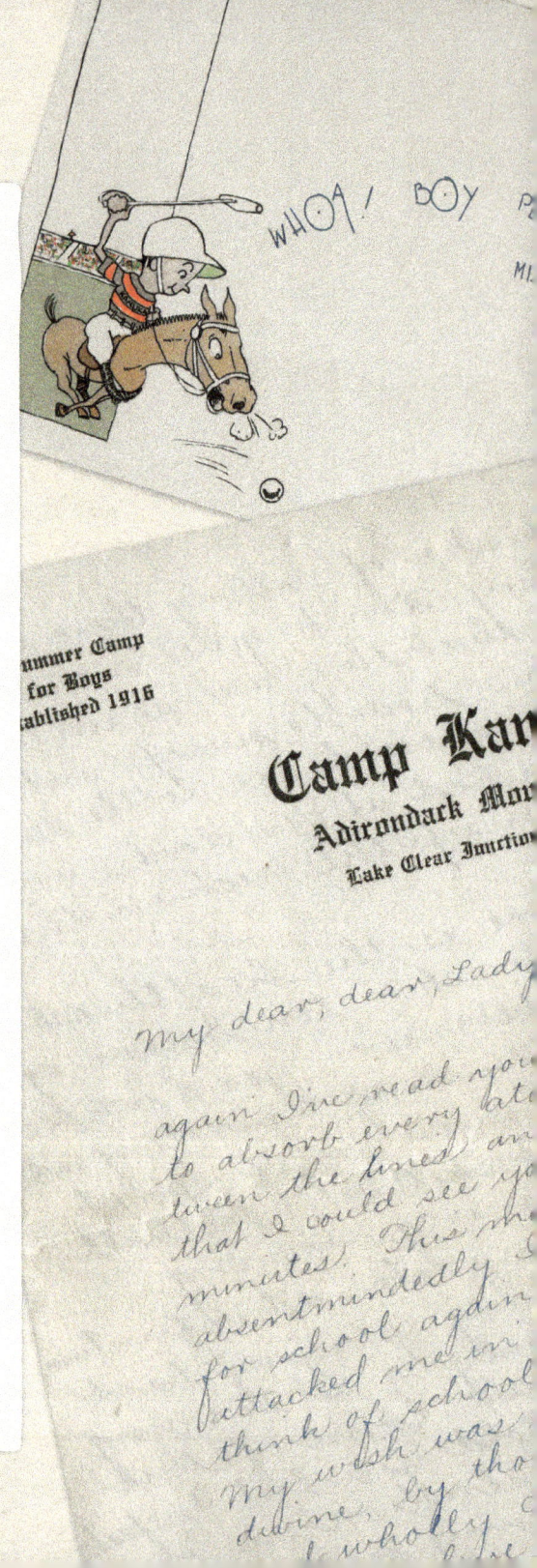

My dear, dear, Lady,

Again and again I've read your precious letter, trying to absorb every atom of love from between the lines. This morning, absentmindedly I wished that it was time for school again, and my little Scorpions attacked me in a body, for they like to think of school as in the distant future.

The life here is a ceaseless round of activity. Foremost among my achievements, I've learned to swim! It's a bit pathetic, isn't it, that I should glory so in something that everyone else takes as a matter of course? On my fifth lesson, I swam about 50 feet without difficulty, using the breast stroke. I think I could have gone further, but the lake was rough, and I didn't dare venture too far beyond the dock, because a wave over my head sets me to sputtering and spoils my stroke.

Do you understand the significance of the title "Little Scorpions" as applied to my quartette? The Little Scorpions appear frequently in that famous cartoon series by Fontaine Fox, entitled the "Toonerville Trolley." I gave them that name the first day, and now no one thinks of calling them anything else. They don't give me any trouble, except they are so untidy. You should see little Kenneth tucking them in bed at 9 o'clock and buttoning them up the back in the morning!

The life here is the healthiest I have ever struck – ten hours of sleep in the open air, good wholesome food (I'm drinking 3 quarts of milk a day), and all manner of sport – baseball, tennis, basketball, football, volleyball, swimming, rowing, fishing, quoits, ping pong, etc. Teaching all morning, playing hard all afternoon, and studying all evening makes a full schedule.

The registration in French has increased, and my present salary is $7 a day or $42 a week for three hours daily work. For the next three weeks I have two students in Latin, which jumps my salary to $54 for that time. All in all, it is the best summer I have ever had – no expense, good vacation, good salary for short hours, and a start in swimming. If Buffalo were only near here, my happiness would be complete!

The teaching itself is going easier. I'm acquiring that blasé professorial air, and incidentally learning more French than I ever knew before. French II begins with the Subjunctive, and it has taxed my ingenuity to the utmost not to be caught napping.

My first letter to you brought me quite a few envelope orders – so that is an additional source of revenue. Tonight I am giving a chalk talk to all the camp in the main lodge. There are in all four Demies here, so that my surroundings are quite congenial. No one has beaten me in tennis yet.

I'm happy you liked your lamp, honey girl, for I spent a lot of time deciding upon it, and more trying to find a Pi Phi crest. None of the Pi Phis in Woodbury had one, and on my trip to Lewisburg I finally managed to find it on some stationery at the Book Store. I wanted to paint directly on it, but couldn't find any medium that would take on that glazed surface. It wasn't much, sweetheart mine, but there was an infinite amount of love packed in it.

Ken x

Monday evening, July 20, 1925, Buffalo to Camp Kanuka

Dear Boy-o'-Mine,

My last letter was quite open and frank, I know – almost too much, so I feared afterward – but that's the way I felt, and I knew you would be glad if I didn't try to restrain my feelings. Aren't we funny, tho, the way we want school to begin, while not long ago a vacation couldn't be long enough to suit us!

Three cheers for the swimming accomplishments! I envy your nearness to the water. I'm just dying for a good swim myself, but no chance here.

Mother & I went shopping the other day for gifts for Father's birthday. But before getting much, we suddenly discovered that Mother's pocketbook had been picked, & she had lost about fifteen dollars! So we had to stop. I guess Father's birthday will be pretty costly this year. Everybody, of course, was just sick about it, but nothing could be done.

Yesterday I had to preach a sermon. Yes'm, but it was only a little one. Father had to give a report of the Conv. in the Lafayette Church, and he made me talk for about five minutes before that whole congregation. Phew! I could hardly stand on the platform, and my voice was so shaky I could hardly talk, but some benevolent souls spoke their appreciation.

I'm not doing a thing anybody could call useful. I sleep most of the time, and then can't seem to get enough. It'll take a lot of resting to get rid of the effects of 208 Taylor Street [Aunt Jennie's house in Lewisburg]. Oh, no, it isn't as bad as that, but a trip like ours needs some recuperation, anyway.

Lots o' love from your "funny"
Lady x

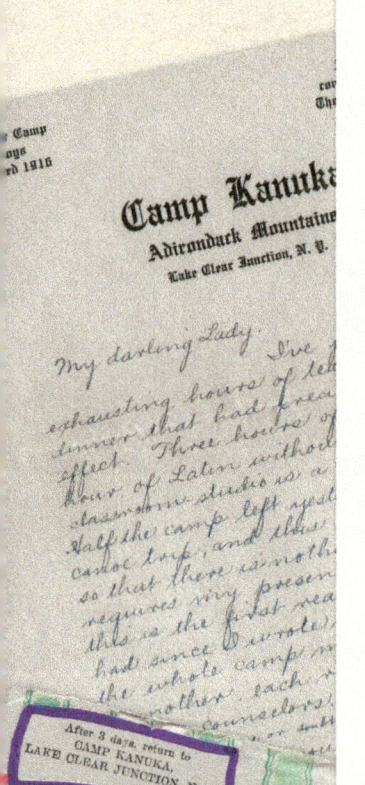

Tuesday afternoon, July 21, 1925, Camp Kanuka to Buffalo

My darling Lady,

I have discovered that my best student in French I is a fellow townsman of yours. His name is Walter Reiman, and he lives at #1 Windsor Ave. [Walt, Ken, and Caryl became lifelong friends.] We are both enthusiastic about the manifold merits of Buffalo. My two most brilliant pupils are foreigners – Miyar, a Cuban, and Vallé, from Peru, are model students, always do more than required, and employ more precise English than the Americans in the same classes.

I should have explained that the polo player on my last envelope had no particular significance, for polo is one of the few sports we don't have here. I had painted one under orders for a fellow here, and it was such a brilliant bit of color that I made another one for you, lady mine.

The envelope idea has made a hit here, and my pens and brushes are kept busy in the little spare time I have. Friday evening I gave the first of my chalk talks, "KANUKA KEN'S KRAZY KRAYON KRACKS." We had a blazing fire, player piano, marshmallows, and chalk. The kids fought for the sketches afterward, and now they're decorating all the bungalows.

My swimming is progressing, and I am learning to use the side-stroke and to dive. The coach scatters five little white butter plates in five feet of water, and I dive for them. So far three is as many as I can bring up at once. I'm not entirely at ease in the water yet, but I'm gradually losing my fear of it. However, the lake is always so cold that no one can stay in very long.

If your globe-trotting should ever bring you in this direction, don't drop in without warning – to me, at least – for we wear only the oldest of clothes and shave only once or twice a week, and you'd be ashamed to admit acquaintance with me – HoboKen!

Bobby received a nice acknowledgment, written on White House stationery, of her birthday card.

This enforced separation is the hardest thing I've ever had to bear, altho it's easier here in the woods somehow than it would be back in the world with people and dances and things.

Always,
Your Ken x

July 22, 1925, Vineland, New Jersey, to Camp Kanuka

On July 22, 1925, Don Streeter, of Vineland, N.J., Ken's Bucknell sidekick in SLIFER & STREETER'S SYNDICATED SIGN SERVICE, pens a letter to Ken at Camp Kanuka. His precise lettering, the address, and the humorous drawing on the envelope of a canvassing note-taker talking to a housewife are clearly the work of another artist in the making. It seems Ken has written to tell Don about his summer job. Don sketches a kicking shoe, addresses Ken as "Kick," and signs off as "Side."

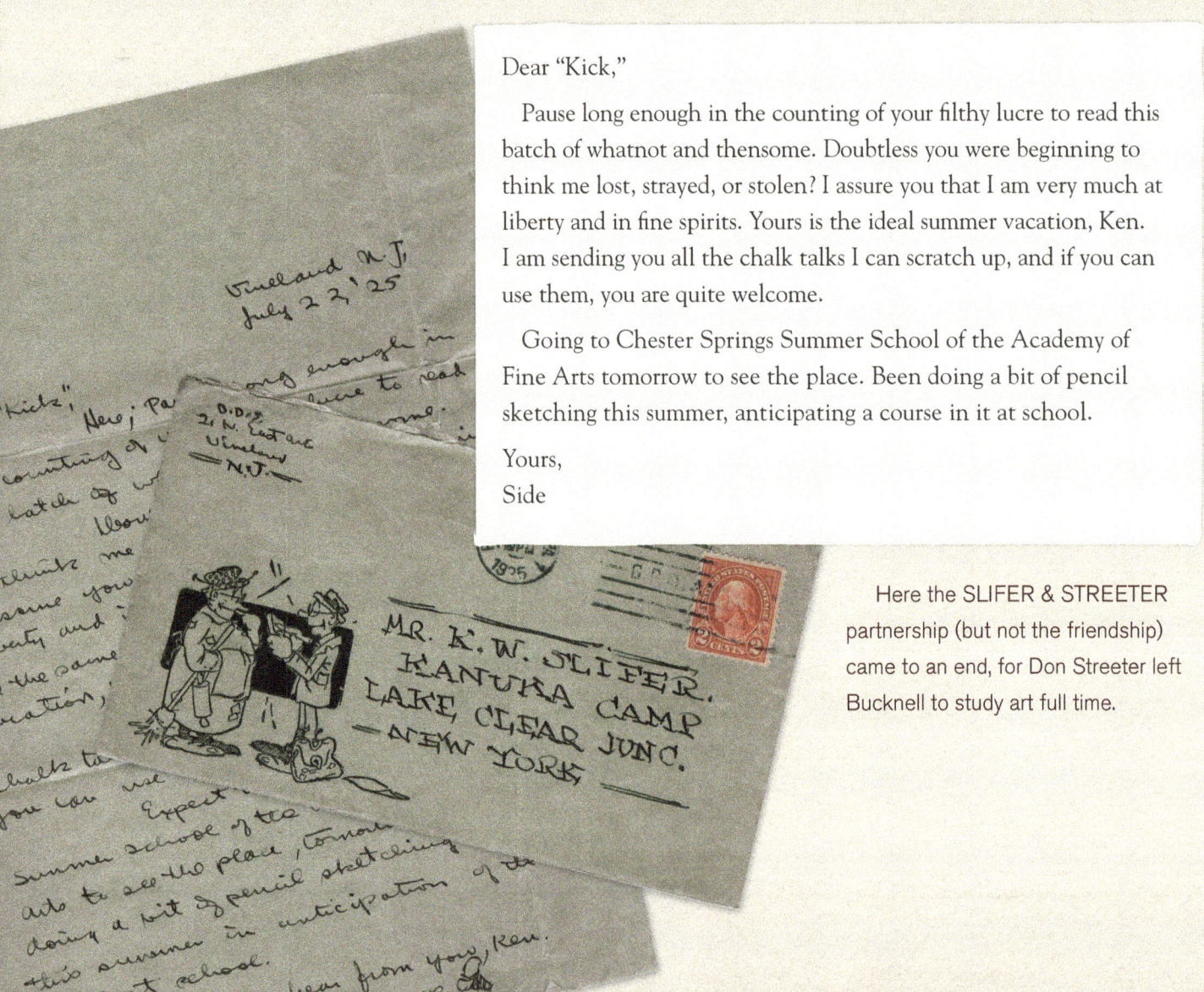

Dear "Kick,"

Pause long enough in the counting of your filthy lucre to read this batch of whatnot and thensome. Doubtless you were beginning to think me lost, strayed, or stolen? I assure you that I am very much at liberty and in fine spirits. Yours is the ideal summer vacation, Ken. I am sending you all the chalk talks I can scratch up, and if you can use them, you are quite welcome.

Going to Chester Springs Summer School of the Academy of Fine Arts tomorrow to see the place. Been doing a bit of pencil sketching this summer, anticipating a course in it at school.

Yours,
Side

Here the SLIFER & STREETER partnership (but not the friendship) came to an end, for Don Streeter left Bucknell to study art full time.

Thursday evening, July 23, Buffalo to Camp Kanuka

My own dear Ken,

How much I liked the dear hillside cottage with its wide-spreading tree and the big round moon. And the polo boy, too. The family always crowds around to see your letters and admire the works of art, and as soon as I've read them they want to know what you're doing. They're interested in everything you do.

Rolland is having a successful summer selling books and expects to make over $100 this week. Mary is giving summer make-up work in Bradford. She has 17 pupils, and earns $45–$50 a week. I'm the only lazy one of our quartet. But I haven't enough ambition to let it worry me. My work at school next year will cover more money than I could earn this summer, and I desperately need nothing but rest just now.

Mother hasn't had an attack since I came home, and even sings a bit now and then, and that's a good sign. Father celebrated his 53rd birthday yesterday, and we had a little home party – no guests. Attie gave him a glove box. Father & I brot several funny things from Seattle. Mother & Attie almost threw away a whole bowl of cake batter, and Rolland almost threw out a big dish of cereal, just because of a protruding black fly that looked very realistic, but was found to be attached to a long pin point.

I send you my very best love and a big wish to see you.

Yours,
Caryl

Saturday evening, July 25, 1925, Camp Kanuka to Buffalo

My precious Lady,

I am quite sure, dear, I never longed for vacation, for that meant long separation. I may have wished for your removal from the Missus' mansion, but for the end of school – never.

Saranac Inn, a large and exclusive summer place, is situated about four miles from here, and a lot of the older fellows run down to the dances there three times a week. I haven't been tempted in the least. Some of my envelopes, drawn for other fellows, have filtered down there and elicited more requests. Today a carload of girls stopped, and the boys came for me with wild tales of millionaires' daughters, but there is not and cannot be any substitute for you, sweetheart.

I have been playing baseball this week. Our big opening game took place today, after a week of arduous practice. I won my berth in a practice game by a clean but lucky single that drove in the only two runs in the whole game.

An amusing coincidence made me laugh last evening. I wanted a box in which to preserve the missives you send me this summer and attacked the trash can in our little store where we sell candy, gum, and all manner of odds and ends. I found a bright yellow box that had held candy bars and departed to my studio. Not until then did I look at my acquisition. It said This box contains 24 Love Nests!

The sketch on this envelope is my newest self-portrait, with the lake and the mountain as mere setting. It is supposed to be symbolical of my newfound enjoyment of the water, at the same time giving you a general idea of my present environment.

As I may have told you I loaned my Demie pin to Harry [Ken's fraternity "son"] to wear home, because the new ones had not arrived when he left. As I have not told you, he lost it, which means that, if I can get one in time, you will have a brand new Demie pin to set above your heart next September 19th.

Your own
Ken x

Tuesday evening, July 28, 1925, Buffalo to Camp Kanuka

Dear One,

Yesterday the whole "D" family invaded the dentist's office, and after he had done his best to put us in shape for chewing rags and other such tough propositions, we drove around town a bit, looking at houses for sale. We're tired of a two-family house, and want to sell if we can. But we probably won't!

The folks dropped me off at Vera's, where I dined and stayed all night. By the way Vera has an awfully exciting and lively position – at the Morgue! Things must be rather dead there, don't you think?

You mos' completely misunderstood my reference to desiring the approach of vacations. I was referring to our kid days, when vacation meant merely a play time with freedom from books.

Too bad you had to visit R.N.D. [Rolland N. Dutton] in Sept. 1923. If it weren't for knowing me, just think of all the thrills you could have meeting those millionaires' daughters and playing the young sheik at those dances. I'm just awfully happy you don't want to go, 'cause it means that you love me so much, and that makes me supremely happy.

There's one thing that you haven't seen about Buffalo – and that's the Falls at night. We went last Saturday, and standing on the Canadian side saw those huge tumbling masses of water turned into every color and shade of the rainbow as those powerful lights were thrown on them and shifted every few minutes. It's a perfectly beautiful sight, and I hope when you do see it I can be with you.

How many more "love nests" are needed to complete the box? If you feel lonesome for love there in the woods, mine is flying to you on the swiftest wings.

Your own
"Lady"

Thursday afternoon, July 30, 1925
Camp Kanuka to Buffalo

Darling,

One bit of news I neglected to mention in my last "billet-doux." I received the same sort of communication from the Dean notifying me of a straight "A" and congratulating me on my "new position in the scholastic life of Bucknell." Aren't we the intellectual pair, tho, lady mine?

I can't sympathize with your statement that it is too bad Fate led me to visit R.N.D. in 1923. If Fate was responsible (Clem says *he* is), that fickle goddess did me the kindest turn she has ever done. I'd be willing to waive the idea of luck or fate and subscribe to the Presbyterian view of "predestination." Whatever agency may be responsible has often had my heartfelt thanks.

Yesterday I laboriously composed a refusal to an urgent dance invitation. A Miss Eden Welsh of Texas and New York was the object of my cold regrets. Enormously wealthy, she travels around in a big Lincoln with a chauffeur and maintains a palatial summer home near Saranac Inn. The invitation came for tomorrow night – a big dance with a California orchestra – at her home, "Tall Pines." I was hard pressed for a plausible alibi. I finally wrote I'd had such a strenuous year at college that I'd come here for complete rest. I couldn't very well announce we're engaged, could I, dear? I decorated the envelope hurriedly and hope it will satisfy her. The boys can't understand my attitude, and at every ball game she attends try to manoeuver an introduction. So far, I've escaped unscathed, but I think I'll stop going. It's a ludicrous situation, but Miss Welsh with all her clothes and cars and millions pales into insignificance beside you, sweetheart. I LOVE YOU!

I am finding that a graceful dive is not as easy as it looks, and I'm sore and aching from hitting the water too flat. When I start head first for the water, the old numbing Fear grips me and twists me into all manner of awkward positions!

Sunday we dress in civilized clothes, and most attend a Presbyterian church nearby, while others, mostly foreign boys, attend the Catholic service. I know I'm putting on much-needed weight; last Sunday I couldn't get my vest buttoned properly, and it was loose when I came here! Sunday the camp comic sheet appears, to which I'm contributing plenty of crazy doggerel and verse.

My regards to your family, reserving an enormous amount of love for yourself!

Your devoted
Ken x

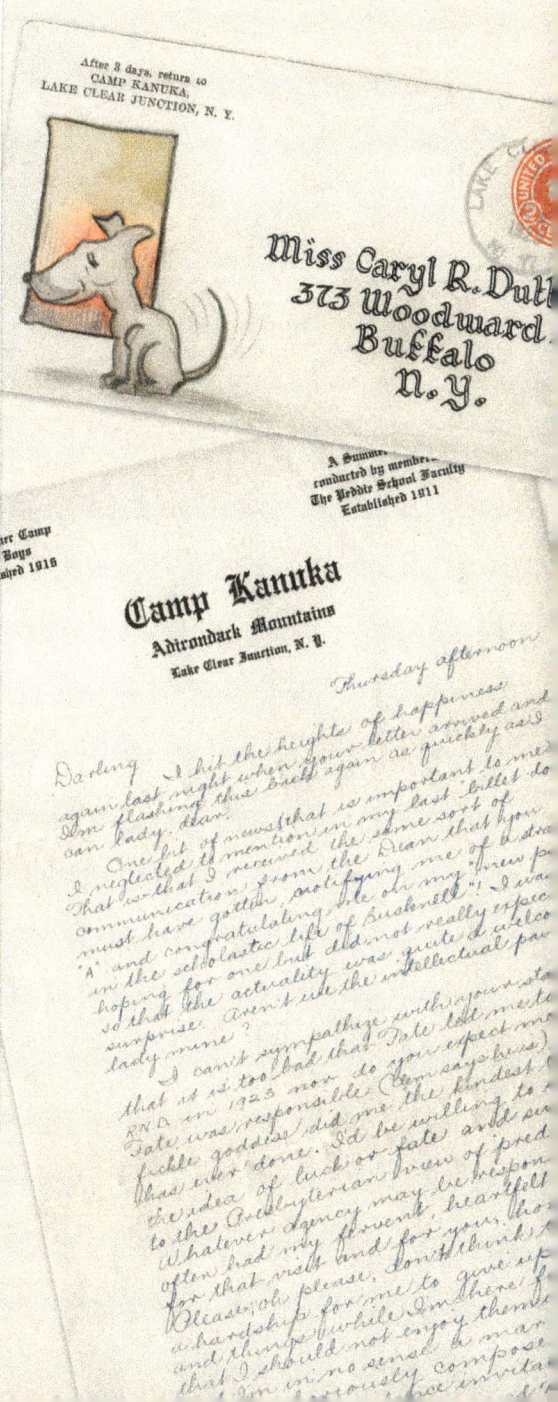

Saturday morning, August 1, 1925, Buffalo to Camp Kanuka

My dearest Ken,

I am just as glad as I can be that you got your letter from the Dean. Mine didn't give me a thrill at all, for beside being the third, it doesn't say I got a straight "A," but merely congratulates me on maintaining an average of "A" for three semesters. I wanted a straight "A" so badly that I was disgusted when the letter came and didn't tell me whether I succeeded or not.

You are such a dear to be so true to me amid all the attractions there. I don't wonder a bit though that they all bargain for your highly desirable presence and attentions. I do myself, and I wouldn't give them credit for any sense at all if they didn't like you an awful lot!

R. and Father are going to bum up to Glens Falls together next Tuesday (4th) and stay at our Camp when they're not invited out. With them, you won't have to worry about clothes and beard, for they'll look like tramps themselves. [Near Glens Falls, where Caryl's father pastored a dozen years earlier, the Duttons built a rustic, one-room retreat on a half-acre rented from their friend Arthur Pike for $1 a year. They called it Pine Cone Inn.]

Yes, R. is surely succeeding. He made $35 yesterday. He stopped at one house the day before and sold two $7.90 Bibles and two $5.00 Stories of the Bible. Of course, that was unusual, but he sells a book at almost every place he goes.

I am having lots of fun slashing up all the cloth that comes within my reach. Mother pulled out some goods the other day that she'd had for herself in a dress some years ago. I pounced on it for myself, since she doesn't use it any more. The joke is that Mother gave it to the dressmaker 6 or 7 years ago to make a dress for me, and she said there wasn't enough goods! I succeeded in beating her to it and made a whole dress for myself!

Please remind yourself you're mos' awfully dear to your "lady" and she loves you a whole lot.

Your
"Lady"

Wednesday evening, August 5, 1925
Buffalo to Camp Kanuka

My dear, dear Ken,

I don't know when Father and R. plan to come up to see you. They were planning to bum, but found Monday night that a Hebrew Christian whom Father knows was leaving early Tues. and going straight thru to Lake George. So they hopped in and rode all the way in a new great big Studebaker.

R.'s old car is working finely. His only objection is that the roof leaks when it rains. But he has been painting it all over, and it looks fine now. When he gets ready to sell it, he ought to make a good sale. He loves to tinker with it & take it apart, and when it doesn't go, for lack of gas, he just gets out and pushes it wherever he wants to go!

Speaking of your personal appearance not being up to the requirement for meeting visitors – I have the same trouble. Besides trying to wear out some old clothes, I'm letting my hair stay the way Nature made it – straight as a poker. Mother says I look disgraceful, but it was coming out so, I thot I'd forego the curls for a while. So don't call on me, either, without warning.

I got a lovely letter from Aunt Jennie a day or so ago. She thot it funny that neither of us had written for so long. Then when we did, I wrote on Monday and you on Tuesday of the same week! She doesn't know how good we are on mental telepathy!

I do want to see you so much. Mebbe I can wait till school opens, but I has me doots.

Caryl

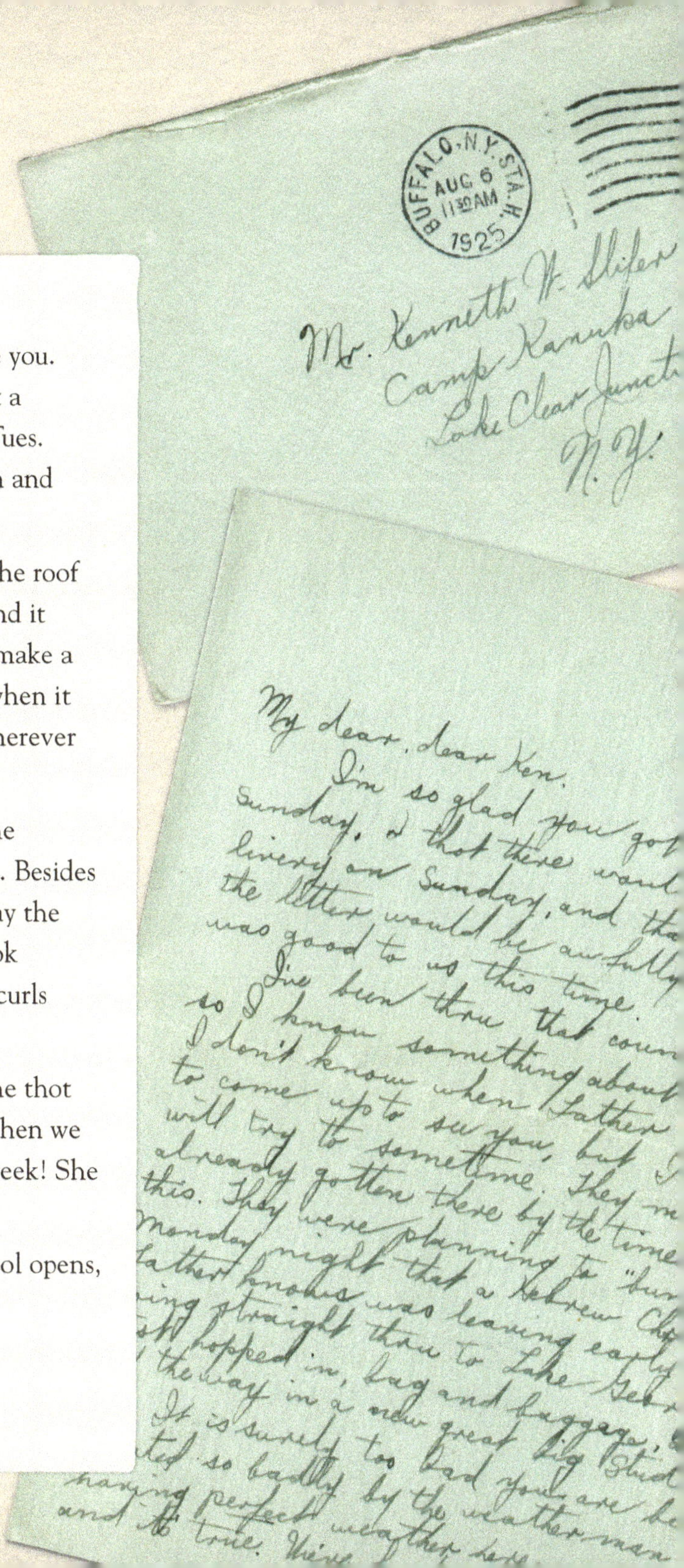

Friday afternoon, August 7, 1925, Camp Kanuka to Buffalo

Dear,

This summer has been much nicer than other summers, for I can be sure of receiving a letter from you every few days. My calendar is marked, not by days or weeks, but by my own dear Lady's letters. Tomorrow we finish reading "L'Abbé Constantin" (in French II), with Lesson 92 in Chardenal's grammar.

The most important bit of news: I have invaded "Tall Pines," met Eden Welsh, and love you the more because of it. Suffice it to say, the best bass fishing in this part of the country is on Saranac Lake, where lies palatial "Tall Pines." Kink Sprout, an ardent fisherman, was offered the use of boats, bait, everything, provided he brought me along. He came to me and pled a long, long time. I suspected a conspiracy, but he insisted fishing was the primary purpose and meeting Miss Welsh a necessary evil. I have spent a great deal of time with him since I've been here and finally yielded, for I believed the meeting inevitable and wanted it over with.

With the best grace I could muster, I met Miss Welsh, altho I did not say, "Delighted." "Tall Pines" is a veritable fairyland, the sort of place one dreams about, and sees only in "Vanity Fair" or in "Vogue." There are all manner of fascinating walks, shaded benches, and little lights in the bushes – honeysuckle, ivy, and evergreens. The boathouse is a regular mansion with a ballroom over it – lamps, big upholstered furniture, speedboats, all kinds of water toys and swimming apparatus – a rather incoherent description, because I was wishing so hard for you, Lady dear. Miss Welsh, reputedly worth 50 millions, was not at all backward or bashful. Further description must wait until I can forestall your "meows" in person.

Kink and I got 15 big black bass in little over an hour. We left immediately after fishing, with me heaving a sigh of relief, for she renewed her pleas to attend her big dance, alleging I didn't look like a nervous wreck. The full story will amuse you when I can tell it personally. I'm glad you trust me, for there's not the slightest danger of my falling for these local samples of "Flaming Youth." Some are good-looking, but that's the only thing they have in common with you.

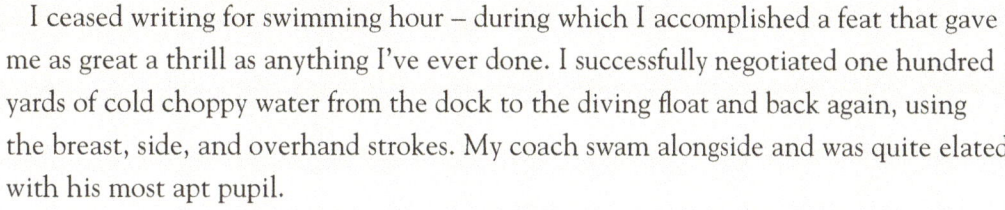

I ceased writing for swimming hour – during which I accomplished a feat that gave me as great a thrill as anything I've ever done. I successfully negotiated one hundred yards of cold choppy water from the dock to the diving float and back again, using the breast, side, and overhand strokes. My coach swam alongside and was quite elated with his most apt pupil.

Rolland and your Dad have yet to put in an appearance. There are four Bucknellians here, and with two more we can challenge the camp to meet the Bucknell team in tennis, volleyball, basketball, or most anything else. If they come today or tomorrow, Rev. E. Herbert Dutton can speak in my stead at vespers.

Any sort of a reunion in the Fall will be delightful. Since I have no expenses now, I intend to spend liberally of my "easy money" for clothes, so I needn't look like HoboKen on this trip, and you will have no reason to be ashamed of me, darling.

Yours for a reunion, with all my love,
Ken x x

P.S. We have a player piano here, and Mother sent the camp 70 piano music rolls of some of our favorite songs from home. It seems almost sacrilegious when I hear our old familiar pieces being ground out all day and most of the night!

Monday afternoon, August 10, 1925, Buffalo to Camp Kanuka

Honey-Mine,

I got an amusing letter from Bobby the other day. She encloses a picture of her "brother's especial and only girl-friend," for my information, she says. Isn't she the funniest and most original girl!

So you have met the famous multi-millionairesse at last! How I should love to see her fairyland-home. You must see everything with two pairs of eyes – one for me. I want to hear all about everything.

I seem to be specializing in thunderbolts or electric shocks this summer. I just got one from Mrs. Sale, announcing that my presence is required at the B.U. Sem beginning Tues., Sept. 8! All freshmen are to come a week early, to get signed up and acclimated before the big rush begins. That means six waitresses beside myself. It will give me a week to get accustomed to my work before the biggest number come. I'll learn all the ins and outs of the dining room when there's no rush of classes, and have time to get my things transferred from Aunt Jennie's and be all settled when the work really begins. Besides, I'll have the grandest possible chance to get acquainted with the 70 or so freshman girls, for I shall be either the only upper-classman there, or one of only two or three. It will make the first few weeks lots less of a nervous strain.

You don't have to spend your money to keep from looking like a hobo. You couldn't look like one. I haven't anything new, so don't buy too much. You'll have to accompany a "Lady" in old clothes, anyway. A sight of you in any kind of clothes – old or new – would make me completely happy.

Most lovingly yours,
C x

Wednesday, August 12, 1925, Camp Kanuka to Buffalo

Dear, dear Lady,

Fate seems to be mocking us at every turn – with your enforced departure at Commencement time and now the cancellation of our reunion. I can see, though, that things are really working out best for you, and so I shan't complain. I am quite sure I'll be able to come up to Lewisburg shortly after your own arrival, and we will enjoy ourselves there as best we can. The main thing after all is that we should be together.

I surmised correctly when I told you the "frivolous females" hereabouts were motivated only by curiosity. They wanted to see a live ham artist in captivity, and they were evidently disappointed, for since our informal meeting I have not been once molested.

The funniest happening of the past few days was the establishment of my Scorpions in the menagerie business. By some mysterious means, they succeeded in capturing an assortment of seven live bullfrogs (all sizes), one medium-sized garter snake, 3 toads, and a number of pollywogs and tadpoles. These they housed in a miscellaneous collection of jars and cans, charging 1 cent for single admission and 10 cents for a season ticket! I made them tickets, and by various expedients they collected 84 cents, and the four of them gorged themselves on candy. A millionaire's son paid 15 cents to see the snake fight the biggest toad! Life was a regular bedlam for two days, for the snake was always getting loose and crawling around, and one was liable any time to find a frog or toad in bed.

Unfortunately, they scaled some sunfish all over the bungalow in my absence, and the smell attracted the powers that be, who banned the whole menagerie. I spent two hours sweeping and scrubbing out, because the kids have only the most primitive ideas of cleanliness. (Incidentally, they upset an aquarium over my best tennis racket! The damage is frightful to relate!)

Bobby and Mother are spending the next two weeks at Drums' cottage [Ken's aunt, Grace Slifer Drum] in Muncy, Pa. Mother is feeling better, and weighs 125 lbs., which is her ideal weight.

All my love is yours, darling,
Ken x x x

P. S. Don't let even a trip to the moon take you from Lewisburg next June, when I'm getting my sheepskin!

Early Friday morning, August 14, 1925, Buffalo to Camp Kanuka

Dearest Ken,

No, Honey-boy, not even a trip to the moon will keep me from Lewisburg when you get your "sheepskin." The dining room wouldn't let me go, anyway, and besides R. will get his sheepskin too, & I suppose the whole family will be there.

Goodness, but I should hate all that menagerie of reptiles, amphibians, and such! For your own peace of living, it's a good thing the "powers that be" descended. I'm so sorry about your racket.

I wish I could get Mother up to 125 lbs. We get weighed every day, but the best we can do is 119 lbs.

"Aunty" Stickle helped me start my latest feminine foolishness – a hope chest, by giving me five beautiful linen towels. I thot under the circumstances it might be appropriate to substitute the name hope chest for my old name for it – "despair barrel"!

Mother says she really thinks I need a slicker! But she says you can't paint on it unless you guarantee to either get it off or cover it up with yellow paint when I'm thru college! Isn't she funny!?

Yours with lots of love,
Caryl

Tuesday afternoon, August 18, 1925, Buffalo to Camp Kanuka

My own dear Ken,

I've been sick in bed since Friday. At first I thot I had an attack of indigestion or poisoning, but now I guess it's been the old grippe. Today I managed to get on my clothes, but I'm not much good. It's disgusting! Here I've been trying my best to gain, and now in three or four days I've lost most all of the results of my efforts. I'm so afraid, too, that Mother will catch my cold, for that would mean weeks of sickness for her instead of days for me. [Mabel's frequent illnesses largely stemmed from chronic asthma, which sometimes progressed to pneumonia.]

Pardon my neglect in not telling you where R. and Father were. They stayed at Camp until Friday, left there, and in one "lift" made Syracuse that night and stayed at the Mizpah Inn. Saturday they got a car a block from the Inn and rode to Canandaigua, and another from there straight to Buffalo, getting here about 4:30! They were sorry not to see you, but it was a long way, and Father didn't dare take chances of not getting back for Sunday morning, when he was scheduled to preach. They put on a kitchen addition to the Camp, and couldn't leave until it was finished. You see, R. is ambitious to get the place all fixed up, for he and Mary are going to spend their honeymoon there. He says it's all agreed and settled!

Oh, please send me a picture of the "Scorpion Family." I'm just crazy to see them all, after hearing so much about them.

What color is your new suit? I'm awfully anxious to see it, but oh, how much more I want to see you. But Ken dear, don't leave home before you ought to. I can have you all year, but your Mother and Bobby will have only two weeks, and busy weeks at that. We must both be unselfish about it.

Lovingly,
Your "Lady"

Friday morning, August 21, 1925, Buffalo to Camp Kanuka

My own Dearest,

Thank you ever so much for sending the pictures. Please, may I have some of the large ones with you in them? The Scorpions aren't half as interesting without you!

How I should have loved to hear your Kracks, Flashes, and Thunder. I'm going to demand a private performance avec papier et plume in the Sem parlor some day – that is, if you will condescend to call some day in that awesome holy of holies, where only the worst of flirts are thot to enter, and where horrible events are seen and said to occur!

Vera wants me again tomorrow night, but I don't know yet whether I can go, unless I'm better. Her little six-year-old nephew, who until a short time ago has lived with them, has just been stricken with infantile paralysis [polio], and they all feel pretty badly about it.

Ken dear, should you say anything to Father before you ask me to take your pin? I don't know whether you ought, so I thot I'd just frankly ask you. I tried to talk with Mother some time ago, but as I feared, I didn't accomplish much. I think she understands my viewpoint, and tho she thinks I'm not grown up yet, I know that neither she nor Father will be surprised at any outcome of your birthday plans. Your yearning for our reunion has an answering response in my own heart, for I love you more every day.

Yours with all my love,
Caryl

No identification, except, "I'm the one in the middle!"

Saturday afternoon, August 22, 1925, Camp Kanuka to Buffalo

My precious Lady,

Our mental telepathy and my faith in you are functioning with a double efficiency now, for I was completely, absolutely confident that your letter would arrive this morning. I love you – until every fibre of my being thrills at the thought, and I want to proclaim it to all the world.

I was interrupted this afternoon to officiate at the camp swimming meet. The camp gives handsome medals in track, tennis, and swimming, and the competition is quite keen. This evening there was a fancy dress parade, with prizes for the cleverest costumes devised from makeshift materials at hand. I was busy "making up" assorted kids and painting all manner of signs. Four of the five prizewinners were entirely my creation, and the Scorpions were voted the best bungalow group. The whole affair was topped by a big bonfire with "dogs," marshmallows, candy, and cake. Most of the camp is asleep now, or suffering indigestion.

I'll delay writing your Father, at least until I can talk with my Mother, and with you, personally. I'm willing to act in every way as you see fit, for I want you, Lady mine!

I'm glad that you liked the Scorpion pictures, and I hope they lightened your illness with a few minutes of amusement. Of course you may have any of them you choose.

I received a funny letter from Bobby today. I think she loves you almost as much as I do!

Tomorrow evening I have full charge of vesper services, and I must give the final address, for by next Sunday a lot of the fellows will be gone. The other directors have all given rather ambitious speeches, so I intend to devote most of tomorrow to preparation.

Next Saturday there is a banquet that Christy Mathewson always attends. Some of the boys take a train that night, but the rest, myself included, will board the train Monday night (Aug. 31), arriving in New York next morning. From that time it will be less than two weeks till I see you again!

Until then – all my love,
Ken x

Tuesday evening, August 25, 1925, Buffalo to Camp Kanuka

Ken, dear,

Your big cousin "T. B." [Thomas "Burns" Drum] has been in Buffalo to visit relatives, as your Mother has probably informed you. Summer surely has agreed with him. With a very good-looking sport outfit, he looked quite the collegiate "hero." (He went to church in knickers, also.) He informed me that on account of drinking at the big Commencement Dance, four Pi Phis have been suspended for a year! [Prohibition, the 18th Amendment, went into effect in January 1920 and was not repealed until 1933, by the 21st Amendment.] I don't like to be unfaithful to our fraternity, but I have to admit, to you anyway, that the standard ought to be better without these four.

We all went to Crystal Beach Monday. We tried both chute-the-chutes, ferris wheel, aeroplane-merry-go-round, and an old mill place where we went a long way in the dark in flat-bottom boats. The last was rather gruesome, but just the place for R. and Mary to go. We went swimming, too.

I got a whole 8-page letter from Bobby today! I was surprised and delighted. It is funny as usual, with a picture of you in the stoutness in which she expects you to appear when you return!

Next Monday you will be leaving our "Empire" for your "Garden" farther away. But it won't be long now, dear. [New York is the Empire State; New Jersey, the Garden State.]

Lots of love,
Caryl

Wednesday afternoon, September 2, 1925
Woodbury to Buffalo

Lady, mine,

The Kanuka banquet last Saturday evening was more than successful. The Directors said a lot of nice things about me and then announced (without having asked me) that I would return next year, whereat the Scorpions rushed over to pummel me, and everybody laughed. It would be much easier next year; an ideal vacation after a senior year that promises to be a strenuous one; and physically and financially it is the best summer I could spend.

I spent most of Sunday planning a "sermonette" for the final vesper service. I used Romans 12:18 as text: "If it be possible, so far as in you lieth, be at peace with all men."

Our train left at 9:45 Monday evening, and I was in charge of the party (16). The kids behaved well, took the berths I assigned them, and I slept peacefully all night. There was a mob awaiting us in Grand Central at 7:45, and it was something of a problem to locate all the poppas and mommas. I succeeded eventually, caught a Phila. express, and got home by dinner time.

We have decided, since I've been home, that I am to leave on Saturday the twelfth, which means, honey girl, that I'll arrive in Lewisburg by the Reading 1:29! Only ten days yet! You must be careful to restrain me, Lady dear, so that I'm not too foolish on the station platform!

I intend to discuss things with Mother before I come back, tho I feel sure she will favor our plans, for she thinks you are the finest, sweetest girl that ever was. I am prompted only by my great and overwhelming love for you, sweetheart,

K x

Sunday evening, September 6, 1925, Woodbury to Lewisburg

My darling Lady,

This envelope design represents, as definitely as they can be portrayed, my thoughts for the last few months – air castles, sweetheart, wherein you always figure prominently. Tall graceful spires lost in the clouds, cool breezes that are borne in from the night, stardust, a wisp of a moon, solitude, and you and I whispering delicious nonsense.

I confided our plans to Mother, and found her graciously sympathetic and understanding. She thinks we are more mature than our years, and that such a step would not be rash or foolish. She esteems you highly, honey, and her judgment is supported by the Drums and my Grandmother. She is willing to trust in us and to do anything she can for us, in the hope that we won't have to wait too long – until Love and Romance lose their first bloom. I can assure you she quite approves, and she's anxious to welcome you and to love you as soon as the opportunity arrives. Bobby, I know, would be utterly delighted to have you as sister.

Clem and Bec got back this evening, tanned and dirty from a week's canoe trip. Gert Hunter and Chick Carter dropped in this evening to "reune," after which we drove out into the country, purchased a big watermelon, and flivvered back to Clem's with it for a welcoming feast.

Here's hoping we can both survive the hours that intervene till 1:29 on Saturday.

Eagerly, lovingly,
Ken x

Monday evening, September 7, 1925
Buffalo to Woodbury

Ken, dear,

I have been thinking ever since Saturday, "This time next week," and it seems almost too good to be true. Tempus is surely "fugiting" now.

Rolland wants to tell you that he will probably be at least a week late getting down to school. He wants to make a certain amount before stopping.

Mary left Friday morning after an awfully busy week. Rolland is angry with me because, at Mary's request, I took her downtown to buy some things she wanted, and thus "monopolized" her for two whole days. Well, he had her most of the night, anyway, for Mary came to bed only one night before 2 A.M. or later! Isn't that shocking conduct?!!!

I think it will be great for you to go back to the camp next year. It surely will be wonderful for you, as a profitable vacation from all points of view.

I am living for Saturday. Five more days!

With happy anticipations,
Caryl x

Women's dining room in Larison Hall where, as head waitress during her junior and senior years, Caryl was in charge of three meals a day, earning a $175 reduction on each semester's bill.[1]

Wednesday p.m., September 9, 1925
Lewisburg to Woodbury

Dearest ~

I don't think I have ever loved or admired any of your drawings so much as this – "our dream castle." It is so beautiful and intricate in its workmanship, and best of all it has a meaning – and a very dear one for you and me. I wish I had your power of expression.

I have been awfully busy ever since I arrived yesterday at 5:30. The dining room has taken almost all my time since then, except for a snatched minute now and then for unpacking. I love my room, even if it is tiny, and I am enjoying the dining room work. The whole crowd will be here tonight for dinner, and I have to supervise serving refreshments at a reception tonight for both men and women.

After dinner: Oh, what a rush I have had! We prepared for 80 at dinner and had 120! I never saw such a hustle to set up new tables, get a waitress, make food out of leftovers, etc. But I enjoyed myself in spite of it all.

With all my love, I am eagerly awaiting your arrival ~
C.

On September 19, 1925, his 20th birthday, Ken gives Caryl his fraternity pin, signifying they are officially "engaged to be engaged." No letters survive from mid-September until the December Christmas break.

Saturday afternoon, December 19, 1925
Buffalo to Woodbury

Ken dear,

Our train was an hour late last night, but Mother was still waiting for me. At lunch we had fifteen or twenty more than the number for whom we had set places. I had to do some hustling to serve them, but we were all thru by half-past twelve. Mr. Warfel was on time, and took us at 50–55 an hour to Milton.

There was quite a crowd of us on the train. A pair of twins – very good looking flappers, from the Penn Art School – spent a lot of time vamping Rolland, much to the amusement of the rest of us. A whole mob of boys got on at Olean from St. Bonaventure and almost overflowed the car. You would have gotten as much fun as we did out of seeing the way Muriel Adams got into the center of things when a young fellow sat down beside her. The whole carful of boys poked fun at her companion and sang to them. I don't suppose Muriel ever had such an experience before in her prim life.

I discovered today that I had mislaid my entrance permit for the conference in Evanston, so I have sent post haste to Grace to get it for me. I guess I was too excited to think straight before I left.

I hope you're enjoying being home again. I'm sending you all the love the mail can carry.

Lovingly your own
Caryl

Wednesday morning, December 23, 1925
Buffalo to Woodbury

Caryl sends two envelopes to Ken, both postmarked 2 A.M., December 24, indicating faith in one-day delivery. One envelope contains a card on heavy stock, showing a beautifully embossed winter scene with the message:

My dearest,

Sunday after dinner, Helen Jackson wanted me to go to C. E. [Christian Endeavor] and church with her. I was worried because I didn't have any good dress to wear, so pawed around among Mother's things, and found a dress of Grandma's that just fit me! Can you imagine? The style was the latest, and since she's much shorter, the length was right, so I donned it and departed.

Monday Mother and I started shopping in search of a dress. We thot I needed one after the previous evening's experience! But I'm so particular that none could suit me, and we came back without one. I had just enough time to eat supper and start back down to the Y.M.C.A., where all Bucknell students (6 of us) were to meet a committee to talk over plans for the Glee Club trip.

I hope the pictures turn out all right. Don't forget I want one of you in your overcoat and hat! I'd sure give a whole lot to see the original! Till I do, all my love to you, dear,

Your "Lady"

This card is signed simply "Caryl." The second envelope contains her letter.

Friday, Christmas Day, 1925, Woodbury to Buffalo

Honey girl,

I had every intention of writing yesterday, but delayed so that I might properly thank you for your Christmas present. That I half expected the book [title not mentioned] didn't make it any the less welcome, and I've hugely enjoyed reading it. It's fun to pick tentative casts from our student body and imagine stage sets for them. Thank you ever so much.

I was the recipient of one gift that will go into your "soap" chest. Mrs. Brown, at the Demie house, sent me a funny, misspelled letter that I am enclosing for your enjoyment. Accompanying it was a good-looking silver gravy ladle! Rogers Bros.! The dear old lady had done things handsomely, albeit prematurely, and had it engraved C.S.! My bringing the "minnue" down signifies my getting the Demie caterer out of bed in the mornings and extracting from him the day's menu, so that Mrs. Brown could order from the store boy. She repeatedly hinted that she was going to do something for me and "Caroline," as she persists in calling you. She seems to think Caryl is merely an abbreviation of the longer name. I know your card of thanks will make her very happy.

My painful public presentation on Monday has not been without its after-effects. Tuesday morning, Gurney Sholl (Delta Sigma, Bucknell '10) called up to say that the Camden Courier was sending a man down to photograph me. He is managing editor or something on the sheet, which is the only really big paper in South Jersey. Fraternity politics again! The photographer came, I was duly "snapped" with sad results, and I am enclosing my only copy of the published picture. Mother was quite desirous of retaining it, so guard it with your life!

I'm now continually accosted by people who want to proffer congratulations. Cautiously I respond, "How come?" If they answer, "Your engagement," I try to blush becomingly, but if they come back, "The medal," I guffaw scornfully. [This medal is not explained.] Somehow the news of our engagement has gone the rounds completely – how I don't know, for Mother and Bobby have not broadcasted it especially. They are all curious to see you – who could charm a bashful, backward chap like myself – that is how I'm remembered. I hope it won't be too hard, when you come down, to be introduced and stared at as "Ken Slifer's girl."

With all the love in the world,
Your Ken x

Friday morning, Christmas Day, 1925, Buffalo to Woodbury

My own dear Ken,

Xmas morning and everything is just covered with a blanket of snow. Merry Xmas! I hope you got lots and lots of things, and all just what you wanted.

Old Santa left me a nice, warm fur coat! I got a pair of shoes for my skates. I knew these were coming, for I had to try them on beforehand. Then there were stockings, handkerchiefs, gloves, a compact, and six lovely silver spoons for our hope chest!

And what do you s'pose landed here all the way from Philly – a mammoth hat box! Yes'm – all black and shiny and with the prettiest blue inside! It's perfectly beautiful, Ken, and far too nice for me, but I'm ever so grateful for it. But honey, the top band has been split in transit, and since you wanted me to tell you if it arrived all right, I must confess this. But I'm sure the store will make it all right. It is such a beauty, and it was so dear of you to send it to me.

Tomorrow Vera is coming to give me another permanent wave. Mary may come next week, but not till after I go. I've written on for a room in a hotel if possible. I think my cousin Paul Harvey (from China, now in Oberlin) will meet me in Chicago and take me to Evanston. I haven't written "Abe." I hope he won't feel slighted! I think your next letter will have to be addressed to Evanston c/o Conference Headquarters, Interdenominational Student Conference. Please, honey, write me as often as you can.

Lovingly,
Your "Lady"

Monday afternoon, December 28, 1925, Buffalo to Woodbury

Careful study of the postmark on the envelope containing this letter – BUFFALO, N.Y., 11:30 P.M., DEC 28, 1925, (hand-stamped by a middle-of-the-night postal worker) – reveals that the year, 1925, but nothing else, is printed upside down. I sent a photocopy of this envelope to a longtime friend of the Slifers' in Woodbury's Central Baptist Church. She was delighted to add it to her vast postmark collection.

Dearest Ken,

Your letter and Xmas card came together this morning, even tho they were mailed three days apart! You surely did get some publicity for your winning of the medal. But goodness, I hope it didn't have such a sad effect on you as appears in this mournful clipping. I dutifully return it to you.

Rolland preached his first sermon last night, in Parkside. He wanted a clerical ticket [for travel discounts] and had to have a license first, and prerequisite for the latter is preaching in one's own church. Hence – the sermon. It was fine, too. He made me proud of him.

Goodness, I'm afraid I won't dare show my face in Woodbury. I'm afraid all the gossips (that is, if there are any) will be ready to pick me to pieces. Better stay away as long as I can – at least, till all the young girls get over their indignation and jealousy!

Goodby, dearest mine, and till I remind you again, remember you have all my love.

Your
Caryl

Tuesday evening, December 29, 1925, Woodbury to Evanston, Illinois, forwarded to Women's College, Lewisburg, with a new postmark of January 6, 1926

My precious lady,

My apologies for the envelope – a strikingly life-like portrait of me in my new sweater [Demie colors: crimson and black] – executed with some old paints of Bobby's. The bare envelope would have been better-looking I fear, but at least there is as much work and love in it as I ever could put in a pretty one. Q.E.D.

I can show a bit more work done today. I succeeded in writing one of my three English themes, and in painting two of 20 small posters for a reader who performs at our church next month.

Mother was delighted to receive your gracious letter of thanks, together with the note from your Mother. We can always be grateful, honey girl, that we have such a sympathetic understanding between our families – for one fruitful source of discord is removed thereby.

Further proof of the value of a college education – specifically my experience as a chapel ticket-chopper. Christmas morning there was a double-header basketball game in the high school gym between the present teams, boys and girls, and teams composed of old alumni

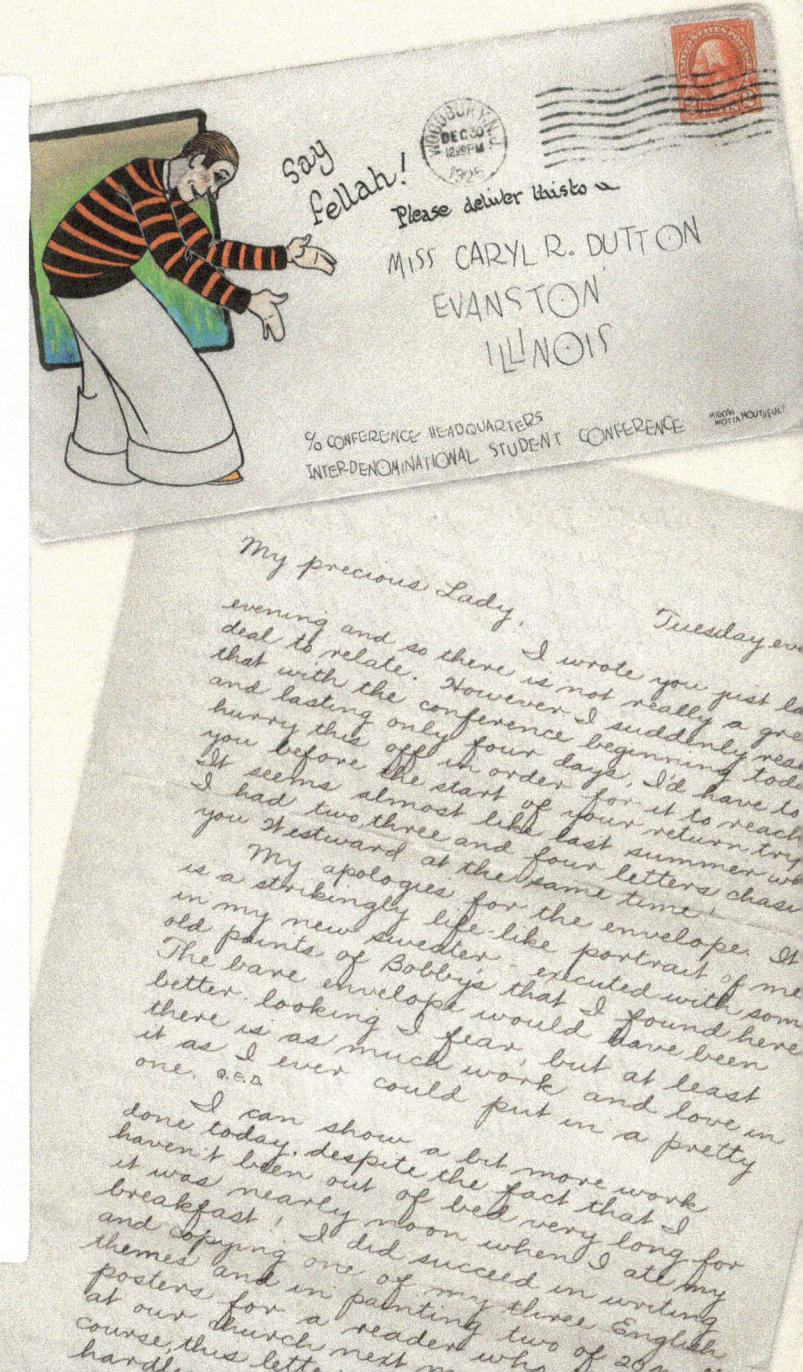

stars. The girl taking tickets was drafted for the alumni squad. I volunteered to replace her and had my ticket money, all of 25¢, for my unworthy services. Another vocation is now open to me – if all else fails, I'll don uniform and chop tickets for the local movie house or the Orpheum in Lewisburg.

   I'm planning to go up to the city either tomorrow or Thursday to arrange for the exchange of your hat box, and I'll notify your Mother immediately of the outcome.

   Another glorious moonlight night! It's not quite so cold, and the skating ice is still superb.

Ever and always,
Ken

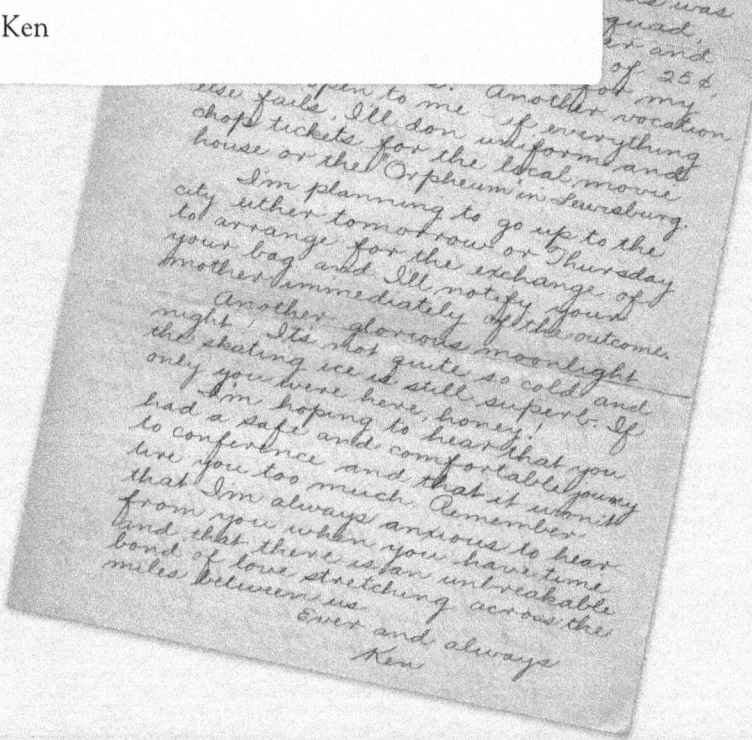

Wednesday evening, December 30, 1925, Evanston to Woodbury

My own dearest Ken,

Helen and I arrived safely in Chicago yesterday morning after a partially sleepless night, and after a little search found my cousin Paul. We talked for a while, then left him and got a train for Evanston, fifteen minutes' ride out of Chicago. Helen and I secured a double room in a home where "coeds" room. The Conference didn't begin until 7:30, so for the rest of the day we explored the town, until we arrived at a movie house, and turned aside there for some amusement. We saw Gene Stratton Porter's "Keeper of the Bees," which was a good picture.

While we were eating supper Abe came up to our table and said he is staying at a Jewish frat house! Oh! That reminds me, I must tell you a good joke. My fatal name almost got me in trouble again, for they took it for granted that I was a boy and assigned me to the SAE [Sigma Alpha Epsilon fraternity] house! We had a good laugh about it.

There are some 900–1,000 students at the Conference, and 200–300 adults who are forced to sit in the balcony and "be seen but not heard."

Thursday morning: The talks so far have been fine, and in spite of our fears, the general body of students is not so antagonistic toward the church. There seems to be a desire to criticize constructively and to constantly question, "What can we do about it?" or "What can the church do to help?"

All my love to you, dear, and one discreet x till I have a chance to deliver more in person!

Lovingly,
Your "Lady"

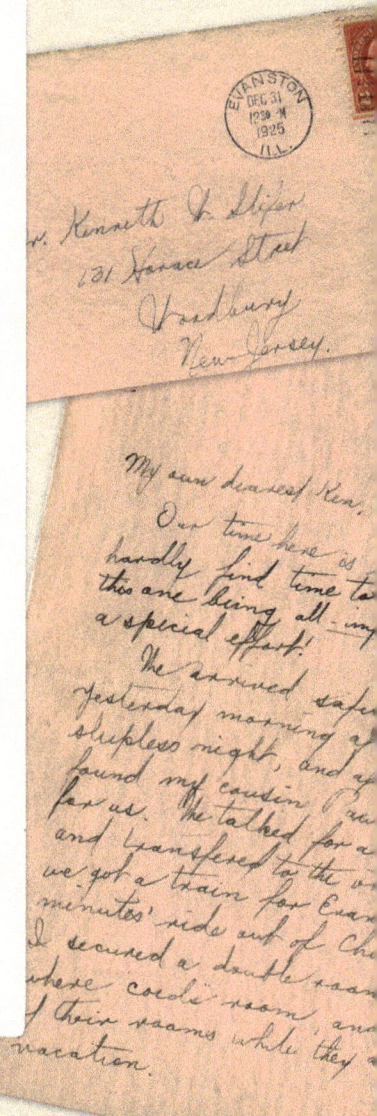

Special Delivery

Miss Caryl R. Dutton
373 Woodward Ave.
Buffalo, N.Y.

"Wal, I may be only a backwoods[man] from Camp Kanuka, Lake Clear Jct., but ef you slick city mailmen don't deliver this here epistle to —

**MISS CARYL DUTTON
373 WOODWARD AVE.
BUFFALO, N.Y.**

Thar'll be trouble, gosh dern it!"

View of beautiful LAKE CLEAR and MOUNT ST. REGIS as seen from Bungalow No. 5, Camp Kanuka, Lake Clear Junction, N.Y.

KANUKA KEN'S KOMIC KARDS — SERIES A, NO. 1

Monday morning

Lady mine,

See how I capitalize on your envelopes and the ideas created first for your amusement? These cards arrived yesterday nearly all gon[e] each. We are [going to St.] Regis this after[noon and a letter] follows this even[ing].

'Bye
Ken

Wednesday
August

[...] must have [...] five mate[...] three [...]

Miss Caryl
373

1926

As 1926 begins, Caryl and Ken are 20. She is a junior at Bucknell, and Ken, a senior, will graduate in June. Caryl has spent part of their Christmas break in Evanston, Illinois, at an interdenominational student conference, returning to Buffalo on January 2. Ken has spent his holiday in Woodbury. Fewer of Ken's letters than Caryl's from 1926 survive, and hers, after this one, are missing until mid-August.

Saturday evening, January 2, 1926
Buffalo to Lewisburg

My dearest,

I arrived home at 8:40 this morning, and Father and Mother met me at the station. Mary is still here, and leaves tomorrow at 12:45. We had a luncheon this noon at the Mandarin to talk over further Glee Club plans, and then Mother, Mary & I went shopping, & I bought a dress & a hat, in order that I may be more respectable in the future!

Yes'm, I have some pennies, tho I don't know yet how many. There are more than 20, though. [Ken and Caryl began a Penny Fund in 1926 for their "Someday." References to regular bank deposits of pennies, and their minute earnings of interest, appear in many letters. When this account was closed two years later to help pay for the honeymoon, it held about $40 – double the weekly starting salary at Ken's job in the advertising business.]

Prof. Robbins dropped in on the Conference for a session on the last day! We surely were surprised to see him. [During my own college years in the 1950s, English professor and scholar Dr. Harry W. Robbins, who by then had co-edited his thick, widely-used textbook, Western World Literature, was still active on Bucknell's faculty.] The Conference was not a thrilling one, but a great experience, nevertheless.

Attie says our chicken dinner is ready, and I simply have to come. Have to stay on the right side of the cook, even if I do come home only at Xmas and Easter!

Most lovingly,
Your "Lady"

Sunday afternoon, June 13, 1926
Woodbury to Buffalo

This letter, postmarked Monday, June 14, 5 A.M., was sent Special Delivery – postage 12¢. Ken explains this extravagance: he's already been home two days following his graduation, without writing to Caryl. The letterhead, on green stationery, bears the seal of CAP & DAGGER, HONORARY DRAMATIC SOCIETY OF BUCKNELL UNIVERSITY, LEWISBURG, PENNSYLVANIA, and the letter is penned in green ink. A yellowed clipping enclosed from the Woodbury paper says "Kenneth Slifer Receives Degree of A.B.," and included in the list of Ken's campus activities is the information that he was class president his junior year and president of Cap & Dagger his senior year.

Old Main College residence hall for men at Bucknell University, where Ken lived in #10 East Wing.[1]

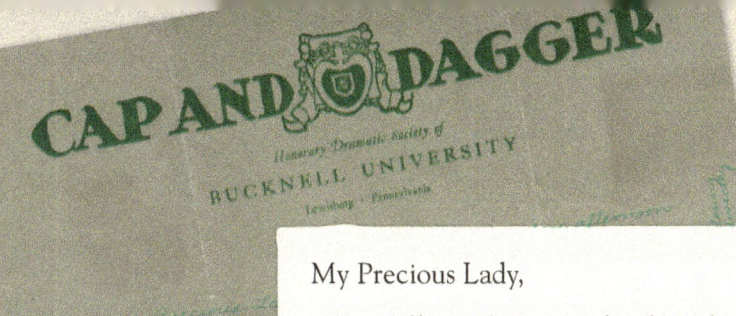

My Precious Lady,

I'm still wandering in the daze that descended upon me last Wednesday when I annexed the sheepskin. Somehow I can't seem to realize that college is all over and that you are 500 miles away! I've had no need to write you since last Christmas – I'd grown so used to our being together that separation came as a rude awakening. I'll try not to be so remiss again.

Our ride to the train was all too brief with you along. On the way back I drove fast and was so preoccupied with my thoughts that it seemed hours later when the Lewisburg bridge [a distance of only five miles] finally glimmered into view. Reaching the room, I packed desperately till 4:30 A.M., finally turning to bed when it was almost broad daylight.

I managed to tumble out after two sleepless nights in succession and succeeded in loading the flivver scientifically so that seat space for three remained. I picked up Mother & Bobby, after overhauling the car and demolishing a big breakfast. The Slifer expedition set sail at 10:30, with a trio of Drums [Ken's aunt, Grace Slifer Drum, and family] booming goodbye. We rolled into Woodbury about 7:30. I fell into bed after supper and slept till dinner time next day.

Friday afternoon sped by in mowing and trimming the yard, which needed it badly, then I tumbled into bed again. Saturday morning my trunk and the huge wooden crate accompanying it arrived. I worked most of the day preparing my room for permanent occupancy – fixing it up, so far as possible, to resemble the one at school. In the afternoon was the opening tournament of the West Jersey Tennis League at our Country Club, and I drifted out there awhile.

New director and three new voices in our choir now, and our friend Mrs. Swift has been moved down to contralto, where she does less damage. Anthem this morning was really respectable.

With all my love to you, darling,
Ken x

Monday evening, June 14, 1926, Woodbury to Buffalo

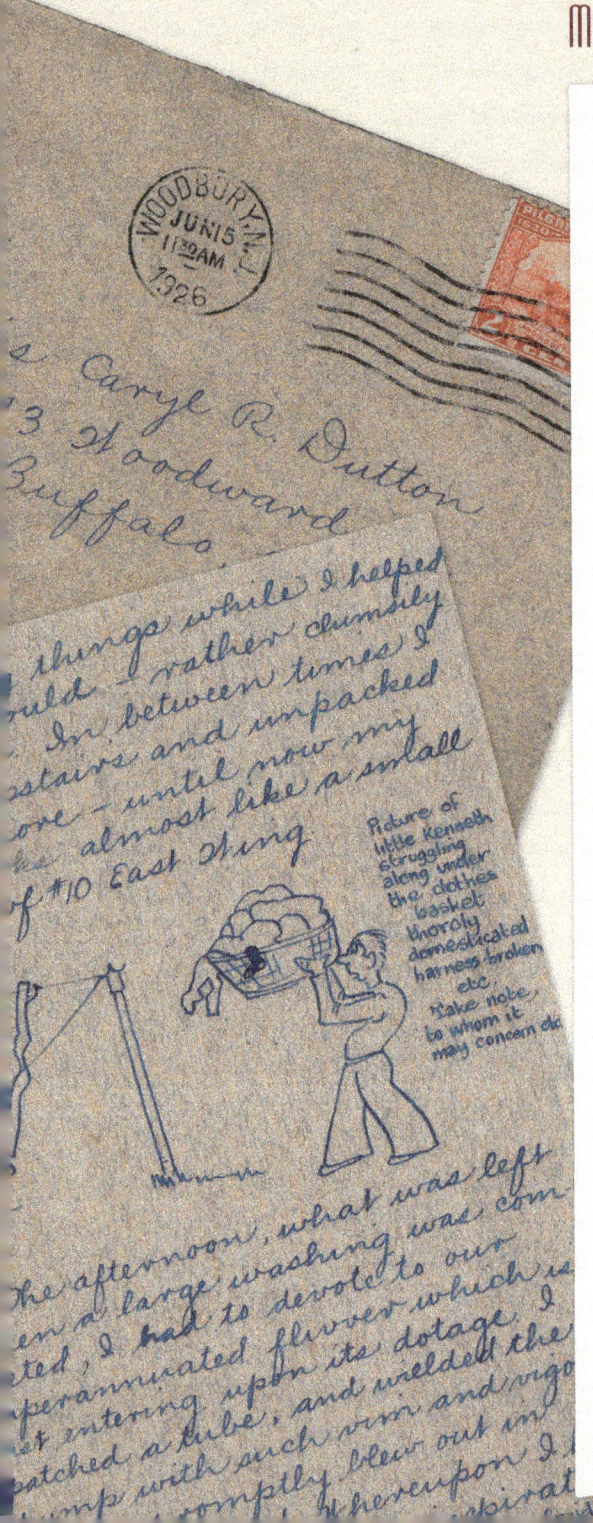

Honey Girl ~

Today has been long, busy, and very, very hot. I spent most of the morning helping Mother with an unusually heavy wash. In between times, I dashed upstairs and unpacked a little more. Now my room looks almost like a small replica of #10 East Wing.

The afternoon I devoted to our superannuated flivver, fast entering upon its dotage. I patched a tube and wielded the pump with such vim and vigor that it promptly blew out in another place! Whereupon I had a brilliant stroke of inspiration and solved the knotty problem by buying a new tire! Simple, wot? Thereupon I tightened brake bands, injected oil, and performed all those gracious "actes de toilette" that mark the cultured, well-bred flivver.

This evening the family Forded the rain to the movies. The feature picture was a comedy, "The Cohens and the Kellys," one of the best all-around pictures I have ever seen. Mother, Bobby, and I were still ridding ourselves of excess mirth on the way home. The picture hovered always between laughter and tears. One scene gave me an especial pang. Two lovers were seated on a bench in some shrubbery. She had several mannerisms almost like your own, lady mine, and as she looked into his eyes and then suddenly flung her arms about his neck to hug him tight – just as you do – oh, sweetheart, I was achin' so for you. I don't think I ever thrilled to a movie kiss as I did then – and it wasn't the end of the picture, either!

Many people have asked about you. The most common formula is, "Congratulations on your graduation" (whereat I smile coyly and mumble something). "I suppose you'll settle down now and marry that sweet–looking (female speaking) or good-looking (male speaking) girl of yours."

Heaps 'n heaps o' love,
Ken

Wednesday evening, June 16, 1926
Woodbury to Buffalo

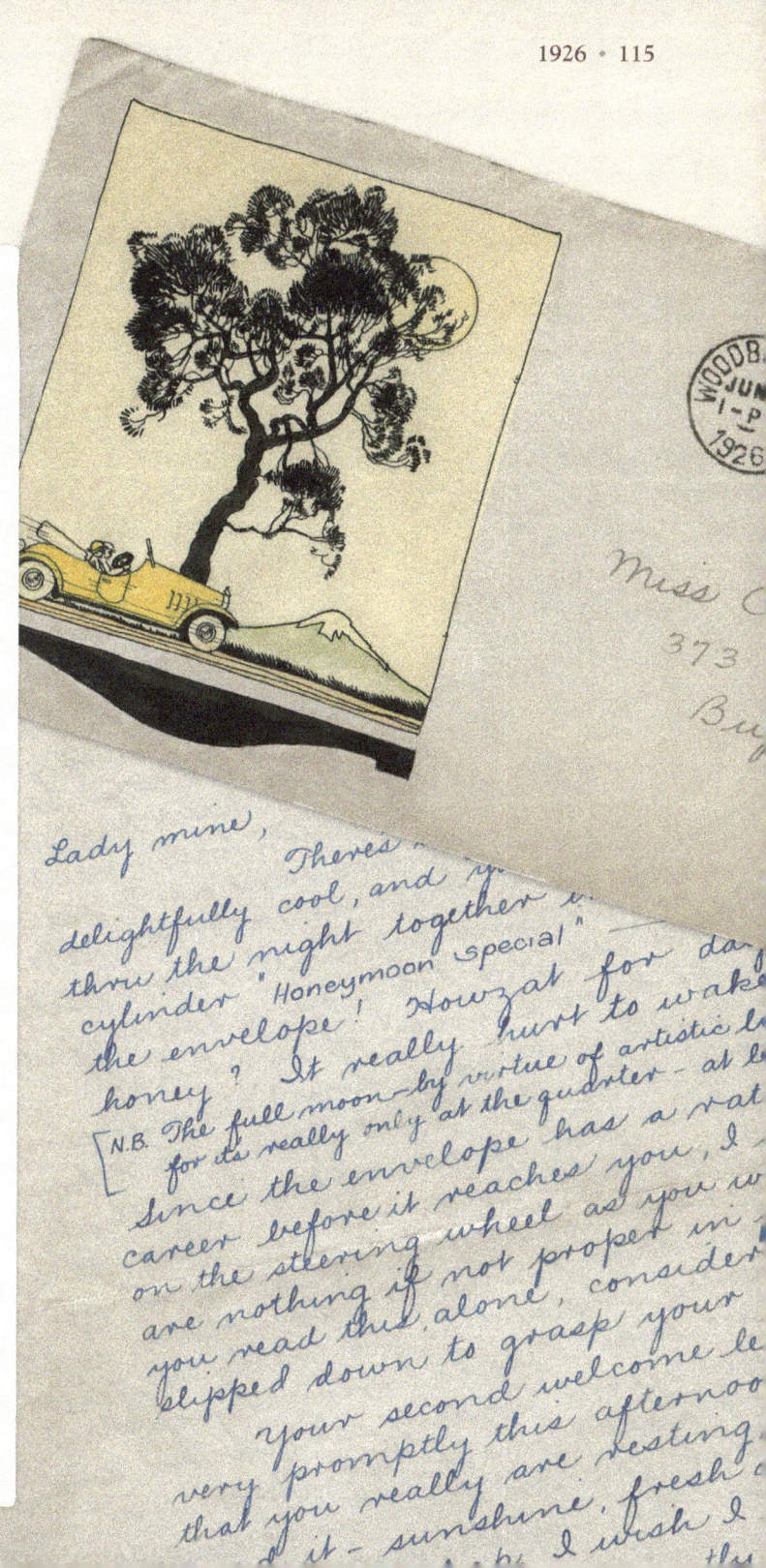

Lady mine,

There's a glorious moon tonight, it's delightfully cool, and you and I are speeding thru the night together in our own 8-cylinder "Honeymoon Special" – but only on the envelope! Howzat for daydreamin', honey? It really hurt to wake up! (N.B. The full moon by virtue of artistic license – easier to draw – for it's really only at the quarter.) Since the envelope has a long public career before it reaches you, I kept my hand on the steering wheel. We are nothing if not proper in public! But when you read this alone, consider that it has slipped down to grasp your own.

Theiss taught us to write newspaper "copy" with one small cross (x) to mark sentence end, two (xx) paragraph end, and three (xxx) the end of a story. I still do it occasionally, and it is a habit I rather like, for you may construe them as kisses, multiplied to infinity. xx

I received a brief but welcome note from your Father just before the boat sailed – he said Rolland was too busy on a tour of investigation to even think of writing. [During the summer of 1926, after graduating from Bucknell, Rolland traveled across Europe with his father – visiting, sightseeing and preaching. Dr. Dutton, whose work among Buffalo Baptist churches included a variety of immigrant congregations, had many contacts on the continent.]

I eventually succeeded in resuming my tennis career on Tuesday evening – not very auspiciously – but then, I was playing the singles champ of the League.

There are 19 pennies in my half of our mutual treasury! I have not yet made disposition of your Commencement gift. I'll think of something – there are several drawing texts I'd like.

With all the love in the world, honey girl, your

Ken xxx

Ken Slifer and his senior-year roommate Rolland Dutton, in #10 East Wing, Ken's "home" all four years at Bucknell.

Sunday morning, June 20, 1926, Woodbury to Buffalo

Sweetheart,

My marks duly arrived, four A's and one B (under Miss Lawson). She announced in advance she would give no A's – doggone her! I was hoping to end my college course with a straight A. I imagine graduate marks, necessarily compiled for Commencement, were sent out first, and that yours will follow eventually. xx

Bobby left yesterday for a camp conducted by the Girl Scouts at Stone Harbor, N. J., along the ocean front. She intends to remain two weeks. xx

Bobby has made an all-around record that has seldom if ever been excelled in this high school, certainly never when her age is considered [she will turn 15 on July 4]. She played on four teams during the year – hockey, basketball, swimming, and tennis – besides acting as class treasurer and athletic editor of the magazine, yet made a scholastic average of 92%. Her drawing was selected as cover design for the Commencement issue of the magazine – which serves as yearbook. She was elected president of the Athletic Association for next year and was made manager of hockey as well. She was selected as the only assistant editor of the magazine, and, the faculty advisor told me, would have been editor, except that the principal had a deep-rooted conviction that only a boy should be editor-in-chief – wherefore they had to find one in the class below her. She brought home a big letter for swimming and refused the captaincy because she thot another girl deserved it more. Obviously, I'm proud of my "kid sister," but my fondest hope for her is that she may grow more and more like your own sweet self. xx

Things are awfully pretty here. All our roses and a lot of other flowers are blooming. The ramblers are a riot of color on the arbor, and the rose trees by the front door are one gorgeous mass of blossoms. The deep yellow tea roses, tho, are my favorites, I think.

I've been playing tennis regularly each evening, and my game, neglected all spring, is steadily improving. I'm expecting Dick Horter down to play sometime in the immediate future. He's working in the same Phila. bank that tolerated me for one summer. xx

My plans, better, dreams, for the future are slowly shaping themselves. I had a telegram from Mr. Black yesterday, asking when I'd be available for a conference with N. W. Ayer Co. in Phila. That represents the absolute summit of my ambitions – it is the biggest advertising company in the world – it IS advertising in the United States! IF I can make connections with such a firm, and IF I can make good, my future is settled and secure. (Phila. is main office. Branches in all big cities.)

IF I do enter the Ayer organization, I intend to go to art school at night, for I have found that they offer splendid courses in night school – 3 nights a week, 7:30–9:30. Whether I use my art professionally or not, it gives me a double-edged sword and will be invaluable even as a hobby. So pray for me, darlin', in the next week or so, for it may mean everything to us both.

Of course, I'll not fail you in Sept. I'd walk all the way from Lake Clear, if necessary, to see you. I'm yearning for you so, honey girl –

Lovin' you always,
K (can mean Ken or Kisses) xx

Wednesday evening, June 23, 1926, Woodbury to Buffalo

Lady, dearest,

I'm so happy, honey, I'm 'most burstin'! I swept Mother off her feet this afternoon in a wild war dance, then dashed wildly upstairs to kiss your picture! Why? 'Cause this was the big day when my business dreams began to come true. Today, Lady mine, I entered the organization of N. W. Ayer & Son, largest advertising firm in the world, tho I do not begin work until September 17, after my trip to Buffalo.

I told you something of Ayer's and of my ambitions in the last letter, but I only half-realized myself the magnitude of their organization, the height of my hopes, and how extremely fortunate I would be if they were to be achieved.

This morning at 8:45, I shot up to the seventh floor of their building at 300 Chestnut Street. Mr. Black had generously arranged for me a conference with the president, Mr. Fry, for 9 o'clock. My card and letter of introduction were sent in, and at 9 A.M. precisely, Mr. Fry came out and led me into his imposing private office. He talked to me quite awhile and then led me down a hall and introduced me to a Mr. Reiker, who hires people occasionally, and is the official "sizer-up." He in turn quizzed me at great length, and extracted a great deal of information from me while I scarcely realized he was doing it. He said also, emphatically, that while Mr. Black's name could gain a very favorable hearing, places were awarded solely on the basis of the individual involved, and that they were flooded with applications from college men – all of which didn't reassure me. Then he added that he thought he could judge character, that I had impressed both himself and Mr. Fry, that my writing, especially, showed promise (I had some of the Sign Service stuff), that I should stress that, since they were overloaded with good artists, and he had decided that both the organization and I would profit by a continued relationship.

Mr. Batten, a splendid chap who is assistant head of the "Copy" department, was introduced to quiz me some more and briefly sketch my duties. I am to be taught the fundamentals in what he called the "detail room," acting as assistant to "ad-writers," studying typography, engraving, etc. During this period of probation, my salary will be $20 per week. At the expiration of this time, which varies from two weeks to six months according to the individual, I am to become a copy-writer with salary raises as rapidly as I justify them. I will be working with the biggest "ad" writers in the country – men who plan the big "Saturday Evening Post" feature ads and similar stuff – many of whom are story-writers as well, tho preferring advertising.

In addition, Mr. Batten said I would have the opportunity to associate with all their artists (men of national repute), and learn all of that phase that appealed to me. In addition to salaries, they insure each employee, without cost, to the amount of a year's salary, increasing automatically as the income increases. They maintain a lunch room at cost.

To encourage saving, they conduct the usual Christmas Club, and in addition a unique benefit fund into which each employee is permitted to pay 10% of his salary, receiving at the end of the year principal, interest, and 66¢ on the dollar, as his share of the company's profits!

Mr. Batten finally reported to Mr. Rieker that he thought he'd found a "kindred soul." Mr. Fry held up a long line of waiting people to officially welcome me into the N. W. Ayer "family," and I departed, walking on air, after Mr. Reiker said, "This may have seemed easy to you, but I turned down 29 applicants before you, and I'll be turning them down the rest of the summer."

Everyone was very courteous to me, from the President down. The whole atmosphere there is so splendidly friendly – the business is established and maintained on rigidly Christian principles – you may remember that Mr. Ayer, the founder's son (dead now), was president of the Northern Baptist Convention several years ago. Mr. Fry, the present executive, is a prominent layman in the North Baptist Church of Camden. It's a superb organization, darling – I could not have found a better destiny if I had molded it myself. Of course I'll have to work hard and long, but I think I'll enjoy it, and if I make good, the prospects are unlimited.

Everyone I've met since has been very properly impressed by my new connection. The name of Ayer is one to conjure with in the business world.

I journeyed to Phila. Monday to replenish my ragged wardrobe – new pajamas, white trousers for tennis, and new socks. Incidentally, I acquired a tricky, mechanical razor strop for 98¢. This morning I stropped up a very old blade and got the smoothest, easiest shave I've had in months.

I'm glad you liked the envelope, Lady. Was all the "stardust" rubbed off our owls' background? Just bought this paper this morning, and have had no time for decoration yet – sorry, honey, mebbe next time.

I am enclosing a lovely letter that I received from Mr. Black yesterday. After my success today, I sent him the most heart-felt expression of gratitude I know how to compose.

Late yesterday, I dispatched your birthday present. I hope you'll like it, tho I'm sorry you have so little opportunity to use it. The press is a new style (to me at least), designed to permit balls to remain in the case pocket – I bought one like it for myself.

Ned Carpenter contributed 4 pretty neckties to my meagre array this week. Bobby reports a glorious time at camp – she won't return till late on Saturday, July 3, while I leave for Kanuka on the Monday morning following.

Hurriedly but happily,
Your own Ken

Thursday morning, July 1, 1926, Woodbury to Buffalo

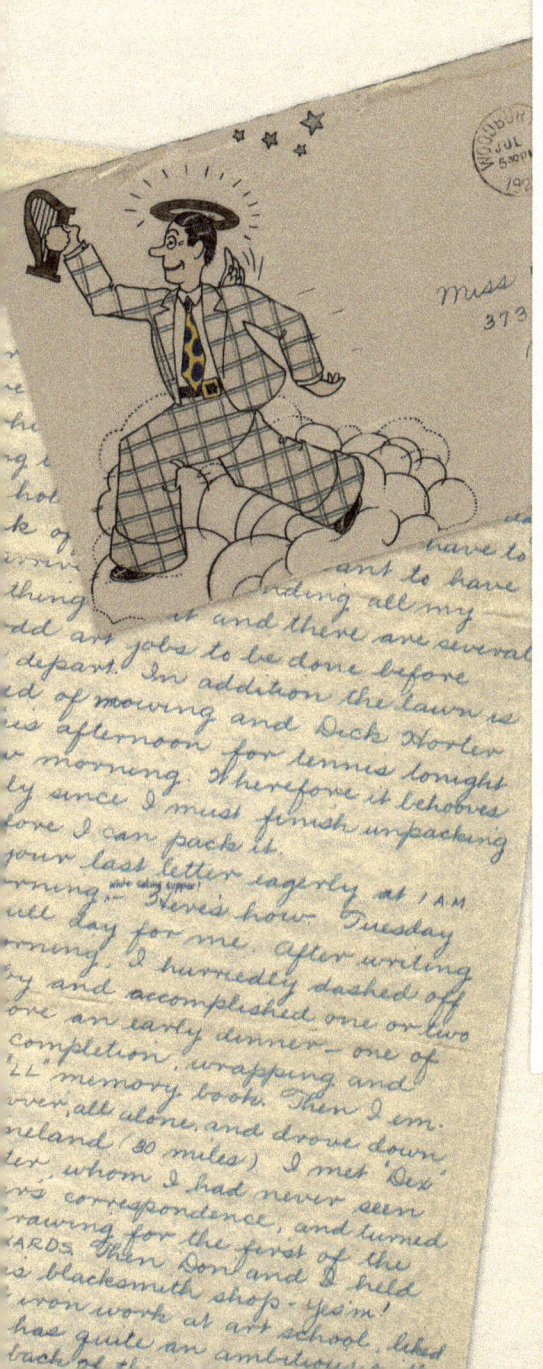

My darling Lady,

You see I adopted your idea for the envelope – I had thot of something similar, but had no time to execute it. Great minds ———! Last painted envelope till I get settled at Camp.

With a half-holiday Saturday and a full holiday Monday, I have to get my trunk off to camp, if I want to have it when I arrive. I'll be sending all my paints and things in it, and there are several signs and odd art jobs to be done before all the tools depart. In addition, the lawn is badly in need of mowing, and Dick Horter is coming this afternoon for tennis tonight and tomorrow morning.

Tuesday was quite a full day. After writing you, I embarked in the flivver and drove down to Streeters' at Vineland (30 miles). I met "Dex" Streeter, the printer, whom I had never seen despite a two years' correspondence, and turned over to him the drawing for the first of the KANUKA KEN'S KOMIC KARDS. Then his brother, my old Sign Service "partner" at Bucknell, Don Streeter, and I held reunion in his blacksmith shop! He studied wrought iron work at art school, liked it exceedingly, and has quite an ambitious smithy of his own now in back of their print shop. He found an old bellows, as well as a lot of tools that had belonged to one of his "greats," and after a little repairing was able to have all kinds of fun hammering out door gratings, latches, hinges, and all manner of similar articles. Don was grimy but happy, as he hammered away, and I too found it all fascinating.

Don Streeter became widely known for his hand-wrought iron work. In 1940, he created stunning hardware and hinges for the Slifers' new home in Woodbury, where my brother David and I grew up.

Returning from Vineland, I stopped at Pitman in time for a tennis date at 6 P.M. Chick Carter, the big gun in Penn debating last year, is quite good. We played until 9 P.M., then dashed off to see "The Bat" at the splendid new Pitman Theatre. The movie was even more tense and nerve-wracking than the stage play. I wouldn't advise you to go if you want to sleep in the next week! After the show, we sat on the Carters' porch for an hour, looked at college in retrospect, and wisecracked. It was after midnight when I started on the lonely drive home, and nearly 1 A.M. when I found your letter, which I devoured (figuratively), before I did the same thing to the contents of the ice-box (literally).

Wednesday morning Mother and I drove to Phila. on a shopping tour, and I finally expended your Commencement present, as well as most of the other money I received, on a good camera – size 1A in a fine folding model, the best I could get in that size. I'd like to have it this summer at camp, and then you may keep it at college, for I won't need it as a working-man. Bobby has had my "vest-pocket" down at camp, likes it, and I thot I'd give it to her for her birthday. The new one shall be OUR camera.

When we returned from the city, I found a telegram, asking if I'd consider an appointment to teach English in Whitman College, Walla Walla, Wash.! Without waiting to ask your advice, I wired NO! That would be almost as bad as my father's job in Alaska!

All the love in the world to you, honey,
Ken x

Ken's mother, Edna Schuyler Shires, graduated from Bucknell University in 1900.

From 1898 to 1900, after graduation from Bucknell, Ken's father, Rob Slifer, taught school on Kodiak Island, Alaska. Rob married Edna Shires in August 1903 and managed to pay for their honeymoon in Britain by publishing collections of his photographs from their trip: castles, historic sites, and the homes of famous writers. During Ken and Caryl's courtship in the 1920s, Ken could promptly send Caryl the snapshots she requested, because his late father's well-equipped darkroom was still in the cellar. In the 1960s, when Ken and Caryl downsized from their large home in Woodbury, Ken donated his father's Alaskan artifacts and pictures to the Kodiak Historical Museum, where there is now a Slifer Room. But during my childhood in the 1940s, I loved being able to pick fascinating things from the mantel in our family room for Show and Tell days at school. Among my favorites were detailed small wood carvings – a whale, a canoe, and a hunter with a bow; a delicate bark canoe, about a foot long, its frame – bits of branches laced together with thongs; woven baskets; and a heavy gray rock worn smooth by time that became a lamp when a wick was placed in a pool of whale oil poured into the hollow in its surface.

Sunday afternoon, July 4, 1926, Woodbury to Buffalo

Honey-girl,

Dick Horter arrived Thursday afternoon, and we played tennis all evening. Fortified by the practice I never had time for at college, I gave him the worst defeat either of us ever handed the other, 6–1, 6–3. Next morning we hurriedly crammed the last-minute things into my trunk. (Despite my early dispatch of it, the freight agent was uncertain that the trunk would reach Lake Clear before me, with Sat., Sun., and a full holiday included in the intervening 5 days.)

I composed a reading list for you, in accordance with your request. I have culled from my own reading those that appeal most to me and might appeal to you in turn. If you are at a loss to begin, you can find nothing better than "Vanity Fair," which most critics regard as the masterpiece of all novels.

124 • Flivverin' With You

Bobby breezed in from camp yesterday, brown as an Indian. Your card to her was delivered yesterday, but we didn't let her see it until this morning, when we had the birthday celebration, with cake, candles, 'n everything. I presented her with my vest-pocket Kodak and 2 rolls of film, while Mother gave her an expensive weekend bag with her initials stamped in gold. In addition she received a big box of candy from the chiefest of her several beaux!

I leave here about noon on Tuesday and reach Lake Clear at breakfast time Wednesday morning. I'll be hopin' for a letter, lady mine, because, you see, I love you so!

All my love, always,
Ken x

Monday, July 12, 1926, Camp Kanuka, Lake Clear Junction, New York, to Buffalo

This is a printed "penny post card" from Kanuka Ken's Komic Kards, Series A, No. 1. The bungalow number must be filled in by each sender.

Monday morning

Lady mine,

See how I capitalize on your envelopes and the ideas created first for your amusement? These cards arrived yesterday and are nearly all gone now at 5¢ each. We are climbing St. Regis this afternoon. Letter follows this evening.

'Bye
Ken

Saturday afternoon, July 24, 1926, Camp Kanuka to Buffalo

Honey-Girl,

All the love in the world is overflowing here for you, sweetheart. I would have poured it forth late last night, but I realized that it could not reach you until Monday, and I employed the time in decorating the envelope. You suggested my painting them in celebration occasionally, and I am certain there is nothing more deserving of celebration than the arrival of the luscious cherries!

All the Directors "Oh'd" and "Ah'd" as I opened the box up in the office and lifted out the first few leafy clusters! Picking cherries is slow work, as I well know, and I enjoyed them the more because you had picked and packed them with your own dear fingers! Each of the counsellors had a few when I opened the box, and then the Scorpions gathered in my classroom, where we feasted till I thot we'd all be sick. Eventually they were satisfied, and departed with bulging pockets, while I invited in our "son," George Roller, and Reiman (the Buffalo boy) to partake.

The box lasted thru my first two classes this morning, before teacher and pupil finally emptied it. Some one of the Scorpions suggested writing you a letter of thanks, and when I reached the bungalow they were writing away in the dim glow of a dying flashlight. Freddy turned over to me their literary productions with the naïve remark, "Mebbe if we thank her for this box, she'll send some more!"

Five notes, all to "Dear Miss Dutton," are enclosed, on Camp Kanuka stationery.

"Thank you for the cherries, they were fine."
Scorpion Lieut. Ralph Straub

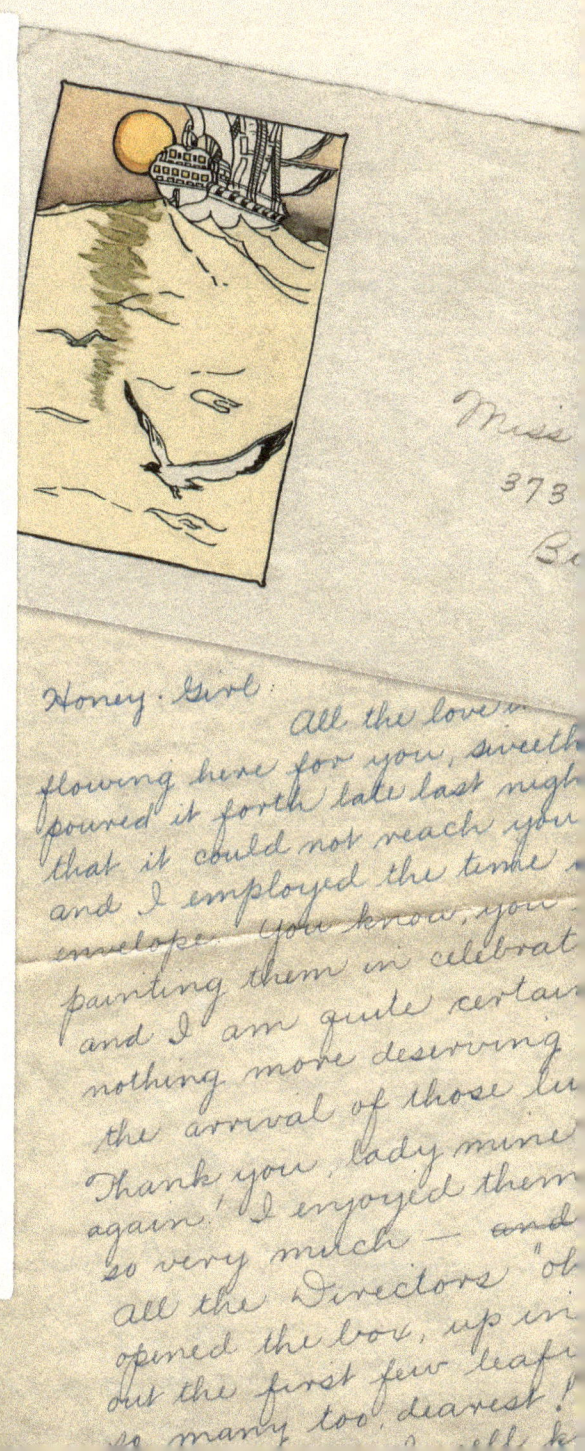

> "I want to cordially thank your exceeding generosity in presenting us with your charming gift."
> Scorpion Captain Freddy
>
> "Ma: Thanx." 'Son'
>
> "Thank you for the cherries, and they were good."
> Scorpion Lieut. Dicky
>
> "The Scorpians are very grateful for the delicious cherries."
> Walton (The Only Private)
>
> I have decided that Carylinian ox-heart cherries are my favorite fruit – and having eaten as many as George ever did, "I cannot tell a lie."
>
> Half the camp set out for Montreal this morning. They return Sunday night, and next morning, another group departs on a 3-day canoe trip. The camp is to be nearly deserted for five days.
>
> Eden Welsh and a carload of her friends drove boldly into camp yesterday looking for a couple of chaps who tutor here. Their conversation was free and easy, to say the least, and they all lighted cigarettes and smoked with the boys! Money doesn't always bring refinement! Q.E.D.
>
> Counting the days till "our" week. Whee!
>
> Lovin' you always,
> Ken xx

Between July 27 and August 12, there are ten envelopes mailed from Caryl to Ken at Camp Kanuka, all now empty. The fate of those letters, like others I was unable to find, remains a puzzlement.

Wednesday evening, July 28, 1926
Camp Kanuka to Buffalo

Dearest Lady mine,

Reiman and I held French class out on the "campus" this morning, and your longed-for letter was delivered there. Fortunately, he received a letter too, so I was free to read the letter.

I read a little while this afternoon, and then rain spoiled my plans for tennis (I am besieged with requests to coach aspiring players, and I try to oblige when I can), so I devoted the time to decorating an envelope for you, darling. The Scorpions invaded my classroom studio soon after I started and hung over my shoulder and table till I had finished – hardly helping the Muse any.

Of course I'll love you in glasses, honey girl, tho' I'm sorry you have to get them. But please don't wear them for the first few minutes of Our Week – I'd prefer to see you first as I remember you, and then I think I can accustom myself to the transformation. Besides, the glasses might get broken in the crush!

Sweet dreams, dearest,
Ken

Ken's warning to the postman says: "Wal I may be only a backwoodsman from Camp Kanuka, Lake Clear J'ct'n, N.Y., but ef you slick city mailmen don't deliver this here epistle to a Miss Caryl Dutton, 373 Woodward Ave., Buffalo, N.Y., Thar'll be trouble, gosh dern it!"

Monday evening, August 9, 1926
Camp Kanuka to Buffalo

Lady darlin',

I couldn't go to bed without having written you – especially in view of the love-filled letter I found waiting for me on my return from Montreal. I devoured the letter, figuratively speaking, and combined with the Scorpions in a literal and voracious attack upon the crisp, sweet-filled pies that accompanied the precious missive. They carried perfectly in their wrappings and were oh, so good! All the Scorpions but Freddy had made the Montreal trip (he went 2 weeks ago), and since we were all hungry from a five-hour train ride, we made ready for bed, then feasted regally. I woke Freddy to give him his. He smiled sleepily but expansively, and mumbled between mouthfuls, with a wink at me, "The Queen of Hearts, she made some tarts . . ." They were especially delighted to find the monogrammed crust. I'm not sure what form their gratitude will take, but I know they concur in my estimate of you – the nicest lady in all the world.

Let me close with the assurance of my eternal love for you.

Love and   x   x   x   your
Ken

Saturday morning, August 14, 1926
Buffalo to Camp Kanuka

After the letter of January 2, 1926, this is Caryl's first surviving epistle from that year. From here on she writes dozens. Only a few from Ken remain; the rest of the 1926 narrative is mostly hers.

My dear, dear Ken,

I am glad about your swimming improvement and more daring feats, but the thing that makes me happiest is that you're overcoming your fear of the water, and gaining a liking for it. It will mean much added joy for us, for I do so love the water, with its sport and its beauty. Someday you must try an aqua-plane. It is exhilarating to ride the waves behind a fast boat. I did it three years ago and shall never forget the thrill.

Yesterday I won a victory for myself. I was downtown from 9:30 to 3:00 and came home without the least semblance of a headache! And I didn't have my glasses on all day, either. Mebbe that's a sign of increasing strength. The main object of our trip was to order a trifle in celebration of the nineteenth of next month [Ken's 21st birthday]. Not nearly as nice a gift as the racquet, but I hope you'll like it. I'm pretty sure it will be a surprise to you, for you've never even said you'd like it. I'm in high hopes.

I love you so, dearest.
Your Lady

Wednesday afternoon, August 18, 1926
Buffalo to Camp Kanuka

Caryl is spending three days in the palatial home of Helen Jackson, whose parents are away.

My own dear Ken,

This place must have scared Uncle Sam, for tho I've watched the mail man come three times, he has failed to leave me anything, and of course I'm quite heartbroken. But I s'pose he was just sort of dazzled by the splendour in which I'm living.

This is a lovely place, and we reign supreme, with a radio, Victrola, etc. The living room is bigger than the Sem parlour, so it's quite luxurious. Last night, Helen suggested we see "The Volga Boatman." We went, but too much fighting, bloodshed, and intensity of action. Splendid acting, but it kept me keyed up too much. Helen has tickets for tomorrow at the Majestic Theatre to see the McGarry players in "Connie Comes Home." Don't you think I'm getting terribly gay? Well, I have to have a spree once in a while.

Rolland and Father sail for home today. Which reminds me that Mary answered Mother's letter, saying she had at last received one letter from Rolland. I think she's awfully brave and forgiving.

All my love, dearest Ken, from your
Lady

Thursday evening, August 19, 1926
Buffalo to Camp Kanuka

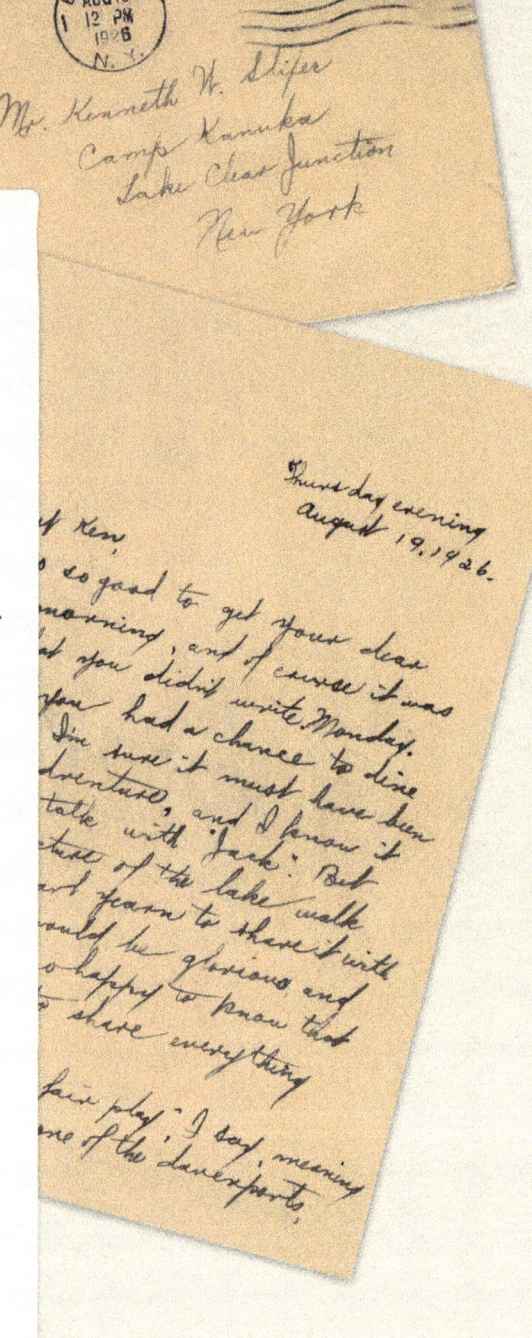

My dearest Ken,

"Turn about's fair play," I say. I sit here on one of the davenports, next to the talkative radio, and write to you in solitude, while Helen and her friend Helen Goulette are washing dishes in the kitchen. You see, they voted to get our own supper here, instead of downtown, the maid being out. So I did the cooking and carving, and consequently rest on my laurels now, while they work.

The three of us went to see the play this afternoon, "Connie Comes Home." Lots of it was very funny, and it was splendidly acted.

Last night Howard Jackson took Helen and me to the movies. I wasn't wild about going again, but I did want a ride in that electric car. We went to the Hippodrome, but couldn't get in, so went up a block to the "Buffalo," a new and gorgeous theatre. We didn't know anything about the picture, but, oh, it was awful. It made me shudder with disgust, and I surely did wish we had stayed home. I don't see why they have to use the moving picture to show such stories of the depraved taste of the money-mad, such as disgusted you in the hotel. I thoroughly agree with you, honey, and when you turn Socialist, I will too. Sometimes I feel "desprite."

I'm so glad you got another letter from school about your good work. I can't help rejoicing that knowing me and spending time entertaining me didn't lower your records, as often happens when men get interested in the ladies!

Oh, my dearest, you haven't the slightest idea how much I love you. I'm Yours!

Friday evening, August 20, 1926
Buffalo to Camp Kanuka

My darling,

When I spoke deprecatingly about my brother's sister, I meant that you had to teach me to be demonstrative in both written and spoken love. I just plain didn't know how, when I first wanted to express my feelings, but now – witness the difference between this summer's letters and last summer's!

When I come to meet you, I'll make the rest of the folks stay out of the station, so I can have you all to myself for the first few minutes. Only ten more days, and then Our Week filled with companionship, joy, lots of heart-to-heart talks, and some cozy times after the other folks have gone to bed and left us together for a while. I have to see enough of you to last all year, and a little less sleep won't hurt me. I'll make it up at school, when I can't have you anymore.

Oceans of love from
Your Lady x

Sunday afternoon, August 22, 1926
Buffalo to Camp Kanuka

Dear, dear Ken,

Don't you think it would be easier if you didn't try to write every day this week? I know you have so much to do, and you can't deny that letter-writing takes a lot of time. This will be a very busy time for me, too, for I want to get most everything done but packing before you come. I have most of the sewing done, but now am working on my two evening dresses. I don't want to buy a new one, but want something good enuf for Prexy's Reception!

I'm wondering what you are going to talk about tonight at Vespers. Whatever it is, it will be splendid and helpful. I wish I could enter invisibly and listen. Don't tire yourself out these last few days at camp with exams and all, cause 'member – I've been storing up all summer for this, Our Week.

Yours,
Caryl

Monday evening, August 23, 1926, Buffalo to Camp Kanuka

My dearest,

Went downtown this morning, stopped at osteopath's for treatments, then on to get material to fix my evening dress.

No, dearest, I won't get too much of the movies or such before you come. Trips with you and without you are two entirely different things – one full of wishin's, the other full of supreme joy and happiness, because you're with me. I warned Mother we wanted some good talks together, and I think we'll be able to do about as we please. When I think of the state of mind and heart I'll be in one week from tonight, I seem bursting with joy and love for you, my own loving and lovable Ken.

Your
Lady x

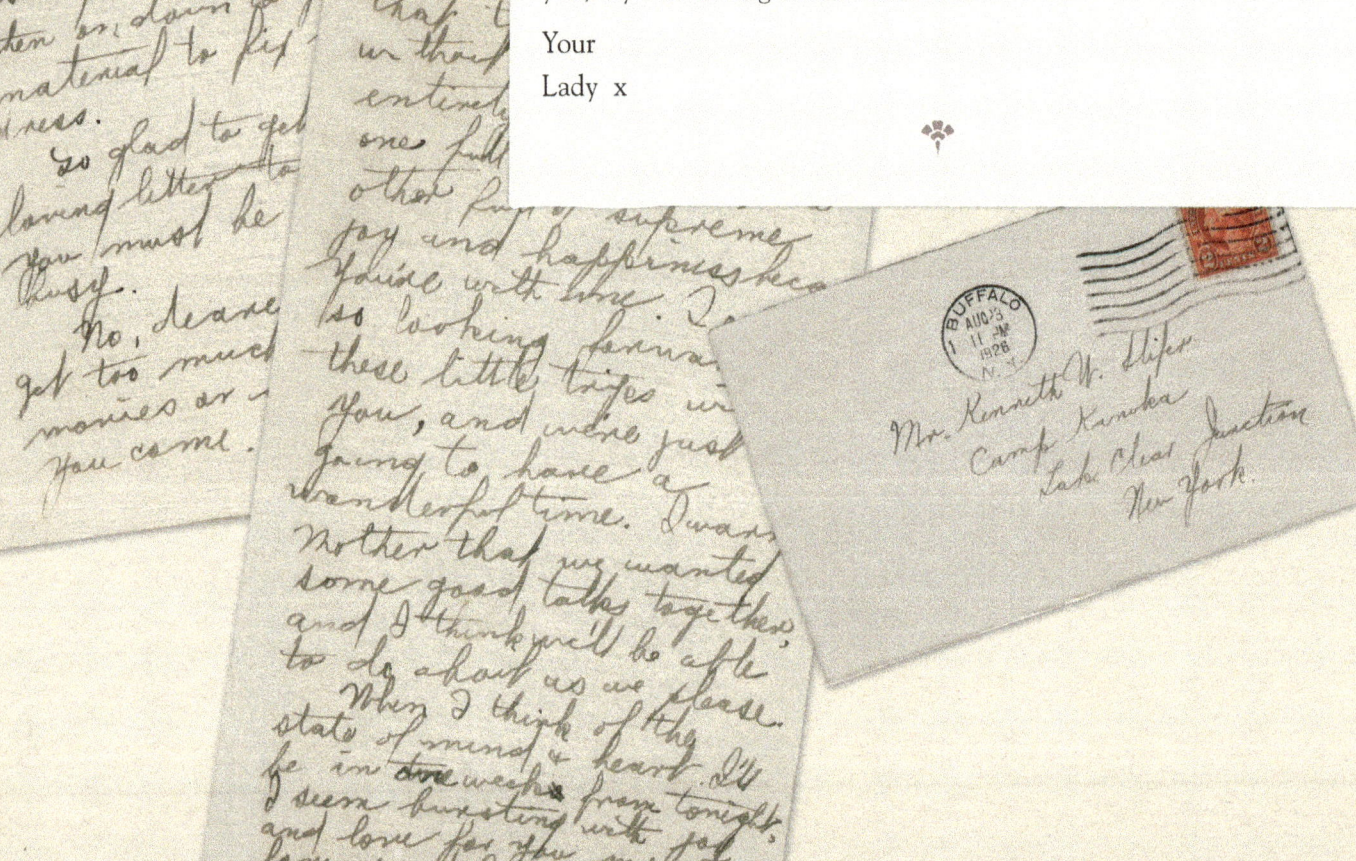

Friday morning, August 27, 1926, Buffalo to Camp Kanuka

My dearest Ken,

Mother and I arose early yesterday to go meet the 8:30 train. We were just leaving the house when the travellers rounded the corner, loaded down with bag and baggage. They took the 6:20, and thot to surprise us, as they did.

Rolland looks like a European, with a "misplaced eyebrow" twirled into a jaunty German moustache! With a healthy, tanned complexion, he doesn't look like the same boy who left home several weeks ago. He proceeded to dump the contents of his and Father's four suitcases all over the house and display the trophies. I had lots of fun parading around in various costumes, made up of an Indian sun helmet, strings of shells and beads, Spanish lace caps, a big silk shawl, and so forth. The silk shawl is a beautiful lavender and white one that Rolland brot home for Mary. She ought to be a tickled girl, for it's a beauty.

What do you s'pose this original young man brot me? An immense complete stamp album in 2 volumes! He has two or three thousand stamps, which he secured over there in packets, and to me remains the task of pasting all of them in, besides transferring my old ones.

Rolland called Mary last night & left this morning to hike to Bradford. This is her birthday, so he was in haste to arrive there. Father goes tomorrow to Glens Falls to preach Sunday, so we will be alone again.

It wasn't imagination that scented my last letter. You see, at last I have matched the perfume you and I liked so much my freshman year, and just for fun I scented the letter with it to see if you would notice it. And you did – you jus' never disappoint me, honey.

Mos' lovingly,
Your Lady

Saturday evening, August 28, 1926
Camp Kanuka to Buffalo

Sweetheart mine,

It seems a glorious, roseate dream to imagine that in two short, busy days I am to start on the long trail thru the moonlight that leads to the dearest, sweetest, prettiest Lady in all the world – to you, darling!

Since it has been so cool here, I chose to place our fairyland in tropical waters. A year ago, in hot and sultry Jersey, I reared us a dream castle among the breezes and the clouds – you see, honey, how the thermometer affects me in planning for us both!

A crowd of the smoking, flask-toting, boy-bobbed, boy-crazy Inn habitués invaded the camp today, to make me more disgusted with our "idle rich," and to make me happier that there are sweet, clean, sensible Ladies like yourself. Their blatant speech and manners, their easy familiarities with the fellows, were more than distasteful – and I turned as from an unwholesome thing to find serenity again in the vast, pure love that is ours. I do love you, dear heart, with all my being, and the remembrance often acts like a balance wheel, when I'm peeved at the world!

Most of the camp – including all the Bucknellians, of course – attended the "Matty Day" benefit baseball game at Saranac Lake today. Christy Mathewson was only 45 when he died in October 1925 (tuberculosis – from mustard gas poisoning in the Great War). Loon Lake was playing Saranac, with Eddie Mahan, former

All-American fullback at Harvard, matched against a present-day Yale star. We had to leave at the most exciting part – the end of the ninth inning, tied at 4-4 – in order to get any supper.

There was a costume dance at the Inn tonight, and I fixed up two of the fellows – and both copped prizes – 2nd and 3rd. Quite naturally, they could not let Kanuka carry first prize away from the Inn! "Spark Plug" Parslow donned my organ-grinder outfit in its entirety – taking 2nd prize with Dickie as his monkey. Bill Blanchard took the elaborate lamp-post that I built for my last chalk talk, and I made him up as an inebriate with a sign: "The Saturday Evening Post."

I have 3 exams to give yet, 45 birchbark menus to make out, packing, etc. in the coming two days! I've lost all hope of painting slickers! I'll be busy, but Time cannot fly fast enough for me till 9:20 Tuesday morning, darling. Good night and sweet dreams, honey-girl. xxx

Your loving
Ken

Ken and Caryl do have that visit in Buffalo. Then they travel together on the train as far as Lewisburg, where Caryl will begin her senior year, while Ken goes on to Woodbury. He will start work at N. W. Ayer & Son on September 17, two days before his 21st birthday. We don't get any first impressions – all of his letters over the next two months are missing.

Sunday evening, September 12, 1926
Lewisburg to Woodbury

My dearest,

It isn't because I haven't been thinking of you that I havn't written, but I've been so busy I hardly knew where my head was. It's all been lots of fun, but strenuous: from 6:30 A.M. till 11:30 P.M. or after, I've been in a rush. It took me so long to get my room in habitable state & to organize my workers. Then each night, and some other times, my services have been required to serve refreshments.

Friday we all went on a picnic to Wolfland – from about 3 to 8:30, and back by moonlight. We played quoits, volley ball and other games, and had a wonderful supper. When we came back several of the girls came up to my room, and we talked till after eleven.

The pictures are really good – but so funny – especially the lunch one at Crystal Beach. Do you s'pose I just bit down on a gritty piece of sand? The hat one is good, tho. I want a set of the pictures, and Aunt Jennie wants one of the hats!

In spite of my haste, all my leisure time is filled with thots of you, my dearest Ken.

Your Lady x

Monday afternoon, September 13, 1926
Lewisburg to Woodbury

Dear, dear Ken,

I am writing to the tune of the old "Vic," which in spite of its age is doing its best to entertain. I got some oil this morning and oiled it up, and I must get some more needles. I'm afraid it's on its last legs now, but I hope there'll be something left for Bobby!

You may remember there is a sizeable alcove just outside my door. Mrs. Manning has given permission to place a table there. Mrs. Sale will furnish an old dining room table, & we can play ping pong to our hearts' content. Do you suppose you could make me two paddles? Maybe I can get a ball at Donehower's [household and sporting goods store in Lewisburg]. I think it'll be lots of fun.

I have yet to buy my books, and then all will be ready for classes. It will be hard to study after this week of everything else but lessons.

All your
Lady

Wednesday morning, September 15, 1926, Lewisburg to Woodbury

Dearest Ken,

My first day of classes is over at last – not the day, but the classes. Perhaps you would like to know how to think of me as I work, so I will copy a little schedule.

	Mon.	Tues.	Wed.	Thurs.	Fri.	Sat.
8-9	Home Ec	Pol. Sci.	Home Ec.	Pol. Sci.	Home Ec.	Pol. Sci.
9-10	French	German	French	German	French	German
10:30-11:30	Philos.	Music	Philos.		Philos.	

As you notice by my schedule, I have registered for one-half hour of music period a week – with Mrs. Wilcox. I do hope it will help my voice some, at least. Aunt Jennie is going to let me practice at her house – when she's not there! – thereby saving me $10 practice-room fee (tho she doesn't know this).

Yesterday I deposited our $3.25, and found an added interest of 4 cents! So now we have $9.49.

You are such a dear to want to celebrate "our anniversary." [On September 19, 1925, his 20th birthday, Ken gave Caryl his fraternity pin.] Thank you, honey – even before I know what it is, I just can hardly wait. The kiss you asked for will be yours on Saturday, also.

Mrs. Sale says that my assistant and I can alternate for breakfasts. That will be great, even tho I have 8 o'clocks every day. But now I can have Sundays off, and I never could before. I am going to do all the head work for the 2 shifts, & my ass't will have charge of all the changing of linen, and some substitute getting. That will be a big relief. We are using 24 waitresses beside myself, and feeding 330 people – fifty more than last year! Phew! You never saw such a mob.

Your letters will be the brightest spots of this year, except the few precious visits I hope you'll make.

All my love to you,
Your Lady

Thursday evening, Sepember 16, 1926
Lewisburg to Woodbury

Dearest,

We had our student convocation this morning at ten, and it seemed awfully funny to be walking up the hill behind the Faculty as a Senior. Dean Rivenburg made the address, the best I ever heard him make.

Somebody has walked off with our ping pong "net," but hope to locate it soon, or find another.

Went to Burns's political science class for the first time today. He was splendid! If he keeps up the whole term like today, that ought to be the best course I've ever taken.

Please don't say anything, but Dwight practically told Vera he doesn't want her any more – after begging her last spring to take his pin & writing her love notes all summer. Poor Vera is stranded, feeling as if the bottom has dropped out of everything. I only hope and pray Dwight may come to his senses soon and find his mistake.

Oh, Ken, if you had ever ceased to want me I don't know what I should have done. You were always so wonderful. I surely can never say I didn't have an ardent lover – even if I did discourage him!

All your
Lady

Friday afternoon, September 17, 1926, Lewisburg to Woodbury, Special Delivery (12¢)

My own dear Ken,

This will have to be your birthday letter, honey, since Sunday's Uncle Sam's day of rest. Wish we could celebrate together. "Our first anniversary," too! I wonder what I'll be doing on our second anniversary! Still loving you, anyway!

Thank you for the paddles. I appreciate ever so much your making them. Our "net" is still missing, but Bill Ware found a piece of beaverboard and cut one the right size. Maybe I'll have time to trim it up tomorrow.

The Home Ec. course I'm taking is household management. I want to know all the scientific methods of making the nicest home for you. The classroom is just outside my door, so I don't have to go far for either reference material or class. Miss Douglas told me that any time we want the domestic science rooms right next to me, we can just ask her for her key. Now when we're out of candy, we can make our own fudge.

I'm afraid all my letters this year are going to be hurried, honey-boy, but you'll have to be forgiving. All my love, dearest Ken, congratulations, and best wishes for the bestest year ever.

Your own
Lady

Tuesday afternoon, September 21, 1926, Lewisburg to Woodbury

My own dearest Ken,

It's awfully nice you're taking musical instruction, because the more you know about music, the more you'll enjoy it. I took a lesson today, & I certainly harmonized with any old sawmill, for squeaks were more in evidence than notes.

Your account of your first business day wasn't the least bit uninteresting. I'm so glad you gave it in so much detail, for I want to know all about it.

I was shocked to hear of your Grandmother's death, tho I know she [Charity Slifer] had been sick for some time. Wish I had time to go see Aunt Clara. What will she do now with the home?

We had initiation last night at Rivenburgs'. Their home is surely beautiful. I couldn't take part in the ceremony but sat by & watched. Tonight we'll have a long meeting, for rushing begins tomorrow, & we must select tonight.

We had a lovely Vesper service Sunday night, receiving the new freshmen into YW. Aunt Jennie gave a little talk, & the meeting ended with forming a complete circle around the living room, each girl holding a lighted candle. There must have been a hundred girls there, & the effect was beautiful.

I'd much rather write you than study, but a long assignment from Burns, including study for a test, makes me relinquish the pleasanter task.

Your Lady

Friday afternoon, September 24, 1926, Lewisburg to Woodbury

Ken, dearest ~

What a hectic period this is, especially with these Pan-Hellenic Rules. I'm not so wild about the group our girls are after – too much looks and not so much brains, I'm afraid. But of course it isn't fair to judge too hastily. The Buffalo girls are out of luck, I fear. I don't think Edna cares, for she wants to be Alpha Chi, but Helen seems to be more our way. I think she would be most happy to be a Pi Phi, but her type doesn't appeal, and maybe she'd be happier as an Alpha Chi anyway.

The ping pong paddles arrived safely Wednesday, and yesterday Billy & I played a few sets. She's quite crazy about it and learns ever so quickly. We expect to have lots of fun, thanks to your help.

Tonight there is a mass meeting [pep rally], and afterward the annual reception at the church. I s'pose I'll come home tonight awfully tired, but happy, for I always have a good time at those receptions. But tonight, dearest, I'll be thinking of that wonderful night three years ago, when you first took me home. I'll never forget the thrill of that night, honey. I can't seem to stop my old habit of searching among the tall men and feeling a queer start whenever I hear the Demie whistle.

Tomorrow afternoon is our first football game. Oh, how I wish you were here to go and share the thrill of that first kick-off. I hope my "rushee" accepts my offer for a date, so I won't be alone. But probably most of the Pi Phis will go together anyway. I will be thinking of you, with all the love I have.

Your own Lady x

Monday evening, September 27, 1926, Lewisburg to Woodbury

My darling Ken,

Vera has been spending the evening with me, studying – or trying to study, against the temptation to talk. Confidentially again, Dwight has become humble & wants Vera to take his pin. Vera feels sure of her own feelings, but after Dwight's acting up can't be sure what his will be. I am advising her to make him wait till Xmas anyway.

As you know, we are allowed one big party during rushing season. Sunday afternoon, we had about 20 freshmen, took them over to Wolf house about 3 o'clock, where Pi Phis hold down a suite of rooms, & there served fruit salad, pickles, olives, rolls, cheese, and potato chips. When this course was finished, we went over to the Suite and had coffee and ginger cake with whipped cream. I forgot to say that over at Wolf house we gave a crazy little skit that in slang phraseology "went over big."

We had a Frat meeting from 6:30 to 7:30, and then I went to church, tho I had a hard time finding someone to go, & finally went, sat, & came home with three different people. It seemed so lonesome without you in church. I missed that gentle pressure of your arm that used to say so much, and the joy of being & worshipping together. I seem to be ever more appreciative of bounties, and thankful, since your love has come into my life, dear.

I s'pose you now know the happy results of the football game we won 53–0. It was quite dull – action always in one direction, except at end of quarters. I had my "date" but didn't care for the girl, & she is now off the list. We have 18 on now, two of whom are upper classmen, & may eliminate more, for we have till a week from Wednesday to rush – then bid day on Saturday.

Ruby Robison is back visiting, with her 6-weeks-old baby boy. Imagine – and just two years ago a freshman! It certainly seems queer.

My love is for you only, dear,
Your Lady x

Wednesday evening, September 29, 1926, Lewisburg to Woodbury

My dearest Ken,

    Billy & I had three fast sets of ping pong this afternoon. Billy is as good a player as I am, tho she doesn't try placement as much, and we certainly had good rallies. Is the table supposed to be marked off like a tennis court, with right & left serving squares? We can do it with chalk if we should.

    Mrs. Rockwell stopped me on the Hill today, & asked if I could spare a half-hour a week to teach typewriting to her daughter. Imagine that! Frances has a portable typewriter & is going to bring it to my room to take her lesson Sat. mornings at 10:00. Vera has a typewriting book and is sending for it for me to use as a text. I almost have to laugh when I think of the variety of jobs I've undertaken since arriving in Lewisburg 4 years ago. Billy Williams and Ethel Hurst have a beauty parlor established, and I'm a minor partner as a water-waver – just for fun, because I enjoy doing it, & don't expect more than one or two customers a month! I'll let you know when my first one hails in!

Till I see you, remember how much you mean to
Your Lady

P. S. I'm studying how to build houses in general & thinking of Our house in particular. Any suggestions, aside from sleeping porch, shower, fireplace, and a big chair?

Sunday afternoon, October 3, 1926, Lewisburg to Woodbury

Enclosed with her letter to Ken, Caryl returns Rolland's typewritten letter, headed Boofalo, 9/26/26. Rolland has entered Rochester Theological Seminary; he describes his class in glowing terms.

Dear Roomie, Brother, Brother-in-law, etc.

There are 17 or 18 in our class (which is exceptionally small). The type of men, I'm glad to say, is far superior to our average Bucknell 'ministerial,' so-called. They are all here for business, but they aren't any bunch of joy-killers or crepe-hangers, either. Don Head was a member of the University of Pennsylvania relay team that competed against Oxford and Cambridge two or three years ago; our next-door neighbor down the hall is a Yale alumnus; and the room across the way is occupied by two big black men, one of them a football star and captain of his college team for two years, the other 6'3" of basketball center prowess.

The men, taken as a whole, are the finest looking group you could find anywhere, and the spirit is simply great. Fraternity politics doesn't stand a show, and the only way you can rate a drag with the profs is by real production.

All kinds of luck in the advertising business. Don't overwork yourself trying to perform the Horatio Alger stunt in less than six months' time.

Your loving roomie, 'Dut'

My Darling,

I know how discouraged you have felt after that refusal. Disappointments are bound to come now and then, and you have all my sympathy & love. But you mustn't feel that you did a "nervy" thing in showing that attempt, for it only showed the men that you were eager to do as much as you could and willing to profit by instruction. Eventually, it may help you to learn more quickly the type of work Ayer & Son do. Build up your "castle" again, honey, right on top of the "ruins," to cover them up, and remember the supports made up of your Lady's love for you, and faith in you and your success are stronger than ever!

Thank you ever so much for R's letter. I surely did enjoy it.

Carolyn Hunt [a sister Pi Phi and the daughter of Bucknell president Dr. Emory William Hunt, a Baptist minister] is to be married on October twelfth in the evening. The Pi Phis are invited to the wedding at the church, but not to the reception, for they have so many friends and relatives. Carolyn surely ought to make a lovely bride. This morning in church she sang a solo, and it was beautiful. After she sings I'd always like to have the benediction and go home. I don't feel so much need for a sermon.

Bid day for us is Friday. We expect to get all 15 girls we are rushing. We have a freshman sister who gets all the "dope."

Honey-boy, your Colonial house sounds most awfully enticing as a home for us. Don't start to build it till I come, anyway. No, honey, even if you found a few thousand dollars blowing around, a license as a Commencement present wouldn't be much good, for I'm not anywhere near ready for you yet. I've got to be lots more rested & stronger, & learn how to cook, and – oh, lots of other things, before I'll say "Yes" to the minister!

Hope the class was 100%. If I were a little boy in your S. S. class, I'd come every single Sunday, & sit there watching your face with adoring eyes, & making resolutions that when I grew up I'd be just as near as possible like my wonderful teacher. Beside being a love pupil, I'm your own

Lady x

P. S. I have your lamp on my dresser, & everybody who comes in admires it. I had lots of fun with Frances Rockwell & her typewriter. I kept her a whole hour, because we got so interested that the clock struck eleven almost before we thot it was 10:30. Went to the movies Fri. night & saw Galsworthy's "The White Monkey." I thot it was very good & enjoyed the whole spree, including a Purity Special afterward. [Lewisburg's Purity Ice Cream Company was a favorite destination.]

Tuesday evening, October 5, 1926, Lewisburg to Woodbury

My dearest Ken,

I'm so glad about the beginning of the class. I hope you really will enjoy the teaching. Sometime you might study the next lesson on Sunday afternoon and add to it all thru the week. I used to do that, because after Sunday School I always felt in the mood to study more, and by the next Sunday, I had so many illustrations and methods worked out, just by thinking about it, that the School hour was too short.

I'm glad you're feeling well, honey. I advise changing your lunch sometimes or you will never again want to see or hear of cheese, rye bread, or roast beef. You are surely being thrifty, and I commend your efforts. Tell your Mother my gaining theory is exploded, for I am down to 115½ again. But I feel fine, except for a desire for more time to sleep beyond my 8 hours, which never seem to be enough.

I forgot to tell you about Burns Drum's remark the first day or so in class. He told us he loved to draw pictures, & he guessed it was due to the influence of his cousin, "who is one of the best artists who ever went thru this school." He didn't exactly wink in my direction, for that would have been too undignified, & Burns is nothing if not dignified, but he shot a knowing smile across the room. Once in a while, he deigns to walk down the hill with me, & of course I feel real big to be thusly honored by my Professor! I am still thoroughly enjoying his class.

Billy and I had some fast ping pong last night. It was too hot to study. She is beating me now & acquiring a "nasty" service. I had to play my wickedest game to get a set of 10–8 from her.

You will probably soon hear from a Demie that they have gotten nine men out of some 13–15, but are expecting 2 more to come. I have just come back from meeting, myself, and am in a rather bad frame of mind due to a high-handed running of affairs, and a rejection of the two girls I wanted most. But we have some nice girls – 17 in all, I think. I am so glad we got Ginny Scully thru at last, for it has been a big fight every year, with heartaches all around.

Goodness, such a long tirade on odds and ends. But in between every 2 lines there is an invisible group of three words, which are foremost in my thots all the time!

Your Lady

Sunday afternoon, October 10, 1926
Lewisburg to Woodbury

Dearest Ken,

Yes'm, I do have relatives in Jenkintown – Dutton, by name, and cousins of ours. They're wonderfully dear people. They have always seemed an ideal couple and are much in love with each other. They have three dear little girls and a beautiful home. [When Ken and Caryl married in 1928, the newspaper account says Caryl was "preceded down the aisle" by one of those little girls, Pauline Dutton, "in the daintiest canary frock, smocked in blue." I have no recollection of Pauline's own wedding, but a family photo from 1942 shows that I, in turn, became Pauline's flower girl.]

All our bids were accepted, of course, and such noise & commotion and osculation you never heard or saw, except on other bid days. I know you're saying, "Those foolish, funny women!"

My precious Pi Phi lamp nearly went up in smoke and sparks this morning when the wires pulled out, and I had to take it apart and cement up the wires again. Now it's just as good as new, I think.

Your loving
Lady x

Monday evening, October 11, 1926
Lewisburg to Woodbury

Dearest Ken,

I am enclosing the calendar I secured last evening. C. E. was led by Edna Craft. She has a genius for speaking, and the whole meeting was a lively session. I stayed for church, and enjoyed that, too. I got a big thrill when the bridegroom himself, plus his father & mother and several pompous-looking relatives, filed into church. Wonder what Carolyn's inward feelings were when she sang her solo for that crowd!?

I have been crazy to see Carolyn's things, for she has an unusual collection, such as few brides ever even hope to have. Mrs. Hunt has asked us to come over Wednesday & see them then. The Pi Phis gave her a breakfast set – tho I'm not sure what that includes. I s'pect the wedding will be awfully pretty.

I want to see you as soon as you come, tho I'd like it better if our greeting could be outside in the dark rather than in the front hall. I will do my best to save a place for us in the parlours. It will surely seem like old times to have a date there with you again.

Lovingly,
Your Lady

Wednesday evening, October 13, 1926, Lewisburg to Woodbury

This stationery is headed FIRST BAPTIST CHURCH, LEWISBURG, PA., PASTOR'S STUDY. One of Caryl's college jobs was volunteering in that office.

My own Dearest,

My thots most of the time since last eventful evening have been on the wedding, which was so lovely as to leave me in a rapturous state of mind. A quadruple quartet in the choir sang the Bridal Chorus from "Rosemaid" before the processional, and then sang Lohengrin's chorus as the processional. There were four ushers and four bridesmaids. The only decorations were palms and yellow chrysanthemums. It was so thrilling to go under the striped canopy, which extended from church door to street.

Carolyn looked lovely, of course, as most brides do. Her father married the couple, assisted by Dr. West, pastor at First Baptist. The funniest part was the way Bill rushed Carolyn out of the church as soon as the last word was said. Honestly, they almost ran up the aisle!

I never was so thrilled by any wedding before – partly because I have always thot so much of Carolyn, but mostly because weddings never had such a personal interest before. The reception looked and sounded very exciting as we strolled past. Most of the people escorted the couple to Milton to the train. They'll spend their honeymoon in Havana, Cuba! Wouldn't that be lovely?! And I s'pose they will go by boat. M-m-m! Just two weeks and they'll be back again, and then the bride must choose her home from three that are on the market! Bill's father gave them a $5,000 check, to go toward the house. I think, too, that there was another $5,000 check. Helpful start!!

I was over today to see the things, and it was overwhelming. Such an array of linen, silver, furniture, dishes, I never saw. The Faculty gave her a $300 silver set, a magnificent gift. Carolyn's mother gave her a purple satin coat, and Tomas (their guide) put ermine on it for collar, cuffs, and all down the front. Tomas has been several years collecting this ermine, and everyone said the cloak is royal in appearance. A wealthy aunt outfitted her with something like twenty dresses and shoes to match, so if there is anything left to be desired, it can't be in gifts!

You have probably known that Jack Hubbard has been dissatisfied with Demie, & last night he wrote a letter of resignation & moved out. The boys feel badly that he didn't come out in meeting & express himself. He will go Phi Gam, of course. There seems to be trouble brewing within the Frat, mostly against your liquor rules [the Demies were observing Prohibition], and Ken, do you know that Burns & Len [Len Coates, a Demie, who would become one of Ken's co-workers at N. W. Ayer & Son and a boarder at the Slifers' home in Woodbury] are two of the strongest leaders in a faction working to abolish that rule? It doesn't seem possible. You will hear it all when you come. I only hope this step of Jack's won't hurt the Frat, but the boys are pretty much broken up over the whole situation.

Well, honey, this will be my last letter before I see you. I can hardly restrain my feelings.

Lovingly,
Your own Lady x

Tuesday afternoon, October 19, 1926
Lewisburg to Woodbury

Dearest Ken,

I had to keep up a rather excessive gaiety after you left, to keep from thinking of how much I lost by your going. I shall keep these memories very dear. Thank you ever so much for the fun of that dinner downtown. Sunday night I went

Larison Hall, women's dorm and location of the "Sem parlor" and the women's dining hall. From her room above the dining hall during the two years she was head waitress, Caryl could see the Delta Sigma House across the street.[1]

to C. E., then came home & wrote a long letter to the folks – so full of our weekend that I forgot all about telling them of the wedding and of Carl Sandburg's visit!

Sem rules surely didn't interfere much with what we wanted to do. Even the bringing of you to my room was a privilege I hadn't even thot of – so soon in the year – without either of our families. I'm glad if you liked it, for so many of your things help to make it nice!

After considerable thot, I asked Vic Meyers to the dance, but he said he was going to be away over the weekend. I finally decided today to ask your worthy cousin Burns, & he accepted with a semblance of real pleasure – which was nice of him. I won't enjoy his dancing, unless he has improved, but we can talk the time away, & probably most of the conversation will be about you, for your Lady is going to have a hard time thinking of anyone or anything else.

Mos' lovingly,
All your Lady x

Thursday afternoon, October 21, 1926
Lewisburg to Woodbury

Dearest Ken,

This will be hurried. Lots of work to do & a quiz to study for, plus pledging from 4–8:00 tonight.

I've been awfully sick since I last wrote. It wasn't the hamburg, but something poisonous here, for many others have been sick. I was too sick to sleep Tuesday night & cut classes Wednesday to spend the day in bed. I feel better today, tho weak, since I've had nothing to eat but an orange in a day and a half.

Yes'm! Dutton-Slifer incorporated have now the sum of $11.67 accumulated in pennies.

I must start studying for that quiz under Docky Lawson. Then I have another under Burns Saturday, so let the old, old news of my love suffice this time, and we'll hope for more news next time. There'll be more love, anyway, for that keeps on increasing every day.

All your own
Lady x

Sunday afternoon, October 24, 1926, Lewisburg to Woodbury

My own dear, dear Ken,

I am enclosing a program from last night, filled in with dances for your approval. Burns was very nice, and I admit that I did have a lovely time. The Lambda Chi House is nice for a dance & had a lovely cozy corner I did so want to enjoy with you. Even an almost full moon shone down upon us.

Burns is greatly improved as a dancer. He is no longer awkward, but keeps beautifully in time with the music & is peppy. His Hawaii trip must have done him a lot of good! It seemed so funny to have to go down to see if my escort was there in our front hall, rather than have him whistle as you always do. [Every evening during my childhood, I looked forward to Ken's Demie whistle, which announced his arrival home from the office.] Burns told me all about his girl in Genesee.

The dance ended about 11:20, & strolling back to the Sem got us here just after the locking of the doors & the departure of the Chief. Finally our Gym teacher came & let us in so that our poor escorts could go home to bed!

Friday I gave my hair a waterwave for the dance, & it must have been a good advertisement, for I got two jobs for Sat. afternoon. I wish I had more jobs like that. It's fun, & an easy way to make a few cents.

The concert on Friday was splendid. We had the Ritz male quartet and a harpist. The quartet sang lots of familiar things, and surely was enjoyed by the students, tho some of the aristocratic profs thot there was too much barbershop harmony!

I just couldn't find time yesterday to get out to Aunt Clara's. It was a lovely day for a walk, but I had so much work to do. Then, too, it would have tired me pretty much & I didn't know how much effort I would need to follow Burns!

I'm glad you're enjoying your work so much, honey, for that makes life so much fun.

All my love to you,
Your Lady

The Demie whistle.

Thursday, October 28, 1926, Lewisburg to Woodbury

My own Dearest,

This has been a busy day, with a test this morning, a chapel speaker, an hour of tennis, and a meeting, with lessons in between. Discussion groups begin next Monday evening, and I think I am to be sent to Groover House to lead a discussion with the 23 freshmen there. We will discuss Prohibition. The leaders' group meeting, both men and women, comes tonight, and probably will take most of the evening.

I entered the "Grace" or "Blessing" contest again this year. Last night the winner was announced; lo & behold, 'twas yours truly!! I about fell over! They gave me $5 to spend as I wish, but I haven't decided what that method will be. I wrote words to the tune of "Savior, Again, in Thy Dear Name We Raise":

> Father, again we raise to Thee a prayer
> In gratitude, for food & loving care;
> Grant us forgiveness for our sins this day,
> And in Thy footsteps, guide us on our way.

I surely feel very much pleased they liked mine best, tho I s'pose by the end of the year I'll be tired enuf of hearing it twice for each dinner.

Thank you for the dear note today,
C.

Caryl's "Blessing" was often family grace before meals when I was growing up, and we used it later with our own kids. But after the Scotts were introduced to the Doxology sung to the tune of "Hernando's Hideaway," that became the grace of choice!

Sunday afternoon, October 31, 1926, Lewisburg to Woodbury

My dearest,

We had that Prohibition meeting all Thursday evening till 9:30, then a senior "sing" till after ten. Most of Friday I was planning the dining room for dinner, and yesterday was filled with all sorts of things.

Oh, honey, I'm ever so glad you can come early this week. I'll be counting time till Friday, & long before eight I shall be hanging out doors & windows with a beating heart, chasing up and down, watching for a big Cadillac to roll up to the Demie house.

Doesn't it seem strange that you should have as a member of your S. S. class a boy who lives in your former home? [Malcolm Thomas, also an active member of Central Baptist Church, bought the large Slifer home from Edna after Rob's untimely death. His son Charlie, the "boy" Caryl mentions, faithfully attended Ken's class for many years.]

The Halloween party on Friday surely was loads of fun. We had a wonderful dinner of candied sweet potatoes, ham, lima beans, peach salad, mince pie, and stuffed doughnuts. Costumes surely were clever. I made mine out of (don't be shocked) a vivid pair of Billy's pajamas – black with big orange and red & yellow flowers. I donned a gay pair of black lace stockings with black pumps. I had a big 3-cornered black tie around my neck. I topped it all off with a black tam I made, and your palette.

Lots and lots of love from
Your Lady x

Tuesday afternoon, November 2, 1926, Lewisburg to Woodbury

Ken dear,

I've been noticing lately that sometimes you use two stamps instead of one [4¢ instead of 2¢], and it makes me wonder whether some of my letters with weighty enclosures have come to you "postage due." Have they?

This morning when I walked into the Sem, I found in my mail box two big letters – one from you and one from Rolland, of all people. This is the first letter R. has deigned to write me, & I surely was surprised.

There's a whole lot of blarney in your congratulatory paragraph, but I forgive you, knowing the state of your heart. It doesn't prove at all that I have such exceptional ability, but it will be lots of fun if I ever can help you with your copy work. I guess we were planned for each other, for I have always thot advertising about the most fascinating subject I know, and it seems as tho sharing that sort of a work-game with you would be just about the most fun I could want.

I had two quizzes this morning – one under Burns, and a mid-semester one in German. At four, I'm going out to play hockey, and this evening have a social Frat meeting.

Aunt Jennie and I had an enjoyable walk to your Aunt's, groping our way for two miles in the darkness amid puddles and deep mud in places. The stars had come out by the time we came back, and they were beautiful. We started from here about six and got back a little after nine. I found Aunt Clara well and as happy as could be expected.

Discussion groups last night were good, tho our numbers were depleted by the Philly trip. I had 1st & 2nd floor Annex, and only 7 girls were home to attend, but we rather completely discussed the drink problem.

Anxiously awaiting your arrival,
Your Lady x

Wednesday afternoon, November 10, 1926, Lewisburg to Woodbury

My own dear Ken,

Yesterday we had a regular cloudburst in the afternoon, and the stream below my window soon quickened into a rushing torrent. [At least once during Ken and Caryl's years at Bucknell, this "rushing torrent" – flooding from the nearby Susquehanna River – completely filled the street between the Sem and the Demie house, to a depth that allowed Rolland to climb to the porch roof of the house and dive in.]

Thank your Mother for me for that Lavender she sent. My perfume holder is receiving much admiration – most of all from me, for I surely do like it, honey. You were such a dear to bring that to me.

After Frat meeting last night, Aunt Jennie and I went down to the Lutheran church to an illustrated lecture on S. S. work in foreign lands. I quite enjoyed it, tho I was too sleepy to derive full benefit.

I found out last night that I broke a rule on Sunday by eating at the Demie house. We must be chaperoned by a member of the Faculty, or by Mother, Father, or married sister! Well, hope I don't get campused for it. Not that a "campus" would matter much with you gone, anyway.

I had a delightful surprise yesterday. The Demies invited me to take one of the two girls' parts in their annual play. They are going to give "Three Wise Fools," and I can tell you more after we have had a meeting of the cast. It will be loads of fun, and I'm looking forward to getting to work on it.

Your leaving left an awfully big emptiness that makes me long for Thanksgiving to approach on wings.

All yours,
C x

The Susquehanna River floods St. George Street between Larison Hall and the Demie House after a major storm. The entrance to Larison can be seen at center (Caryl's room is above the entrance).[1]

Friday afternoon, November 12, 1926
Lewisburg to Woodbury

My own Ken,

I am becoming more humble each day, as the recent series of events leaves me breathless. I thot I was having a good time this year in a quiet fashion. Then, along comes the grace contest prize, the Demie play, and now a 3rd honor that almost took me off my feet. We have a live, organized, functioning athletic association this year. Wed. night they had election of officers, and out of a clear sky they nominated & elected me for the presidency. In many ways it made me happy – not the honor of it, but the evidence it gave that my efforts to be more of a friend to all, this year more than ever before, have in part succeeded. You know how I hated to come back this year, and you told me I must learn to smile. Now, if I can go on as I have begun, I can make this the happiest year of college.

Your prayers have helped, dearest, and, oh, how I love you for them and your love!

Thank you, dear,
Your Lady

Sunday afternoon, November 14, 1926
Lewisburg to Woodbury

My dear Ken,

I wonder what makes you think I might be playing the "lead" in the Demie play. No'm, I'm only the governess to the heroine. The date is somewhere in the first week of February. You won't have a chance to see your lady star, but I hope to be able to carry out my part creditably, at least.

Last night I took a chance on "Subway Sadie" at the movies & enjoyed it thoroughly, in spite of the title. It was awfully funny in parts. (Next time Burns remarks in class that he hasn't been to the movies for so long he hardly knows what they're like, I'm going to throw a book at him, for he was there last night & also two weeks ago. I hope he caught the meaningful glance I sent in his direction!) After the enjoyment of a Purity Special, I went early to bed like a dutiful "Semite," and slept 9 hours. Consequently, I went to S. S. this morning. Imagine that – after a year & a half of absence!

I tried to digest the camera instructions the other evening but was too stupid to see thru them. I tried 2 pictures of my room & took the film to be developed. I don't expect them to be any good; my light was too weak. You must explain the camera all over again at Thanksgiving time.

Lots of love,
Caryl

Ken (center) and Bobby (right) and friends in the Slifers' small front yard with "Lizzie" behind them in the driveway.

Sunday evening, November 14, 1926, Woodbury to Lewisburg

Honey, mine,

Please understand, the sketch on the envelope expresses my recent gay exuberance and deep-felt admiration for your charming, adorable self. I couldn't let your newest deeds pass by without visual recognition – if only this congratulatory toast to your health in a brimming flagon of cider!

I think the Athletic Association success is as sweet to me as to you – I'm so proud of your swimming, tennis, hockey, and basketball prowess – nor do I feel it wrong to ascribe such an award in part to prayer. I so thoroly enjoyed my four years at Bucknell that I wanted you to have the same fond memories of The Hill. One joyous year to link you closely to the old campus will be an additional bond between us, in the

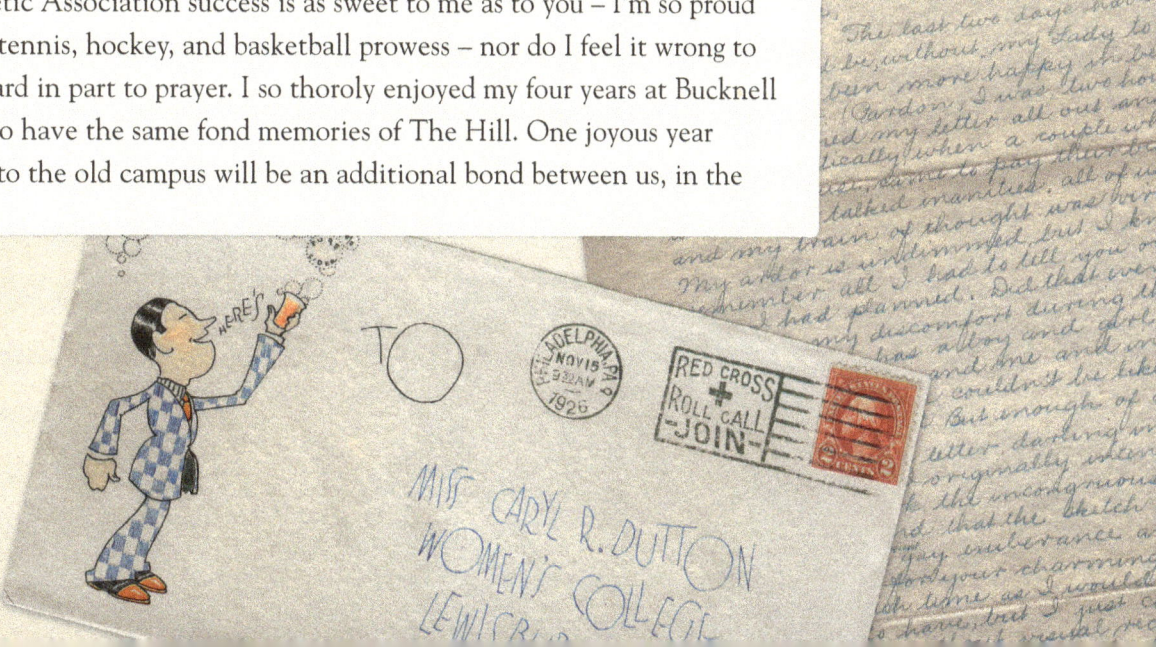

precious and intimate companionship we hope to enter soon. I didn't want you to leave our Alma Mater with a sense of dissatisfaction, and my highest hopes bid fair to be realized. (I was concerned in the same way about Rolland, but I'm afraid he's beyond salvation, with little interest in college, fraternity, or anything else.)

May you continue to have the happiest, gayest year of all your 21!

Yesterday Bobby and I played football with a round brown cookie can that spiralled beautifully, and had a riotous good time for an hour at least, as we used to do.

This afternoon Mother, Bobby and I went for a delightful drive, over roads we hadn't travelled in a long time. In Mullica Hill, we stopped to see some friends who have just finished remodeling an old house built in 1785! The exterior is still rather shabby, but inside it is charming, and you just must see it while you're here – to complete your Home Ec course, if nothing else.

With oceans of love to my lovely, talented Lady,
Her own devoted Ken

Tuesday afternoon, November 16, 1926
Lewisburg to Woodbury

My dear Ken,

The toast that greeted me last night is surely a very nice one. My, but I was delightfully surprised to find a painted envelope again! I surely do appreciate your taking time from your busy days. And it was so dear of you to take the news in that way. I don't think I can ever feel toward Bucknell, Frat, or friends as warmly as you do, but I can honestly say that I am enjoying them all.

It surely was a shock to all of us to hear about Paul. [Paul Wilbur Slifer, Ken's 15-year-old cousin and the only child of his Uncle Conard, died November 15, 1926.] It is awfully hard on his father and mother. I have tried to get Aunt Clara [a trained nurse], but couldn't, so I think she must be over there with them.

We had a brief meeting of the cast and got some books. I don't think I'll need to bring the book with me Thanksgiving, for I only have a few short lines in the play. We have first rehearsal tomorrow night at seven. The stage work is going to be complicated, to adjust to our limited stage and scenery. I have to go to Senior indoor hockey practice in a couple of minutes, so I must hasten.

With lots of love,
Caryl

Thursday afternoon, November 18, 1926, Lewisburg to Woodbury

Dearest Ken,

Mid-semester exams are piling up thick and fast. We had one in German, but have one in Philosophy tomorrow, and also in Home Ec., and one in Political Science on Tuesday. I'm trying not to study too hard, so that I won't be exhausted for vacation time. This afternoon I was studying Philosophy, and reached the saturation point to such an extent that I crawled under the covers and slept almost an hour.

Yesterday I was out playing hockey from 3–4, and watched the Freshman-Junior game from 4–5. The field was one mass of mud and puddles, but the girls played right thru it all, regardless, and tho the spectacle was awfully funny, the poor girls were all just about soaked by the end of the game. There was plenty of excitement and good playing, and the game ended 2–1 for the Juniors.

I got the pictures today. Yours are splendid, but mine weren't any good.

All my love to you,
Caryl

"Almost Sunday evening," November 21, 1926, Lewisburg to Woodbury

Darling,

I have an Executive meeting tonight after church, and the work I ought to do is so extensive that I'm almost overwhelmed. I've been working most of today as well as yesterday on a long mid-semester quiz given in Home Ec., to be worked out & answered over the weekend. I had hoped to spend at least an hour on Pol. Science in preparation for a quiz, but couldn't find even a minute.

Tomorrow afternoon we have hockey practice, and Tuesday we play a game! Yesterday noon we played the Sophs and won 3–0. But we almost froze. Br-r-r-r but it was cold. I think we play the Freshmen on Tuesday. We are handicapped, for we have only nine on our team.

I'm so excited about going to see "The Student Prince" with you, honey. You don't know what a treat it will be to me, & I don't s'pose I'll be able to tell you, unless actions speak louder than words!

I had a wonderful time yesterday all day. One class, hard study, and a typewriting lesson till 12:00, hockey game 12–1:15, lunch till 2:00, football game and freezing atmospheres till 4:30, dinner, then movies to see Richard Dix in "The Quarterback" (dandy picture), & back to the Sem to a dance which the K. D.'s gave to all the Sem. We had a 4-piece orchestra (men), lovely decorations, & one of the peppiest times I've had this year. [As a child I loved to ask my mother to demonstrate the Charleston, then watch her whiz sideways across our kitchen floor. But I never could master it.]

Friday night I had lots of studying to do, but nevertheless Vera & I invaded the Home Ec. kitchen, made a big batch of fudge, & then devoured a 1/2 pint of bisque ice cream apiece, with choc. sauce, & choc. cake. Goodness! It's a wonder we weren't sick, but we weren't.

It's time for C. E. I wish I could go out to meet the Demie whistler, and go with him to church. For Thanksgiving, and next Sunday, I'll be there with you.

Your Lady

Monday afternoon, November 29, 1926
Lewisburg to Woodbury

My own Darling,

The spell of last night is still upon me, for I can think of nothing else but you. I know it has never been so hard to leave you as it was this time, and after these short days together, I feel that you mean lots more to me than ever before.

I do hope it wasn't too much of a strain on your Mother. I don't want to increase her burdens one bit. Words are awfully futile, but within a few days I shall try to express to her my gratitude for all that she did. I learned to know & love so much more both your Mother and Bobby.

The trip back was uneventful. After cleaning up a bit, I went to the kitchen, and the Chef fried me an egg, which I enjoyed with buttered potatoes, raisin bread, and cocoa. I have been over to Mrs. Phillips' for a little vocal work, and am now using strenuous will power to settle down to study again. Well, honey, all the love in the world is yours, from your own

Loving Lady

Friday afternoon, December 3, 1926
Lewisburg to Woodbury

Dearest Ken,

Oh, honey, what joy you give me by the promise of your company on the eleventh! I did so want you to come, and even now, I'm afraid you are doing what your Mother would advise not doing.

But I'm so glad, glad, glad! I just long to throw my arms around your neck in an ecstatic hug. I do hope it won't be too much of a strain on you or faithful "Lizzie." Yes, the dance is formal for men. If any bad creases occur, I could press them out for you.

I have been busy with Xmas gifts, which I'm making for Home Ec. I guess I got the fever hard, for I'm making a yardstick holder like your Mother's, six holders for hot things, 2 pairs of shoe covers for traveling, and two handkerchief holders.

If the snow isn't too deep, we shall play a hockey game tomorrow afternoon. Hope we have better luck than Bobby, tho a loss wouldn't mean so much to us as to her team.

It just seems too good to be true, honey, that you'll actually be here with me, & I'll see you again only a week from tomorrow. And only a week ago, we were spending the evening together in Philly. Oh, honey, looking backward or forward, life is one constant joy because of you.

Always your lady,
C.

Sunday afternoon, December 5, 1926
Lewisburg to Woodbury

My dear, dear Ken,

This is surely quite a letter-writing day, for I have already written your Mother, Rolland, my folks at home, and now you – best of all.

I am more inclined than you to find justification for Rolland's visit to Kitty's home. You see, Father & her father have been friends since early boyhood and worked for years together in the same factory. That made a bond immediately when the four met on shipboard, and they were together from then till they left Paris. I do think Rolland makes a little too much of it, & I'm afraid if I were Mary, I should be awfully jealous of the liking which Rolland professes to have for Kitty. I'm just glad, dearest, that you don't find any special interest in other girls, but I can see reasons why Rolland would be glad to avail himself of Kitty's invitation for refuge for the night and a chance to exchange experiences of the summer. We hope, anyway, that he wrote Mary assuring her, for the slightest reason, that his visit and fun meant nothing that concerned any lessening of his love for her.

Your own
Lady

Tuesday afternoon, December 7, 1926, Lewisburg to Woodbury

My own dear Ken,

If you only had some idea of what wonderful letters you do write, and what immeasurable joy they give to Your Lady! When you enter the Copy department, if you write advertisements half as full of thought pictures and lovely appealing expressions as you use in writing to me, you will be a perfect success! As I read, I lived over again last Sunday with you before the fire, until it was so real it almost hurt.

Tonight we have special chorus rehearsal, tomorrow fraternity meeting & student government meeting, and Friday a Xmas party, which Home Ec. class 103 is giving to class 101. Next week is Artist Course on Monday, Oxford debate on Tuesday, "Messiah" given by the choir on Wednesday, Xmas party here on Thursday, and mayhap a dance on Friday. Our national Pi Phi Grand Vice-President is coming tonight to visit our chapter. We have a tea for her tomorrow afternoon and meeting in the evening.

This morning the thermometer registered ten degrees below, so you can imagine that it was a bit chilly. But my room has been nice and warm, and with red and green plants in my window sills, a narcissus in bloom, its fragrance permeating every corner of the room, and half-completed Xmas gifts spread about, I feel in the bestest of Xmas spirits.

Love to your Mother and Bobby, and all possible love to my own dear Ken from

His Lady

Thursday evening, December 9, 1926
Woodbury to Lewisburg

Honey-Girl,

I didn't get home from the office till nearly 9 o'clock – I'm jammed with work just now, as most of us are. I painted this envelope since reaching home and eating – so there's not much time left for letter-writing.

I'm not able to give you full details of our trip yet. We cannot leave Phila. till 10 o'clock, which means 7:00 or 7:30 at Lewisburg! Sorry, but I'll dress as fast as I can after saying hello x x, but we may be a little late to the dance. I can't tell you, darling, how very happy, happy, HAPPY I am to be traveling toward you again! I bought new patent leathers 'n everything

Oceans of love to you, sweetheart, and all the affection in the world till I see you.

Your devoted
Ken

Friday afternoon, December 17, 1926, Lewisburg to Woodbury

My dearest Ken,

Yesterday I had charge of decorations for our table. I bought, cut, and sewed white material in the shape of immense canes, a yard high, then stuffed them with newspaper & wrapped them with red & green paper strips to look like candy canes. We stood them in the middle of the table & decorated the rest of the table with various red and green formations. There surely was a lot of exclaiming about these canes. Our table being in the center of things, no one could help seeing it.

The whole party was just lovely. The girls in evening dress looked so pretty, and each table was fancily decorated, the candles on each table being the only light in the whole room. We had a delicious turkey dinner, ending with mince pie à la mode.

In our ten-cent gifts that every one at the table gave to some other, anonymously, I gave Mrs. Phillips a big onion; she's always wishing for onions in everything. One of the girls gave me an auto, with a verse about joyriding with you. Vera got a very suggestive cigar (!), with a verse about patience being a virtue! After the dinner, I went with twenty-five or so others to sing carols at different profs' homes.

"Messiah" Wednesday night was beautifully given. I never heard the choir sing so well. At the debate with Oxford, Commencement Hall was packed, and The Bucknellian says almost a hundred were turned away. Our men put up the best arguments, but the other men surely had the sense of humor. My goodness, I never heard such a string of puns and jokes – one right after the other – and many of necessity impromptu. Those Oxford men were surely clever. Everyone greatly enjoyed the debate, but especially the accent and jokes of our visitors, judging from reports!

This time tomorrow I will be speeding homeward. Joy! You know, honey, how much I love you, and how completely you fill all my thoughts.

Your own
Lady

Sunday evening, December 19, 1926, Buffalo to Woodbury

Dear Ken,

I was afraid yesterday, when the mail failed to be delivered to the Sem, that I was missing a letter from you, but fortunately you wrote here instead, and homecoming seemed so much more complete with a letter from you awaiting me.

Several people have asked about you, and many seemed to think that of course we would spend Xmas together! I wish we could, and your own wish only makes mine deeper. If you'll just send Santa's sleigh along, I'll be only too glad to jump in and ride to greet you with a frosty kiss that nevertheless would hold plenty of warmth.

There is winter in real earnest here. The snow is piled high as a result of a blizzard on Thursday. And tho the thermometer is not so awfully low, yet it seems bitter cold as compared with Lewisburg weather.

Father is on his way home from Boston and New York, so have not seen him yet. He thot he might get back this morning, but he didn't. At 4:30, we went to a song service at the Delaware church. A choir of seventy-five voices sang carols of all the centuries and all nations.

The Demie dance was lovely. I spent most of the afternoon and early evening locating a pair of silver stockings and turning up various hems to the required and cooperating lengths, but finally was ready on time. The house was beautifully decorated with a lighted tree on the porch, all the lights embowered in pine branches and red crepe paper, and the railing of the stairway all covered with the pine, with little colored lights peeping out here and there. The dance was lots of fun, but not half so nice as the one the week before, with you.

Always your own
Lady

Sunday afternoon, December 26, 1926, Woodbury to Buffalo

Ken fortuitously drew the name of "Little Johnny Frazer" for the office Christmas party gift. John became one of the Slifers' closest friends. When he left Ayer to become Reader's Digest's India/Pakistan correspondent, he wrote articles on figures such as Mother Teresa and Mohandas Gandhi. Eventually, we also enjoyed John's visits to our farm.

My precious Lady,

I never appreciated before how little of the day is left when business has taken its toll – 7:30 A.M. to 6:15 P.M. Every moment was precious this pre-Christmas week, and I worked till at least one or two o'clock each night. I had a very enjoyable Christmas, but I'm heartily glad that "it comes but once a year."

I thank you, dearest mine, for the Christmas remembrance, that combined with the sentiment on its lovely card to make me very, very happy. The scarf is very good-looking, and exactly the sort I had in mind, honey-girl.

Thursday evening, after the church party, I set about concocting my offering for the Detail Bureau Christmas party next day. The 15 men in Detail had previously placed all our names in a hat and each drawn one, for whom a ridiculous present was to be purchased at a maximum price of 25¢. I drew the name of the youngest chap, who is still attending college at night, but who is very capable and likeable, and ranks next to the Chief of the bureau. One of his largest accounts is "Canada Dry Ginger Ale," and that was the germ of my idea.

I purchased a small wine bottle of wood, with a wooden nipple attached on a stem, containing a whistle that emitted an unmusical squawk. Then I carefully prepared a burlesque of the "Canada Dry" bottle that was quite accurate in miniature. The whole was painted the same green as the real bottle, and the top gilded roughly to represent the gold foil seal. I drew rather faithful imitations of both labels on the bottle, caricaturing all the printed matter, coat of arms, etc. For example, the product name CANADA DRY PALE GINGER ALE became KINDA DRY EMACIATED GIN OR ALE, and the whole was carried out in the same spirit. Then I lettered this bit of doggerel on a card and wrapped everything carefully in a holly box.

Best wishes for good spirits at Yuletide

> To Little Johnny Frazer,
> Who has never used a razor
> We dedicate this jug of gin or ale.
> We attached a large-size nipple
> So that our John could tipple,
> As befits his age – which ends
> this trifling tale.

The fellows also asked me to draft a letter to accompany the offering we presented to production manager Harry Batten, who controls the destinies of Detail men and the other bureaus of production. He's a good skate, young, energetic, and aggressive, with lots of money and a sense of humor. (The Victor Co. presented him with a special Orthophone Victrola, costing $1,000!) I took some time composing it, and all in all it was well after 2 A.M. when I finally fell into bed.

It seemed a lot of work for a little fun, but that one morning's nonsense accomplished more for me, I think, than several weeks of serious, earnest effort could have done. My burlesque bottle was unanimously adjudged the cleverest offering in the bureau. Frazer was quite pleased with it, and he helped me unconsciously by showing it to everybody – to the artists who admired my bottle, and to the writers who laughed at my verses.

But the biggest thrill came when "Santa" read my letter to Batten aloud. It elicited several hearty bursts of laughter and a lot of compliments for me – AND Paul Lewis, head of all Copy Department and a demi-god in the advertising world, said "Very, very clever, Slifer." Rapturous, ineffable, sublime thrills! It was worth a long night's work to draw a laugh or two from the powers that control the pay envelope, and I'm happy for what it may mean to our future, honey-girl. The results may not be tangible soon, but the whole episode drew their favorable attention to me, and I cannot fail to profit by it if I stay awake and on my toes.

The whole proposition grows more like a game each day, dear. It's fascinating, and I'm playing to win – for the adorable Lady who is my partner.

Thank you, Lady-love, for the pictures. The one of you without a hat is the nicest I've ever had of my precious sweetheart. I've carried it ever since, and I want to shout to everyone: "See, here's my Lady!"

Ken adds no signature because there is not one centimeter of space left.

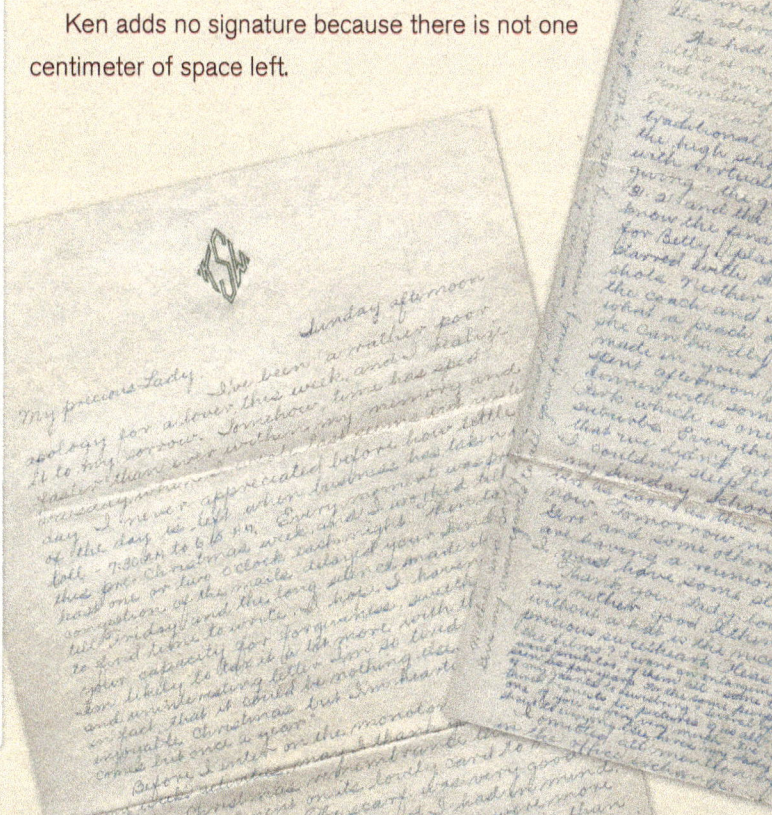

Tuesday afternoon, December 28, 1926
Buffalo to Woodbury

Dearest Ken,

I'm so glad, dear, if you really liked the scarf. I could have bought ready-made a more dainty one, but since you lovingly said that one I would make might be more valuable in your sight, I did my best to pick out a satisfactory material from the meagre supply that I found.

Oh, honey, as if you could like it half as much as I like my gift. It's just beautiful – so lovely I rather stand in awe of it. [No word on what it was.] You do have such good taste. Thank you just ever so much.

I did enjoy your description of the Office Party gift. That surely was clever – the letter must have been, too. I hope it does help you a lot. I can appreciate the thrill your recognition must have given you.

I'm glad you liked the pictures. Everyone here liked that one without a hat, and Mother and Rolland had several printed. Would you please have one of you alone finished for me?

Among my gifts I found candy, silk stockings, handkerchiefs, washcloths for school use, aprons and some salad recipes for the hope chest, some of the various cosmetics I had previously selected, Pullman slippers, silk bloomers, and a beautiful bath towel set, which I shall safely put away for Our Home.

The worst part of this vacation is this old book report and term thesis, which I have to write for Home Ec. I've at last finished the book, but haven't started the report yet. I wish I could get it done, for then I could really enjoy my vacation. (I've been working on it all day today.)

Sunday morning Mother and I went to Parkside, where Mother had to give a talk on the World Tour. The first stop is in Poland, where Father visited this summer at the home of John Sus, a man whom we knew here in Buffalo. His two children, born in America, are here now, sent back for proper food, clothing, and education, and Mother used these two children as a sort of object lesson.

Friday night the Jacksons come here for a New Year's party, and Saturday night Duttons, Johnsons, and Stickles descend en masse upon some hotel for our annual New Year's dinner.

Give my love to your folks too, please, honey, also from my folks to you (especially from Attie).

Your Lady

1927

Caryl and Ken, both 21 as 1927 begins, will spend most of this year far apart – yearning and writing constantly. For unknown reasons, only a handful of Ken's letters survive. However, these do include some exquisitely painted envelopes. Most of the year's events must be inferred from Caryl's letters.

Sunday afternoon, January 2, 1927
Woodbury to Lewisburg

Darling mine,

It was a shock to realize after I'd finished the envelope that by virtue of the holiday this could not reach you till Tuesday, when you'd probably be in Lewisburg. Moreover, the design, appropriate to the Christmas season, would seem out of place back on the college campus. I'm sending it to you anyway, honey-girl, for I assuredly don't want to hold it till next Christmas!

Our own New Year's Day was quiet – nearly noon when Bobby and I finally came downstairs in 1927. A little ping pong, and this envelope, consumed the afternoon, and the evening we spent with our neighbors, the Wellbrocks, listening to the N. Y. Symphony, McCormack,

Elman, and the rest of the Victor artists. (Radio, of course.)

This morning was filled by Sunday School and church (communion, too). After dinner Mother & I counted and wrapped the coins in the month's church collections for nearly three hours. One of my boys is in the hospital for a leg bone infection, and yesterday we entertained his baby brother (9 mos.), while his mother went to see him. Mother wanted the baby to have an airing, so I went along to lift the carriage up and down curbs. Everyone stared, so I'm afraid I'll have quite a job explaining that it was a borrowed baby!

The pennies continue to pile up, and I'll probably have 4 or 5 rolls to add to the fund at Founder's Day. I'm longing so for the day when I'm economically able to make you mine.

I'm hoping my love may help you to start again on the last lap, with renewed vigor and enthusiasm. I'm so overflowing with thoughts of my dear lady, and you may be certain of my deep and enduring love for you.

Devotedly,

Ken x x x x x ⟶ x

Wednesday evening, January 12, 1927
Woodbury to Lewisburg

My darling,

Listen carefully, for this is a real, genuine, honest-to-gosh, bedtime story.

Yesterday morning early, before the writers and artists began to drift in to the office, I noticed a large painting in one of the offices, and stopped in to look at it. While studying it, the owner of that particular sanctum entered breezily and genially as usual. (One of the highest paid men in the organization – writes most of the Camel-Prince Albert stuff and a lot of Victor as well – he is a prince of a chap.) We considered the painting a moment while he told me the story behind it, then suddenly sez he, "I understand you are to be with us in Copy soon, Kenneth."

I nearly fell against the wall as he went on: "Yes, I believe you will be moved up when the new office across the hall is finished." I thanked him for his unexpected "star of hope." I wasn't worth much as a Detail man the rest of the day. I was busy dreaming dreams – You – My Lady – My Wife – our castles in Spain – Someday. (S'pose we must call them Ayer-castles, now!)

Today I kept speculating on what I'd been told yesterday – and growing more and more dubious as to its possibility – all precedent would be shattered if I moved up so soon. Ayer personnel are fair and just, but rather conservative. Reasoning thus, I decided to table my hopes awhile yet, but another chance encounter with the same man led me to query him a bit. He thought his story authentic and well-founded, and added that such a step was inevitable in the near future, in view of the empty office and a real need for extra men in the department. He promised to sleuth a bit and report definitely. Sometimes, dear, working for you, knowing the greatness of your love, I feel as if I could win the whole world – with your trust in me – my lovely, precious Lady.

I've enjoyed this confidential chat with you, honey-mine. Try to imagine that you are cozily snug in my arms and drifting off to dreamland with a good-night kiss from your own lovin'

Ken

Monday morning, January 31, 1927
Philadelphia to Lewisburg

My own sweetheart,

I shall cherish for a long time the memory of my last lovely glimpse of you before the Demie House as we started home yesterday. You were charmingly radiant, and your fine, dark, aristocratic beauty stood out against the background that the other girls afforded, like a delicate, gracefully slender orchid against a bank of – uh – dandelions. I know only that I saw a rapturous, ravishing vision – the dear, precious Lady whom I love and worship with all my soul.

Devotedly,
Ken

P. S. I could taste the lipstick half the way home – I found it pleasant, though. x x

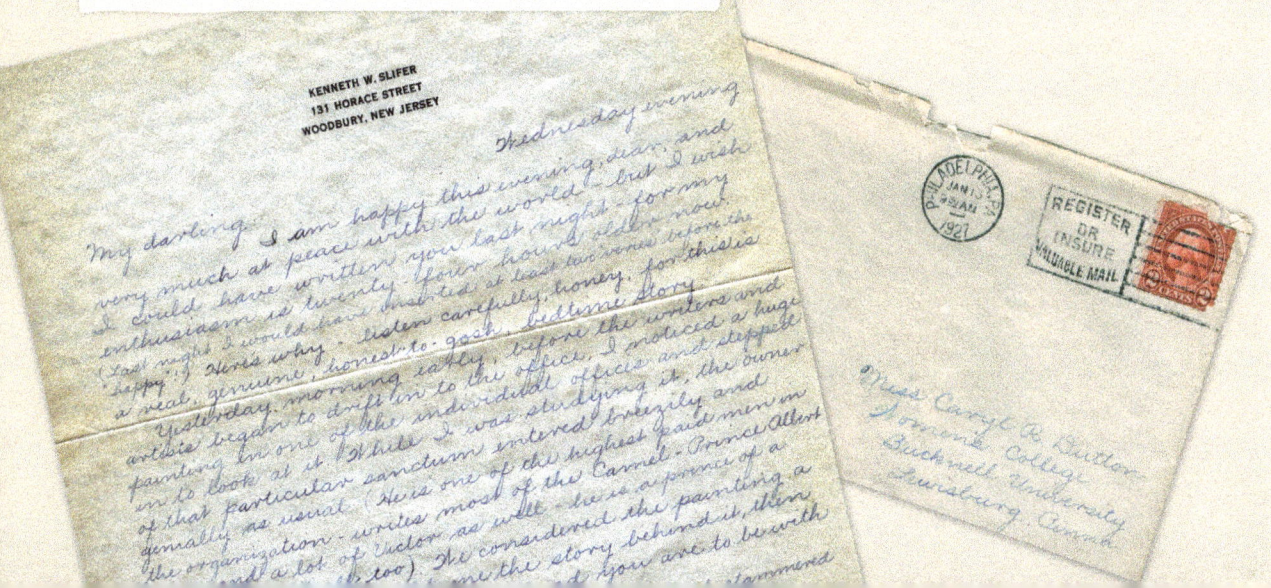

Thursday noon, February 3, 1927
Philadelphia to Lewisburg

My darling Lady,

I'm sorry, dear, that you found my note insincere and flattering. Truly, honey, I have never so rejoiced in your love as in the last few days. If only you could know how ravishing you really were as I said goodbye! It may have been just your love welling up and overflowing – "the beauty of the soul revealed" – but sweetheart mine, you were beautiful – and that's as heartfelt and sincere as my love for you – what higher pledge can I offer?

While I carried a rapturous vision for many, many miles, you looked critically into your mirror and saw only a stray curl or a bit of a shine on your nose, overlooking completely the radiant being who had kissed me goodbye. And so you label my letters "blarney"! Please, precious, won't you understand! It's LOVE, dear, wholesouled, tremendous, all-engulfing!

Last night I worked awhile on my memory book and then obliged one of the neighbors by making a fourth at bridge.

The high school has finally assigned point values to all student offices and set 25 as a maximum for one student. Bobby had previously dropped a couple jobs, but she still has 56 points, and is quite perturbed at the prospect of giving them up!

Just because it's the last lap, honey, please don't overwork this semester. Keep well and fit for that happy Someday when we face the world together – wholly each other's!

Your own – always,
Ken

Sunday afternoon, February 13, 1927
Lewisburg to Woodbury

Both this envelope and the letter are written in purple ink and appear at first glance to have come from Ken. However, the decorations are actually painstaking cutouts, pasted on by Caryl. Whatever her glue, more than eight decades later every edge holds firm.

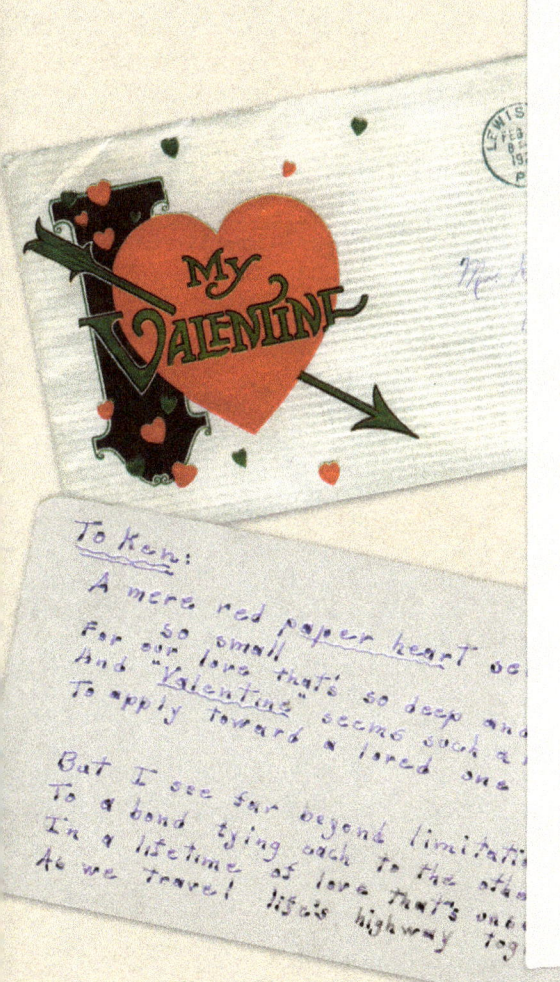

My own Ken dear,

I couldn't find a printed Valentine that suited me at all, so I thot I might make one. I can't paint, but I can use a pair of scissors – hence the envelope. Please accept it as a sincere greeting. You have often said I acted as if I were afraid to show my love for you in public, so I have published to the whole world the fact that you're mine!

To Ken:

>A mere red paper heart seems a symbol so small
>For our love that's so deep and sincere,
>And "Valentine" seems such a meaningless name
>To apply toward a loved one so dear.
>
>But I see far beyond limitations of both
>To a bond tying each to the other,
>In a lifetime of love that's unselfish and true
>As we travel life's highway together.

By his Lady

Yesterday after two classes, a typewriting lesson, and an hour of basketball, I spent an hour or so in play rehearsal, then came back here and worked fast and furiously on a pile of neglected textbooks. I spent so much energy that I needed recreation in the evening, so I invaded the movies again. Then Craftie came home with me and

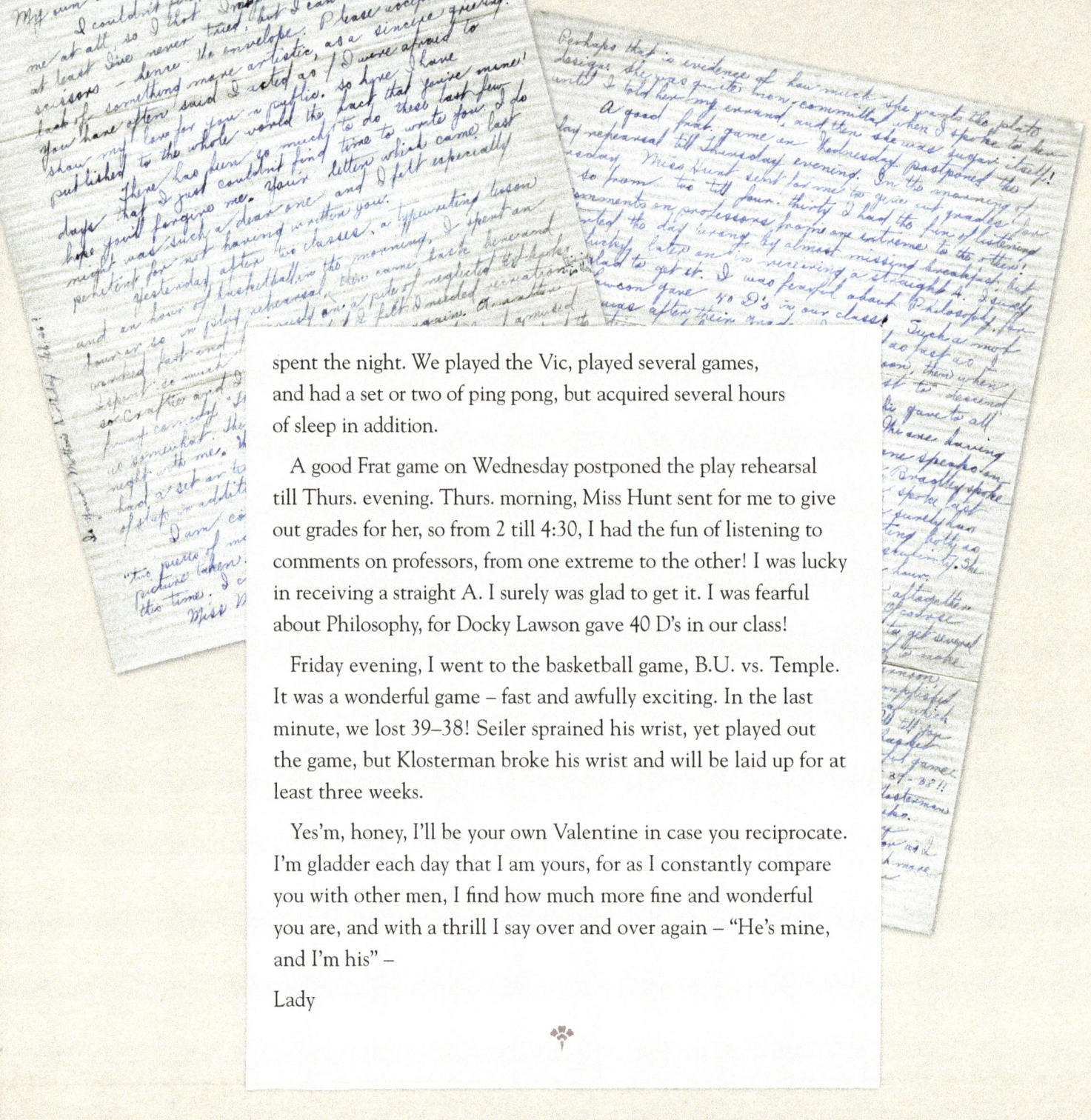

spent the night. We played the Vic, played several games, and had a set or two of ping pong, but acquired several hours of sleep in addition.

A good Frat game on Wednesday postponed the play rehearsal till Thurs. evening. Thurs. morning, Miss Hunt sent for me to give out grades for her, so from 2 till 4:30, I had the fun of listening to comments on professors, from one extreme to the other! I was lucky in receiving a straight A. I surely was glad to get it. I was fearful about Philosophy, for Docky Lawson gave 40 D's in our class!

Friday evening, I went to the basketball game, B.U. vs. Temple. It was a wonderful game – fast and awfully exciting. In the last minute, we lost 39–38! Seiler sprained his wrist, yet played out the game, but Klosterman broke his wrist and will be laid up for at least three weeks.

Yes'm, honey, I'll be your own Valentine in case you reciprocate. I'm gladder each day that I am yours, for as I constantly compare you with other men, I find how much more fine and wonderful you are, and with a thrill I say over and over again – "He's mine, and I'm his" –

Lady

Sunday evening, March 27, 1927, Woodbury to Lewisburg

My own sweetheart,

An hour ago I finished re-reading your most recent letters. Ever since I've been reviewing successive events as our love came into being, powered, & deepened into undying devotion.

Then, for the first time, I got out my diaries and read the record there – from our first meeting up to our engagement and beyond. Those matter-of-fact entries (I was chary of exposing my heart for anyone to see) hold a world of significance yet, while memory is still fresh – and I read avidly, eagerly – pausing now and then to relive the more sacred moments – our first kiss – the stealthy whispered good-nights in the black darkness of the hall – the time we sat in the big chair, with your hair let down about us – the night we first watched the embers die away – the incomparably happy, holy feeling of our engagement day, and my faltering, heartfelt prayer in the Sem's oft-profaned parlors. These things and many more drift back to me, honey, dreaming thus of you and the story of our love. All of them combined have stirred up anew in me the deep insatiate craving that oft-times grips my soul – for you – the cool, clinging caress of your lips, the soft stroke of your hand on my sand-paper jaw, the exquisite hollow in your throat that God made for me to kiss, the little tendrils of hair at the nape of your neck, you, yourself, gracious, charming, sweet and pure – oh, Lady, precious, how I love you and want you! The mere thought of you carries me out of myself! Sweetheart mine, you're such a dear. x x x

After a lengthy, loving revery like this it's hard to come back to the simple chronicle of everyday facts – Woodbury from Elysium – corned beef and cabbage after nectar and ambrosia! Perhaps it's just as well, for the last few days, while very busy, have been uneventful.

Would it grieve you unutterably, Lady mine, if I could not attend Commencement proper? Mr. Batten has said that in all probability I may have a two months' leave of absence to go back to camp. In that event, I could not possibly demand more vacation in early June. I'd like very much to be present when you annex the diploma, Summa

Cum, dearest, but I think that two months' camp overbalances that brief pleasure. First and foremost, I can make considerable money, and second, above all pleasurable appeals, comes the continued development of my swimming.

I have ever with me the innate, utter longing for the glorious day when you are mine and I am forever and always your own

Ken x x x

P. S. Tomorrow evening I attend the battle for the N. W. Ayer & Son bowling title. Our Dept. (Copy) meets the Composing team from Printing Dept. for the championship in the finals, each having won its league. Excitement is intense and elaborate; costly prizes are at stake.

Friday, May 20, 1927
Philadelphia to Lewisburg

The envelope has no outer decoration, but its contents are important, and the yellowed and torn edges indicate frequent handling. First, the fragile hand-printed copy of the telegram Ken sent Caryl earlier in the day; then three fanciful pasted-up pages of cutout illustrations with Ken's captions portraying the arc of his career at Ayer; and the accompanying letter, written at work after hours.

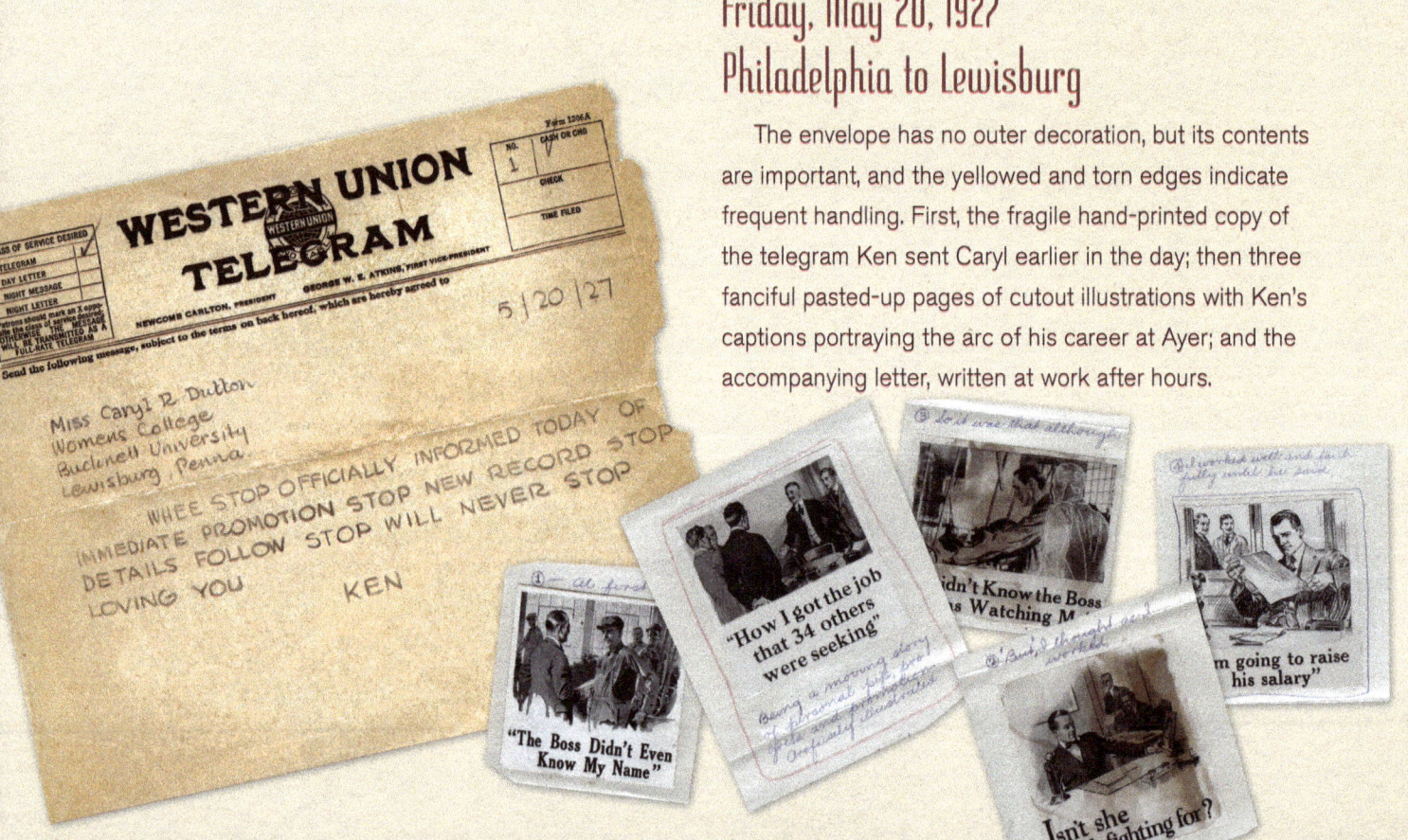

Honey-girl,

This incoherent jumble [the paste-up], tossed together for your amusement, is indicative of my exuberance at the good news I received today! I was called into Mr. Batten's office and told abruptly but courteously to get my accounts in shape to transfer to other men – by Monday. I am to go at once into one of the nicer offices with one of the finest writers in the Dept. – entirely without a preliminary course in the "small mammal house"! (The latter term is derived from the sign over the monkey house at the zoo, and denotes the large office where four of the younger writers are always in training.) Incidentally, my term in Production Bureau (8 months) has been shorter than any man who's ever gone thru here!

I am to start at once to take over the International Correspondence Schools account (a very large account – from which I selected my clippings above), in order to free one of the oldest writers for work on the new Ford account. It will be a big assignment, but I'm going to do my darndest for you, dearest mine, and for our Someday!

I haven't time to enthuse any more, for I'm due to meet Mother for our visit to the Academy and "Iolanthe." Suffice it that I love you whole-souledly, unutterably, as I never loved you before!!

Ken x x x x

Sunday morning, May 29, 1927, from Caryl in Lewisburg to her family in Buffalo

"Last from college" is penciled at the top, in Mabel Dutton's handwriting.

Dear Folks,

Can you realize that one week from today, your youngest worry will be adorning herself in cap & gown for Baccalaureate Sunday? Just now I'm worried about exams, for three difficult ones stare me in the face. After the last exam, I'm going to start washing, ironing, mending & cleaning my whole wardrobe, preparatory to Ken's coming!

It was awfully nice to get so many missives from home this week. The two letters, card & laundry were surely appreciated. The cakes are delicious, too, & I am enjoying them to the full! And thank you so much for the generous check. I surely do appreciate it. I wish I had asked you to get some felt strips in Buffalo for making hats. They have some here, but no white or tan. I have no hat to wear home but a big tan one, which is not good for driving. I'll have to let it go till I come home. I asked Bill, man-of-all-work, about crating the chiffonier. He said he'd charge a dollar. That seems a lot. Maybe R. could do it for me.

Now, about your arrival, Mamie [Caryl's pet name for her mother], could you get here early enuf to go to Symposium with me? Several of the girls are taking their mothers this year, & oh, I'd love to have you go. That could be my commencement gift to you.

This morning at the Methodist church I heard Dr. Babcock. He preached to war veterans and Scouts on "The old men dream dreams, & the young see visions." I got more out of this sermon than from any 10 of Dr. West's sermons at the Baptist church.

Loads of love,
C.

Wednesday afternoon, June 1, 1927
Lewisburg to Woodbury

Honey-mine,

I feel like a bird released from its cage – tho I'm a bit weary from trying the bars! My worst exam is over, and only one more left. Besides that, I am a lady of leisure! At last I am "fired" from the dining room – forever! Mrs. Sale called me in last night and said as soon as I could transfer my job, I could be free. It couldn't be done till after lunch, but now I am head-waitress no longer; my first free meal tonight!

Lovingly,
Your Lady

Friday evening, June 17, 1927
Buffalo to Woodbury

The next two letters from Caryl reveal that Ken made it to her graduation ceremonies, and then to Buffalo for a visit, but that he did not go back to work at Camp Kanuka, where he'd hoped to earn extra money that summer. His promotion may have changed that plan. Although Ken continued writing faithfully, only two of his letters survive from the rest of 1927.

My dearest,

I did so enjoy having you for those commencement days, and then for an all-too-brief visit here. Oh, honey-mine, these next few days are going to be hard for us both, after the joy of recent days, but writing will help some, and I hope to do that often. Did you say goodby to Attie, dear? if you didn't, you ought to drop her a card.

We've had an awfully sad thing happen since you left. Yesterday noon Uncle Stickle left the office for lunch and drove off into the country, telling no one where he was going. About five o'clock, under the influence of liquor, he was driving at full speed & ran into a girl on horseback, killing both instantly. Swerving aside, he raced madly on till he was caught ten miles farther.

Oh, the whole thing is like a nightmare that seems madly impossible. No one knew that

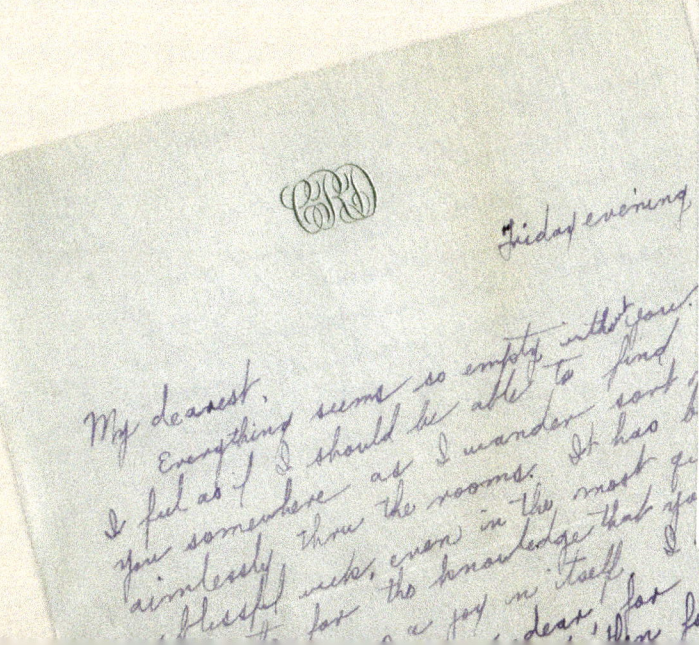

Uncle Stickle drank, & then the fact that he went on without stopping makes the situation far worse. He is in prison now, where he must remain till September when the Grand Jury meets, but even then I fear there is no hope for him but a long imprisonment. He was crazed, of course, or he never would have done such a thing, but oh, it is terrible. We all feel stunned by it.

With all the love in my heart for you,
Your own Lady

Sunday evening, June 19, 1927
Buffalo to Woodbury

My own Ken dear,

After dinner I slept awhile, then went with the family to see the Stickles. Sam [the Stickles' son] had been sent for, and all three are staying at the daughter's home. What an awful burden these poor folks are bearing these days. If only he had been killed, it would have been so much better for all.

Those who are working on the case are trying to secure a month's mental examination, hoping the decision may be insanity, for then the commitment will be to hospital rather than Auburn prison. According to every evidence, he arranged all his belongings beforehand, intending that day to drive his car and himself to destruction. No one who wasn't insane would ever plan that sort of thing. It is far worse for his family than for him, of course, and remember them all, dear, in prayer.

I've been trying to see the funny side of this trunk business, even trying to conquer the pang caused when I thot of my 4-year memory book. But yesterday I opened the drawer where I had put your letters and realized that all your painted ones, which I treasure so much, are also in the trunk. Fearing I might never see the old trunk again, I just sat down and cried. I s'pose it was awfully silly, but I've loved those letters so and never before left them out of my suitcase. I surely hope I can trace it soon, for it worries me a lot, and the loss of it would be far greater in treasures than in money value.

Oh, how I wish I could come tuck you in and clasp my arms tight about your neck while I kiss you good night. More than ever I long for you with all the love of which I am capable.

Your own Lady

Monday evening, June 20, 1927, Buffalo to Woodbury

Ken dear,

I am happily relieved, for my trunk has at last come! I nearly went thru the roof when I saw the express truck outside this morning. My room has been topsy-turvy all day but now is nicely cleaned up. I have moved the desk; put the cretonne covers, which I had at school, on my bureau, desk, and chiffonier; and changed most of the pictures to allow addition of the big blue skin [diploma] and palette. I still have to sort out the accumulation of four years and bring my memory book up to date.

Days, weeks, and months must just fly by, dear heart, till I can be for always your very own

Lady

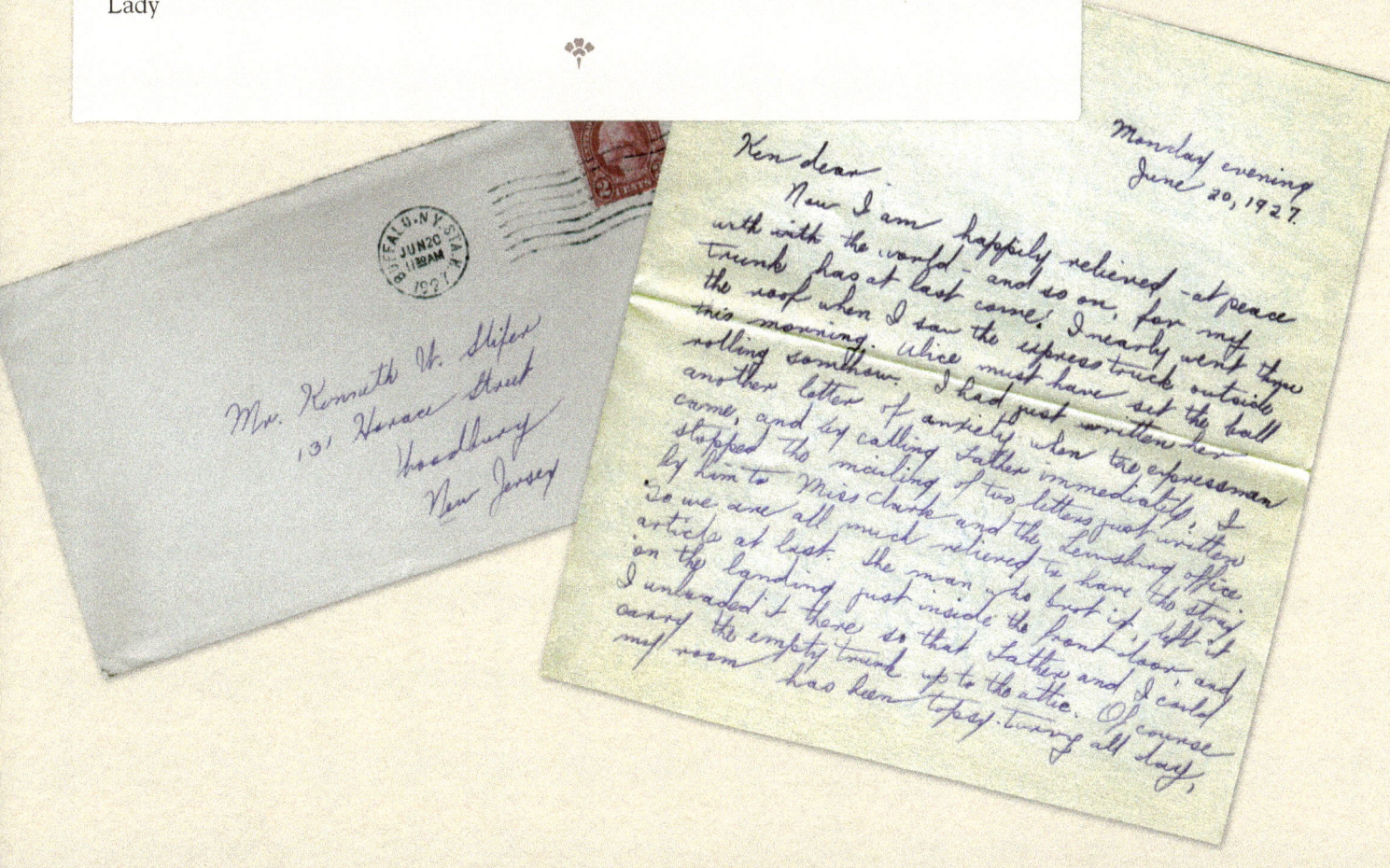

Tuesday evening, June 21, 1927
Buffalo to Woodbury

Rolland, attending seminary in Rochester, holds a student pastorate in Conesus, New York, about forty miles from Buffalo. His engagement to Mary Schilling will be broken off sometime soon, but no letter exists to explain exactly when it happens.

Ken dear,

Rolland was here for a few hours and left after dinner to go back to Conesus. He gave us glowing accounts of the wedding and reception of one of his parishioners, tho poor Mary arrived too late for the service. The path of that couple seems strewn with thorns, and I feel so sorry for them. On the way back, Rolland had one tire trouble after another, and after four in the morning had to drive seventy miles on a flat tire. Fate doesn't seem very kind to them, even when they are together.

I wish I could have peeked in at the party Bobby gave. I know she looked lovely. It gives me a pang, tho, to think of the total absence of entertaining allowed to me in my own home during high school. Perhaps that is why I long so for our home, where we can have our own friends come, and entertain them.

Your own loving Lady

Wednesday evening, June 22, 1927
Buffalo to Woodbury

Dear Sweetheart,

Is it really a whole week since we were returning from a glorious day by the lake, completed by a ride in the moonlight, and several precious, never-to-be-forgotten hours here?

Today Mother, Aunt J., and I went shopping, then went to the Great Lakes Theatre to see the picture, "A Million Bid," a strong love drama, well played and tense. The vaudeville was not in the same class – stupid.

I have been getting more gifts – a perfectly lovely pink nightie, very lacy and feminine, from Glens Falls folks; another lovely luncheon set from Mr. & Mrs. Jackson; and from Helen two Century editions of Scott: "Ivanhoe" and "The Talisman," bound in beautiful soft dark blue leather, to start our library. Folks surely have been generous to me.

Well, dear, it's easier to drag myself from this letter than it was from your arms a week ago, but I'd ever so much rather face the harder task. Goodnight, sweetheart. *

From your own Lady

P. S. The letter to Attie was just the thing, and quite delighted her. So dear and characteristic of you.

Saturday morning, June 25, 1927, Buffalo to Woodbury

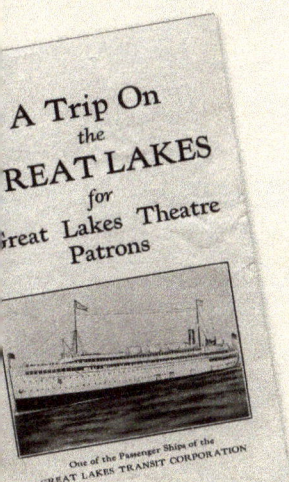

Dearest-mine,

I was most undignified in my expressions of delight when I learned of Bobby's great achievement. [Caryl likely refers to a list or a newspaper clipping from Ken of honors Bobby won when she graduated, at 15, from Woodbury High School.] My, but that is something she will be proud of all her life.

This is a hastily written letter, for I am going on a picnic today with the Parkside church. They asked me to bring cookies and olives, so I made some chocolate raisin cookies this morning. Want a bite?

Your own Lady

Monday evening, June 27, 1927, Buffalo to Woodbury

My darling,

Now your senior partner has advanced in age a bit [Caryl turned 22 the previous day], but you'll soon catch up. I doubt if I was asleep yet when the 26th began, but after daylight, I was awakened by a telephone call from Rolland, congratulating me and chatting over long distance! At breakfast, Father and Mother and Attie gave me a box of correspondence cards, a pastry brush for my hope chest, and a lovely blue silk umbrella. I also received a traveling correspondence case in rose leather, with a writing pad, envelopes, stamp folder, address book, letter opener, and calendar.

This morning Mother, Attie, and I had our eyes examined. The doctor told me I would have to wear glasses now only for close work, or other times when I feel I need them. After the examination, I donned dark glasses and stumbled downtown with Mother to do some shopping.

Rolland is coming home Tuesday or Wednesday, and expects to take me back with him to Conesus, to stay over Sunday. That will be fun. Mother will remail your letters to me if I go.

Lovingly,
Your Lady

Tuesday evening, June 28, 1927, Buffalo to Woodbury

My dearest Ken,

How could I write anything but a love letter to one so dear as you, who writes such beautiful letters! And yet it is true that this last period of companionship with you has more completely opened the floodgates of my love than years of writing could have effected. It seems impossibly perfect to love so completely, and be loved by one so dear as you, my Ken. After four years of growing into each other's lives as we have done, with the first love growing steadily deeper and finer till nothing seems complete without the other, we should surely be happy as two lovers could be, in that Someday of ours.

Of my visit to the dentist this morning: I am very much alive and thankful the old tooth is gone. Until late afternoon I lay down most of the time, not so much because of my tooth as because of a bad headache and a dilated pupil of one eye, which blurred my vision. Mother gave me a pill later in the afternoon, and I was able to go to a Delavan Avenue Church picnic in the park.

Gifts are still descending upon me. Today I received a lovely set of lingerie in pale pink. Folks have surely been well-advised, as well as generous in their gifts.

I love your letters so, darling, and read them over and over till the sweetness of them fills my own heart for you. I am unutterably happy to be

Your own Lady

Wednesday, June 29, 1927
from Conesus, New York, to Woodbury

My own darling Ken,

Before I finish this, I shall probably be interrupted to accompany Rolland to his lecture on Palestine. We drove from Buffalo here to Conesus in "Elijah's Chariot" – the old yellow Ford truck! We had plenty of room for luggage in the back, and with a few cushions the seat was quite passable. Rolland gave a splendid talk later in the day that kept children and grownups interested and quiet, under heat more excessive than any we have had so far. I've been thinking of you in the heat of the city. I hope it hasn't been too withering.

We'll be away most of August – probably near Lake George most of the time.

I must say goodnight – wishing, however, you were here, that I might throw my arms about you, hold you close, and pull your head down to its pillow, dearest.

Your very own Lady

Thursday evening, June 30, 1927
from Conesus to Woodbury

Honey-mine,

This morning I tried to write some thank you letters, but with three little children talking to me all the time and the heat dulling my thots, it took me all morning to write just two. I have two more I simply must write, and besides them, I had hoped to pen a few lines to Bobby, Aunt Clara, and others.

Rolland worked on an old mimeograph most of the day, cleaning it for use. In the afternoon, we dressed for swimming. Piling three other girls in the back of the truck, we drove seven miles to a good place to swim. The lake bottom was rocky, but we had a lot of fun in spite of it. A flat tire on the way back had to be pumped up four times, but we finally got home. After supper, Rolland hauled out the little old reed organ that belongs with the truck, and a whole bunch of children gathered round it to amuse him while he worked on tires!

No one else has seriously thot of retiring yet. They are all downstairs listening to the radio. But I like to be alone with you, so I ran away to talk to you a bit, before jumping into bed. Your going this time has left an aching emptiness. I realize now how perfectly glorious it is to be

Your Lady

Saturday afternoon, July 2, 1927, Conesus to Woodbury

My dearest,

Tho I've loved and wanted you before, I never longed for the "cage called marriage." But now I begin to long for the day when life will grow full and glorious because you are constantly by my side. I can close my eyes and feel your lips on mine, see the glow in your eyes, and feel your arms tighten about me. But then, I open my eyes, and my dream lover has vanished, leaving only a lingering sweetness within my heart. Come back, lover-mine, won't you?

Your typing is fine, but I know the process must be laborious. [Throughout his life, though he produced the equivalent of volumes of creative writing on typewriters, Ken signed his typed personal letters "The Two-Fingered Typist."] I wish I could teach you, but I fear that will have to wait for our Someday.

I didn't have a chance before coming away to get my new glasses, but I don't need them much here. I fear, tho, that health and strength won't cure my eyes, for astigmatism is a matter of eye deformity, and not weakness. It is slight, however, and I'm glad of that.

I've had quite a time getting to bed here, for no one thinks of retiring before midnight, when the radio men say their last words. But every night, I've said farewell and retired earlier than the rest.

Yesterday afternoon we all went swimming. A ride back in wet bathing suits thoroly cooled me. In the evening, the church had a supper & social, tho the social was more an entertainment than anything else. People of all ages entertained the rest. I sang 2 solos! Rolland sang, & I played for him. Some really clever things were given. This is a community of splendid folks. No wonder Rolland likes it here.

Your own Lady

Tuesday evening, July 5, 1927
Buffalo to Woodbury

Darling,

I surely was glad to hear of the commendation on your first copy. Of course you can make a living for us by writing. With your natural ability and love of your work, you can accomplish miracles.

Tomorrow your lady starts school again! I enrolled in Hurst's Business School. It seems crazy for a college graduate to go to business college, doesn't it? But it will keep me busy for a month. From 9–1:00, I study shorthand and typewriting; from 2–4, I take bookkeeping. In all of these subjects I move ahead as fast as I can cover the necessary material. That's the kind of school I like.

Mother and I took Rolland to the station this morning with plenty of luggage, bound for work at Camp Kanuka. Thanks to his clerical discount, his ticket was less than six dollars!

It was lovely of your Mother to enter so generously into your plan for my visit. I wish I could say now, "Of course I'll come." We'll hope for it, anyway, won't we, dearest, for I just can't live till next summer without seeing you again. I love you so.

Always your Lady

Wednesday evening, July 6, 1927
Buffalo to Woodbury

Honey-mine,

It's too bad the lovely weekend for you at the shore had such painful after-effects. Being an advertising man yourself, you should have been fore-warned as to the havoc of the burning sun and have provided yourself with any of the famous feminine preventatives such as Pond's or Honey & Almond!

My first school day is over, and I find a solid morning of typing and intensive shorthand, and 2 hours of steady bookkeeping and figuring, tire my arm quite a bit. They planned to give me 2 hours each of typing and shorthand but soon found that my typing doesn't need much training, so I'm going to take 3 hours of shorthand. The bookkeeping was lots of fun – only 4 of us starting in together, and I can go as fast as I like. See how well I'm trying to prepare myself to be budget-keeper for you, partner-mine!

I'm learning to drive a gear-shift car. Father let me drive from the park home tonight. I was so scared. The car seems so big and powerful, and the traffic is awful! But I'm going to swallow my fears, and really learn before I get too old! I must be able to drive you around next time you come.

Yours,
Caryl

Thursday evening, July 7, 1927
Buffalo to Woodbury

My own Ken,

Mr. Reiman called today to say he had witnessed the safe arrival of his son and Rolland at Camp Kanuka. Does it make you feel blue, honey-mine, to be in advertising rather than camp-tutoring?

I deposited our check today, with additional pennies. The fund now amounts to $21.25.

I've been in school only 2 days, but was promoted today! Elementary folks are on the 4th floor of the building, advanced on the 3rd. I'm now on the 3rd in a class that keeps me hopping every minute.

When a fresh note comes each day from you, I can't read one as many times as I used to, but not for worlds would I give up these daily notes, for which I live in hopes all day.

Lovingly,
Your own Lady

Over the next several weeks, Caryl becomes alarmingly ill and suffers terribly during the rest of July, with a slow recovery throughout August and into September. Excerpts from three letters to Ken, Buffalo to Woodbury, begin to recount the nature and course of her illness.

July 11, 1927

Monday evening:

Your "senior partner" is an aged and infirm old lady today – at least, you would think so if you could see her crawling about the house. My throat has been quite sore all week. But with no other evidences of cold, I think there must be poison in my system, for yesterday when I got up, my knees were stiff. They gradually loosened up during the day, but this morning they were so stiff and painful I had to clumsily fall out of bed and support myself from one thing to another to walk!

Imagine that – from a 22-year-old! It was almost funny, the way I had to maneuver to rise or sit down all day. I think it must be caused by this throat, for it is so sore today that I could eat no lunch. Nature plays funny tricks. I don't like to feel 95 in my knees and 18 everywhere else!

July 15, 1927

Friday evening:

Because I love you so, I have tried hard to get stronger, but when I feel so unaccountably wretched as these last few days, I get awfully discouraged. Sometimes all my efforts to "eat, sleep, & be merry" seem so vain, but I'll keep trying, and perhaps someday the results will show favorably.

Saturday morning:

The only other news I have, you won't like. I couldn't get out of bed this morning, too stiff and sore and weak from head to foot. The doctor came a little while ago. He thinks I'm OK from my head down, but above that — (You've heard of such people, haven't you?). He thinks there's trouble in my mouth or nose – sending poison all thru my system and causing this arthritis. I have to have my teeth x-rayed, and my nose & throat examined by a specialist. If poison has been circulating, it's the best thing possible to reveal the source, for then I shall be rid of this tired feeling that has become discouraging.

July 17, 1927

Sunday evening:

I'm still in bed, with no improvement, tho I'm trying to be optimistic. This is a case of "making hay while the sun shines," for my left arm was almost useless today, & I thot I better write you before the right one went back on me! (I hope it won't.)

We had a lovely chicken dinner today, and Father carried me out to the table and back. My legs are totally useless, so the folks have to treat me like an infant. Honestly, I have to laugh sometimes, in spite of the pain, at the queer maneuvers we have to go thru to move me even a few inches. Just think how wicked and nasty I must have been inside to cause all this trouble! But won't you come and sit beside me, hold my hand, and tell me you love me? I want you so, my darling.

Monday evening, July 18, 1927, Buffalo to Woodbury

Dearest-mine,

Today the pain has almost gone from my knees, and I can move them around. It is so funny what only two days in bed can do to you, for I feel as if I'd been down for weeks. What a glorious relief it is to be back on one's feet again! I can walk a little and this afternoon managed to get dressed & come out on the porch. When I walked out this morning, Father said, "Well, age before beauty, huh?" Mother thinks it would be advisable for Father and me to go to Clifton Springs for a week of thoro examinations and treatment, but Father hesitates on the expense end. We may do it, tho.

There's a possibility of my getting a school office position after all and perhaps in a school within walking distance of home. The hours would be fine – only 9 to 3:30 on school days, at $5 a day, but no pay, of course, when there's no school. That's not so good. Besides, I'd like a chance to use either shorthand or bookkeeping, or both, for which I'm paying good money.

Again tonight, dear, when sleepy-time comes, I s'pose you'll seek your swinging bed in the silv'ry path of the moon. Watch! Honey-mine! The old man in the moon is an enchanter, and his spells work witchery with lonely lovers. My downy cot is also in his silv'ry, bewitching path, and tonight, able to resist no longer, I shall yield to your loving call, steal out into that shining way, then down again to where you're softly resting. A light kiss to rouse you, and my eyes shall shine their loving message into yours, and arms and lips reveal the love that longs to overflow. Before the old man hides his magic path I must leave you, yet you will know that I'll come back to be with you always, for I am

Your own Lady

Tuesday evening, July 19, 1927, Buffalo to Woodbury

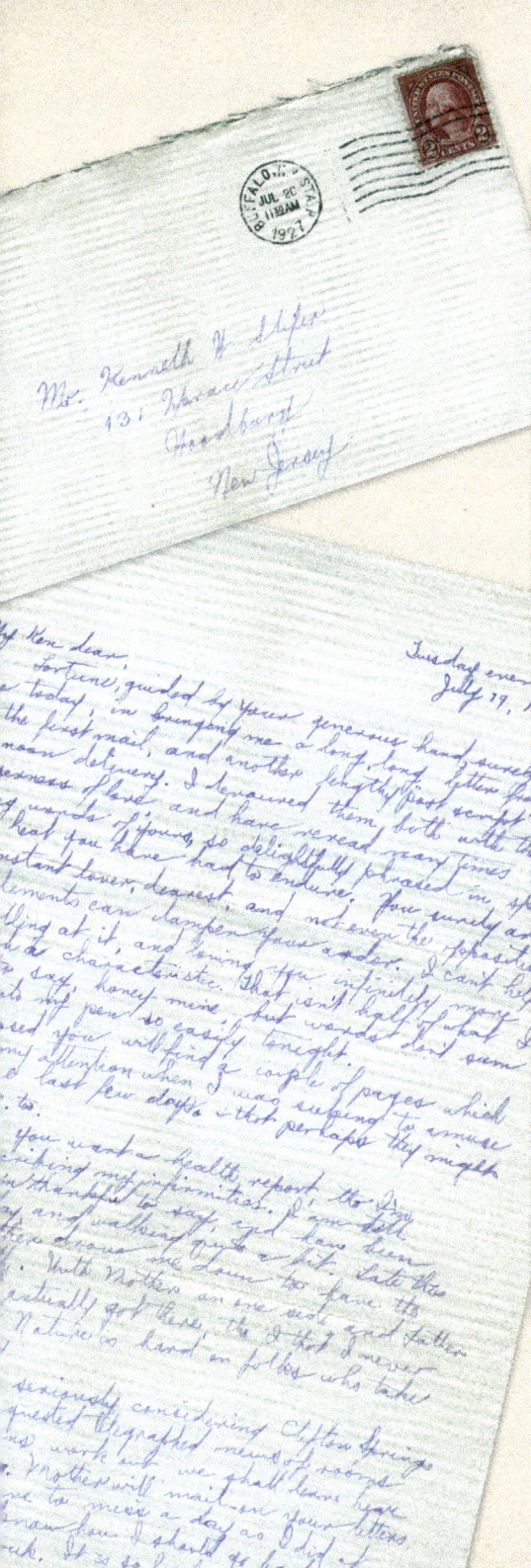

My Ken dear,

I s'pose you want a health report. I'm improving and walking quite a bit. This morning Father drove me to have the x-ray of my teeth. With Mother on one side and Father on the other, I actually got there!

I'm so glad your advertisement was favorably received. I feel confident that all of them will be.

I know how your church must feel about Mr. Hatts' demands, but aside from the train fare, I don't think his requests are unusual. Father always had his moving expenses paid, and few ministers have less than a month's vacation. I s'pose that's why the two weeks you have seems so short to me.

You express a wonder at the freedom with which I often write you now – so different from my formal, reserved style of the past. It has taken me four years to learn to know you well and feel absolutely free with you. I must have built a formidable wall about myself and my feelings. It's about down now, and I can write easily the thots of love I've often thot, but never could express. I've always loved you, sweetheart, since first I met you, but marriage two years ago would have been largely an adventure, and not so completely the attainment of the beautiful dream I now have of full companionship with you. Oh, how sweet it is, dearest Ken, to be

Your own Lady

Wednesday evening, July 20, 1927, Buffalo to Woodbury

Dear Sweetheart,

I knew the news of my illness would worry you, but I knew you would want to know if I was sick, and then I wanted the sympathy of the one who cares most.

Tomorrow morning we go to the nose and throat specialist. The x-ray showed two suspicious teeth – one the dentist has been working on ever since Xmas. Isn't that the luck! I s'pose it'll have to come out, and mebbe the other one. Now if the specialist rids me of this catarrh, mebbe I'll be an operatic star yet!

This morning Mother and I cleaned a lot of my dresses in gasoline. She did most of the work, but I stood by and took it all in – the smell, I mean! [For decades, because many fabrics were not washable, the dangerous – and sometimes deadly – practice of home dry-cleaning in gasoline or kerosene was common.] After lunch and a nap, Mother and I dressed and walked about five blocks to a committee meeting. I was pretty tired before it was over, but I am no worse for the effort. It's just awful to feel so "wobbly."

Should I get the school office position, I'd begin September 6, the day after Labor Day, eliminating the possibility of driving up with your folks. I don't like that, but even if the remuneration isn't the maximum I could earn, I would appreciate Saturdays and part of every afternoon for sewing & such – and then I could come to you at Xmas, for I'd have 2 weeks' vacation.

It seems such a short time ago that I felt two years of working after college would be no hardship at all, in waiting till you were better fixed financially, but now that same period of time seems so much harder and longer as I realize the happiness it will mean to completely belong to you as

Your own Lady

Friday morning, July 22, 1927
Buffalo to Woodbury

Dearest,

Forgive this brief note, honey-mine, but I can't write any more. Some of this nasty poison must have gotten into my stomach, for I was awfully sick yesterday & last night. But I am better now.

I felt sick yesterday morning so made myself go to the specialist. His verdict: my tonsils are bad & must come out. I'm waiting for the doctor's decision as to when I'll be strong enuf. It must be soon, for I fear I'll never rid myself of the soreness till the pus is out. It transfers itself all over, & now my shoulders & arms move only with difficulty. I hope I can have my tonsils out tomorrow – if not, I'll wait until Monday. Mother will write you, if I don't. Pray for me harder than ever, won't you, dearest. I love you so.

Your own Lady

Saturday evening, July 23, 1927, "At Home!"
Buffalo to Woodbury

My Darling,

I'm still at home, not at the hospital where I feared I'd be. The Dr. came last night & said he wanted me first to have this suspicious-looking tooth out. At 3 p.m. I went thru the ordeal – it was a bad one – enuf to cause all my trouble, the dentist said. It had fastened to my jaw & came out like a piece of granite! Now there will be one less for us to worry over & you to pay for, when I get my false teeth! On closer examination of the x-ray, no other teeth look bad, so this is the last of such troubles for a few months.

Yesterday was Father's birthday, & we had a wonderful broiled chicken dinner to celebrate. Unfortunately, my internal volcano of recent eruption refused to look upon it favorably!

Good luck in the tennis! [Caryl returns Ken's information sheet on Ayer's Annual House Tennis Tournament, minus the coupon, which Ken had cut off to sign up. Matches will be held: "on the clay courts of the Merion Cricket Club at Haverford. The firm will pay the necessary 'greens fees.' Entrance fee for men's singles will be 75¢. This will cover the cost of tennis balls and other incidentals. Each player will have to provide a white shirt, white trousers, and rubber-soled heelless shoes. Get down your racquet and oil it up. With Tilden's recent defeats in Europe, our Davis Cup chances are rapidly decreasing, and it is the obvious patriotic duty of every loyal citizen to get his tennis game in shape."]

Always your Lady

Sunday, July 24, 1927, Woodbury to Buffalo

This letter, on Ken's engraved KWS stationery, opens not with a salutation but with the lush verse from a poem by Nobel Prize-winner Rudyard Kipling that inspired the coloration of the painting on the envelope.

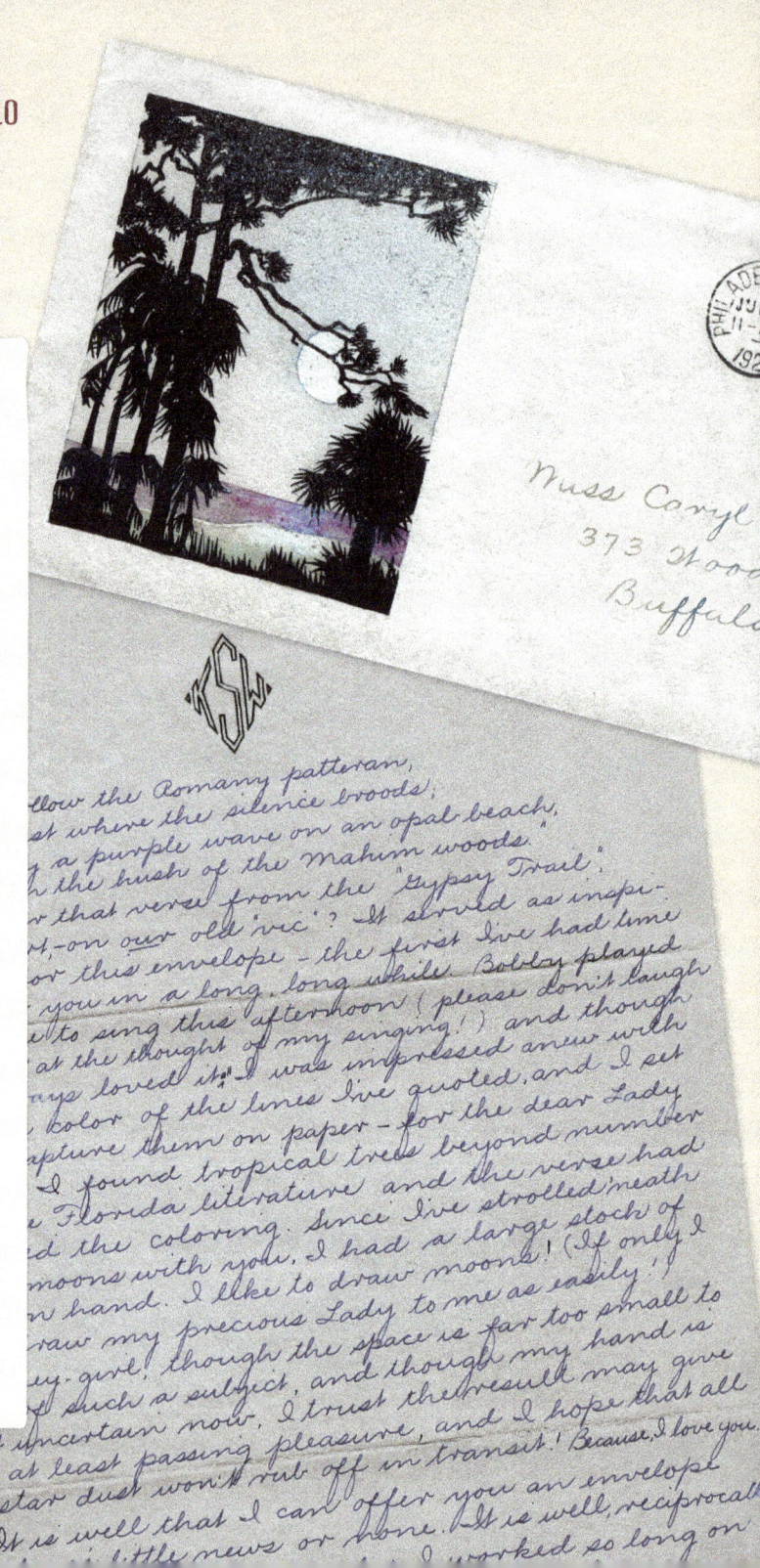

> "Follow the Romany patteran,
> East where the silence broods;
> By a purple wave on an opal beach,
> In the hush of the Mahim woods."

Remember that verse from "The Gipsy Trail," on our old Vic? It served as inspiration for this envelope. Bobby played it for me to sing this afternoon, and I was impressed anew with the rich color of the lines I've quoted and set out to capture them on paper – for the dear Lady I love. [Over many years, beginning in her childhood, Bobby accompanied sing-along gatherings with family and friends.] The verse provided the coloring, and I like to draw moons! (If only I could draw my precious Lady to me so easily!) I hope that all the stardust won't rub off in transit!

Bobby drove off to play for Woodbury Country Club in the West Jersey Tennis Tournament at Haddonfield. She has a complete new sports outfit – tricky white hat, white flannel dress, blue and white blazer, and white shoes and stockings. In that, she looks far more than her scant sixteen years and is a bit awesome, even to her brother.

The latter part of the afternoon and evening I spent at a pleasant task – sorting and arranging your letters. Now, dear, everything you've ever sent me is neatly arranged in chronological order in one drawer of my desk – from a note postmarked Wilkes-Barre, Nov. 30, 1923, clear down to the last letter I have, dated from Buffalo July 21, 1927.

I re-read a lot during the process, and I moved in a happy revery for several hours – and often I smiled – at the earlier notes in particular. As late as Jan. 2, 1925, you addressed me as "Dear Ken," and signed yourself primly, "Yours sincerely." Doesn't that sound funny now, darling mine? It's very hard to realize that endearments did not always leap easily to your lips and mine.

The most precious group comprises your messages of love since we said good-by in Buffalo last month. I cherish them all, but I was surprised to see on re-reading how casual and matter-of-fact some of our letters have been! A stranger would guess our engagement came this June, for it seems to mark a new era entirely. Then does love most truly manifest itself, and your heart infuses its very self into your words. More keenly than ever has this review made me realize the wondrous beauty of our new companionship – the glory that is to be.

Your own adoring
Ken

Sunday, July 24, 1927, Buffalo to Woodbury

Sweetheart mine,

Give three cheers, Ken-boy! Let a glad smile erase the worry on your dear face. Physically I'm not in a jig-dancing state, for I'm flat on my back with a temperature of 102; but mentally, I'm in joyous condition. First, because this tooth – or cavity – which has raged unmercifully all night & day, is lessening, and I am in a saner state of mind; second, because my joyride to the room of horrible instruments is indefinitely postponed. Dr. says a jaw like this shows sufficient reason for all the trouble I've had, so he'll wait till I'm well again to examine the tonsils.

I forgot yesterday to mention your advertisement. It is fine, honey, & splendidly done, according to my novice judgment.

You think your Lady looks "sweet" even in illness, but you'd be sadly disillusioned by this terrible specimen. My hair is perfectly straight, pulled back tightly, and my face is swollen and drawn to one side, so as to produce a queer distorted effect. But I'm going to get well and be a regular "picture of health." In another day or so I can eat solid foods again, & then I'll gain fast.

At times, Father has helped me out to the davenport & played the Vic for me. Music is maddening when you're longing so for your lover.

Your Lady

Saturday evening, July 30, 1927
Buffalo to Woodbury

Ken, my darling,

I am waiting for the dentist to come reopen the gum for draining of poison. All the germs came together for a heated convention & don't like to be disturbed! I dread the process, yet it's for my own good. But how glorious it is to be able to hold a pen and think coherently for a brief chat with your own dear self. How I have longed to talk with you, but dearest, I've been awfully, awfully sick – sicker than I ever was before or hope to be again. It has been a nightmare, but I thank God I am better again.

Folks have been wonderful – calling by phone & in person, and Father and Mother have weakened themselves in tireless, uncomplaining waiting on me. I don't know how I shall ever repay them.

Always your own Caryl

Sunday evening, July 31, 1927
Buffalo to Woodbury

My own dearest Ken,

I have progressed a lot in the last twenty-four hours, and tho the pain only ceases under medicine and I am generally weak, yet I am happy to be able to get out of bed and amble about a bit.

I must get well fast now, for we'd like to leave for Glens Falls a week from tomorrow. Father's Sunday to preach there has been changed to the twenty-first. We'll spend the interim at the Camp and at a resort on the lake, unless unexpected invitations come, or an opportunity to rent a cottage cheaply.

Ken, dear, I wonder if we sent Attie down, if you could meet her in Philly and take her across on the ferry to the Camden train. She wants to see her Mother in Salem and would get into Philly at 8:21 A.M. either this Saturday or next Monday morning.

Tomorrow I'm going to have a feast. I plan to read over all your letters of the past week! I'm eager to really see what's in them. Then I'll have to write a 10-page letter to answer all at once. My head doesn't work much yet, and I can't write much, but my heart is longing to overflow to you. I want you so.

How beautiful the painting is, dearest, that you did for me. I've kept it where the calm beauty of the scene could lend its restfulness to my feverish spirit. What a dear, ideal lover you are, sweetheart, and How lucky I am to be in boundless love.

Your own
Lady

Monday evening, August 1, 1927, Buffalo to Woodbury

Ken dear,

Today brot me another cheery note to help send me farther on my way to health. How much you've written me this past week; the pile of letters I read thru this morning said so much I want to acknowledge. It isn't possible to make you feel how much I appreciate your faithfulness.

My family looks a bit relieved now. I let them have undisturbed sleep last night, for even under drugs & so-called pain-killers, I didn't sleep more than 2 or 3 hours at a time before the folks had to get up to get new doses. They wouldn't let me move alone after I fainted one night trying to wait on myself.

This afternoon an answer to the doorbell revealed 3 Delavan girls with a huge yellow "sunshine box" full of gifts. Each package is beautiful in yellow paper; a cute clock drawn on the outside tells the opening time. I never got such a thing, and it is so exciting. The one I opened tonight was a cute basket filled with paper violets, with cunning chocolate dolls hidden in the flowers. I don't want to be sick, nor am I glad I was, but I shall never forget the goodness of everyone. I humbly thank God for such people.

Will I be with you, in your arms, a month from today? Oh, my Ken, how I long to be there!

Your Caryl

Tuesday evening, August 2, 1927
Buffalo to Woodbury

My Dearest,

Three packages from the sunshine box proved most interesting today. At 9:05, I found a shopping-list notebook with pencil – something I'll make use of. At 12:25, I unearthed a box of Kellogg's "Pep," a bowl to eat it in, a box of dromedary dates, and one of Nabiscos. That was fun! And at 8 this evening, I unwrapped an embroidered tea towel, which I'll delightedly add to my hope chest.

Tonight, cousins of Father's – Mr. George Dutton & Wife, of Philly – took us for a ride in their car. Good to be out again – even if I do travel about like a woman of 80! My tooth is taking its own sweet time subsiding, but I got thru today without "dope" to deaden the pain. I hope my facial muscles relax soon. I can't laugh (even smiling is stiff work and one-sided), and I talk as if I had a hickory nut in my cheek.

We have an invitation to a wedding in Glens Falls, so we must carry evening clothes. Shucks! as the flapper would say. We'll need a trailer for all our stuff!

My greatest incentive for growing health is to be fit and ready Someday to be

Your Lady

Thursday evening, August 4, 1927
Buffalo to Woodbury

Dearest,

Father took me to the dentist's today to have the tooth socket opened again. The gum and teeth stay so sore, but there was no pus this time, so that's probably the last treatment.

This evening we drove over to Aunty Stickle's and tried to comfort her a bit, but she certainly is in awful trouble, and we can't help much.

Please forgive me, honey, if this is a shorter note than ever. I hope that our guiding star will bring our paths together before many more weeks have passed. Always, my love is all yours.

Caryl x

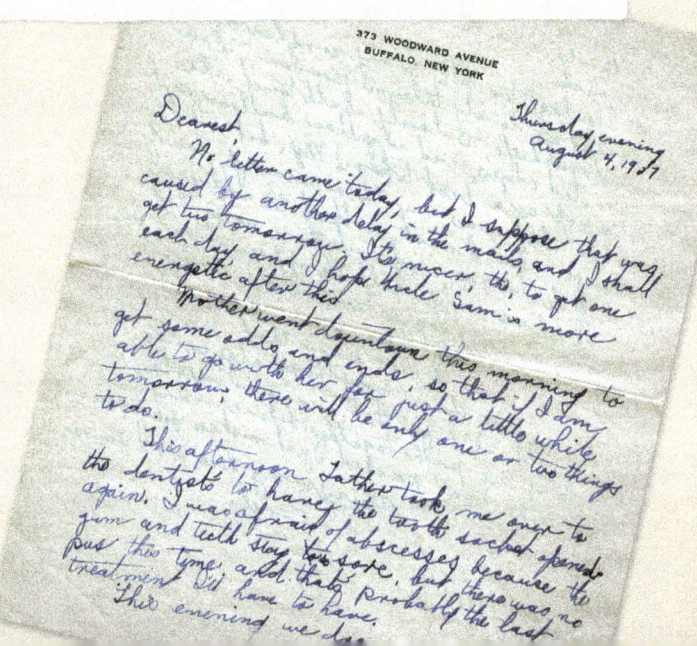

Saturday evening, August 6, 1927, Buffalo to Woodbury

My Dearest,

You just mustn't sympathize so hard as to get sick yourself! I can't fully recover in a few days from a 3-week siege. It may be months before I can completely rid myself of the poison, but each day gives me more strength, and life at the Camp will do me good.

Yesterday I changed places with Mother at the nursing business. Late morning we went downtown and shopped, but Mother was tired to begin with. At 4 P.M. I left her to do an errand & came back to find her in the oppressive heat of a department store, faint with a heart spell, struggling hard to breathe. She got worse & couldn't walk to where she might get air. With the help of several floorwalkers, we carried her to the door, & I never was so relieved as when Father got her to the car. Now, tho she moves slowly, she gets around the house. If only she'd take better care of herself, she wouldn't have these spells.

You deserve a medal for checking on Attie's train time. We all appreciate it. It's a problem to get her anywhere, and you filled that need. I told Attie I'll be horribly jealous Monday, when she's trotting around Philly with my Ken!

Uncle Sam won't let me write more without making you wait another day.

Your own Lady

Tuesday evening, August 9, 1927
Northville, New York, to Woodbury

Dearest Ken,

I never thot tonight's letter would be postmarked from any place but the old Camp, but we had so many delays today that when we landed in this place after dark and found we had 40 miles yet to Glens Falls, we decided to stop in a tourist home for the night.

This morning we struck a bad detour outside Seneca Falls and were glad we stopped last night before reaching it. At Auburn we mailed your letter, then hunted up the prison. Tho too late for visiting hours, they admitted us. The rules say no women visitors allowed, but they gave all of us a pass to the waiting room to which they brot Uncle Stickle. The experience made me feel awful, but he was glad to see us.

We had lunch in Syracuse and then had a blowout to fix. Everything combined to delay us, but we are enjoying the trip nevertheless. It's a lovely bright moon tonight.

Your Lady

Thursday morning, August 11, 1927
Lake George, New York, to Woodbury

My dearest Ken,

This old camp was a mess to fix up, but Mr. Pike came up last night to do odd jobs and add some humor to the occasion. Later on, Dr. and Mrs. Sweet drove down from Lake George to visit. We are going to their cottage for dinner tomorrow. This is surely the most glorious spot, tho. As I sit here writing, I can look up to the left to the very tip of French Mountain, and to the right, way over miles and miles of beautiful lowlands, to the Green Mountains of Vermont.

Remember, dearest, the depth and greatness of love for you within the heartbeats of your own

Lady

Friday morning, August 12, 1927, Special Delivery (12¢)
Lake George to Woodbury

My own Sweetheart,

A real love-feast is the only expression I could use in the joy of four of your dear letters. There's a world of love in each beautifully worded sentence, and it makes me yearn so for you. A surrounding such as this on the side of the mountain amid the pines, the glories of sunrise and the reflections of sunset, the enchantment of moon and stars, is almost maddening to the loneliness of love, without the sharing companionship of you whom I love so dearly.

We are lazy most of the time up here, tho Father insists on doing too much work. He and Mother are now lying down – Father stretched out on the grass and pine needles, Mother on a couch swing. Mother has donned her bathing suit to get a good sun bath, and the costume looks sort of incongruous!

Thank you for the long letter from Rolland. We all enjoyed it. He is certainly trying to return to your good graces, isn't he? He hasn't written much of anything home.

You ask about Mr. Stickle, and I will tell you all when I come – confidentially, for your ears alone, for in respect to the family, we have agreed to say or do nothing to make things harder for any of them.

I'm so glad you and Attie met all right. Thank you for the timetable.

Your advertisements are just splendid, honey-mine, and I'm just awfully proud of you.

I too wish you could fly from the hot bricks and run to me and the beauty of Nature. It can't be long before life assumes a new meaning, in the full companionship of my dear Ken and his own loving

Lady

Tuesday morning, August 16, 1927
Lake George to Woodbury

My own darling Ken,

Yesterday I was bemoaning that mail is so irregular here. Father said, "That's one of the prices to pay for a quiet, restful camping experience. I don't attempt to keep in touch constantly with the outside world."

"Yes," I replied, "that's true enuf, but what difference does it make to you, when you have the most important thing right next to you!" That silenced him, for he had to admit I was right. And it is hard, honey-mine, to watch them so happy in each other's companionship, and to be longing so for yours.

You may wonder at my saying I find little time to write up here, but we get up late, and there are so few conveniences. It takes twice as much time to wash, dress, and eat. And there's a lot to be done to fix up the Camp, for it's been uninhabited for so long. We can't do much after dark, for our light is not very brilliant. I can't be alone long enuf to think as I want to when I write you. Not much solitude can be obtained in a one-room establishment, especially when it's too cold to stay outside long!

We had a delightful visit with the Blacks. We planned a steak & corn roast in the open fireplace before the Camp. The Sweets came along, so we invited them to join our picnic. Such a jolly crowd! The stories Mr. Black has without ceasing, and those contributed by the rest of the crowd, kept us laughing. We set a long table on the grass in front of the Camp and all sat around feasting on delicious foods.

A load of congratulations on your tennis success. I surely hope you win the finals. But I honestly will be glad when the season's over. A little exercise is the best thing for you, but not the overdose you've given yourself. I'm afraid the real cause of the illness you suffered recently was that you played so hard in the excessive heat. Please won't you be a little more moderate, for your Lady's sake?

Last night Nature was gloriously beautiful. The air had been clear thru the day, and by moonlight it was a magic scene. The moon is waning, but still almost round and of a deep yellow. The sky was strewn with lovely dark clouds, each with a silver lining, and the stars shone as I have never seen them before, in competition with a full moon.

Somehow the thot of the glider on your porch has fascinated me, and ever since your first mention of it, I have dreamed longingly of coming to you, of finding you lying there in the light of the moon, and of stooping to place my arms about you and lay my lips on yours.

Adoringly, your own
Lady

Wednesday morning, August 17, 1927
Glens Falls, New York, to Woodbury

My dearest Ken,

Yesterday after supper we drove around to the Baptist parsonage in Glens Falls, and Mrs. McDowell, the pastor's wife, took us all thru the house – the first time, for me, since we moved out twelve years ago. My, what childhood memories all the nooks and crannies of that place recalled!

Many of the guests at the wedding were young folks I had known years ago, and they're all so grown up and different, and several are now married and have little children. Of course, I know I must look queer to them too, but it sort of gives one a strange feeling to see the changes a few years have brot.

The wedding was lovely, and Father assisted in the ceremony. I'm glad we could be there, but I'm going to steal you away in desperation pretty soon. Next year being leap year would be a very good time!

Always,
Your Lady

Thursday morning, August 18, 1927
Glens Falls to Woodbury

My Dearest,

At the wedding the other night I renewed acquaintance with one of my old friends who is engaged to an advertising man in New York City. She knows the terminology of the business and is fascinated by it all. We had an interesting time exchanging news. She expects to wed around Xmas time.

Yes, honey, it does make one feel envious to see these younger folks just starting in college. I wish I might have had some of the preparation, socially especially, that most folks now have when they enter college. It would have been so infinitely helpful to me. I think I'm just beginning to grow up now and arrive at the point I should have been three years ago.

You don't need to blush, dearest, when I term you an "ideal lover." I'm of too practical a mind to really think you perfect. But you're the dearest thing in the world to

Your loving Lady

Sunday evening, August 21, 1927, Glens Falls to Woodbury

Dearest mine,

Darkness is fast closing about me, but I love to sit here as long as possible, in a big rocker with a stone for a footstool, facing the distant valley. In such a place as this, all days are Sundays – Lord's days – when every turn inspires with awe and worship.

This morning we arrived in time for part of Sunday School before church. I surely enjoyed every minute of it. Father preached a good sermon, but as is often the fate of ministers' families, I had heard it twice before, and I felt as if I wanted to prompt him now and then!

After church we were invited to the home of friends, and there enjoyed a lovely dinner with splendid folks. I get homesick for Father to have a church again. I've felt lost ever since going to Buffalo, as far as a church life is concerned. What a host of friends Father and Mother have here. It is a lovely tribute to their ministry here. We can't ever be pastor & wife, but I hope we will be able to work together a lot in whatever church we have. This isn't a Sunday mood, either – just a wish I always have.

My, how your desire for a trip to the Bucknell stadium arouses an echo of longing in my own heart. I did so love those football games, mainly because it meant a whole afternoon with you – in a crowd, yet wondrously alone and happy. Doesn't it seem like a long time since we had parlour dates at the Sem?

Thursday, a childhood friend is coming after me in her roadster, and we're going joyriding where fancy may take us, and end where hunger bids. I hope the weather is fair, for it will be quite a lark.

You may not know how to think of the Camp, so . . . Constructed for a refuge years ago, when Father needed to get away for rest & study, it's a plain, oblong room, with a door and 2 immense windows front & a door on the side. At first there was a place for 6 bunks, which fold down when not needed, but we have 3 of them up now at the back, a "double-decker" on the right. (I sleep "upstairs.") The right end of the room is bedroom and boudoir, while the left is dining room and kitchen. We also have a stove, 2 tables, and a curtained-off portion for clothes. We added a wash stand to the furniture because living in suitcases was cramping, and we increased the lighting facilities from 1 to 3 lamps. Father & Rolland put a roof on the side porch 2 years ago, building the floor with stones. Father leveled the floor with soil & pine needles, surrounding it with rustic railings, so we have an outdoor breakfast room hard to excel.

Now, honey, are you eager for me to come this Saturday? I can't give you any definite train time, but the New York-Philly trains run every hour. I would take the Pennsy, arriving at Broad Street Station. The folks think I'm "deserting the ship," but such an old spooning couple as they are ought to know how much I long to be with you. I shall come to you with love such as I never felt before. There's been a great change since you came to me in June, and I am gloriously happy for that – since I'm yours.

Caryl

Sunday afternoon, August 21, 1927, Woodbury to R.F.D. #1, c/o Chapmans, Lake George

This is the last of Ken's 1927 letters that survives. Enclosures include notes from Ken's mother and sister, urging Caryl to visit them.

From Edna:

I want you very much to come to visit us, if you are able, and be here to go along to Lewisburg when I take Roberta up, on Sept. 7. Do hope you are feeling better. Tell your Mother I shall do my best to have you in bed in good time, for I warned Kenneth he wouldn't dare keep you up late. Hoping to see you the last of the week, I am

Sincerely yours,
Edna S. Slifer

From Bobby:

Caryl, if you don't come, this family will simply mourn, bathed in wet and salty tears, with which we would be likely to ruin the furniture. So at least, dear coz, be kind enough to spare the furniture though you care not for us. If you're feeling just so-so, I promise to be your personal maid. Please don't say you're not coming!

Ardently Awaiting, Eagerly Expectant,
Bobby

Sweetheart mine,

I'm sending you a ship to bring you to me. An airplane would have been more practical and a bit faster, but planes are so prosaic and colorless to this blasé world. Besides, there is a lot of water between us, so my caravel is at least appropriate. May good winds speed it Southward!

Mother and Bobby want you, truly, and they each wrote a personal note. Now, honey, will you believe that we all are eager to have you? Mother thinks, too, that your advice and example will be invaluable to Bobby. After all, she is a bit too harum-scarum at times, and a little guidance from the Lady she so admires will help a lot.

News is conspicuously absent in this letter, because the thought of your coming has blotted out all else. What utter joy when you come to your own loving

Ken x

Thursday morning, August 25, 1927, Lake George to Woodbury

My Dearest,

Such a lovely note from you – with that lovely painting. It is so pretty, and the cabin lights enticed me to go within and sail whither its builder and guide should swing the prow. Any other frail craft would have sunk. But tho the storm left its mark, the good caravel still floats strong and sure, and soon will bear me homeward bound to you.

It's delightful to be wanted not only by you, but by your folks, and all my doubts vanished when their letters came. My folks have been discouraging me about coming, saying I wasn't in good shape for visiting, but Dr. Sweet said it wouldn't hurt me a bit. I'm getting better by leaps and sleeping myself out, so I won't need so much when I come! I hope your dear Mother won't send me to bed too early, for I must have some hours with you alone, just to live on in the days beyond my visit.

We had such a good time yesterday. We arrived at Sweets' cottage and under the trees by a beautiful rushing brook cooked our dinner. Goodness, I never saw folks eat so much! Jupiter Pluvius frowned upon us while we ate, but nothing daunted, we shook off the drops with good Baptist fun, & after dessert gathered up our stuff and ran back to our cars to drive home & dry off.

A world of love from your eagerly anticipating and loving
Lady

Caryl, Edna, and Bobby drive from Woodbury to Lewsiburg in the Slifers' flivver. Bobby is to begin her freshman year at Bucknell; Caryl will visit old friends on campus for two days and have the last look at her alma mater for some time before taking a train back to Buffalo.

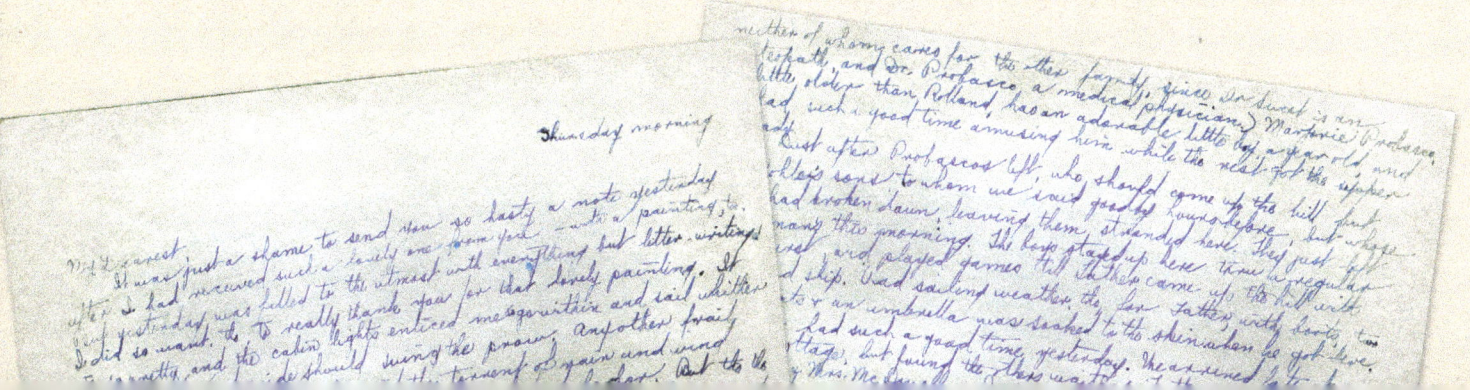

Thursday, September 8, 1927
Lewisburg to Woodbury

My Dearest,

Such busy, busy days! Of course, I'm trying to pile a whole lot into a few hours – seeing all the folks I've known. But honey-mine, I've had lots of chances to dwell happily on recent days with you – tho they did fly so fast. Thank you for all the endless things you did for me during my visit. Only your heart can ever know my full appreciation, for ears could never hear the half of it. It was so hard to leave you, dearest, and my heart ached so all day as the miles increased between us. Instead of the hasty farewell, I wanted so to hold you in a clasp that would never let you go.

Tomorrow noon I take the various lines homeward. I've had long enuf to look over the new class, greet old friends, have a good visit with Aunt Jennie, & now I can't get home too soon. Twelve tomorrow will see my last look on the old campus for awhile.

For ever,
Your Lady

Friday morning, September 9, 1927
Lewisburg to Woodbury

My Darling,

Memories, honey – just memories of you everywhere! Someone just went by whistling your own old tune, and I started immediately thinking it was you. We arrived just in time for dinner Wed. night, but I was too excited to eat, for many familiar faces greeted me. After dinner I found Bobby quite settled in her new room. I went over to the reception in the gym. Lots of fun, but I was weary when I finally tumbled into bed.

Thursday I ate breakfast while talking to your mother and your Aunt Grace Drum, made several calls, & served lunch for old times' sake. Wandered around all afternoon, then ate dinner at the Sem.

Had breakfast at the Sem this morning. Called Aunt Clara and had a good talk. Thru Aunt Jennie, secured Harry Pierson's flivver to drive me to Milton. I can get my lunch here first. Miss Clark refused any payment for meals, which favor I surely appreciate, since it is seldom done. Check from home awaited me, so your $5 is returning via your good Mother. Thank you, dear.

All yours,
Caryl

Saturday evening, September 17, 1927, Buffalo to Woodbury

Written to arrive on Monday the 19th, Ken's 22nd birthday.

Dearest Ken,

Many happy returns of the celebration of that day that gave you to the world, sweetheart, and began a life now so infinitely dear to me. A day of memories for us too, dearest – two years of companionship 'neath a pledge of each to the other for life. A birthday kiss from so far away is rather unsatisfactory, nevertheless two lips I press firmly here * for you to touch with your own.

The penny fund has amounted to $24.25. Is that increasing fast enuf for you?

Rolland came home late, night before last, and stayed till this evening. He has just left in his new car! A friend from seminary nearly wrecked the other one, so Rolland turned over to him the remains and bought a Buick – same year – for $150. It looks fine, with new tires and many up-to-date devices, and runs like a charm. He bought it with his Kanuka money and surely is proud of it.

Buffalo friends may not be as anxious as I to see Bucknell on Homecoming Day, so don't count on seeing me, but of course if I can come, I surely will. I wrote Aunt Jennie a crazy letter, in which I mentioned that if lovelorn lovers like ourselves ever met at Lewisburg, we would appreciate using her davenport!

Delavan has a pastor now, Frederick Bone. He was given a "call" the Sunday after we left, and I think he will do splendid work there. Parkside Baptist – or Central Park as I should call it – has as yet no pastor.

I've been thinking of your completion of a year at Ayer's. I only hope the succeeding years may be as happy for you in your work there.

Always in love with you,
Your own Lady

Sunday evening, September 18, 1927, Buffalo to Woodbury

My own Dearest,

Perhaps it is foolish to write each other every day. Our families think so. But how more lovely each day seems with a message from your own dear self! Sundays are less bright for that very reason. I've been thinking how glorious Sundays will be in our Someday. A whole day with you – in thankful worship, at church and home, and in happy companionship. How much more precious Sundays will be then!

This morning we drove to a small village where there is a Baptist church. It was an ideal day for a drive – not sunny, but a balmy, fresh atmosphere. We drove leisurely home, stopping a few times to pick wild flowers and buy bunches of asters. [Asters were Caryl's mother's favorite flowers. In 1901, Mabel and Herbert married under a bell of asters, on her father's farm near Auburn, N.J. In the 1970s, I spoke with an elderly gentleman in our nearby Woodstown Baptist church; he remembered attending their wedding as a small child with his parents and recalled the fun of throwing rice at the newlyweds departing in a horse-drawn buggy.]

Curfew must have tolled long ago. Goodnight, sweetheart, and may the boundless love of your Lady for you help you to do and dare great things.

All lovingly,
Your Lady

Wednesday morning, September 21, 1927, Buffalo to Woodbury

Throughout college and for years thereafter, Caryl's hair – when unfastened – was waist-length, thick, and dark. As a small child, my own bob with bangs was the same color. Once I went to a big Halloween party in a little-Dutch-girl outfit made by my mother. She fastened her own hair, which not long before had been braided and then shorn, into mine, so that two fat pigtails hung down from my starched white cap. I won the prize for the best costume – a huge thrill.

Sweetheart mine,

Yesterday was as full as I thot it would be, only worse, for I didn't get a bit of work done. I started in the morning to wash my hair and never had such a job with it. Buffalo water is so hard it makes soap sticky instead of forming a lather. I worked till I was all tired out, and it was still a sticky mass I'll have to rinse more this morning. I finally had to dry it and put in combs so I'd have a little wave for the luncheon to which Mother & I went, but I've about decided that if I keep my lengthy locks, I'll go where I can sit in a chair and let someone else do the work.

The picture album came this morning. I love all these pictures of your childhood and baby days. I love best the one you gave me, where you are holding the kitten in your lap, and your chubby little face is all puckered up into the funniest, dearest smile. I long to pick you up & hug you to pieces, but then I realize it is really you, and that dear little fellow has grown to splendid manhood, and mine to love forever!

It will seem funny to address you at #19 instead of #131, but I suppose I'll soon get used to it. [In October 1927, the Slifers' house number, 131 Horace Street, became 19 North Horace Street. The letters do not explain this change, but Horace Street had been divided between South and North by Delaware Street, which ended a few miles beyond Woodbury, at the Delaware River.]

With an overflowing love for the dearest of all men – my own beloved Ken.

His Lady

Saturday evening, October 1, 1927, Buffalo to Woodbury

Here ten days of letters are missing, though the lovers have been writing constantly. Caryl has been ill again.

Sweetheart mine,

Yesterday I had to crawl out of bed and advance from position of patient to that of nurse, for Mother had two bad teeth extracted. I wasn't very useful or energetic, but was thankful to be able to wait on myself and also help Mother. She got along nicely tho.

Anyone who saw me yesterday would have thot I had joined in the big fight last week, for I had a swelling in two places on my face and was fearing painful boils, but the beautifying effects of iodine applications seem to have humbled their pride, & I think they will slowly retreat!

Honey-mine, would you mind either having some copies made of that Crystal Beach picture of me, or send me the negative, please. I want four or five to send away. [Ken kept a framed enlargement of this, his favorite snapshot of Caryl, on the wall for the rest of his life.]

Caryl

Sunday afternoon, October 2, 1927, Buffalo to Woodbury

My own Ken,

This morning, Father had to preach at the Indian reservation. Mother and I walked over to Parkside 'neath the warmth of a July sun! The supply at Parkside was our first candidate, Rev. Reynolds of Rochester, a man well advanced in years, but of ability that has built his church there from 200 to 800 members in fourteen years. He gave us a splendid sermon, and the church was better filled than it has been for years. We will surely try our best to get this man.

I just got my dress & shoes off, ready to lie down, when the front doorbell rang – an unusual occurrence for Sunday. Frantically, I dashed back to my room & dressed, getting my dress on backwards in the haste, and got to the door at last. There were Aunty Stickle & George, come to take us out to see the mansion his millionaire brother is erecting. I sat down and did the duties of hostess to them for an hour, watching my nap recede & disappear!

Now I'm getting so much better, even tho not well yet (plagued poison won't be placated). Father can't yet see how I was so wretched one night & on my feet the next. I thot it was some new medicine I got, but now I know. It was you – your love – all the power of loving prayers centered on my sickness, pulling me up to my feet, out of pain to strength, out of discomfort to rest.

I am growing to feel that each day is giving us a greater appreciation of what our Someday will be, and when it is at hand, I feel sure we shall both have gained by waiting, and have acquired an appreciation for & love of each other such as few have attained ere they stand at the altar, dearest. x

Your Lady

Monday evening, October 3, 1927, Buffalo to Woodbury

My Sweetheart,

I'm just specially bubbling over with gratitude tonight, honey-mine, not only for you and your love, but to you for this trezyure box I found today! Oh, my! I was like a child with an advance Xmas present! This funny pirate on the outside looks as if she needed a more complete dressmaker! We had a good laugh over the box. Then I lifted the lid expectantly, and – whee! What a find! All kinds of funny, bumpy packages in lots of colors, with the nicest hand-painted cards attached to each!

Counting the first day today, I opened a square, red package and found the man with a lot of faces! Among the other bundles, I found a tiny one unlabeled, then another & supposed they were chocolate drops – but lo, one was and the other a cream drop! Oh, aren't they the cutest little dolls. As if it could be too childish or foolish! Why, what are we all but grown up children, anyway? I'm having a perfect lark with these funny things & can't tell you how delighted I am. Oh, honey, thank you loads & loads.

So glad for continued good news from the office. You surely are making good splendidly, dearest, & I'm so proud of you. You're such a dear, & oh, so precious to

Your Lady x

Undated, but postmarked Friday, October 7, 1927, Buffalo to Woodbury

Ken mine,

Last night's reception at Delavan Avenue Church – as thanx to Father for serving as interim preacher & welcome to Mr. Bone, the new pastor – was a very nice affair. Mr. Bone & his wife seem to be fine folks – the wife especially, who is a delightful little Scotch woman with a lovely accent. The reception consisted of entertainment with speeches, followed by a more informal gathering with refreshments.

There is really no need of my writing Bobby, for I told her that our relationship would be unaltered by her choice of college group! She would have been foolish to do otherwise, but I can't help thinking that if only I had been there, she & her friends too would probably have been Pi Phis.

I'm so lonesome for you, Ken. Each day gets harder without you.

Your Lady

Saturday afternoon, October 8, 1927, Buffalo to Woodbury

My dearest Ken,

"Sanny," my old high school friend, is to be married today in the big Presbyterian church just a few blocks from us. That makes the third of my friends to change her name this week.

Thank you for sending me Bobby's letters. I'm so sorry she had to have such trying experiences with Pi Phi. She will be far happier, not only with her own group, but with the rest of the Alpha Chi personnel, and I am glad for her sake. Do you now understand why it was so difficult for me to find the happiest sort of relations in my own fraternity? You always thot me a bit peculiar because I couldn't, and yet now you see how they have slighted your sister, & it shows how blind the present group is to real worth. Don't think that I feel the least bit irritated toward Bobby, for she's done the wisest and best thing. I wouldn't have advised her otherwise. You think I'm awfully silly, but make allowances for a different temperament & a totally different college experience from yours. I heartily sanction what she has done.

No news as yet about visiting Bucknell. I hope, but do not expect, for I am at the mercy of others, & have no idea whether they will come. However, I shall be gloriously happy if I can see you then.

Lovingly,
Caryl

Sunday morning, October 9, 1927
Buffalo to Woodbury

This envelope is postmarked October 12 – Caryl's busy father absent-mindedly carried the letter in his pocket for three days before mailing it.

My own Ken,

I'm envious of "Sanny's" privilege today, of attending church with her new husband. I wonder what makes me jealous of all brides! Could you guess? The wedding was lovely. The church is large and wasn't more than half full, but there were a good many people even so. The minister read the whole ceremony. I didn't like that nearly as well as Father's method of speaking it, with a bit of change for each occasion.

Thank you for the book suggestions. I'll try to get them from the library. I've been reading "We Must March," a splendid novel built around the life of Marcus Whitman, first American settler in the Oregon Territory. I think you would enjoy it. Honoré Morrow is the author.

Always
Your Lady

Monday evening, October 10, 1927
Buffalo to Woodbury

Sweetheart mine,

I'm sure you must be getting to the place where if someone should mention the term "tonsils," you would lose chips from both shoulders and pitch into the nearest victim. Next Monday, however, is the date set for certain, and nothing but severe sickness will alter it. I couldn't see the doctor till last night, and he declared me not strong enuf yet, and said he wanted another week to build me up.

Thank you for the I.C.S. amusement. You seem to be quite as successful – serious or foolish. Imagine Whoofus an artist!

Phew, but it's cold here! I wish my furry coat weren't quite so conspicuous. I'm freezing in my light coat, but no furs seem to have blossomed out yet, except in the zoo.

So you have a radio! That's just great. I know you'll enjoy it a lot – if you & Len & your Mother can agree on the times it is to be used. You know, they say hundreds of divorces are caused by the radio!

The North Park Church dedication service was most interesting and Dr. Pierce was splendid. He spoke to two congregations and held us spellbound by the stories he told of his experiences, the forcefulness of his personality, and his stirring plea for missions. What an inspiration for the members of his church to live under the messages he must give them each week! This sort of thing I missed a lot when I was away at school.

Word has been received from Mr. Reynolds, of Rochester, that he will accept a call from our church. He is a man who seeks service in hard work when he is willing to leave the splendid church where he is and come to our small one. We surely need such a man.

'Ray Bucknell, for beating Penn State! The team must be profiting by the new coach. Wouldn't you love to be at school now? If fate keeps me here over Homecoming, I'll be disappointed, but not because I'd miss a game. Thinking of that weekend is like seeking an oasis in the desert. Separation is so hard, dear.

All lovingly,
Your Lady

Tuesday evening, October 11, 1927
Buffalo to Woodbury

My Dearest,

Perhaps I may not be able to write sanely tonight, for I'm in an exalted mood. I fared forth with Mother this morning to attend a meeting of the women mission workers and women folk from all Bap. Churches in the city and this Association. Such a gathering of inspiration and thrilling character is held each month. The missionaries gave splendid reports of their work and stressed the needs of each field. After lunch, Miss Long, our newest missionary, gave a résumé of her life and call, and so lovely was her personality, so simple yet beautiful her story, that we sat in reverent silence for several seconds following her last word.

The afternoon speaker was Miss Wallace, assistant to the Stewardship Secretary of the Northern Bap. Conv. Charmingly dressed, and with a most attractive face, she's the kind that fascinates at first acquaintance, and forces admiration. (If I were a man, I certainly would like to offer her a home!) She travels all over the U.S., spending weeks in different cities speaking on Stewardship. She made me want to empty my pockets then & there & give her a check for the rest!

Last night I dreamed we were united again. Somehow, when I awoke, it seemed as tho you really had been with me. The sweetness of having you stayed about me long after the dream had vanished. I wish I could find you more often like that, dear.

Your Caryl

Wednesday evening, October 12, 1927
Buffalo to Woodbury

Dearest Ken,

Mother just handed me the enclosed account of her wedding, for you to read & return, please. It seems strange to read about an event so long ago like this. Notice "tied the nuptial knot"!

We planned to go to Delaware church tonight to hear Miss Wallace speak again, but bad weather kept us at home. Instead, I hemmed & pressed skirts (still going up), and made a hat.

You surely are a "Konstant Ken," so lovingly faithful to me. I must admit you fell in love with a hard-shelled heart, which only your loving persistence pried open into the depths within.

Loving you ever,
Your Lady

Saturday evening, October 15, 1927, Buffalo to Woodbury

The first clipping from Ken describes groundbreaking ceremonies for the 13-story N. W. Ayer & Son headquarters at 210 West Washington Square, Philadelphia, and pictures a model of the building to be completed in 1929. Ken worked there until his retirement in 1966. In the late 1990s, the building was sold and remodeled into luxury condominiums complete with concièrge and limousine service. Some of the units have since brought $8 million.

My very Dearest,

Thank you so much for the enclosures. The new Ayer building surely looks splendid.

The radio must be a real ornament in the house. Where did you set it up?

Phew, I hope the permeating perfume of this house doesn't penetrate this paper! We've been dry-cleaning coats, hats, and dresses in gasoline, & the odor is terrific! You may be glad you're so far away!

Yesterday Mother & I went downtown with Father to look at kitchen stoves, to exchange my stockings, get my hat stretched, and buy some other odds & ends. Why must you always worry about yourself when I buy something new, honey-mine? You always look wonderful! Don't you know a girl must have at least 3 dresses to every suit a man has! My dress is a reddish-brown satin and wouldn't be warm enuf for a cold football game. The hat is light to harmonize. The shoes, patent leather pumps, and stockings I probably shall wear. So don't worry about a new suit. I like the ones you have. You might put away the money, unless it's really needed now, for our Someday! Every dollar will help. I've just added twenty more pennies to our fund!

Your year being now well passed as a business man, you spoke of a possibility of a salary raise. Have the powers that be conferred it yet? They should be interested in bringing our Someday a little nearer, & just think how much more valuable to them a staid married man would be!

Before long, I'll be able to cast my first vote. Father, Mother, & I went around to register last night. They signed me up, but not knowing whether I was illiterate (!), I had to go back this morning to present my college diploma! I took Attie too, and helped her laboriously sign up!

Ever longing for you, dreaming of you, praying for you, loving you, I am, as I'll always be,

Your own Lady

Tuesday evening, November 2, 1927, Buffalo to Philadelphia

Caryl forgoes a salutation, beginning instead by impersonating a newspaper reporter.

Copy from Local Social Gazette

Miss Caryl Dutton, recently suffering from a tonsillectomy, has now sufficiently recovered her former strength and health as to resume her social obligations, and today was present at a luncheon given at the home of Mrs. Hatch. (There! – wouldn't I make a good reporter?)

I did go out today for the first time & walked 6 or 7 blocks to the home where another meeting of our women's society was held. My eating wasn't very successful, but quite creditable, considering, and I enjoyed the occasion. After a business meeting, two of our missionaries gave splendid talks.

I am gaining visibly now, and you might recognize me once more. Yesterday I tipped the scales at 113, and I'm going to watch the increase till I'm even with Mother, who weighs 123. Watch the race!

I enclose a clipping from a Rochester paper that tells of our wonderful new pastor, Mr. Reynolds. It is a long-felt dream come true. With this man at our head, we won't know ourselves within a year. The Rochester folks are reduced to tears because he's leaving, so you know how fine he is.

What a clever idea – to build a Hebrew house! Those boys will never forget that lesson. I'd like to be one of those little boys listening to you each Sunday, and on Monday nights at your YMCA group meetings. Can't you just see me sitting there with adoring eyes, drinking in your every word?

No, I don't agree with you at all this time, when you want to keep me from that sermon on husbands. As if he could present any kind of a man I'd want more than you! Nobody would want a perfect man. That would be too monotonous, and I love you so much I wouldn't want you different. My dear, dear Ken, I'll always want you till you're mine, & after that I'll be supremely happy & be your

Lady x

Friday morning, November 25, 1927
Buffalo to Philadelphia

My precious Ken,

You must have had a jolly Thanksgiving, with the family all reunited. We certainly had some experiences of our own! Dr. Price, Sec'y of the Federation of Churches in Rochester, invited us all for dinner. So yesterday morning, in the midst of a cheerless rain, we started for Rochester at a fine rate for about 45–50 miles. Suddenly something in the engine broke, and it sounded as tho the pieces were being churned about. The rain was just pouring down like everything. Finally, we hailed a car & begged a ride for the three of us, & leaving our car locked by the side of the road, on we went to Rochester.

There we took a trolley to Eastman Theatre, where the Thanksgiving service was being held. We got there in time for the benediction, found the Prices and Bucknell prof. Dr. Wood, and in their two cars finally reached the Price home. They have a beautiful place and do quite a bit of entertaining. We went to a dinner crowned by the presence of a 12–14 pound turkey! Dessert came in the form of ice cream, moulded into a turkey, ear of corn, orange, flowers, pear, banana, etc., all in very natural colors. The round table made a jolly group, and all conversation was for everyone. All too soon we had to leave a big crackling fire to get well on our way home before dark.

And such a ride! After 25 miles, we found our car, backed up to it, and tied it to Rolland's bus. Already dark, still raining hard, & bitter cold, on we went – R & Mother in his car, Father & I behind, trying to keep the road, tho we could hardly see. Besides a heavy fog, which almost hid Rolland's car, the windshield froze, & we could steer guided only by a blur of light thru our glass caked with ice. Once the rope broke, & somehow we shot off the road, over a ditch, and into a field, while R rode off down the road. And so I say, "Some ride!" Fortunately, we arrived home safely, stiff & cold & well aware of nerves, but alive nevertheless, & none the worse for our exciting experience.

Loving you so,
Caryl x ——— x

Saturday afternoon, December 3, 1927, Buffalo to Woodbury

Dearest-mine,

Blessings came in bunches this week, and I have three of your dear letters to answer with my one.

I realize how much bridge is played in social groups; you may teach me sometime, for I want to share everything with you. I should greatly enjoy playing, for I love games, but my folks' objections have made me avoid the game. I dislike to hurt them in anything.

Our Thanksgiving turkey was a bit expensive. We must have churned up our car, for the bill on it is over a hundred dollars! Poor Father is staggered. Nice Xmas gift!

It's a relief to know Rolland has written you about Mary. I wondered how to tell you adequately in the limits of a letter. I'm so sorry for the whole affair and for both of them. Of course you have only one side of the question, but you know Rolland well enuf to surmise the rest. I pray this may not have been, as he thinks, the great love of his life, but that there may yet be waiting a real partner for him. Those two were never fitted for each other, and it is well the truth was recognized before too late.

I must start out now to reach choir rehearsal on time. It's a cold night, but the exhilaration of walking with you would make me forget the cold.

Your own
Lady

Monday morning, December 5, 1927 Buffalo to Woodbury

Dearest Ken,

Somehow I caught cold and am greatly disgusted at the fate that keeps a round of such events coming my way, but such a mood won't cure the old germs, so I'm on the warpath!

We had a splendid service yesterday morning. Church was fuller than I'd ever seen it, and we had a sermon that was fine in tact, in appeal, and in challenge to service. It is so good to have a pastor once more, and especially one so full of plans and pep. We had Mr. Reynolds & his wife here for dinner, and we like them ever so much.

This isn't the least bit of a satisfactory note, but I wanted you to get something tomorrow.

Your own
Lady x

Saturday afternoon, December 10, 1927
Buffalo to Woodbury

Precious Ken mine,

There is a minimum amount required before the best economy can make marriage possible. I don't want to be a burden upon you as a "dependent." I'm just hoping the road to success may enable you to "keep two" before long. No privation would be too great in return for companionship with you.

As to Attie, she is recovering slowly, and feels pretty well, tho her ankle bothers her somewhat. She was never in bed, tho that's no sign she wasn't sick – for if she can crawl around, she will. Her worst troubles are neuritis and high blood pressure. She can't eat meat, & we have an awful time feeding her!

Mid-afternoon yesterday I finished my coat. Some job, but it won't have to be done again for 2 years. The old interlining & padding were threadbare & shredded, but now my coat feels like a downy quilt. Mmm, it's nice! [More linings and years later, photographs show Caryl still wearing this coat.]

Last evening Mother & I played games. I taught her "Sweetheart Rook." Tho it's really "Sweetheart Bridge," she doesn't know that. She liked the game a lot.

I'm delighted you want to share your business interests with me. I'd feel hurt if you didn't. I'm head-over-heels interested in everything that concerns you. It's part of my love for you and one thing I never could understand as lacking in Mary's love.

Loving you dearly,
Your Lady

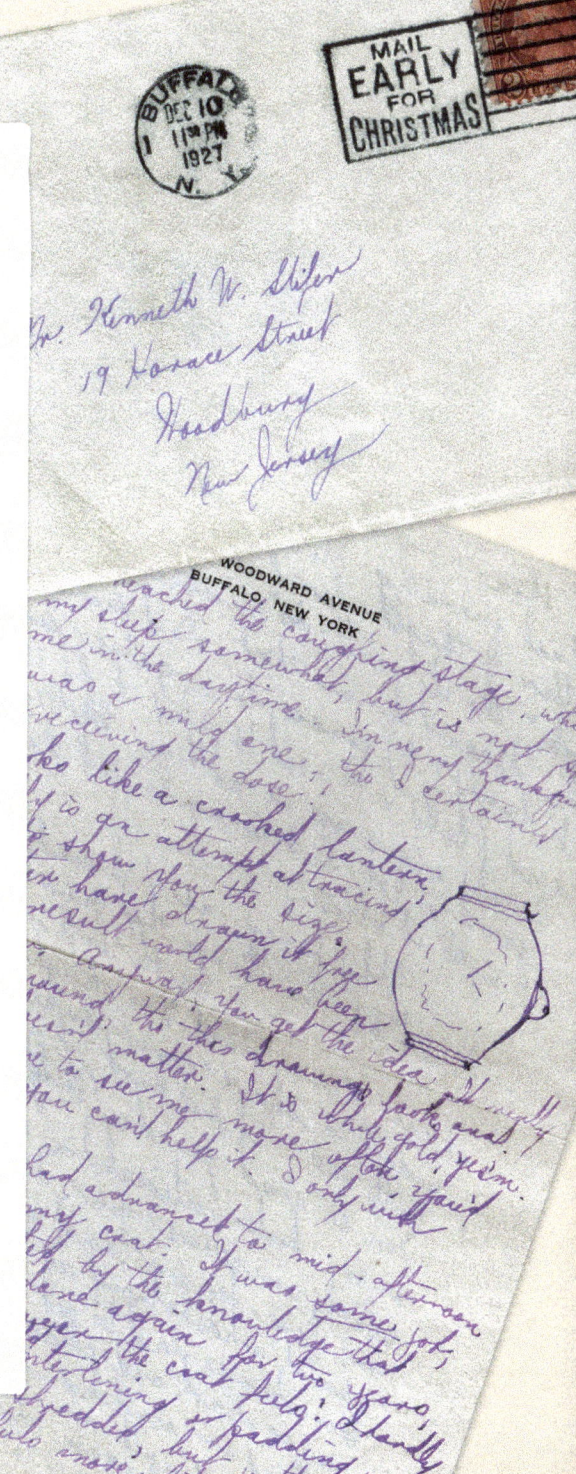

Thursday evening, December 15, 1927, Buffalo to Woodbury

My Dearest,

Old Santa had lots of assistance this evening. We've been wrapping and labeling Attie's gifts to her South Jersey relatives. It would be more fun if we could be there to see them receive the gifts.

Mother had a missionary luncheon today and used the "Bargain Counter" game from your "sunshine box" as a main part of the entertainment. The folks were crazy about it, and I plan to use it next Monday. It was some struggle tho, to print 24 copies on this awful typewriter! [For this game, Caryl uses the typewriter she had at college, but all her letters from home are handwritten.]

In connection with your work: while in New York, Father had a fine visit with Mr. Black, who mentioned he'd be glad to give you frank criticism on your work, if you sent him proofs from time to time. It's fine to have him so interested in you, and I imagine his years of experience could help you a lot.

This letter of Bobby's is certainly smile-producing! She surely has a funny streak in her! Do you know how she knew of R's break with Mary? I suppose that means it is generally known around school.

Speaking of "our" home reminds me of growing eagerness to buy things for my own home! I won't care if it's just one room at first. Really, I think I'd rather have just one. Then we could better appreciate a larger home. But the most important part of our Someday is You; where you are, I want to be too.

For ever,
Your own Lady x

The Holidays
BY ANNE CAMPBELL

THE Holidays are coming now,
   The happy time of year.
The world is gay with holiday,
   And green and crimson cheer.
   (If only you were here!)

So many crowding tasks to do,
   There is no time to sigh.
Time rushes so I scarcely know
   How fast the moments fly.
   (If only you passed by!)

There's laughter in the winter air,
   There's gladness in the hum
Of open fire whose flames aspire
   To warm a heart grown numb.
   (If only you would come!)

Caryl tucks Bobby's letter of December 11 into her December 15 missive and returns it to Ken. Bobby penned four delightful pages of news and nonsense on heavy, folded stationery, clearly a handcrafted gift from Ken. Cut precisely into the upper left corner of page one is a stylized letter S inside an oval, both perfectly edged in gold ink.

December 11, 1927

Dear Buddy,

Realizing all of your responsibilities as head of the house, maître d'hotel, and garde-malade, I scarcely expected a missive from your tender, delicate hand. Incidentally, there is still a Sunday morning delivery at the Sem, and I enjoyed bien receiving une lettre.

Paul Confer is giving us his Sunday afternoon concert à la flute. He's now playing Christmas carols à la jazz. If you note signs of haggard imbecility, the people upstairs are playing a Vic to drown out Paul, and we, between the two, receive the results of the delightful mixture.

As you know, Friday night produced the Prom and Geddes. [Ken's fraternity son, Geddes Simpson, of Lewisburg.] The gym was in the best condition I've seen it. The decorations, orchestra, and favors were all good.

Last night, rather foolishly I suppose, I went to the movies with Van den Bree – Phil Murray escorting Peg. Coming home, I established myself as an ideal escortée in Phil's eyes by ordering a lemon coke and two pretzels (7¢). As a result of last evening, the room now contains another decoration in the form of a red and gold sign. The artistic addition is really remarkable. We tried to get a "No Smoking" sign, but it wouldn't come off. I can remember your sign, demonstrating the virtues of Reading Pretzels!

We've gotten (editorial we) a silly spell of personifying les meubles de notre pièce. My alarm clock is Theophilus; Peg's is Pegasus; my lamp is Stygius; the bridge lamp is Marcus Flavius; the Vic is (Vic) Troilus; the trunk is Elephantus (Elly, for short); the waste basket is Cylindricus (Silly, for short). There are a few more, but I'll spare you the harrowing details. Oh yes – Caryl's old chair is Comfortabilis, Tabby for short. If you visit us again you will be expected to address each piece by its particular nomenclature.

I'm being dragged to the Christmas cantata, given by the Glee Club, by Ken Haines. The only reason I didn't turn him down on the plea of too much work is because he would think I no longer deigned to go out with a non-frat. Between you and Ken Van den Bree & Ken Haines, I should soon be immune, don't you think?

Next Wednesday is due a long research essay for English; Thursday, a report; Friday, term thesis in History; Demie dance in the evening; and Saturday – Home – probably on the 1:50 from here, if my exchequer is reimbursed by that time.

Did you know Dut's engagement was busted? I s'pose you did.

Because page four has no room remaining for a signature, Bobby goes back to the top of page one and writes in a box: "This is the end – Love, Bobby"

Saturday evening, December 17, 1927, Buffalo to Woodbury

Darling mine,

You should see the snow we're having! The effect is magnificent! Trees droop like weeping willows under the snow that burdens every limb. The world is fantastic – not like the fairyland that sleet-frosted twigs transform, but like a white weird world of jagged mounds, mysterious in their mantles of deep snow. I anticipate keenly the walk I shall have to choir rehearsal tonight, plowing thru the drifts 'neath an interlaced blanket between me and the leaden sky. What fun to take such a trip with you joyously sharing the lark!

The house has assumed a festive air. I have been decorating profusely front room, dining room, stairway, and we really look like Xmas. Yesterday, I bought a much-needed bathrobe – one of the things I've helped buy, or pointed out, for myself, so Santa won't have many surprises for me. I concocted a package for #19 (ex-#131), and sent it today, in hopes it might reach you by Sunday.

If I don't say goodby now, the Dutton cafeteria will close for the night, and there's nothing wrong with my appetite these days. I'm getting pep by the pounds, tho the supply is soon exhausted.

Your own
Lady

Monday morning, December 19, 1927, Buffalo to Woodbury

Dearest Ken,

Yesterday there were things I had to do to get ready for the invasion of Bucknellians tonight. The table is ready now in red and green paper, fancy napkins, red "crackers," and favors I had a lot of fun making yesterday. I made a big chocolate cake and a vegetable-gelatin salad, so the heaviest labor is over. The crowd will consist of Vera, Craftie, Helen Bell, Esther O'Blenis, Ann Sprout, Mother & me. We're going to the Hippodrome this afternoon, then scramble back here for eats & fun. Too bad we didn't plan a sleigh ride. It's glorious weather and heaps of snow everywhere.

I liked the latest advertisement a lot, Ken. Language surely flows beautifully from your ready pen.

Ever so lovingly,
Your own Lady

Tuesday morning, December 20, 1927, Buffalo to Woodbury

My Darling,

You deserve a big letter this morning, but I'd much rather give you a big hug and kiss, in congratulation for the raise to $30 a week. How glad I am for you, and for us, dearest. It may mean more than we think and make possible an earlier companionship than we've dared dream. We'd have to do some close figuring. Putting aside our plans for a June 26 "birthday" wedding in 1929, we could consider September 1928 and still use the Sweets' "Bonnie View" cottage on Lake George for a honeymoon. But we have loads of time to think and plan.

Wouldn't it be interesting to inquire about the cost of tiny unfurnished places near Philly? The nearer we could get would save more carfare, and that's a big item. I'm going to have some fun with a tentative figure of $35 a week, or $1820 a year, and see what happens. I'll send the results sometime. I hope I can get work soon so that I can save for our home, too.

We had a lovely time yesterday. Five of us Bucknellians met at the "Hipp" and sat thru an enjoyable performance. The picture, "Figures Don't Lie," was awfully funny. The vaudeville was too, and since we sat in a section of the theatre all by ourselves, we wise-cracked to our hearts' content – but to our sides' despair! It took ages to get home, so we didn't have supper till seven, but everyone was starved and did justice to the meal. We ate by candlelight, as I love to do. After supper we played games, including Bargain Counter and had so much fun we forgot the hour till after eleven. Father played chauffeur thru a glorious snowstorm and returned all safely to their fond parents. It's loads of fun to give a party like that, but I've never done very much of it. Helen Bell said to tell you I'm a good cook!

This afternoon our Women's Society is having a Xmas party at the home of one of our wealthy members, and all the missionary girls & missionary pastors' wives are invited to receive our gifts to them. Vera & I are going to help entertain by giving a little Americanization pantomime.

I like the way we used to do our French – 'member? – a kiss for each page – or was it each paragraph? Anyway, the latter was best, even if I did tease you a lot about it!

Your
Caryl

Tuesday evening, December 20, 1927
Buffalo to Woodbury

My Honey-Boy,

Our Xmas party today was a huge success; 51 women present! Not all the missionaries could come, but the gifts were divided among those present & absent. How happy they were to get such a surprise! The house is beautiful – so spacious you almost get lost – but a real home. Beside a lovely fireplace was a tall lighted Xmas tree, gifts beneath it. Besides Vera's & my offering, there was a solo, the reading of a Xmas story, and a recitation by a lovely woman more like the kind you dream of than those in actual life.

I'm sleepy, honey. I long to slip into your arms, dearest, and drift off to dreamland with you.

Lovingly,
Your own Lady

Friday morning, December 23, 1927
Buffalo to Woodbury

My own Ken,

Yesterday your big box arrived. I can hardly wait to see what's inside. We shall probably have our gifts tomorrow evening, so I'll not have to wait much longer.

Aside from odds and ends yesterday, I slashed up old issues of "The Bucknellian." I got so interested reading over old articles that my progress isn't rapid, but I did manage to finish my senior year memory book. I'm going backward. How funny the oldest ones are going to sound by the time I get to them! Doesn't my freshman year, and your sophomore year, seem ages away?

I see your point about Mr. Black, but his motive isn't to criticize your literary style. His wide experience and broad practical knowledge put him in a position to judge things as a whole. His viewpoint would be that of a good business man studying your method of attack in "selling your goods." He'd appreciate your sending him a sample of your work once in a while. He sent us a lovely box of candy yesterday.

Lovingly,
Your Lady

Saturday afternoon, December 24, 1927
Buffalo to Woodbury

This letter, though written December 24, was enclosed with Caryl's letter of Wednesday, December 28, having been returned to her for postage due. It is included here to maintain chronology.

> Honey-mine,
>
> We have our Xmas dinner at 4 o'clock; we invited Mr. Reynolds and the Bone family. As soon as the crowd disappears tonite, we'll have our gifts, spread out now under the tree! We hadn't had one for years. I had so much fun decorating it. To me, Xmas just has to have a tree, or it isn't Xmas!
>
> No time for stockings or anything else tomorrow morning, for I'm going caroling. The choir meets at the church at 5:30 and ends up at one of the homes for breakfast. We had rehearsal last night, so we'd all be at home tonight. I went home alone in a blinding snow storm. I love a snow storm, don't you, honey?
>
> Oh, I'm so eager to see your new suit, dearest – to see you in it! I know I'll like it. The suit would be an inducement to visit you, but your own precious self is all the inducement I need, always.
>
> Your Lady
>
>

Monday, December 26, 1927, Buffalo to Woodbury

Precious sweetheart,

On Christmas Eve, the turkey dinner was great; Mr. Reynolds is so jolly, and the Bones had their share of fun. They have 2 boys, one 10 and pretty as a girl, the other an attractive high school boy. After dinner, we cleared the table, played ping pong, then everyone joined in a game of anagrams, the funniest & liveliest I ever played! Little Freddy Bone timed us, giving each just a minute to think (time-out for wisecracks). We were having such a gay time we never thot to notice the clock till after 10:30. Our guests gasped at the lateness of the hour & dashed off to their sermons, leaving us to our gifts at last.

Now I am the proud possessor of a link bracelet for my watch. It is so pretty, and matches beautifully. I just had to open that package first. Thank you ever so much. The picture for our home is ever so pretty! It makes me think of Maxfield Parrish's work, and I'm happy to add it to our hope chest! (Now you won't dare call it a "soap chest" anymore!) I've always wanted a silver set. When I saw this beautiful one your mother gave me, I just oh'd & ah'd. And Bobby's flower was à propos. Mother gave me a flower for my other hat, & I've put a snap on my coat collar & one on each of the flowers, so I easily can change to suit the hat! I also got "Quelque Fleurs" toilet water, an ivory penknife for my purse, a recipe card box, a silk bag (such as I never carry!), a buffet cover set, 2 lovely pillow-slips with colored embroidered baskets on them, and a hemstitched set of pillow slips from the Sweets. Old Santa surely was generous.

When my Baby Ben alarm set up a protest at 5 Xmas morning, I had to force myself out of bed. But in ten minutes I was dressed and stole out of a sleeping house into a foggy, bitter cold morning. At church I found heat and other early risers; soon 32 of us set forth in several cars. Too cold to even hold a hymn book, I had to stay in the car at two or three places to thaw out. We had a jolly time tho, and so much humor flew around that by journey's end we had to be assisted out of the car, we were so weak! In spite of the huskiness you would expect in a choir after an experience like that, the church people insisted they'd never heard the choir sing as well for the morning service. But we were all in the spirit of it. The sermon was fine, also the afternoon exercise at which the children took part & were so cute.

Tuesday morning: Rush! Rush! I'm going joyriding with mon frère and must hurry.

A glorious day yesterday. The Johnsons invited us to a noon dinner at their home. Rolland got back from Conesus just in time, bringing with him Gladys Jones from Keuka Park. She's an old friend of ours, and Johnsons' too, so we all had a wonderful time together. [This is the first mention of Gladys Evangeline Jones. On June 19, 1929, Rolland and Gladys were married in the Conesus, N.Y., church he had served as student pastor during his seminary years. Ken was best man; Caryl was matron of honor.]

Oh honey, Rolland's in a mad rush to get off. We'll be back tonite, & I'll have to continue then.

Ever so lovingly,
Your Lady

Wednesday morning, December 28, 1927, Buffalo to Woodbury

Dear, dear Ken,

To resume my discourse, I was speaking of Gladys Jones. You've heard me mention Gladys and her sister Lois. Rolland took Gladys to help him at his church service this Sunday, then brot her back to Buffalo Monday. She stayed with us thru the evening, and then we took her over to Auntie Stickle's to stay with her. She's my idea of an ideal girl – so sweet, charming, and talented.

Yesterday Rolland had to go to Conesus to conduct a funeral. He dislikes to go anywhere alone, so he persuaded me to go with him. We took Father's car, to try out the new engine parts on a long trip, but couldn't drive over 30 an hour, so it took us ages for the journey. I stayed at McVicars' during the funeral, then we started back about 3:30. After we left Conesus, Rolland said, "Want a lesson?" I said, "Sure," so we changed seats, and I drove all the rest of the way home! Rolland made me stop every once in a while, back or drive into driveways, turn around and so forth, so I had a pretty good lesson. Now all I need is practice to familiarize myself with the shifting and emergency processes, and I'll make my application for a license. I was tired last night tho, for the roads are bad ice ruts much of the way, and we drove over an hour after dark.

Such a dear clipping of the father reading to his little boy before a blazing fire. Never in all my life have I found a love for little children such as has been aroused since learning to love you, and dreaming with you of a home of our own Someday.

Your
Lady x - - - - - - - - - - - - x

Thursday morning, December 29, 1927
Buffalo to Woodbury

Dearest-mine,

Yesterday I entered the business world again. Father called, said Miss Vail's assistant was sick, and asked me to come to the office to help. I thot despairingly of the loads I have to do, but left them behind and went. I worked steadily at stencils, mimeograph, typewriter, etc., & was very ready to go home at 5!

Mother & I went to prayer meeting last night alone. Father was under the weather after a tooth extraction, and Rolland had four theses on his hands. We had a good service, but I was so sleepy I could hardly keep my eyes open.

I'm glad we can use frankness toward each other in everything. It makes things much easier. I knew the bracelet was expensive and declared as much when you insisted such a gift was not enough. I thot you would buy thru Ayer, which would have been less. Too bad I'm such a costly possession, honey!

Loving you so dearly,
Your Lady

FINDS A 'PRINCE CHARMING'

Viennese Girl Discovers Fiance is Son of Sears-Roebuck Head

Chicago, Feb. 9. — The story-book romance of a poor but beautiful girl who pledged herself to wed a son of one of America's wealthiest merchants, unaware of his vast fortune, comes true here Sunday with the wedding of Miss Renee Scharf, of Vienna, to William Rosenwald.

The bride is the daughter of Victor Scharf, an inconspicuous Austrian portrait painter. The bridegroom is youngest son of Julius Rosenwald, owner of Sears, Roebuck & Co. Miss Scharf while traveling [in] America. The youth has a $5,000,000 and is also [heir to a] fortune. At the [... will] present a [...] 000,000.

Rev. and Mrs. Elwood Herbert Dutton
request the honor of your presence
at the marriage of their daughter
Caryl Rushton
to
Mr. Kenneth Wilson Slifer
on Tuesday, the fourth of September
One thousand nine hundred twenty-eight
at seven-thirty o'clock
Central Park Baptist Church
Buffalo, New York

At Home
after October first
Woodbury, New Jersey

I LOVE YOU

W. F. FOCER, DR.
FURNITURE
PITMAN, N. J. Sept. 27 — 192_

BOORUM & PEASE COMPANY
MANUFACTURERS OF
Standard
BLANK BOOKS AND LOOSE LEAF DEVICES
NEW YORK
ESTABLISHED 1842   INCORPORATED 1892

CAP AND DAGGER
Honorary Dramatic Society of
BUCKNELL UNIVERSITY
Lewisburg · Pennsylvania

My own sweetheart   Sunday

This won't be as long as a couple Sunday letters, for the evening is well and I want to get to bed in good time in order to be fit for my interview with Mr. Lewis tomorrow. The daylight hours since dinner I've spent in charge of the Demi delegation to take to the convention of ΦΔΘ on May 19. At Founder's Day assembled alumni asked me to go with President Abraham as alumni representative. I didn't think I could afford the time and money, but charts instead. I've done this before, so it's easier for my interview this year...

1928

In 1928, Caryl and Ken, both now 22, find themselves overwhelmed with longing. They continue to write daily, almost frantically, and use asterisks for kisses. However, few of Caryl's letters survive from this important year – although there are eleven empty envelopes from Buffalo.

Sunday evening, January 1, 1928
Woodbury to Buffalo

My Ladysweet,

Your Ken has been unusually devout today with four church services to his credit! I taught Sunday School class from 9:45 till 11:00, attended church till 12:30, helped Mother with her bookkeeping as treasurer this afternoon, led Young People's from 7:00 till 8:00, and then sat through church again till 9:15! Stars in my crown and all that sort of thing? I've surely shattered all my own previous personal records today.

I used to wonder about caring for Mother. She must have divined my thoughts, for she said I must not let consideration for her delay our marriage, and that she'd be glad to offer us the house but felt young couples should be alone. So, though I'll not dare go far from her and don't know how she plans to manage by herself, I'm glad she disposed of some of my misgivings.

Saturday I hurried home from the office, and after doing several jobs for Mother, I bathed, shaved carefully in preparation for New Year's Eve festivities at the country club, and donned my evening clothes with relish. Bobby was eager to wear her new ensemble – pale green taffeta silk with facings in front of pale yellow; bodice closefitting, décollettage round front and back; skirt bouffante, hemline scalloped. She looked most attractive.

At 9:30 we set sail in the faithful old flivver. The dance was unusually nice. At least a hundred couples were there. There's something about a formal affair that appeals to me – & all club dances are formal, except in midsummer. The music was very good, and we both enjoyed it hugely. I had a popular partner, and men from the stag line cut in repeatedly, while I had lots of requests for dance-exchange.

At midnight a wild burst of confetti & yells announced the New Year. Otherwise, none of the noise that rocked the old garage at college dances. At home by 1 A.M., we threw together a meal of our own and found it lots of fun – dining in the kitchen in full evening dress! It was 2 A.M. when we reached our beds.

This afternoon I took Bobby to Philly to catch a jammed 4:35 train back to Bucknell. It's nine now, and I haven't even touched the mass of steamship material I brought home from the office.

I want you so! I'll keep on craving you, carissima, until I am at last your very own

Ken   *———*

Thursday afternoon, January 5, 1928
Philadelphia to Buffalo

My Lady dearest,

My letters are likely to be increasingly irregular as this steamship stuff develops. It will take a deal of quick and thoughtful work to meet the first insertions, which are close upon us. I may have to work in the evenings sometimes, and I'll certainly have to study after office hours. If I can make good on this project, our chances will be immeasurably increased.

I must confess too, dear, that your own hopes have renewed mine wonderfully. Let's plan our hardest for September, and things will work themselves out somehow!

Loving you dearly (though hurriedly),
Ken *

Friday morning, January 6, 1928
Philadelphia to Buffalo

Lady o' mine,

Last evening was glorious – crisply, comfortably cold with a brilliant moon that made me forget all my good resolutions and go skating instead of letter writing! I felt no little pang, watching couples swing over the ice hand in hand, thinking of how much I'd enjoy it with you.

Soon I'll mail the booklet describing the Ayer Saving Fund. I can at any time withdraw 50% of the principal I have paid in, but until two full years are up, I cannot draw on the $66^{2}/_{3}$ additional amount the house credits me, nor draw more than my own 50%, without losing the house share. In December, I'll have $700 available, but in September, I dare figure only on $275.

I'm enclosing your book list, Ladysweet, with a few personal suggestions checked. As to the bureau set, I think white would be safest, since you have it. It seems strange and intimate to be selecting things for "our room." I pray that it may materialize before too long!

Loving you always,
Ken *

Friday evening, January 6, 1928, Woodbury to Buffalo

My darling Lady,

I succeeded in getting to Wanamaker's today – spurred on by the news you'd not yet sent the bracelet on its way. Now you may safely send it to me, sweetheart. The salesman said they were out of the 7/16" width bracelets but would have a new supply in a few days.

I'm enclosing a check for the 175 pennies I hurried to deposit in the bank this morning. I really had 176 but kept the extra one for "seed"!

We're listening to the Princeton Triangle Club presenting their current show, "Napoleon Passes," at the Phila. Academy of Music. It's most amusing and tuneful. I like so much to think you are lying in my arms here in the shadows, listening to the music with me, my lips meeting yours, or brushing your cheek as I clasp you close. I love you, want you so!

K

Tuesday evening, January 10, 1928, Woodbury to Buffalo

My precious Lady,

Today has been the busiest, most intense since I've been a copywriter! The most involved of my assignments was preparation of a statement of copy policy for American-Hawaiian steamship company. "Copy policy" consists in analysis of a new account, decision upon objectives that seem paramount, and a careful outline of advertising procedures to achieve the objectives.

Yesterday, Mr. Warren asked me to try my hand at it. I had only the vaguest idea of what was required, but I thought and wrote furiously all morning, for it had to go off to San Francisco tonight by air mail! I had to suspend activity to supply a small "rush" campaign for Boston chain store papers on Tetley Tea, necessitating a telephone conference with one of our august New York reps. (Both American Telephone & Telegraph Co. and Western Union are our clients!)

Mr. Warren asked me to rewrite several sentences of my initial effort and said he was well pleased with the memo as a whole. I was elated and typed like mad to make all corrections complete by 4 P.M. Plans Dept. kept the phone buzzing intermittently to ask for it, and I found it all very exciting! Then I checked on my Tetley Tea layouts, which the artists had hurried through. I was ready to stumble home when the bell rang at 5. I'm going to bed now; mental weariness has made me tired physically, too. I'll save your dear letters till Sunday and answer their questions then.

Sleepily, lovingly,
Ken *

Thursday, January 12, 1928, Philadelphia to Buffalo (Ken's heading: "8 FLOOR ZUP!")

Lady mine,

Last evening there was a union meeting of the churches, including 150 men and women who volunteered to serve in a religious census of Woodbury. I was drafted for the Baptist complement. It must be completed by Sunday afternoon, but I can't see when I'll find time. Tonight I expect to escort Mother to the movies, Friday evening Len and I are going to the Temple-Bucknell basketball game, and Sunday, besides the census, I must speak in church at the morning service – part of the Northern Baptist caravan ritual. Doggone!

It's very good to think that Someday we'll not need to write each other – ever! It's hard to make my love pulse through a typewriter key, sweetheart, and there's always the chance that I'll be interrupted and have to leave the machine. But hurriedly now, while no one is looking, I'll whisper that I love you dearly, and add one lone, lingering kiss   *   !

Always,
YOUR Ken

Friday morning, January 13, 1928
Philadelphia to Buffalo

Caryl, dear,

Time was when I wrote you almost as much as you deserve, but alas, poor Yorick! I've been thinking I'd have to get a secondhand typewriter, probably a portable, for occasional work at home in the evenings. Will you bring yours when you come to me in September?

I'm concerned about the ambitious program you are following, Lady mine. Even though we are eager for the consummation of our happiness, it must not be at the cost of your own health – for then we could not half enjoy each other. Please don't overdo things, honey.

Bucknell defeated Ursinus last night on the latter's floor, and tonight we see them tangle with Temple, here in the city. It was an epic struggle last season, and there are sure to be a lot of Bucknellians at the game.

I'm so very eager to be for always your own loving

Ken   *   *   *

Saturday morning, January 14, 1928
Philadelphia to Buffalo

My own Sweetheart,

I'm chancing the old fountain pen again this morning – after a series of machine-made missives.

Tomorrow afternoon is the church census, so I'll not be able to write before evening. I assume your formal business education ended yesterday. If they supply a diploma, you'll have a formidable array to present to prospective employers! Incidentally, your bookkeeping/budgeting training will be invaluable to us later. It will be a case of my earning and your spending. You are accepting a big responsibility, Ladysweet!

The game last night was disappointing: a 29–18 defeat for Bucknell. Wild & rough throughout, the referee lost control almost completely toward the end. Temple foul tactics brought occasional "boos" even from the Temple cheering section. Tonight will be very different – cleaner, faster, for Haverford men are traditionally & thoroly gentlemen. Lots of Bucknellians were at the game – and I was elected cheerleader! We made lots of noise. All in all, quite a reunion!

Loving you dearly,
Ken   * ——— *

Sunday evening, January 15, 1928, Woodbury to Buffalo

My precious Lady,

Writing you, and nothing more, is hard when I want you so wishfully! I want to hold you close, feel your lips cling to mine, the warmth of you against me, breathing the fragrance of your lovely self. Then to slip off to sleep while you tousle my hair and stroke my face, myself, with your cool, white hand! Oh, Ladysweet. Someday I shall have you, and life shall be supremely sweet!

Last evening Len went direct from the office to Haverford – a charming old Quaker school, with the highest scholastic standing, that has produced some notable alumni. I met Mr. Meader (fellow copywriter, Haverford '13) in Philadelphia. He was in college with Christopher Morley & knows him well still. Meader himself has written and illustrated three corking books for boys (pirate-adventure stories). An interesting traveling companion, as you may imagine. [While growing up, I looked forward every Christmas to receiving the latest, specially autographed Stephen Meader book, which I usually devoured before the day ended. Slifer grandchildren still have some of them.]

The game was fast & clean. Our outfit played superbly, to win by a 45–25 score. The officiating was good, the crowd courteous and sportsmanlike, even in defeat. The team and the Bucknellians present were treated royally. The whole evening was a tremendous contrast to the Temple tangle.

Taught my Sunday School class this morning, then spoke in church. Hurried home for dinner and from there to my job as census taker. For about 3 hours I interviewed Catholics and Protestants, Negroes, Jews, Italians in a hundred North Woodbury homes. By now I am some census-taker – and how! I wager I'll be called on to direct the national census in 1930!

The Hawaiian honeymoon is a glorious prospect, sweetheart, but I shall be quite content with you an' Lake George, because I love you & shall always be your own adoring

Ken *

Tuesday morning, January 17, 1928
Philadelphia to Buffalo

Lady o' mine,

Our YMCA group team defeated the North Woodbury All-Stars 30–20 last evening! It was after ten when we reached home, and I spent an hour hunting a box and wrapping material for the bracelet, which I sent you this morning. The clerk assured me it is exactly 7/16" wide at the clasp, and it seemed precisely that in comparison with the other.

Two dear letters from you last evening – that I shall try to answer tonight.

Very hastily and VERY lovingly,
Ken *

Wednesday morning, January 18, 1928
Philadelphia to Buffalo

My own Lady,

These hurried Noiseless notes (the whole office is equipped with Noiseless typewriters) are woefully inadequate, but I can't conceive of any other solution. I'm too busy to push my pen as lengthily as I used to, and with the work that's waiting for me, it would be impolitic as well. Evenings are overfull, and I don't dare write love-letters late, or I'm too sleepy next day to write the letters that are to buy us bread and butter!

I had no thought of bowling last evening, but Mr. Warren, the acting captain who asked me to appear, is my supervisor on American-Hawaiian. All in all, I had little choice. The only consolation for me was that I raised my average some three or four points.

A kiss for you, dear   *   !

Longingly,
Ken

Thursday evening, January 19, 1928, Woodbury to Buffalo

My precious Lady,

I didn't read my newspaper this morning and stopped only for lunch at noon. I wrote furiously all day, as a telegram approving our preliminary plans on American-Hawaiian arrived yesterday, asking also for 4 advertisements at once. They must be mailed Wednesday, so I must complete copy by Saturday and allow 3 days for layouts. It was hard, slow work, for advertising ocean freighters (to the public) has never been attempted, anywhere. I ground out two ads entire and formulated ideas for others. Mr. Warren approved one, rejected one, and approved my tentative plans.

I'm sure everything will be alright for "Someday" in September – if we can swing it financially! If we can see any conceivable way to scrape through, let's take the plunge, precious mine. (The radio orchestra is playing the "Wedding March"!)

Do just as you like in regard to the job, honey girl, but I'm not marrying you for your money! I don't want you to overwork, and I do want you to be happy in whatever you undertake.

Your own
Ken

Sunday afternoon, January 22, 1928, Woodbury to Buffalo

My own Sweetheart,

It's twilight, dear, the witching hour – and I'm longing so for my Lovely Lady. Just now I'd like to have you here to run your hands through my hair in your own loving, gentle way. I've given myself a shampoo with Packer's Pine Tar Soap! My hair feels so tingly, healthy-clean, and it's so soft and fluffy that you should find it a more pleasant caress than usual.

Friday evening, Len and I worked at the office till six, then went to the annual Auto Show. It is one of the things no enterprising young advertising man should miss. I've never seen so many beautiful cars in any other show – some of them sensationally so. And every low, long roadster made me wish for my lovely lady beside me – an open road – and a moon!

Today was so invigorating I went skating in the afternoon. I've never done it, but until last year and this I'd never been limited largely to Saturday and Sunday for exercise – with ice on Sunday only. I can't see any difference between skating and walking or motoring – except it's better exercise! So long as it doesn't interfere with church duties! I had a royal, happy, healthful hour on the ice. I can't feel like a reprobate, for I've gained rosy cheeks and a tremendous appetite!

I'm glad the second bracelet fits satisfactorily, sweetheart. I s'pose you had to have a link taken out. I didn't like to do it without being sure of the size.

Don't overtax yourself – even in a Democratic cause, dear! I hope something more congenial turns up – more lucrative, also. And don't worry about the money – that's my job!

The more I think and plan, dearheart, the more I believe we'll not need to write – after September. I'm counting, wishing, dreaming so.

Loving you dearly,
K

Tuesday afternoon, January 24, 1928, Philadelphia to Buffalo

Lady, dearest,

At last, a breathing spell! I worked on my A-H ads over the weekend and satisfied the supervisor by noon Monday. Before Thursday night, when they start for San Francisco, I must write a long memo to accompany them and make sure the layouts are all they should be.

While I was laboring on the steamship stuff, my other accounts piled up, but after a full week of sustained writing, I feel like a little celebration. My first campaign, and all that sort of thing!

Thank you for the information on the Buffalo News advertising contest. However, the first rule said, "Professional advertising men and newspaper employees are excluded from the contest." So it hardly would be ethical to compete. Moreover, I know nothing about the institutions and products to be advertised. Most laymen (and most contestants) will put together a string of synonymous superlatives, without regard to the facts involved.

Copy, to us, however, presupposes a comprehensive knowledge of the article at hand, and definite assurance of superiority. We cannot say baldly that Blank's coal or Ex's bedsprings are the best – without knowing and being able to prove it rather conclusively, or without qualifying it to read best for a certain purpose, or in one respect. (Quoted from "The Ethics of Advertising," by the eminent and well-known copywriter, Kenneth W. Slifer.)

Last night we took the kids to the Camden "Y" for a swim. Tonight I must design a picture postal for a Demie Founder's Day announcement and paint a poster for a missionary affair at church.

I'm sorry the ring I gave you (a year too soon?) keeps you from finding a position. Just think of the wonderful openings you'd have if I hadn't shackled you so! I'm fishing, for I want you to say you prefer me! The wonder of it never grows less.

I'm reasonably sure we can find a small apartment for $35–$40 a month. We ought to be able to manage that. Moreover, there are houses – five or six rooms, with bath – listed to rent at $25 and $30. For a house, we'd have to add $12 or so a month for water, electricity, gas, and coal. Fuel would be a big item if we started in September, and probably we could not swing a house.

Remember the newspaper clipping I sent you, announcing the engagement of the pedigreed chap I met in the tennis finals? He was married Saturday in New York; there were 3,000 at the reception afterwards. One of the presents was a big Nash convertible coupé. The finest present I expect is a gold-plated wastebasket to hold all my rejected copy! Let's hope for a flivver to take us to Lake George! If only we could do our wishing together – it's rather rough doing it alone!

Your own
Ken

Wednesday afternoon, January 25, 1928, Philadelphia to Buffalo

My own Lady,

This really must be a hurried note today. Last evening's letter was the loving, wistful sort that I always like to get, and it deepened my yearning for you – if anything could.

I'm beginning to believe a Someday in September will come true! The $8 I put in various house funds each week, I don't count as available for debts, but I've determined upon $35 for a month's rent. As to savings, we can take the 10% the Ayer fund allows – $3.50 weekly. Besides 4% interest, they add $66^{2}/_{3}$ cents on the dollar, the same as a weekly salary increase of $2.16.

Back to my desk, with a kiss * for you and the assurance that I'm loving you dearly,
Ken

Caryl's response to the above letter is gone. However, on the back of Ken's envelope, she pencils a tentative budget based on his getting a raise to $35 a week: Benevolence $3.50; Savings $3.50; Shelter $8; Food $12; Clothing $5; and Carfare $3. Though there's no category for miscellaneous expenses, she includes their tithe.

Friday morning, January 27, 1928, Philadelphia to Buffalo

Lady, darlin',

Eureka! My American-Hawaiian campaign was completed and is on its way to San Francisco by air mail. Mr. Warren agreed the layouts were most effective and added, "You've done an equally fine copy job, boy." As a precaution against possible loss, we had photographs of the layouts made, and everything finished up nicely at two minutes of five!

Last night Mother and I took my Sunday School class to the movies! "The Big Parade," said to be the greatest of war pictures, is superbly directed, and there are some splendid scenes. But good as it was, it left me strangely unmoved and dispassionately calm, principally because you weren't beside me, clasping my hand and sharing every emotion with me.

Wanamaker's is staging the greatest furniture display ever attempted. There is a Spanish villa furnished in every detail, and there are 50 or 60 model rooms in various styles – most bigger than our whole house! The smaller apartments were called "Little Budget House" A and B. Printed estimates showed the cost of each room and each piece, even to wallpaper, curtains, and labor. They were way beyond our budget, but I shan't care, if I can only be forever

Your Ken *

Saturday morning, January 28, 1928, Philadelphia to Buffalo

Bobby Slifer drew a high number in the dorm-room lottery and had to choose from among a few rooms on the top (fourth) floor of the "new dorm." The Alpha Chi suite was on the second floor. Construction of the New Dormitory for Women began in 1927 and was completed by the spring of 1928. In 1931, the new women's residence was named Hunt Hall for the Rev. Emory William Hunt, Bucknell president from 1919–1931, encompassing the years Ken, Caryl, and Bobby were undergraduates. I lived in Hunt Hall during my own junior year, 1952–1953.

Hunt Hall, the "new dorm" for women where Bobby lived on the top floor her sophomore year, was completed in 1928 – this side faces the Sem quadrangle.[1]

My precious Lady,

Bobby was unlucky with room assignments. Drawings were held this week, Freshmen last. She drew 96! Her only choice: five rooms on the top floor of the new dorm, with a $50 increase in cost! She and Peg got near each other and will use one room as a study, the other for sleeping.

Yesterday I was assigned The Joseph Dixon Crucible Company, makers of every conceivable kind of pencil, notably Dixon's Eldorado drawing pencils and Dixon's Ticonderoga for ordinary use. It's a sizeable account and has been handled thus far by one of our best writers.

Last evening Len and I listened to Galli-Curci as she made her radio debut in Victor hour. I heard her once in person, but I enjoyed this almost as much. She's simply marvelous! Sharing the program with her was Pablo Casals, called the greatest living cellist by musical authorities. It was a superb concert, as you can imagine, and our cabinet reproduced it flawlessly.

All my love,
Ken

Sunday afternoon, January 29, 1928, Woodbury to Buffalo

Honey mine,

I'm all alone in the house, as you were when you wrote the loving, yearning letter that made me so happy yesterday. I've read it eagerly, hurriedly – slowly, patiently – trying to draw all the love from every line. And what a world of it I found, dear heart! The last perusal fired me with a fierce, wild longing for you that is almost desperation! I wandered upstairs, half-hunting for you, conscious only of the intensity of the yearning in my heart. Oh honey, I must have you soon!

A fine, driving snow started yesterday and was still whirling down in gusty blasts when I went to bed. I'd shoveled our walks, but the storm continued, and the mocking wind covered my tracks in no time. This morning we rose to find a dazzling white world. On the level there were 18 or 20 inches of snow; elsewhere the wind had wrought drifts of 3–4 feet. The tall evergreens in front of the house were gorgeous, and I wished mightily for camera film.

I shoveled our walks, cut thru 2 waist-deep drifts to dig the driveway clear from the garage to the street – wide enough for the flivver, & broke a path to the track in the middle of the street, so Mother can get out. Helped a couple of neighbors who got stuck and finished by tunneling a path to each clothespost in the back yard. I came in at 1:30 – 3½ hours of continuous shovelling! My arms ache from the tons of snow I lifted, but it was good exercise, and I enjoyed it.

It's great fun to plan definitely for our honeymoon. I knew we'd need a car, and I've been calculating. Our old bus (five years!) would hardly be adequate or reliable. We may get a new one, but I don't know. Clem is planning to get two new Fords – a sedan and a coupé, so he can drive one to the office and leave the other for Bec. I'd like a coupé – for a honeymoon! They seem so delightfully intimate, and there's loads of luggage space! I feel as if I can solve any problem, overcome any obstacle, so eager am I to be your own adoring

Ken *

Tuesday morning, January 31, 1928, Philadelphia to Buffalo

Lady, dearest,

We're slowly digging ourselves out of the snowdrifts, but there is not a great deal of vehicular traffic yet. More snow is predicted, and the few remaining records will be shattered in that event, for this last storm was the heaviest since 1893!

Last night, after our Stunt Night program at the "Y," Len and I came out to find ten kids lying in ambush. We had a royal snow battle that was all sorts of fun – Len and I against the mob. We were a bit handicapped by being dressed in good clothes, but we went to work with a will and succeeded in tossing all of our adversaries except one into assorted snowbanks.

I rather thought you'd like the Chalfonte-Haddon Hall Hotel series, for they really are well done. John Frazer was down there last weekend for "atmosphere," and is to go for several days in February. Of course, he was a guest of the hotel, and they assigned him a double room with bath, for which the normal rate is $28 a day! Fancy that!

The engraved invitation is self explanatory. N. W. Ayer & Son's new corporate headquarters, under construction on West Washington Square, is progressing rapidly. The steel superstructure is up eight or nine stories, and they are beginning the masonry work. Hence the official cornerstone exercises this Saturday. It gives me a thrill to realize that when the dedication ceremonies are held next November or December, you'll be mine and can go with me!

Two bits of information for which you asked are, respectively, the commutation and straight rates on the West Jersey and Seashore division of the Pennsylvania Railroad. Commutation is $7.86 per month. Single straight fare to Phila. is 35¢, BUT the railroad, to cope with bus competition, has begun a rate war, in which they sell a round trip to the city for 40¢. Anything else to help you in your tentative budgeting?

Remember I have been giving one dollar a week to the church, in addition to my Sunday School offering of 20–25¢. Country club membership is about $30 a year, including tax. I'd like to keep that if I can, for it's the only real exercise I (and we) can get. But no matter. I'll sacrifice most anything to have you, honey. I want you so!

Lovingly *
Ken

Wednesday morning, February 1, 1928, Philadelphia to Buffalo

Caryl, mine,

I went bowling last night, happily raised my average two or three more points, and escaped the immediate danger of ending up at the bottom of the league.

I had to take this out of the machine this morning, in order to write a brief bit of copy for Dixon's Ticonderoga pencils. It was a rush job – part of a four-color page.

Did I tell you that I got an electric waffle baker for Mother's birthday? We tried it out at once, and it made the most luscious, crisp waffles faster than we two could eat them!

Of course I don't think you were foolish to start the wedding invitation and announcement lists. I don't know how many invitations I'll want, for they demand a present in return, and most of my friends are poor, but there are a lot of people I'd like to have receive announcements.

Bobby is to move into her new room this week. Exams are over & I imagine she acquitted herself creditably. Her mid-semester grades showed three A's, a B and a C. The last in Math, which she loathes as heartily as I. The B was in English under Prof. Coleman – and is nothing to be ashamed of. Her calendar of dances for the spring semester is formidable.

Our local Demie alumni club expects to take two or three carloads to Bucknell for Founders' Day, Mar. 2 and 3. It won't seem like college without you, but I'll go back with the gang, if only to see Bobby and the boys at the house. Oh, Ladysweet, I love you, want you always!

Ken *

Monday evening, "Rather late" February 6, 1928, Woodbury to Buffalo

Sweetheart mine,

I'm a medical phenomenon – with two colds at one and the same time! I start to cough and stop to sneeze! The combination has put me in bed. Sunday I'd added a bad cold in the head! After two church services, I cooked dinner, did the dishes, and went for a walk in an effort to throw it. This morning I felt rotten, but went to the office, did a couple of things that had to be done, and came home at noon. A visit to the osteopath's, hot bath, hot lemonade, and bed again. I'm sitting in the bathroom where it's warm, eating graham crackers and milk! It's late, I have a little fever, and I don't dare risk being chilled. I'll not go to the office tomorrow, so my letters are likely to be delayed. Don't worry, honey-girl, and remember that I love you dearly!

'Night,
Ken *

Tuesday evening, February 7, 1928 Woodbury to Buffalo

Caryl, darling,

I slept till noon, then dinner, and another visit to the osteopath. (Our osteopath is Carl Fischer, former intercollegiate tennis champion, ranked #7 in the United States. He's a peach and has a tremendous practice here.) I felt like myself again, though he found a wee bit of fever.

My heart is full of many, many things tonight. Whether I can pour them out to you as I want, I don't know. My own room is too chilly for a semi-Demie-invalid, and I never write freely with the paper held on my knee.

The possibility your parents might not approve of our September plans had not occurred to me. My mother, if she has objections, has not voiced them. She trusts our discretion and judgment and will be reconciled to any plans we make. However, I quite agree with your folks that your health does not warrant the arduous employment campaign you mapped out for yourself. Your own letters suggest you are tired and nervous. Because of your condition for the last year or two, I cannot feel you ought to work at all in the months that remain. And the money gained might easily be wiped out by doctors' bills. We must be well, precious mine, for a few osteopathic treatments would blow our budget sky-high.

If God wants our lives to fuse in September, He will make it possible – how, He only knows! I can say this and face the prospect of postponement, because I love you so. Yet I want you as I've never wanted anything – with an intensity that's almost maddening! Paradoxically, it's because I love you that I ask you to give up part of your plans to bring us together! There'll be no "obey" in our ceremony. I wouldn't dare order the senior partner anyway (!) but you may know, dearest mine, this is my earnest wish: Leave the lucre to me to provide. That's my job. I'll get it if it can be got – even if I have to crack a safe! Meanwhile, you're to worry only about recipes, napkins, bridal veils, and things like that – at the same time building your adorable self into physical fitness for wifehood – and motherhood. Isn't that a sensible way to look at things, dearest? And will you understand the infinite tenderness in my heart?

Our "needs" will be simple, so long as we have each other, but we'll make sure they're provided for before we start. I believe we can work out a presentable budget on $35 a week, with some $600–$700 besides. I enclose the story of a family of six who live on $14 a week! The discussion has been raging in the "Letters to the Editor" column for some time, but this is the most amazing I've seen, though a number of people reported family incomes of only $20–$25 a week – and wrote eloquent English, too! I think we'll be able to manage for a few months, at least!

Have you ever asked your parents how well fixed they were at the start? I know my own Mother and Father had little more than love to live on. I can remember desperate days when I was just a kid – yet Daddy was well on the way to being wealthy when he died.

I'm enclosing the carbon of a report on my first four American-Hawaiian advertisements. It is especially interesting, as the client had refused to approve the schedules prepared by our Plans Dept. and was in a negative frame of mind. Another step up the ladder for us, Ladylove!

Oh, precious, I love you, long for you so infinitely. Your own adoring

Ken *

Wednesday afternoon, February 8, 1928, Woodbury to Buffalo

My own Sweetheart,

It's a dull, foggy afternoon. I'm all alone in the house and yearning so for you! It was raining this morning, and the doctor said irrespective of how I felt, I should not venture out. My conscience ought to hurt me (nothing else does), and I feel fully fit! I'm suffering seriously from a bad case of dislocated razor! My three-day beard makes me look like Comrade Ivanitch himself. I don't suppose you'll allow me such luxuries – nor am I likely to ask them!

I've told you nothing of Ayer's cornerstone ceremonies – an impressive service, attended by 500–600 employees and 100 invited guests. Dr. Barbour of the Seminary gave the invocation. Mr. Fry, as president of Advertising Headquarters, delivered a short address, reviewing the history of the firm and relating anecdotes from Mr. Ayer's life. A tremendous assortment of articles was placed in a metal box and sealed in the huge cornerstone. Included was Mr. Ayer's well-worn Bible, wrapped in an American flag. The oldest employee, who entered the organization in 1877, assisted Mr. Fry in spreading the mortar for the stone. Then a closing prayer, by the pastor of the historic Presbyterian church that fronts Washington Square.

I have been lucky to win my way into an organization like "Advertising Headquarters." It stands supreme in the field I like best – and is almost as unique among all business, for its principles and practices. It is growing rapidly – expanding always – and you and I shall grow with it!

All my love, dear *
Ken

Friday morning, February 10, 1928, Philadelphia to Buffalo

Lady of mine,

My advice against job-hunting came just too late, didn't it? I can hardly expect you to give up the job with Remington Rand at my request, but if it lasts into April, and you come to me in May, it might suffice for the season. I imagine you'll want to spend most of the summer getting ready for the ceremony itself in September.

I looked over last evening's paper and found a little story (I'm enclosing it) about Anne Campbell, who was <u>your</u> discovery and whom we've enjoyed together.

The enclosed statement shows my balance in the Beneficial Fund on January 1st – a little more than a year's savings at $2 a week. At the end of next year, I'll have $450 in this fund and be eligible for complete withdrawal without losing profits. By September, I'll have $200 in the Xmas fund. With that – whatever you have, and my two-weeks' salary, as well as what is given us – we ought to be able to squeeze out a honeymoon and start housekeeping.

What an enigmatic brother you have, Caryl mine! I've wondered at his inviting feminine guests to your home before. It isn't done – in our community, at least – without a tacit engagement, or an elaborate function for which a girl comes from afar. But for two student pastors to bring two girls all the way from Rochester, at night and unannounced, is startlingly unconventional. What a pair of ministers they'll make. Do their congregations know of these escapades? Our own would lift the roof. I can't conceive of doing such a thing or of Mother's countenancing it.

But I've said too much already on a disagreeable topic. Forget it all, please, honey-girl, and remember only that I love you with all my heart! I'm longing so to be your very own

Ken *

Sunday evening, February 12, 1928, Woodbury to Buffalo

My own Lady,

I've spent the afternoon writing to Mr. Black. I told him our hopes and plans as carefully as I could. It was good for me to think things through and evaluate them. I chronicled our finances and asked his advice and opinion on it all.

'Scuse me for a few moments, dear. Your old friend, John D. Rockefeller, Jr. was just speaking over the radio, as a guest of Collier's hour. He spoke well and interestingly on "Character in Business." He has a very pleasing voice and clear, clean enunciation. [In earlier years, Caryl's father served as associate pastor of Fifth Avenue Baptist Church in New York City – renamed Park Avenue church and later Riverside Church – attended by the Rockefeller family. When Caryl's mother, seriously ill, had to be hospitalized, John D. Rockefeller took care of her bills.]

Friday evening I helped Mother put new seats in the kitchen chairs. The operation moved her to reminisce of the early days, when those two chairs (secondhand even then) & a typewriter chair were all they owned. Whenever another couple came for dinner, Daddy sat on a rickety old stepladder! She said if you and I were married now, we'd have more to start with than they did. There's no question of her good wishes for us, honey, though she has most to lose of us all.

I was mos' sorry to learn in yesterday's missive that your budget letter had gone astray! I've seen nothing of it yet, but hope it will turn up after the labor and love you put into it.

   Here's a kiss, dear Lady mine,
   Will you be my Valentine?! ♡

Lovingly,
Ken

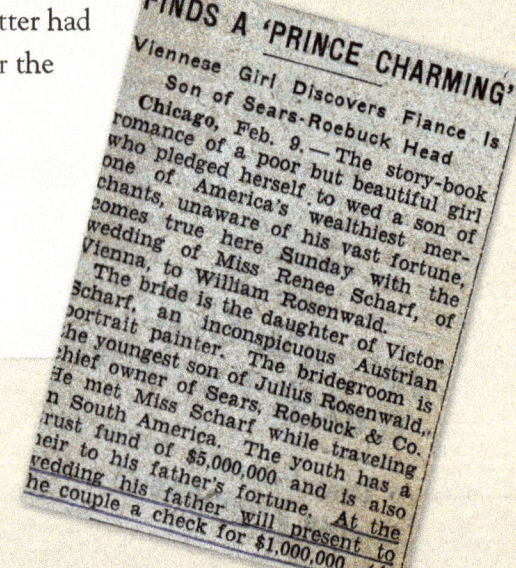

Noon on Valentine's Day, Tuesday, February 14, 1928
Philadelphia to Buffalo

Lady, darlin':

The rush now is to clean up the Dixon pencil schedules. Many companies furnish portfolios showing a year's advertising to their salesmen to display to dealers. For portfolio purposes, all advertising must be complete early in the year. I'm writing the last of it now – advertisements that will appear next November and December! My supervisor on this account said some very nice things about my copy and approved all of it without changing a single word! I'm learning, sweetheart, and it's going to bring me YOU!

I'm glad you find your position so enjoyable, Lady mine. If one must work, it's fun to work at pleasant tasks. I hope the regularity of your routine will have the healthy influence you expect of it. I'm wishing things for you, as I wish for you! You have said nothing about salary.

Bobby writes that the new dormitory rooms are very nice. By shifting and trading, she and Peg have rooms directly opposite and are combining in a bedroom-study arrangement. Mother's birthday is Feb. 26, and she expects to treat herself to a weekend in Lewisburg as celebration. I'll be there the next week, so Bobby will have lots of entertaining to do!

Adoring you so!
Ken *

Lady, darlin':
I was busy at the "Y" till ten-
honey, and had no chance to write. This morni
one and I've only a few moments left of my l

The rush just now is to clean up the Di
Many companies, Dixon included, like to fur
ing a year's advertising to all their sale
them it to dealers. For portfolio purposes then
be complete early in the year. I'm writing
advertisements that will appear next Nove
supervisor on this account is one with wh
fore, though I defeated him in the tenni
He has said some very nice things about
of it without changing a single word! He
caption for one piece, but has altered
I'm learning, sweetheart, and it's goi

The letter that you wrote on Frid
Friday morning and spoke in the first
evening hour!) did not arrive yester
since you sent it to the office, and
able to write in return, there is no
find another at home this evening?

I'm glad that you find your po
Lady mine. If one must work, it's
tasks. I hope that the regularity
healthy influence that you expect
you, as I wish for you! . . . You

I know that I would have en
always do anything with you. An
going to insist that you hide y
that you are not drafted for a
you beside me that I don't war

Bobby writes that the new
Good bed, big dresser, table
finished in mahogany. . . Ro
hooks. . . Wide window sill
sort of thing. By shifting
directly opposite now and
study arrangement. Mother'
to treat herself to a week
be there the next week so
to do!

Len and Mother ask c
forget because I have s
self!

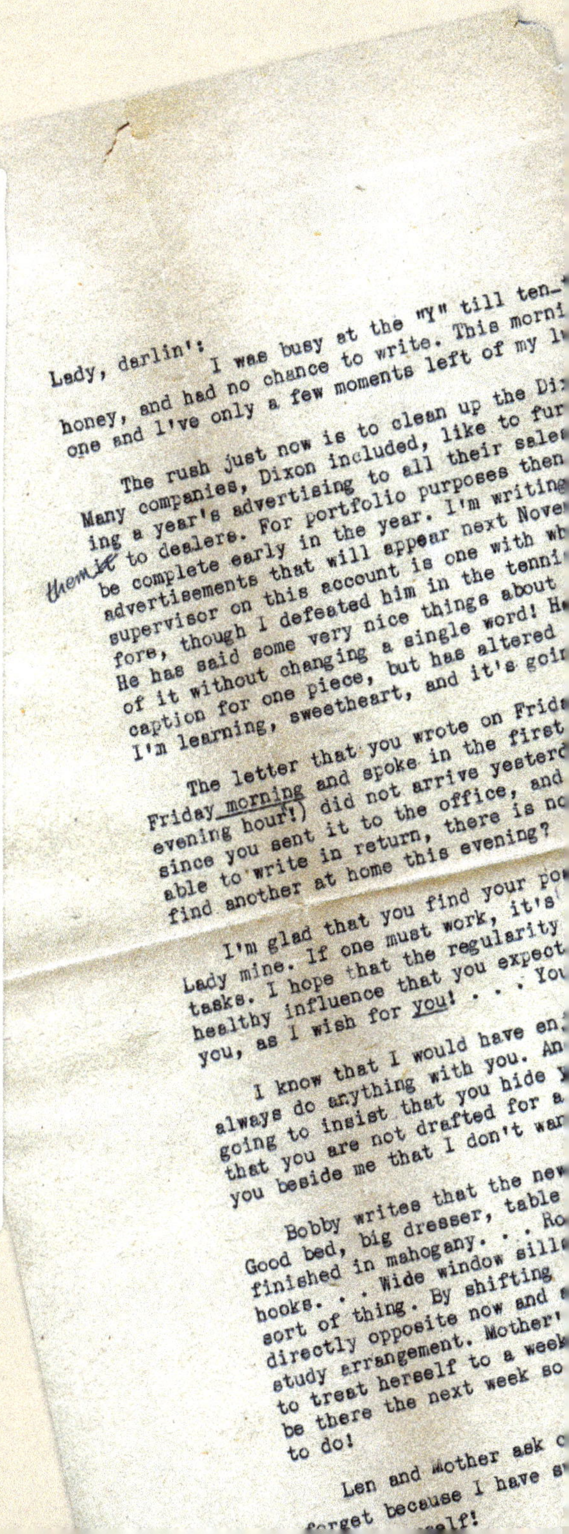

Wednesday afternoon, February 15, 1928, Philadelphia to Buffalo

Lady mine,

   I think I can cram everything into one paragraph – except my love, and I shan't attempt that, for I expect to take my lifetime to tell it to you! I went bowling last night and did not reach home until 10:30. It was stormy, but that seemed to help my game, for I rolled better than ever to lift my average several points. I took the final Dixon advertisement to the supervisor today. He liked it, said "That's darned good copy, boy," and sent me away with an OK and his blessing. "The Jazz-Singer" has been playing in Philadelphia for eleven weeks – almost a record, so it must be good. I find it absorbing these days to read the classifieds "For Rent" and dream. In the Woodbury Times alone there have been five advertisements in the last three weeks, offering unfurnished apartments of two rooms and bath for light housekeeping. I'm sure we'll find something to suit us. Oh, precious mine, days and nights are filled with dreams, because I love you so.

Ken *

Thursday evening, February 16, 1928, Woodbury to Buffalo

My precious Lady,

   Before I began to write, I took my drawing pen and made your Valentine look like you! I transformed corn-colored curls into rich, dark tresses. I left you a bit of a wave, tho, for I thot you'd like it. I darkened your eyes, brows and lashes till you look very much as you must have about 1911! [That year, Caryl was six.] The Valentine, nice as it was when you sent it, is infinitely improved!

   I've been afraid these last couple years that I was not a gentleman, because I did not prefer blondes! This month's Atlantic removes my fears for all time. It announces a new volume by Anita Loos, as companion to the other. [Her first book was "Gentlemen Prefer Blondes." In 1953, our whole family enjoyed it as a movie musical, starring Marilyn Monroe.] It is titled, amusingly and reassuringly: "But Gentlemen Marry Brunettes"! Since that is precisely what I proposed to do, a great load is lifted from my buzzom, and I can face the world, a jaunty gentleman once more!

Much LATER: It's 11:30, honey, and things are upset here now. Len received word that his uncle was killed in an Atlantic City auto accident today. I've been loaded with instructions regarding his work at the office tomorrow, and Mother is getting him something to eat.

I'm sorry you have a cold. Of course I'd be happy to sit by your bed and hold your hand as I read. And if I stopped reading occasionally for a kiss and a caress, would you object? Our day is coming closer. Then when I've read you to sleep, I can lie by your side the long night thru, as your own adoring

Ken *

Friday evening, February 17, 1928, Woodbury to Buffalo

My darling Caryl,

A world of pent-up love for the dearest, most adorable Lady ever. Is it enough?

Your salary seems munificent to me, dear, remembering how long and hard I worked for $20 weekly. Even though it lasts only into April, it will be a sizeable contribution to our joint fortunes.

My first four Dixon pencil ads were returned today, "OK without change." They are part of the Saturday Evening Post series, reproducing handwriting, so they must be brief yet crammed with meaning – just the sort of stuff I like to do. The client's letter was equally short and significant: "Copy has the convincing crack of a rifle shot." Several people through whose hands the letter passed complimented me on it.

I've been reading "Green Mansions" by W. H. Hudson this week. It's a modern classic and quite unlike anything else that has been written. I'd revel in it with you, because I'm loving you so,

Ken *

Sunday afternoon, February 19, 1928, Woodbury to Buffalo

Ken writes on letterhead of the WOODBURY HIGH SCHOOL YOUNG MEN'S CHRISTIAN ASSOCIATION. Names on the masthead include Kenneth Slifer, Secretary, and his close friends Walter Hunter (Gert), Treasurer, and Roy K. Clement (Clem), Assistant Leader.

My own Sweetheart,

I wonder if you'll mind some odds and ends of stationery I have lying around? I've no personal paper, except the monogrammed box you gave me, and that's rather expensive for daily notes. This particular assortment, printed as it is, explains itself. I've hundreds of envelopes to match – relics of high school days when I was always secretary of something. Whether it was my handwriting I don't know, but I was a perennial scribe. In college, strangely, I never held a single secretaryship.

I've finished "Green Mansions," a peculiarly poignant and beautiful romance that carried me out of myself as books seldom or never do. Hudson, an eminent English naturalist as well as author, in vivid, imagistic description surpasses anyone I know. Locale and setting almost become characters in the simple, moving story. It carried me to the sheerest ecstasy of love and brought me perilously close to tears – as nothing printed has done for years. Galsworthy, in his introduction, calls it a "prose poem," and it assuredly is. Perhaps you are familiar with it. In that case, you'll be interested to know how it affected me. If you do not know it, I envy you the joy of reading it for the first. When I'd finished the book and closed it slowly, the quiet of the fireside sent a tremendous wave of longing surging through me. I wanted you close against me, with your lips meeting mine lovingly, lingeringly. My arms ached with emptiness.

Then from eight to nine I sat quietly, listening to the New York Symphony Orchestra. But what a hunger in my heart! I wished for you, waited for you. But you didn't come to me, not even in my dreams when I went to bed to look for you there! Oh, Caryl sweet, I said I could wait another year, if need be, but I was untruthful to you and to myself. I need you, crave you, honey, and I must have you. I must! *

Your very own
Ken *

Wednesday evening, February 22, 1928
Woodbury to Buffalo

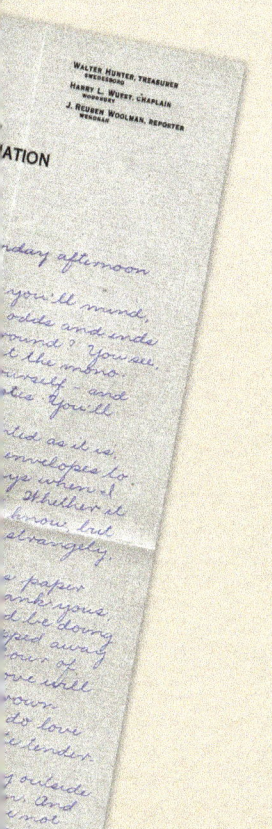

My precious Lady,

This weekend I'll yearn for you. Mother leaves for Lewisburg Friday, and Len goes to girlfriend GG Saturday at noon. I must be my own cook and companion, which isn't much fun, for I'm a gregarious soul. Won't you come stay with me? We'll sit by the open fire while the radio plays softly and talk of the thousands of things that lie ahead of us. I'm craving your kisses … and you, with a maddening intensity!

I had a ride in a new Ford today, and what that bus will do! Got home from the office early and met Gert Hunter driving a glistening new sport coupé out Delaware St. Of course he picked me up. They already have a Packard and Jordan in the family but added the Ford as an auxiliary. Mr. Hunter [Walter's father] is mayor of Swedesboro and received the first new car delivered there. Gert had been trying it out and was wildly enthusiastic. He offered to chauffeur for us in May. I've always wanted to ride in the rumble seat of a fast roadster with you! (The Ayer Ford has done 74-miles-an-hour in tests!)

It's late, honey. I've told you little in this note, but I had to write to tell you I'm lovin' you dearly,

Ken *

Caryl's meticulous proposed budget, in her tiny handwriting, is reproduced here. It presupposes a raise for Ken to $35 a week and is answered by comments in his letter of February 26.

K and C's Budget

Larger items included:

Ayer Fund	• 10% each week
Carfare	• $7.86 per month
Insurance premium	• $80 a year
Country club	• $30 per yr., or $.58 per week

Note: According to budget form,

"Shelter" includes:	taxes, rent, fire ins., etc.
"Operation" includes:	fuel, light, help, laundry, furnishing, phone
"Advancement" includes:	clubs, mag., newsp., educ., doctor, gifts, <u>autos</u>, amusements, books, vacations.

Budget Proper

Benevolence		$ 3.50	< (We might more rightly ask God's guidance & blessing if we tithe. All of our religious giving is included, tho some withheld each week for various benevolent demands, & not all given in Sunday collections.)
Savings – Ayer		3.50	
Shelter		9.00	
Food		10.50	
Clothing		2.00	
Operation			
Carfare	2.50		< ($2.50 carfare would allow 1 round trip to the city a week for me, if necessary. $.50 should cover laundry if I do the lighter things. How much is your telephone a month?)
Laundry	.50		
Phone	.50 (?)	$ 3.50	

Advancement			(Does your Country Club fee include any privileges for a wife, or would I have to join separately to use the courts?)
Newspaper	.12		
C. Club	.58		
Misc.	.76	<	(76¢ may be used for any kind of amusement, tho it isn't very much. With an occasional trip to the movies, I thot we'd be only too glad to spend our evenings together, alone, in our own little home.)
Ins.	1.54	3.00	
Total Balance		<u>$35.00</u>	

Any items such as Country Club & Insurance, which will be paid in lump sums, may be deposited with our savings each week, accrue interest, and thereby earn for us, until the total is to be paid.

For the first, we must spend the minimum for everything & save what we can for emergencies. Leftovers from allotted expenses, I'll put in a fund for entertaining guests, a luxury now & then, gifts, and so forth.

Any other items which I may have forgotten, please remind me of & we'll try to fit them in, tho our budget won't be much more elastic.

Submitted respectfully on this nineteenth day of February, 1928, by the "Senior Partner."

P.S. You spoke a while ago of paying $8 into various House funds a week. Why is it so much, dear, or is that explained in the booklet I haven't read carefully yet?

Sunday afternoon, February 26, 1928, Woodbury to Buffalo

My darling Caryl,

I've chosen the biggest piece of paper I could find, for I have much to tell you. Probably I'll forget half of the news I have, for the things in my head are likely to be swept away by the flood of love in my heart! The consciousness of my hunger for you dominates all else.

The long-planned American-Hawaiian conference materialized on Thursday. Mr. McPherson of A-H (a keen, likeable, eloquent Scotchman) & Mr. Watson of our San Francisco office had been in session with men from Plans Dept. all morning. When discussion veered from schedules and estimates to copy, Mr. Warren & I were asked to join them. It was 2 P.M. when we entered, nearly 5 when we left. In general, the A-H people liked the copy & layouts very much. The real thrill came late in the afternoon. Mr. Warren explained that since inter-coastal freight advertising is an entirely new venture, no one, even in our expert organization, has the background to handle it as well as it should be done. He added that I should be sent to San Francisco and back on an A-H boat, to absorb "background and atmosphere"! To which Mr. McPherson calmly replied, "Nothing could be more easily arranged."

Though I'll hardly get a round trip to San Francisco, which would take a month, I'm reasonably sure of some sort of voyage – through the Canal.

I've dined for the day – well, if not wisely. I heated a huge slab of meat loaf, warmed a can of asparagus tips, and candied two sweet potatoes. Lettuce salad & celery, with 5 slices of bread & butter and 3 glasses of milk completed my first course. Half a cream-apple pie & another glass of milk served as dessert. One full quart of milk in all. I then went walking for an hour – for some fresh air after the stuffy atmosphere of the house. It would be superfluous to say I intend to eat nothing else before bedtime. But you must not think either, after reading my menu, that the hunger I referred to on the first page was a craving for food!

I found OUR budget, as you had conceived it, very interesting and ingenious.

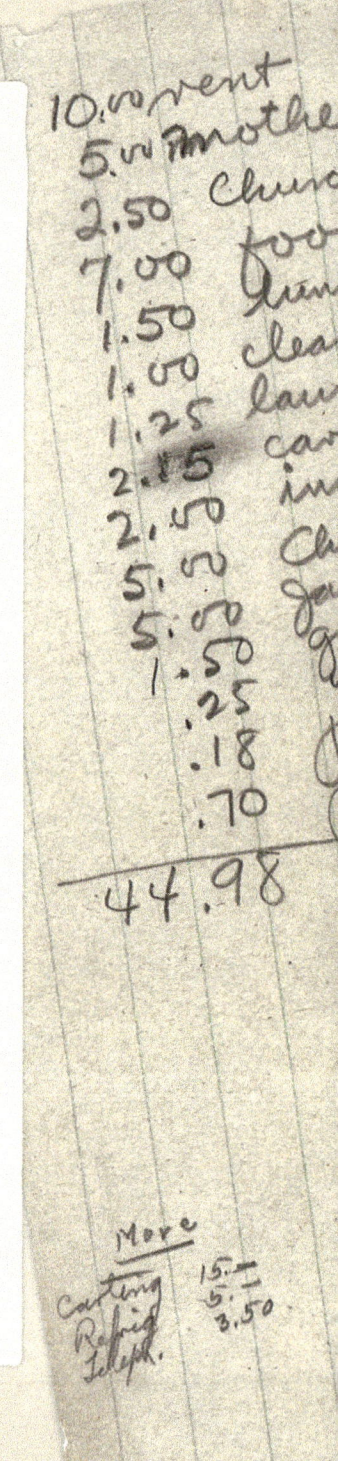

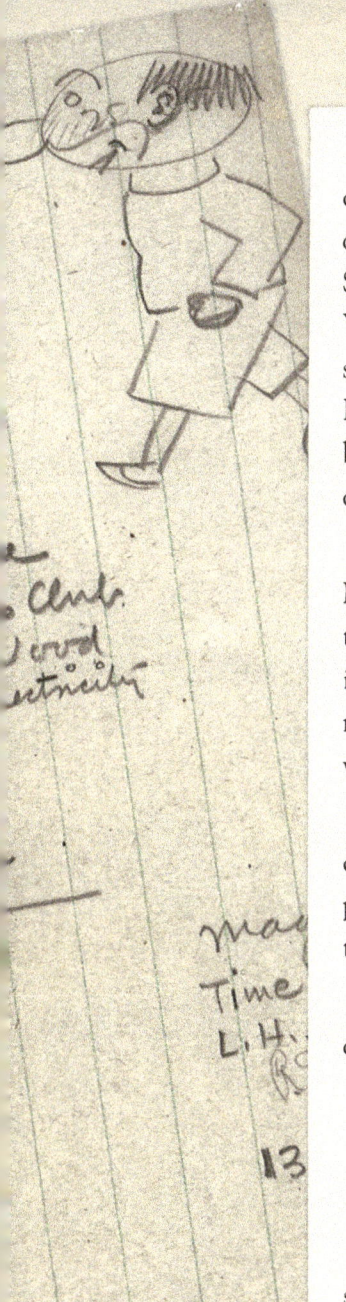

I confess I had not expected us to tithe. I've never done it, though I've come close, counting what I spend on my class and "Y" group plus church and Sunday School offerings. There will be church benefits and suppers to be included, & special S. S. offerings for every holiday. One has to contribute something once a year to the YMCA and the Boy Scouts. At the office, I'm obliged to join the Red Cross and subscribe to the Welfare Federation of Phila. If we can stretch a "tithe" over all that, I'll be glad. I should think $2 a week to the church direct would suffice, the balance being deposited until we have occasion to withdraw it. In the church here, there is only one family giving more than $2 weekly now!

I was thoughtless not to include Country Club membership for you in my figures. Membership for men is $25 a year, for women $12. There's 10% war tax, making the totals $27.50 and $13.20. I share a locker with a chap, for which the yearly rental is $5. I can get by without a locker & save the $2.50. Membership includes tennis, regular dances, 8 or 10 a year, and musicales and lectures occasionally during the winter.

Mother is not here, so I cannot ask her what the phone costs. It is conceivable we could do without it for a while, if we are pressed. I shan't need it for any business purpose, and it will leave us more to ourselves if people can't call us for meetings and things. But circumstances will decide that.

We may even cut under the budget in rent. Yesterday, in the window of a real estate office, I saw listed:

      Apartment: 3 rooms and bath - $30
      Apartment: 4 rooms and bath - $40

What they looked like I don't know of course, but we can't be too proud.

You've done a splendid job on the budget, precious mine. I have little else to suggest, and I certainly can't improve it. Here's a long, luscious kiss for your labors * !

If only I could give it to you myself! I'm very glad that you're eager to come to me. I shall be waiting with arms wide stretched.

Lovingly, lengthily yours (lonely, too)
Ken *

P.S. I thought I'd explained my $8 weekly savings: $5 in a Christmas Club and $2.80 in the Employee Beneficial Fund. I have 193 more pennies collected. Shall I send them on when I've reached 200?

"Toosdee" morning, February 28, 1928
Philadelphia to Buffalo

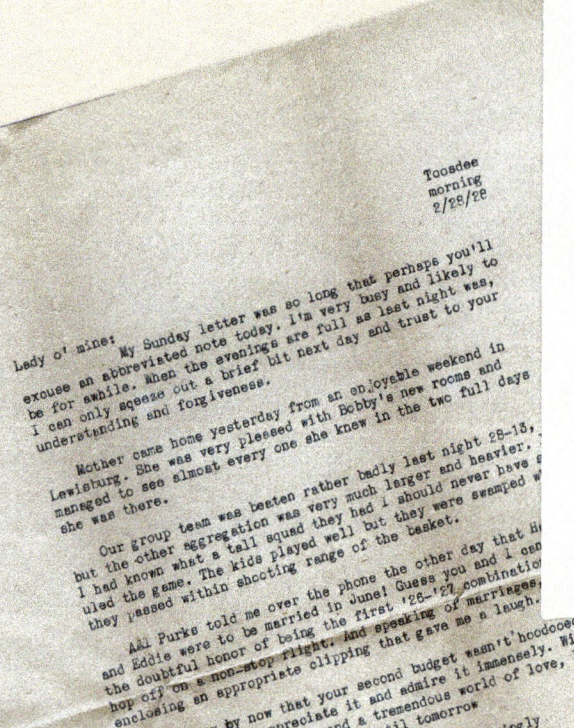

Lady o' mine,

Mother came home yesterday from an enjoyable weekend in Lewisburg. She was pleased with Bobby's new rooms and managed to see almost everyone she knew in the two full days she was there.

Our "Y" group team was beaten rather badly last night 28–13, but the other aggregation was much larger and heavier. If I had known what a tall squad they had, I should never have scheduled the game. The kids played well but were swamped when they passed within shooting range of the basket.

With these few scraps of news and a tremendous world of love, I'll ask you to be content until tomorrow.

Hastily, lovingly,
Ken

Tuesday evening, 11:30, February 28, 1928
Woodbury to Buffalo

My own sweetheart,

I can't write you the long, love-filled letter you deserve, for 6:30 A.M. comes, oh, so soon these days! But when you're mine, there'll be another hour added to every weekday – and two or three on Sunday! (Letter time, of course.) I'll need it all, for the joy of having you will make time pass so much more quickly!

I raised my bowling average about a point tonight, but the team lost two games out of three and is now tied with the other Copy Team for the cellar position.

I was sorry to learn of Attie's stroke, honey. If a funny card or anything else of the sort would help, please tell me. When I was about 10 years old, it was my experience to find Grandmother crumpled up from a stroke, babbling wild incoherencies that frightened me fearfully.

Another busy day at the office tomorrow. But I can write you from home.

Lovingly, longingly,
Ken *

Wednesday evening, February 29, 1928
Woodbury to Buffalo

Caryl, darling,

I'm full of ships & sea, wind & stars, pilots, compasses, binnacles, forecastles and all that sort of thing! I've tried all afternoon and evening to think of an effective name for the monthly bulletin that American-Hawaiian intends to issue. Mr. Warren wants one with all the rich flavor and color of the sea. I thought of a number this afternoon but none quite satisfied us. The one we want will come, though, and will seem inevitable and ridiculously easy when it does arrive – they always do!

I was sorry to know that headaches are still annoying you. I hope the glasses may do all you hope for them. It's not pleasant to know you are feeling wretched and needing me. I'll be happy when you're near enough for me to comfort you with kisses and caresses.

I'm working intensively to get things cleaned up for the weekend in Lewisburg. It promises to be a record-breaking Founders' Day. Nearly 50 alumni announced their intention of returning. Two or three carloads of us leave the city at noon Friday, reaching the house at supper time. Demie play and smoker that evening, convention next morning, banquet that evening. Campus weekends are strenuous, with little leisure or quiet for love-letters. But I'll try, sweetheart.

Loving you dearly,
Ken *

Thursday evening, March 1, 1928, Woodbury to Buffalo

My Ladysweet,

What a dear, love-filled letter I found here this evening! Sunday I'll tell you the full story of my weekend in a long letter. Working intensively all morning tomorrow, travelling from noon till six, play & smoker all evening, will scarcely leave time for a note.

I brought a dozen roses to Mother tonight – an extra, belated birthday gift. The waffle baker seemed so prosaic, I thought it would be nice for her to have them over the weekend.

If I have time to stop at the bank on my way to the station in the morning, I'll deposit our pennies and enclose a check with this. If it's not here, I didn't have time for it Q.E.D.

Mother says the phone is $2.25 a month, which is a shade more than the 50¢ a week you had estimated – only $1.00 a year more. She thinks your budget is splendid!

You didn't notice I said only one family in the church gives more than $2 a week. Mother tells me three families give more. Our congregation is poor on the whole, though I don't suppose many are tithing. The wealthy people in Woodbury are Episcopalians or Presbyterians. Ned Carpenter and his father are about the only well-to-do members we have.

Now I must pack my bag, take a bath, & tumble into bed – to dream of you, sweetheart.

All my love to you, precious mine,
Ken *

P. S. Glad Attie shows improvement.

* K_{isses} K_{aresses} K_{en}

Sunday evening, March 4, 1928, Woodbury to Buffalo

My precious Caryl,

I found one loving letter at Lewisburg, another awaiting me here. What a dear you are! A great weekend for Delta Sigma and a rousing Founders' Day – the largest crowd ever, except for our 25th anniversary. I enjoyed it all, but Lewisburg seemed strangely empty without you.

My biggest surprise came when I walked into the Demie dining room Friday evening and saw Rolland there. He had two boys from Conesus with him. They'd driven down that day and started back at midnight Saturday, after the banquet. I didn't rebuke him for not bringing you – but the things I was thinking!

Mother told me last week to thank you for her birthday card, so I'll say "Thank you" for her, before I forget. She was particularly appreciative of your sending it to Lewisburg.

I'm loving you so, Caryl sweet. Goodnight *
K

This old town seems mighty blue Without You!

Monday evening, March 5, 1928, Woodbury to Buffalo

My dear, dear Lady,

There's so much news to tell that love may be almost crowded out. To plunge into the story, eight Demies set sail from Philadelphia, 46th & Market Sts., in two Cadillacs, at 12:45 P.M. Friday. In our car, Al Purks chauffeured for Mr. Sholl, Dick Horter, and me. The three with Mr. Robey were all old-timers. We reached the

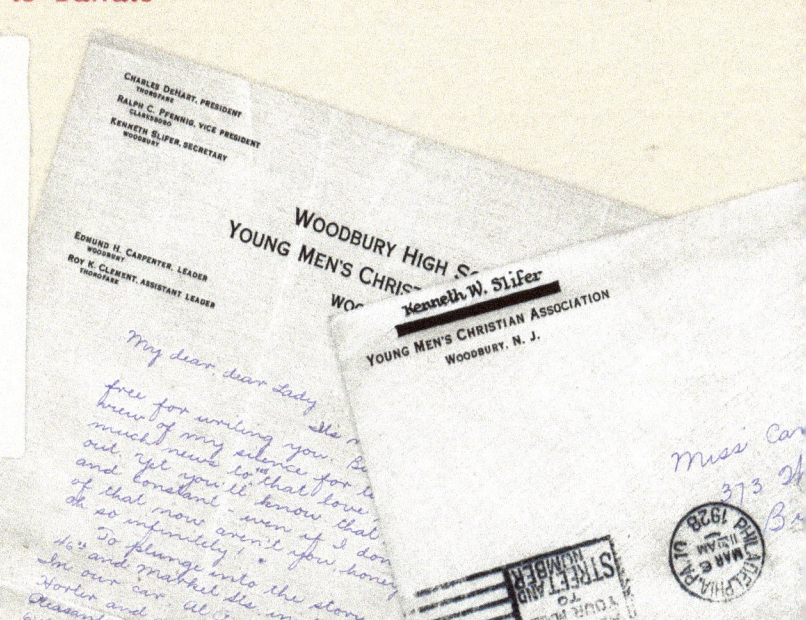

Demie House about 6:15 and were mauled and mobbed by the chapter and a number of alumni already assembled (including Rolland).

While we were eating, Bobby called. I went over for her at 7:30. A look around, and then we departed to Bucknell Hall. The play The Sky Riders was an entertaining farce – with an ingenious plot; a clever freshman did a fine bit as a Japanese house boy. The play didn't end till 11. I left Bobby at her building and went on to the smoker. Pretzels, punch, bridge & secondhand cigar smoke till midnight. Then Geddes Simpson and I went home to bed.

Up at 8 Saturday morning, barber shop shave, and breakfast at the Demie House. About 9, I wandered up the Hill, visited my old room, talked to a couple of professors, found Bobby in the Library, and took her over to the Sem for a bite of breakfast. Guy Payne has changed everything around at the Collge Inn again and has his counters arranged cafeteria fashion! Convention at the house at 10 – active chapter and alumni. It was an interesting session, with a new house and Phi Delta Theta occupying the center of the discussion. I made a speech explaining the progress of the nationalization movement for some older alumni.

Just before dinner, I walked out to the stadium, and after dinner, Mr. Sholl and I toured the new dormitory under Bobby's guidance, visiting the Alpha Chi suite and the Bobby-Peg suite on the fourth floor. The trio of us drifted over to the gym then, saw the end of football signal practice, and watched the Demie-Kappa Sig basketball game.

Bobby and I called on Mrs. Phillips a few minutes after the game. I talked with Rolland and Burns awhile, then went back to the Sem to chat with Bobby. As we strolled into the parlors, she remarked that no one would be there at that time of day. BUT in those dim depths, we found Vera and Bahr on one davenport, Cal and his girl on another. Just like old times.

Banquet at the Cameron House at 7:00 – 80 men sat down to it. The speeches were unusually fine, and I enjoyed it all. Rolland copied down two pages of stories to use in sermons! He left then for the drive back. I was just as glad you didn't have to take that long night ride with him, even though I wanted so to have you!

'Fraid I just must stop, sweetheart. I'll finish the story in my next note. Tomorrow is a hard evening, with a basketball game and swim in Camden.

Always YOUR very own,
Ken *

Wednesday afternoon, March 7, 1928, Philadelphia to Buffalo

My Lady dear,

It was nearly eleven when I reached home last evening, and I've been busy finishing up several ads for Mr. Cecil to take to Scranton tonight.

I'd reached the banquet in my chronicle of the weekend. I sat between Rolland & the Rev. Hobart Evans '21. Neither smokes, so I didn't suffer as much as usual at such functions. There were a lot of speeches, as there always are at a banquet of Demostheneans, but I enjoyed them almost without exception.

Geddes and I went off to his house soon after midnight. Our car was to start back at 8:30 next morning, but when I first saw the light of day, it was 20 minutes after 8:00! By the time I'd said farewell to Bobby, I had to ride off without breakfast! My hunger was appeased when we stopped for a huge dinner in Lancaster. Home at 5:30, supper, unpacking, and BED.

Yesterday the phone rang, and a booming voice said, "Kenneth, this is Mr. Fry. Dr. Hunt (Our exalted Bucknell President & Mr. Fry's personal friend) is in the lobby to see you!"

I calmed myself, straightened my tie, and trotted down to see the Bucknell brass – President Hunt and my old biology prof. Docky Stewart. Mr. Fry chatted with us a little (they evidently had just finished a conference), and then left us. Docky and I talked quite a while before he had to depart for another date uptown. It was good of Dr. Hunt to take time to see me, and I appreciated it immensely, for I've always admired him. He said Mr. Fry told him I was doing splendidly.

I mailed a card to Attie today that may amuse her a little. It is not particularly appropriate, but it was the best I could find.

With all the love in the world for you, sweetheart, I'm always   *   *   *
Your own Ken

I'm enclosing check for the Penny Fund. How much now?

Thursday morning, March 8, 1928, Philadelphia to Buffalo

Lady, darling,

I haven't told you the story of the American-Hawaiian bulletin. With Conrad and Masefield and Melville at my elbow for reference, I ground out twenty-five tentative titles. From that list, we chose "Supercargo." The position of "supercargo" originated in the days of the packet and clipper. The uncertainty of sail, the dangers of the elements, and the slipshod handling accorded merchandise, made freight transit by water hazardous. For that reason, merchants who shipped together by a certain vessel employed a representative to oversee the stowing and handling of cargo, to take precautions for its safety, and to see it was delivered on time. The supercargo was a ranking officer of the ship, responsible only to owners of the merchandise entrusted to him.

Modern methods have largely removed the necessity for a supercargo, but the term is still current. It has the full flavor of the sea. To shippers it signifies vigilance, care, and the complete reliability of A-H service. Art Bureau worked out an effective format and design, and the preliminary dummy went off to San Francisco yesterday.

Good to know your blood pressure reached normal, for a day at least. Now we'll do our darnedest to keep it there! I hope two cold days in succession didn't give you the cold you feared. I'd be happy to warm you, sweetheart! My arms ache to have you close within them. Then, snug and warm, we'd lose all track of time, remembering only love, conscious only of each other. I know I need you – I think you need me. And we shall have each other soon!

Your adoring
Ken * * *

Friday afternoon, March 9, 1928, Philadelphia to Buffalo

My precious Caryl,

I had to escort Mother to the high school operetta last evening. The performance was unlike anything we ever dreamed of in my school days. Settings and costumes were gorgeous – representing months of work and creative effort. Voices were hardly of operatic calibre, but with a couple of graduate students playing the leads, they got by quite passably.

It was nearly 11:30 when we reached home. Wherefore another newless, loveless note from the office today. I never seem eloquent in my noon hours, after eating – even though I eat sparingly! [Ken's standard lunch: a glass of milk and a sandwich or a large cinnamon roll, total cost 20¢, at Philadelphia's famous Horn & Hardart Automat. This cafeteria pioneered the field of vending machines. Choosing items from rotating, glass-enclosed shelves, then inserting the required number of nickels in front of each, made food in that slot magically available. Occasional Horn & Hardart meals provided an exciting treat during my childhood.]

Tonight I must run out to the settlement house to make sure of the magician who is scheduled for our "Mystery Night" program at the "Y" on Monday. Perhaps I can pick up a few skulls 'n things from my medical friends for atmosphere.

Tomorrow, Len & I will see our first game of professional ice hockey – fastest game in the world – at the Arena in Phila. A friend gave us tickets – $3.30 each, centre section, on the aisle! Oh, I want us to share things like this – and everything else – my life through.

Always * *

Ken

278 • Flivverin' With You

Saturday, March 24, 1928, Philadelphia to Buffalo

After March 9, two weeks of letters are missing. In the envelope dated March 24, Ken sends Caryl a one-sentence note and page proofs of three Dixon Eldorado pencil ads he's written. Double postage (4¢) was required.

A world of love for you, dear,
KENNETH W. SLIFER
but little time to tell it! *

Sunday evening, March 25, 1928, Woodbury to Buffalo

My precious Caryl,

I'm proving my love for you tonight with a rigorous and convincing test! I'm here in my room writing, while Collier's Radio Hour goes merrily on downstairs. That's the one hour I try always not to miss! They have the most diversified and entertaining hour on the air. Music, vocal and instrumental, stories from the current issue of Collier's dramatically told by a fine group of "air-actors," and a distinguished guest speaker. I've heard Commander Byrd, John D. Rockefeller, Jr., Gov. Al Smith, Edgar Guest, Bruce Barton, etc. Tonight's address is to be by Eva Le Gallienne, who does splendid things in her Civic Repertory Theatre in New York. And Eddie Rickenbacker, famous war ace, also will speak. So you see, if you haven't before, I do love you dearly!

The day has been extra full. I spent most of the afternoon as chauffeur for the lady in charge of the Sunday School Home Department, distributing quarterlies. Then, up to Clem's with pledge cards, to settle up. (We worked intensively Friday evening, and I cleaned up the loose ends yesterday. I wasn't fearfully proud of our total collections, but we did well comparatively. People are nice when they know you represent the "Y," but I loathe that sort of banditry!)

After supper, Len arrived from Lewisburg and spent an hour telling all the news. One pertinent bit: he saw Mary Schilling revisiting the campus, with a man in a coupé, and wearing a diamond ring! Can you illumine our puzzled souls? Rolland took his ring back, didn't he?

Honey girl, you're part of everything I do, think, and feel. Tonight, striding back from Clem's, toward a rich red and purple sunset, with a silver wisp of moon overhead, my heart was aching to have you there, with your arm linked through mine (even if it isn't proper!) and pressing against me, in the eloquent, unspoken caress we know so well. Oh Caryl sweet, your Ken loves you with such fierce intensity, with such infinite tenderness, that no one else could ever enter in!

Your very own
Ken *

Tuesday evening, March 27, 1928
Buffalo to Woodbury

My own Dearest Ken,

Today was slightly shorter, but hardly noticeably so. "Cudworth" is as fierce a boss as ever. He doesn't smoke or swear, but give me Mr. Hemphill, with all his smoking & swearing!

I like the Dixon ads very much. Of course, I prefer letters to ads, but when there's no time for letters, an ad written by you is next best.

Mother got a permanent wave today – one of the stores was selling them half price, so Mother thot she'd save me time now that I'm so busy & not energetic either. It's a very pretty wave. I'd like one myself, but would rather wait till nearer September so that I can look my nicest for you!

After writing you last night, I went right to bed, for last week was so full & strenuous I've been especially tired, & I don't want to retard the gaining process. I wanted to sew, but health is more important than holes or hems. 'Bye, dear, and a goodnight kiss for you!

> Your love, my Ken-dear, is a boon
> God gave me when I needed you.
> By night your love, dear, is the moon;
> By day, a glimpse of heaven's blue.

Your
Sweetheart

"Wenzdee" morning, March 28, 1928
Philadelphia to Buffalo

Lady o' mine,

A dozen sorts of apologies! Monday evening, I went to bed at 8:30, for the preceding week and weekend were most strenuous. I expected to write you from the office yesterday, but a phone call sent me into Art Bureau as soon as I got back from lunch (even before the noon hour ended), and the rush continued. In fact, I worked till after 5:30, before going up to the bowling alleys.

This morning, I resolved to make amends, but there's little to tell. Last evening, I bowled (last match of the season) and hurried home to hear the last of "Trader Horn" on Eveready Hour. I've been reading him in snatches as preparation for his only American broadcast. Have you read his book, honey? It's full of flavor and rich philosophy.

I forgot to tell you of the fascinating Squibb movies. Non-technical explanations and carefully-planned pictures showed the culture and preparation of diphtheria Toxin-Antitoxin, of smallpox Vaccine, and of Scarlet Fever Toxin. The Squibb Biological Laboratories furnish the bulk of those supplies to the medical profession. All the best minds of the Ayer organization were there, about twenty-five of us! A-hem! But seriously, there were only three writers included, so my invitation must have been made with a definite purpose.

I can appreciate that it was hard to see the Remington Rand [six-week salesman training] school dissolve. I'll be glad to look over the class book you helped prepare and the mementoes you gathered. I never had the slightest desire to be a salesman until the last six weeks, when I fought a fierce urge to enter the employ of Remington Rand! I'm sure I wouldn't waste a single minute at that school! How lucky those boys were! But they seem to have been properly appreciative.

Oh, Ladysweet, the best copywriter in all the world couldn't find words to phrase my love for you! And since I'm far from that, I can't either! What a poignant heart-hunger your fragrant note unloosed last evening! My darling dear, I LOVE you so! *

Always   *   *   *
Ken

Thursday afternoon, March 29, 1928
Philadelphia to Buffalo

Caryl, dear,

Your Ken is getting big and brute-like, Lady mine. Witness my collar size. When I entered college as a child, I wore a 14½ collar (which Len & other acquaintances still find free and full). By Commencement, I was wearing a 15. But in the two years since, I've moved through two successive sizes! Months ago, 15½ shirts were too small for me, but I had a lot with plenty of wear left in them. Last week I was lucky enough to sell six shirts, and now I'm replacing them all with 16s. No one I know, except Rolland, wears as large or larger a collar. And since a large neck is typical of wrestlers, prize fighters, and the lower orders of male mammals, I must be lapsing into the primordial, reverting to type, and all that sort of thing!

Mr. Black's answer to my letter of two months ago arrived at last yesterday. It is splendid and most encouraging, even tho he said precisely what I expected. [Mr. Black's letter, saved among the Slifers' important papers, is included below.] With so much helpful advice, September just must come true. And our own love is so strong and fine we're sure to make a go of it. I have to hope, you see, to make these days endurable.

I shall always be, if not eloquently, at least lovingly yours,
Ken *

Dear Kenneth:

I purposely delayed writing in reply to your letter of some weeks ago, because I hoped I might see you face to face. It now seems unlikely, so I shall say just a word here.

First, I believe you and Caryl can get along on the salary you name as hoping to receive by next fall. It depends more upon the two young people concerned, than upon $5 or $10 more or less of a weekly salary. Some couples would starve on what others would thrive on. Careful budgeting, persistently followed, is worth an extra $5, or even $10, a week more.

The salary you name does not leave much margin to take care of protracted illnesses, but there it is assumed you do not start with an empty treasury. Furthermore, unless N. W. Ayer & Son have changed their policy, you would be carried on their pay roll for quite a time, at full pay. I was receiving $100 a month when I married in 1901, got along on it (My, but we did have to count the pennies!), and had great joy in doing so.

As regards securing that salary increase, what do you think of this method? Casually tell the proper person of your hopes concerning marriage; tell him that the consummation of your plans depends upon your salary. Say that you have no desire to use your hopes as a lever to secure an unearned increase, but that if it is probable you shall be earning more at that (a stated) time, you will plan accordingly. In short, it seems to me some such approach would introduce the subject in a way to secure a sympathetic (metallic as well as sentimental) hearing.

The idea I am trying to convey is that you can avoid a plain, straightout request for a "raise." That form of securing a raise is usually questionable.

Married men usually are worth more than single men. They are steadier, must be steadier. Further, it is usual to give fuller consideration to needs of married men.

I hope you did not feel that I was intruding advice in my former letter. I did not mean to do so. But my own experience of married "blessedness" has been such that I want those I love to have the same or similar experiences. It's God's appointed way for full earthly happiness for His regenerated children, and those who enter upon that road, hand in hand, with hearts full of love for each other and trust in Him can't fail of happiness, even tho' the Heavens fall. (See Psalms 37 – 4 & 5)

Your training (Caryl's also) has fitted you to start on a fairly small salary. I feel sure you can make it go. Were Caryl my daughter, I should gladly trust her to you on $35.

Our love to you all, and may the good Lord prosper you in your work and hopes!

Always your friend,
HAB

P.S. Naturally, I am happy because you were good enough to share your confidences with me.

Mr. Black's name appears as Howard A. Black on Ken's list of wedding invitees.

Friday afternoon, March 30, 1928, Philadelphia to Buffalo

My own lady,

A note to tell you I love you & to assure you I'd write reams if I could. Last evening was filled with kids 'n' things, and today has been busy without much being accomplished. We made lead soldiers last night, popped corn, listened to John Barrymore, Norma Talmadge, Charlie Chaplin, Douglas Fairbanks, et al. on the radio, and had a general good time. It was the most pleasant evening I've ever spent with the class. Tonight I'll write the letter you deserve for the loving missive that came yesterday. Len's kid brother is here; they invited me to go to a show, but I declined in your favor – because I love you, Ladysweet, so infinitely and so very constantly.

Ken * * *

Friday evening, March 30, 1928, Woodbury to Buffalo

My precious Caryl,

I could match your "Saint Patrick's paper" if I really cared to. But far more important than the color of your letter, honey, was the love I found in it! There is something strengthening in the knowledge that we share the same tremendous, tumultuous longing, the same fierce yearning for each other.

Probably our hearts and heads were guiding each other's, for the same superb moon streamed down on us both, and it must have linked us a little. Your heartfelt plea to come to you almost takes me out of myself, precious mine. There's a desperate urge to do the things you ask – and the things you left unspoken. June shall find us free to whisper to each other the half-thoughts we dare not trust to paper. Oh, darling dear, I love you and want you so unutterably! *

Last Saturday was so warm and bright I couldn't resist getting out my tennis racquets to look them over. Strings are all unbroken, but one bat is so loose it must be restrung for any sort of play. $6–$8 for that, and $1.50 for balls – expenses we didn't figure into our budget! But I'll have all supplies for this season and be earning more by the next! Incurable optimist!

An intensive membership drive added 60–70 new members to the Country Club. A lot don't play tennis, but there is certain to be added activity on the courts. I signed up Betty Wilson and Gert Hunter (remember, they're not both girls!) and have prospects for the week that remains.

If you'd mentioned Mary's retention of the ring before this, I'd quite forgotten it. Her attitude is inexplicable. Mother, Len, and

I were not a little puzzled by it. There is no apparent justification for such a stand, and it rather scatters the shreds of sympathy I thought I felt for her.

A letter came from Rolland yesterday. He surely is busy with his church. But he's growing more wordy all the time, more like a "professional" old-school preacher. Very possibly it's the right technique for the people of Conesus, but it's so different from the clear, conversational style of advertising (which is also what I like from the pulpit) that it will never appeal to me.

Miss Agnes Danhower, secretary to the head of our dept., is leaving to be married. Writers report to her when they leave for any special reason, or take a day off. She's responsible for attendance, or at least knowledge of our whereabouts. She's a charming girl – 26 or 27 – and so pleasant that everyone likes her. So Printing Dept. has made a nicely bound blank book, and each writer and artist in the dept. is filling a page with sketch, verse, or sentiment. I didn't have long for the job (I enclose my "Lines"), but I think my production is up to the average. Some of the effusions, though, are very clever. A group of craftsmen like ours are capable of amusing flights. I'm sure she'll treasure it.

All my love, sweetheart,

Ken * * *

Tuesday afternoon, April 3, 1928, Philadelphia to Buffalo

My own Lady,

Agreed! We must do something about Uncle Sam. He's getting too careless altogether. You received no note Saturday – I got none – and we both, I assume, found two at home Monday evening. From Friday evening to Monday evening is entirely too long to be letterless when one's in love! There's only one remedy, and that is to remove the endless distance that makes notes unnecessary. Let's try that soon, honey, for I'm getting desprit!

I planned to write during my lunch hour, as I usually do on Toosdays (which come after Mundees when we have "Y" meetings). But it was such a delightful day, Len and I decided to walk across the Delaware River bridge. With chocolate bars for sustenance, we set out, striding confidently with the air of conquerors. It's half a mile to the bridge, and the structure itself is two miles end to end. We walked to the middle, admired the scenery and the horizons, then hurried back, arriving about five minutes late. Your brilliant mathematical brain can easily figure we walked a good three miles in the hour at our disposal. It is a really interesting trip – one that you and I can enjoy together when we are feeling especially healthy, husky, and hikey!

Last evening we journeyed to the gym with the high school outfit. Chick Carter had brought down two of the Penn wrestling team, and they gave an hour of demonstration and instruction. Following the matwork, the crowd chose two teams and played basketball. The high school kids are in pretty good condition, and Len and I were hardpressed to keep pace with them. I'm a little stiff and sore today, but it was fun and corking good exercise. It helped toughen my feet, too, for tennis season. They usually blister a bit when I wear sneaks for the first.

Remember, won't you, that your Ken is loving you, adoring you, wanting you always.

K * * *

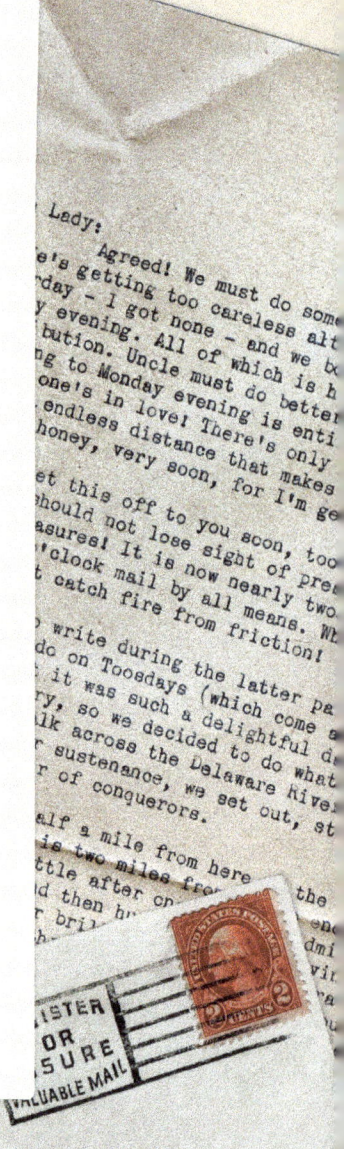

Tuesday evening, April 3, 1928, Woodbury to Buffalo

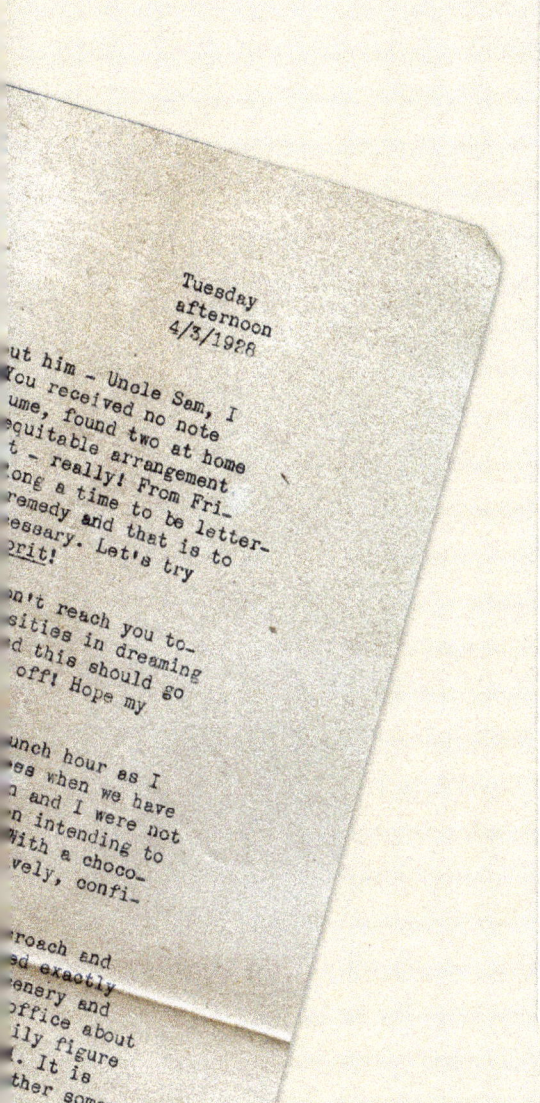

Dearest mine,

Your noontime note arrived on schedule today. This half-sheet of paper I found in my drawer is just what I need, for it's been only six hours since I sent you a letter. And the basketball last night, and the bridge hike today have left me exceedingly tired – healthily so, of course.

I'm glad Attie is improving steadily. Give her my regards, please. The radio will help entertain her, and I know it will give you all pleasure. It will be good to feel sometimes, when I'm listening to an especially fine program, that you are hearing it, too!

Congratulations are in order for the Pi Phis. Bobby refereed the game in which they won the championship, and she gave me a graphic account of it. It carried me back to the days when I stole stealthily down the hill to watch my Lady play.

It will be good when Mr. Hemphill comes back to end your present "reign of terror." I shall be almost as glad as you are! One thing is encouraging. If you can like Mr. H. so well, in spite of his smoking and swearing, chances are that you'll be kind to my more flagrant faults. *

What glorious days and nights these last few have been – and a gorgeous moon! My longing deepens to a desperate intensity! I'm hungering for you, honey, because I love you so.

Always
Ken * * *

Thursday afternoon, April 5, 1928
Philadelphia to Buffalo

Caryl mine,

Sometimes, remembering the effort that we must make to maintain our schedule to write, I think it would be better for us to forego a good part of it. But love answers, "Long evenings, lots of them, without a letter from my Lady? What a ghastly proposal!"

The painters began work on our house yesterday, and there were a lot of odd jobs to be done so they could work uninterruptedly. I pried the duplicate house numbers (the former 131 and the newer 19) off the porch pillars, took awning hooks out of the window frames, and demounted an old clothes line arrangement from the back porch. I carried all the window screens down from the attic, patched two where the football had gone through, and built a wire corral to hold the leaves I expect to rake out of the shrubbery.

What a glorious moon there was last night, honey! Just on the strength of it, Len spent 35¢ to call up GG! Then, a little before bedtime, we took a couple of turns around the block. It was like a real summer evening, made for lovers.

My desk in the corner here behind the door is poorly placed. It's growing warmer every moment, and perspiration puts a damper on my eloquence. Ladysweet, I think of you always.

Your very own
Ken * *

Saturday morning, April 7, 1928, Philadelphia to Buffalo

My own Caryl,

I hope you don't object too seriously to the lack of seriousness in this missive – or to its brevity, which in this case is NOT the soul of wit. I hope the card I sent yesterday will reach you before Easter Sunday. I want you to have it, honey, for a tremendous world of love went with it. I do love you, adore you, Ladysweet!

Last evening Bobby & I drove to Merchantville to visit Dave and Marian Jones just as a great red moon rose over the horizon, & drove back around midnight, when it was high in the heavens. Oh, it was a gorgeous night. The drive was nearer 15 miles than the 8 or 10 I told you. We played several rounds of bridge, then grew childish & amused ourselves with Parcheesi & Hearts for the rest of the evening.

ALL my love is yours, precious mine.
K * * *

While You Love Me

By ANNE CAMPBELL.

WHILE you love me as you do,
All my heart is bound in gold.
Arrows cannot pierce it through!
Like those doughty knights of old,
I am guarded by the might
Of your love, which is my light.

While you love me as you do,
Magic armor seals me 'round.
Should it rain, the skies are blue.
Fragrant paths my feet have found.
When the sun steals far away,
My heart whispers of the day.

While you love me as you do,
In my spirit there is peace.
Faith is blossoming anew!
All my troubled doubtings cease.
Tranquilly I walk abroad,
Loved by you, and loved of God!
(Copyright, 1928.)

Sunday evening, April 8, 1928, Woodbury to Buffalo

My own sweetheart,

What a gorgeous Easter day this has been – and how I've wanted you to share it with me! A hard storm last night, and a new, fresh sunny morning, seemed symbolic of the Resurrection. Our special Easter offering at Sunday School amounted to more than $500. We have only 200 in the school, and since most are of modest means or actually poor, it was a generous outpouring – an average of $2.50 apiece. Our Junior Department (in which I am) turned in $60.11, from 40 boys and girls. We were elated at the showing. An overflow congregation at church, and a fine service. Fifteen to be baptized this evening.

Yesterday afternoon was so fine, Len and I labored lustily in the yard and around the house. The painters had finished with house painting just the day before, so we took off storm doors, put up the porch enclosure, washed all downstairs windows, put in screens, and gave the garage a thorough cleaning – taking out everything in it. We were grimy and tired when we finished, but we accomplished quite a bit.

Early in the afternoon, Eleanor Pierce invited me to a big party for the evening. She's a Mount Holyoke graduate, engaged to a Haverford chap who won the Middle Atlantic college singles title, and is now in Yale Law School. I played tennis with him twice last summer. Eleanor is a peach of a girl, clever and attractive. We were in high school together, and she lives only two blocks away in a rather large home. Her party list had been "couples," and one chap could not come. She needed another man desperately, so I accepted.

It was an elaborate affair – formal – about 35 or 40 guests. Eight bridge tables of 4 each, and two or three who did not play. My winning streak remains unbroken; my score brot me second prize – a good-looking case of real leather containing score pad, pencil, and two fine decks of cards.

At midnight the tables were set up in a long row, and a lavish supper served. Home a little after 1 A.M. Then I tried to write verses and paint Easter cards for Mother, Bobby, and Len, but I was too tired to go on, so I tumbled into bed.

I'm sorry your father is unhappy in his work in Buffalo – glad that a new opportunity has come when he wants it. Naturally, I shall tell no one but Mother about it.

It is good of your folks to offer us furniture, but I'm afraid that shipping it to Philadelphia would be prohibitive. You might select a few pieces that you want most. But I doubt if the expense for it all is within the range of our bankbook. And I'd like you to have a piano, and keep up with your music. Underneath everything, sweetheart, is the feeling that I'd like to start with just our own things, that we'd picked for ourselves – even if we have to sit on soapboxes and eat from a card table! Foolish perhaps, but I'll think it through more fully.

Oh, Caryl precious, I'll be so glad when I can have you in my arms and talk to you – rather than across 500 miles of space. Eager to be your own

Ken

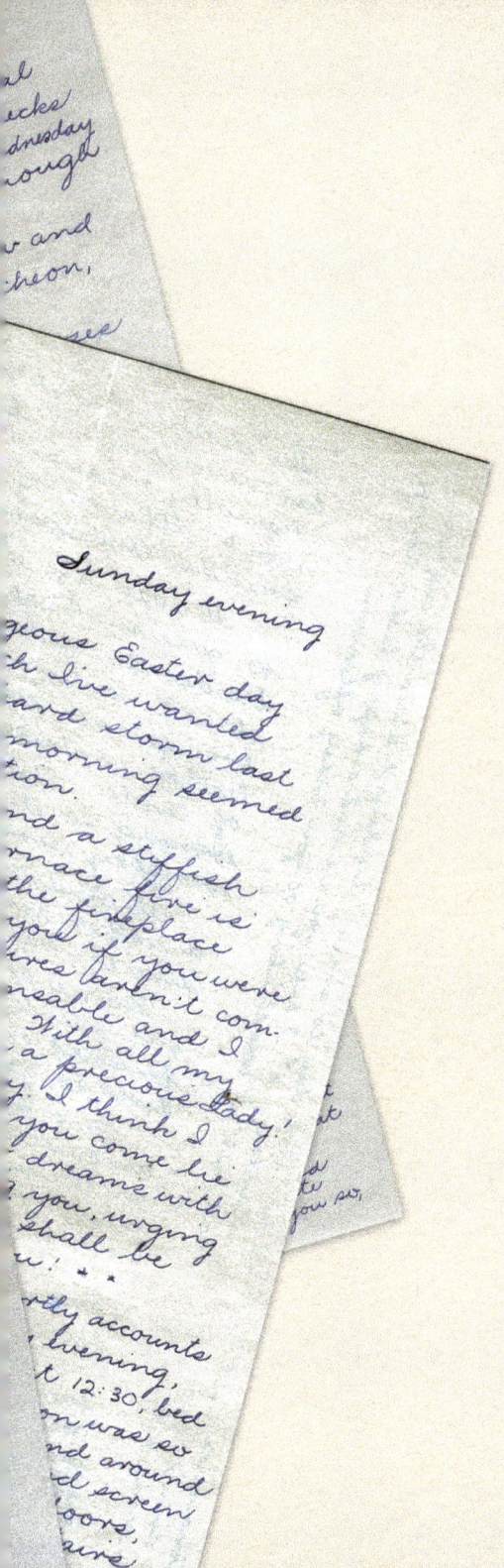

Thursday Noon, April 12, 1928
Tonawanda (near Buffalo) to Woodbury

Caryl's first typed letter, from her job with Remington Rand.

My Precious Sweetheart,

Can you smell the smoke? Well, I can – mos' awful much, for Mr. Hemphill is back. But I'm awfully glad, and you should have seen how the morning whizzed by. He's given me lots of odd jobs that are fun.

I got up discouraged this morning, for I actually felt weak after a long night's rest. I am baffling to myself, and generally disgusted. Because I'm wanting September so hard, the strengthening process seems desperately slow. But I have good news. I have my license at last! Mother called to tell me, and I almost shot thru the window. But I had to be circumspect, since Mr. Hemphill was sitting right here. When I told him, he said, "Well, you can't go riding this afternoon."

But now we can take turns driving on our Honeymoon! I'm so delighted I don't know what to do. Now, please teach me to drive the flivver. I've forgotten all you taught me long ago, Lover-mine – when a squeeze of my arm as I was changing seats with you nearly made me steer into a telephone pole! I've started to think ahead to the time in September when we'll be driving along the road together, with two weeks of heaven ahead, and no foreshadowing thot of goodbyes. Then we can sit as close as we like when we're shooting along the road, and give ourselves up to complete happiness.

No hope of the school going to Buffalo. But from the viewpoint of everyone concerned, except me, the school is far better here – a little ways away from the wicked city! These men aren't allowed to bring their wives along, and six weeks away from the influence of home leaves room for loads of things. The school will start here, then move several blocks nearer Buffalo, but still in North Tonawanda. The moving will lend a little excitement, and even if the building is a wreck, I won't have to suffer long. How carefree I can be, with a life-long job awaiting me!

The other day, when I mentioned something about being tired, Aunt Anna said, "Yes, I suppose when you're married, you'll lie in bed in the mornings and let Ken get his own breakfast."

And I said, "No sir – it will be too much of a privilege to eat breakfast with him!" I don't want to miss anything with you, dearest, cause I've longed for those times, and dreamed of them so long.

Loving you so,
Your Caryl

Sunday evening, April 22, 1928
Buffalo to Philadelphia

A small card; the envelope is missing, as are the previous ten days of letters.

> Sweetheart mine,
>
> I love you, love you, <u>love</u> you, dearest Ken. I've a longing growing greater as the days & months go by. Oh, how can I wait till June – for the feel of your hands, your lips, your face, your hair – You once more.
>
> No news. Nothing except choir rehearsal last night, a ride into the woods in search of flowers this afternoon, & a solo part this evening in church.
>
> Does a sense of loneliness ever almost overwhelm you, dear, leaving you despairing in your longing? Well, that's the way I feel – I want you so. You've become so dear to me, and the separation is increasingly hard to bear. How could I ever wait for you till June 1929? I'm so glad you're going to let September find me for always
>
> Your very Own *

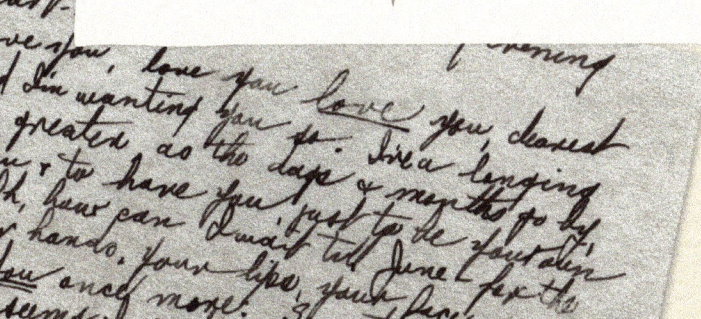

Tuesday afternoon, April 24, 1928
Philadelphia to Buffalo

No letters from Ken exist since his missive of April 8, 1928. In the interim, he was given a big project that he refers to as the "Advertising Advertising" assignment – a series of 14 separate pieces about the advertising industry to be published in magazines and newspapers in 1929. He relishes the important job for "the glory (and cash) one accrues," as well as for "the earnest work," because it will help lead to Caryl and Ken's Someday.

> Dearest mine,
>
> I've been working steadily at the "Advertising Advertising" assignment, but I still have eight pieces to do, and only five days left. With all the routine jobs as well, it will mean steady, earnest work. I may even have to work thru noon hours, if they are to be finished on time.
>
> We had a good attendance at the group meeting to hear Senator Francis B. Davis [N.J. State Senator, 1924–1931, from Gloucester County, where Woodbury is located] – president of the Senate and one-time acting governor of the state. He was earnest and interesting, and pleased the boys for more than an hour. He explained the organization of our state government, and then told stories – dating back to the days when Woodrow Wilson was governor of New Jersey. Len and I were quite impressed by his manifest honesty and sincerity.

I wish I could believe that all our state officials were of equally high calibre.

I'm glad that you enjoyed "My Maryland" so hugely. But structurally and musically, I thought it much weaker than other shows of this type – and I saw it presented by the original cast. It is so luridly melodramatic! But I have no right or wish to spoil your pleasure, by imposing my own opinion. Too, that I went to see it with Mary didn't help to make me appreciate it any the more. You and I are likely to differ often in matters dramatic and literary, but it must not, will not, make any difference between us. It's just one contrasting trait of character – no more important or significant than our varying reactions to typewriter and fountain pen. I've always liked your letters, Lady mine, but you do write unusually fine ones on the machine, while I struggle along despairingly with the same medium.

Oh, darling dear, when days are busy, hurried ones, I want you, love you, most. My head aches for the precious pillow that only you can give, for the soothing caress of your lips and fingers.

My Ladysweet, I love you!
K *

Wednesday afternoon, April 25, 1928
Philadelphia to Buffalo

My precious Lady,

Last evening's fragrant note was so full of love, so full of you, that I can't let it pass without this brief answer. I'm sure I caught your mood, dear, for I go through it so often myself. Days – and nights – when there's little news. Just a despairing, driving love that urges one to write. And an aching longing that baffles expression.

I came home tired and worn last evening, wanting you, oh, so desperately. And the perfume that clung to your card, the words upon it, stirred me tremendously – then soothed me somehow. It seemed almost to give me you for a moment. But Ladysweet, I cannot be content much longer with letters. I must have you in my arms again or I shall crumple with the strain. I'm waiting, living only for June – and you. Then – September, and the joy of life together!

Always your own adoring
Ken * *

Friday afternoon, April 27, 1928, Philadelphia to Buffalo

My own Caryl,

Excitement yesterday was occasioned by my being assigned four new accounts. They are, in order of importance, New Haven Clock Company, International Salt Co., Western Pacific Railway, and Robb-Ross. The clock schedule provides for half pages in the Saturday Evening Post and similar magazines in black and white, with full color pages next winter, to announce a new line of alarm clocks. The salt and railway accounts are self-explanatory. Robb-Ross manufactures maple syrup and kindred products, about which I know nothing now.

I'm glad to have the added assignments, for I think I can handle them all right as soon as the Advertising Ad series is finished next week. I'll be a busy boy, but the more work one can accomplish, the more glory (and cash) one accrues. My Ad Ad job is nearly finished now. I have eleven done and three full days to do three more.

A telegram from Geddes yesterday says he made the relay team as anchor man. Which means he's the best quarter miler in school now. We must be proud of "our son." This morning he called to assure me he'd come down for the night. They run this afternoon and again tomorrow.

Tonight, Mother, Geddes, and I will go to the high school senior play – Booth Tarkington's "Seventeen," the logical sequel to "Penrod," which Bobby's class gave last year.

Mrs. Buttolph acted with characteristic lack of convention in announcing our engagement for us! Characteristic too that she should misspell my name. That's nothing new to me, though it never has been done in an engagement notice! You'll have to get used to such mistakes, dear, for our last name can be rendered (and is) in seventeen separate ways.

Adoring you so,
K * *

Ken adds: "I am enclosing a poem that caught the strength and glow of our love."

LOVE IN LIFE

WITH some it is the brief flare of a match,
Cupped with both hands against a flow of air
Or a quick-taken breath.

With some it is the great blaze of a beacon
Built on a headland
In a storm;
Flattened by blasts,
Dragged sideways by gales,
Roaring upward in lulls;
Spit at by spray,
Licking up sleet,
Climbing on rain,
Blazing all night in the storm!

— Abbie Huston Evans

Saturday evening, April 29, 1928, Philadelphia to Buffalo

My precious, precious Caryl,

Oh, honey-girl, I do love you, adore you so! I know I do, for only a tremendous love could make me write a letter as long as I think this will be! After writing all day as "work," "job," it's not much fun to do the same thing all evening! But I like to write to you, sweetheart, because I want my life to fuse with yours forever. *

The weather is pertinent to discussion of my chiefest news. A cold rain yesterday and a lashing, driving storm from the northeast. Today a drenching, penetrating drizzle that became hail, so tennis was rained out for the fourth successive week, and the local season is still closed tight. In place of the tennis, I visited two doctors! No need for alarm, dear. The outcome of my double consultation: I'm to be operated on and a small piece of bone cut from my nose.

You may remember my telling you months ago I was beginning to sleep with my mouth open at night – and for some time it has seemed increasingly difficult to breathe through my nose. The nasal passages, I thought, were becoming constricted. During exercise, they could not deliver an adequate amount of air and clogged at the first sign of cold.

Today our family physician examined me and gave his opinion (it proved correct), then sent me to a nose-and-throat specialist who practices in Philadelphia but lives in Woodbury. The latter explained that the septum bone between the nasal passages is projecting more and more into the left nostril, partly cutting the passage of air. It can be cut away readily without ill effect and is the most common operation (next to tonsil removal) he is called on to perform.

Your Ken will go under the knife May 16, in the splendid private hospital here. The doctor will come from the city to operate. I missed a pun: Local operation, with local anaesthetic!

The most painful part will be paying for it! Doctor's fee, including examination and dressing for several days afterwards, is $50. Cost of operating room is $10, and bedroom for one night about $6.50. At least $65 out of my savings!

Sunday afternoon

The cost is a blow to me, but apparently it is necessary. The doctor has known me since I was a kid, knows I'm anxious to be married, and I'm sure the fee is minimum. But that is just the sort of thing that makes me fearful of marrying on so little. If either of us gets sick, the cost may run far beyond our tiny reserve. Our budget could not stretch even over a sum like $65. Yet, I don't know how I can live longer without you, Ladysweet!

Vacation notices were posted, and selection of dates is supposed to be chosen from the period between June 4 and Sept. 8. Time outside of that is by special permission of a member of the firm. Accordingly, I plan to see Mr. Lewis the latter part of this week to ask whether I can expect to be making $35–$40 by summer. I hope to find him sympathetic, but as the time comes near, I'm increasingly apprehensive. I'm progressing as fast or faster than the other young writers but don't know whether I'm yet worth $35 a week. This profession is intricate – and can only be learned by slow, patient work and experience – in which one's mistakes are expensive for the firm. But I'll try to be tactful and not too frightened, in my interview.

Your place card was certainly effective dear. What a clever, adorable Lady you are! It will be fun to go through life with such an ingenious, resourceful – and good-looking – wife! Your characters were well done, too, and I found them as indecipherable as any Chinese laundry ticket I ever saw. Fact is, I puzzled over the card for fully five minutes before I read your letter and found the explanation.

I hope you have been able to get everything in readiness for another school – without tiring yourself too much. It was a real responsibility that Mr. Hemphill handed you.

Geddes was with us Friday night, and he, Mother, and I went to the senior play. Settings were effective and elaborate, and the kids certainly eclipsed by a big margin any of the plays we gave in "the good old days." Careful coaching had done a lot, and this year there were two dogs on the stage, both of whom behaved themselves perfectly. They allowed themselves to be mauled and manhandled with good grace, and the Peke yapped just when he should.

Oh, darling dear, sleepy time serves always to intensify my longing for you! The memory of you, the fragrance of you, the beauties of you, the pulse of your heart 'neath my fingers or lips, the soft, sweet beauty of your breasts, the cool, lingering caress of your arm around me – a hundred things come back to carry me out of myself! The combination of spiritual love and physical craving is a powerful one that I cannot long withstand. My Ladysweet, I love you, reverence you, want you for my own for always.

Ken * *

Tuesday noon, May 1, 1928, Philadelphia to Buffalo

Sweetheart, mine,

Five P.M. is the deadline for my 14 "ADVERTISING Advertising" pieces of copy. I'm halfway through the very last now, but it must be finished and turned over to the stenographers in time for them to type it nicely and get it back for my OK. So I don't dare take time for a full letter now. I've put a deal of work and thought into it, for it means a lot to me – to both of us – and I think it's a good series. There's a real thrill to thinking that when they begin to appear in magazines and newspapers in 1929, you will have been my very own Lady for several months!

It was a dear and amusing card that I found last evening. Where did you find the letters, honey? You must have juggled them amazingly from their original form. My clever, resourceful Lady! I do love you, Lady mine, with all my heart.

Ken * *

P. S. Baseball in the gym with the "Y" group last night. I hope to play tennis for the first time this evening. We can now, with daylight saving. But it will probably rain again!

I have 200 more pennies for you, dear. I'll send a check, as soon as I find time to write it.

Wednesday, May 2, 1928, Philadelphia to Buffalo

My precious Lady,

For the first time in two weeks, I can write without the stifled, harried feeling of working under pressure. Last evening, I turned in a full fourteen advertisements for the Ad-Ad series. I'm hoping several are good enough to warrant a place in the annual collection. I'll know nothing about their fate, tho, until the edition appears in the fall. Now I am comparatively free, and glowing with the consciousness of a real job, carefully completed.

We finally pried the tennis season open last evening. My first opponent ranks a notch above me on the tennis ladder. Our game was of a calibre much higher than expected on opening night. My service broke hard and fast. Ground strokes were rather wild. I won the first set 6-1, dropped two others 1-6, 5-7. A strenuous dose for a début. This morning I was so stiff I could hardly fall out of bed! Exercising all winter – basketball, baseball, and several swims – I thought I was in good shape. But tennis tears at muscles nothing else will touch. We'll have to work to keep young together! Neither office work nor house work is conducive to physical fitness.

I shall go up for the Demie house party next week. Len wants to take GG, Al Purks intends to take a carful, Chick Carter would like to see Bucknell, Bobby wants me to come. Ken Van den Bree (Demie freshman) is eager to take Bobby to the house party, as he does everywhere else, and I don't like to claim her from him. I shall be a dignified alumnus and go as a stag (not stagger) to watch the boys and girls enjoy themselves, reminiscing of the halcyon days when I was in college. Bored, superior air to cover an aching heart!

Your last note sounded as if you were tired and nervous. Such a round of activity as you recounted! I want you well and happy when you come to me – for your sake and mine. Oh, my Ladysweet, I love you! And I'm longing to show you, tell you, with my lips, my arms, myself!

YOUR Ken *

Thursday afternoon, May 3, 1928, Philadelphia to Buffalo

Caryl, mine,

If you're to get this tomorrow, I must rattle along as fast as I can. I imagine you're glad to see the school begin again, for the variety it brings to the daily routine. I'm glad, for it dates the period until you come to me: June 9. Wishing for the end of school more eagerly than I ever did as a kid!

Of course I'll buy you a canal boat – or any other kind of a craft – Someday. Let's make it a yacht so we can get completely away from the rest of the world.

Last evening I went to prayer meeting with Mother, then play practice until 11 P.M. Church functions prevented rehearsals on the Tuesday-Thursday schedule this week. Tonight, I expect to play tennis and work the stiffness out of me.

Bobby spent last weekend with Phoebe Bloomfield, Alumni advisor to the Alpha Chi chapter. That's all the news, except I love you dearly and always shall!

Your Ken *

Friday afternoon, May 4, 1928, Philadelphia to Buffalo

My precious Lady,

I came in this morning resolved to make a desperate attempt to see Mr. Lewis, but he was in a conference all morning. Now he has put on his hat, lit his pipe, and gone out, presumably for the afternoon. I wish the matter were settled, for I don't relish the problem of broaching it. I've never had my heart and happiness so dependent on a single man and a single situation.

Just now is the worst possible time to even breathe the suggestion of a raise! Yesterday it was announced that R. J. Reynolds Co., makers of Camel cigarettes and Prince Albert tobaccos, and our largest single client, cut their advertising appropriation from nine million dollars to less than a million. Agencies charge straight 15% commission, and large as Advertising Headquarters is, a slash like that is perceptible. Mr. Lewis went to the council of war from which the announcement came, and he's probably not recovered yet. The new building, too, is another reason why I don't expect to be greeted with open arms.

My tennis rose to mid-season heights last night. I trimmed the club tennis chairman – two love sets! Something I'd never done. I ran my string of games to 14, before he took one. My service was breaking sharply, my ground strokes more accurate, than any time I can remember.

Honey girl, I love you, want you always,
Ken *

Saturday morning, May 5, 1928, Philadelphia to Buffalo

Caryl, darling,

Mr. Lewis won't be in today, so I can't see him till Monday. I'm half-glad, half-sorry. It is an ordeal to ask anything of him, for he has the steeliest blue eyes, the most disconcerting gaze, I've ever faced. I've never met anyone who so ruffled my composure. Most of the young writers find him as unnerving as I. In reality, he's not the granite figure he seems. So somehow I'll stumble thru my story But it would be easier to face anyone in the whole agency – even Mr. Fry.

I hope the showers hold off, for it's to be a gala afternoon at the country club – open house and reception for new members, with tennis and golf matches, bridge under the trees and on the porches, tea at 4, and a dance this evening. You should be here as a new member! If you're not feeling well enough to play, you could sit in the new wicker furniture for tennis spectators and watch awhile; then I'd join you at tea time. Wouldn't that be fun?

The fragrance of your Tuesday-Thursday letter made it all the more precious to me. With the love in the letter, it helped bring you closer. The moon is gorgeous every evening, the yards like fairyland. Apple blossoms everywhere, pink and white. In Jennings' yard beside our porch, there is an apple tree, a cherry tree, and a pink dogwood in full bloom – and a huge, blazing bed of tulips. Oh, sweetheart mine, if I could only have you!

Adoring you,
Ken *

Sunday evening, May 6, 1928, Woodbury to Buffalo

My own Sweetheart,

Since dinner I've been drawing charts for the Demie delegation to take to a province convention of ΦΔΘ on May 19. At Founders' Day, the assembled alumni asked me to go as alumni rep. I can't afford the time and money, so I'm making the charts instead.

Thank you, honey, for the clipping and my other "personal" mail. It is a bit startling to have hotel rooms offered us. [The offer probably results from Caryl's engagement announcement in the Buffalo paper.] Luckily, the managers know nothing of our financial status!

I've been thinking, though, we must stay one night at a really nice hotel on our honeymoon. That should be, most fittingly, our bridal night – on the drive across New York State, Buffalo to Lake George. We surely can splurge a bit once, and it will be a new experience for you – with a world of new delight. Oh, darling mine!

If I'm granted the salary increase, it will be possible to get any two weeks we want. September 3 will be alright too, for our wedding day. The only objection I can think of is that it is Labor Day – perhaps an advantage, being a holiday. But here Labor Day is a noisy, disagreeable holiday – with all roads traffic-choked. It may not mean that in Buffalo.

I shouldn't begrudge the cost of the coming operation, but added to other amounts due then, it's an imposing total. $65–$70 for the operation; $50 on my Stadium pledge; 40-odd dollars as my biannual insurance premium. I owe Mother $25, and vacation expenses. I need a new light suit. My other one is three years old. And I must start hunting for a wedding ring! What a struggle it all is, precious mine!

Yesterday the thermometer touched 90°! I played two sets of singles, then one of doubles. The latter was a sorry exhibition; we were fearfully tired before it ended – not far from collapse. Ice water & a cold shower afterward felt great. I'm a couple of shades darker today from the sun.

In the evening, Mother and I drove to Mullica Hill for a supper & strawberry festival at the Baptist Church there. I surely stowed away the shortcake! Perhaps you haven't had strawberries up there yet. This was my fourth attack upon them!

I must tell you more of the beauties of blossom time here. Apple trees run the length of every yard on this street; the fields behind used to be an orchard. Lilacs are gorgeous and bursting with fragrance; lilies-of-the-valley are opening. The maples, poplars, and willows are a bright, fresh green. It's glorious, darling mine, needing only you to make it perfect. All of me is aching for you, precious mine, eager to be forever your very own

Ken *

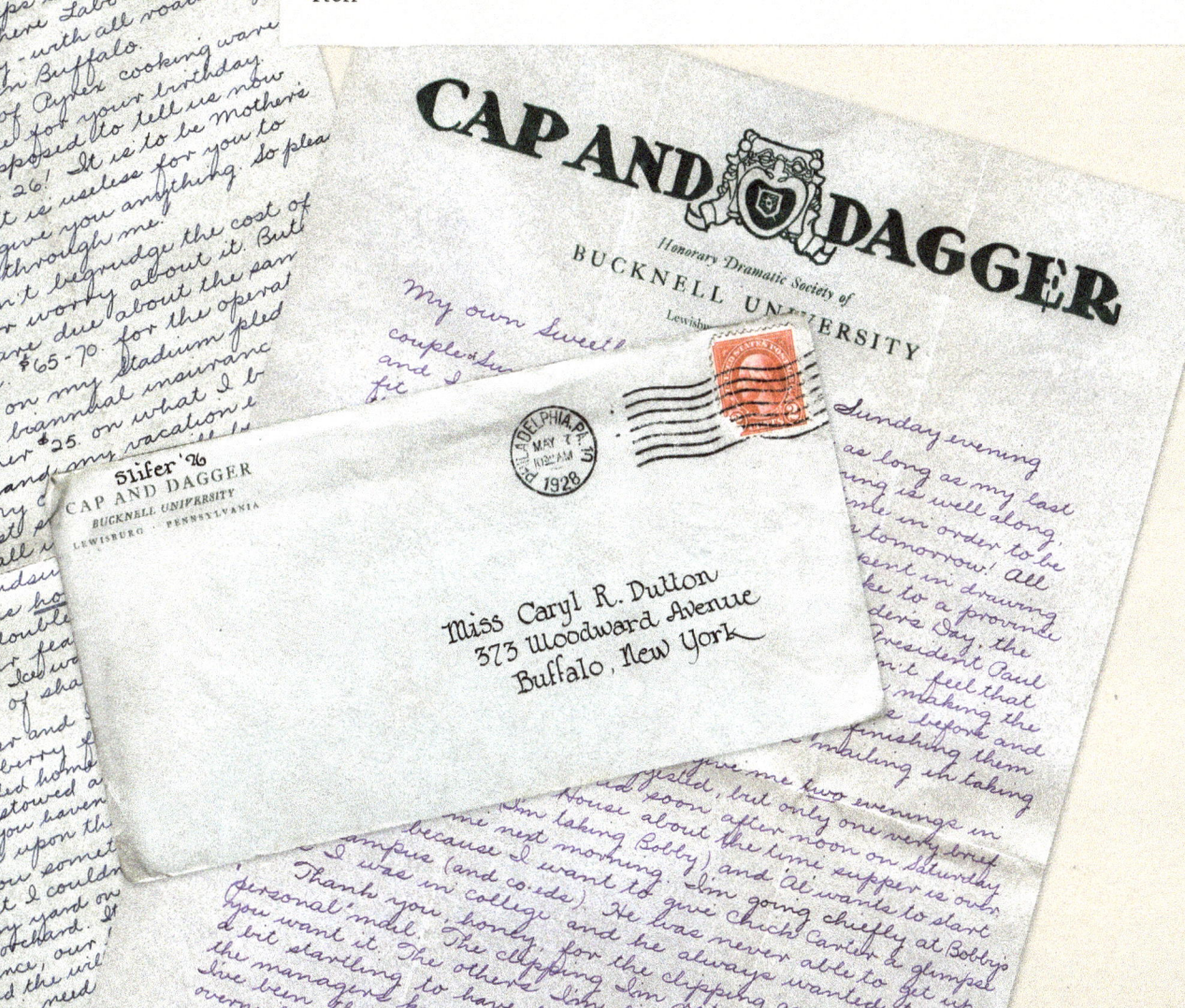

Monday noon, May 7, 1928, Philadelphia to Buffalo

My precious Caryl,

It's all over, darling mine, and I'm "woozy" with happiness! I haven't had a coherent thought since 11 A.M., and my hand is still trembling. From the cryptic telegram I sent, you must have deduced that I saw Mr. Lewis this morning – with eminently satisfactory results. I came to the office this morning – a raw, rainy "blue Monday" – resolved to do or die. I haunted the hall grimly until I was sure Mr. Lewis was free, then trotted in. He greeted me cordially and asked me to sit down! A trifle tremulously, I told him my story and asked for a modest $35 a week. He smiled sympathetically, kindly, and the great Stone Face was gone forever. Sez he: "Of course! I've been hearing very fine things of you, Slifer. By September I assure you that you'll be receiving at least forty dollars a week, if not more."

He asked me how old I was, said I was a bit young, but added that he favored young marriages generally. He encouraged me to tell him all about you and our plans and was altogether so nice I wanted to kiss him or something! I'd do almost anything for that man now! Oh, darling dear, I won't be able to think sanely for a week. Forty dollars as a minimum figure seems immeasurably more than thirty-five! We won't need to worry quite so much, and perhaps we can get a bit better apartment. At least, I'll go hunting with a lot more vim.

You might have been dismayed had I told you the chiefest reason for my forebodings: A Penn grad who's been part of this organization longer than I was getting only $25 a week. Not only was a requested raise refused, but Mr. Lewis told him he hardly deserved what he was getting! Knowing his experience, I was honestly afraid of what my own reception might be. I've been writing only a year, and I have a terrific lot to learn yet.

Mr. Batten told me to take as much time as I needed or wanted for the operation. What a company to work for! I shall probably be out at least a week.

My Ladysweet, I'm tremendously thrilled by all this because I love you, want you with all my heart and soul! And now I'm going to have you always and ever!

Ken *

Thursday afternoon, May 10, 1928, Philadelphia to Buffalo

Precious mine,

Last evening's happy note told me you received my telegram. I haven't calmed down yet! Life with you seems in prospect so sweet and joyous that it will be one glorious adventure. I'm likely to be always a bit breathless that the beauty and loveliness of you should be mine forever!

I worked till 11:30 last evening to finish the second and last of the charts I'm to deliver at the Demie house this weekend. Tonight is play practice. Tomorrow, bed early in preparation for the trip to Bisonburg.

Just now I'm struggling with eight small ads for Bell's Poultry Seasoning – sold widely in New England. Tough work for a poor male. Won't you come give me some of your sage advice?

Please get yourself a really nice new evening dress. Such a charming Lady deserves an equally pretty trousseau – and this dress, in particular, will have to do yeoman service afterwards.

Somehow I think it should be either lavender or silver – that's the way I dream of you. I'd like a close-fitting bodice with full skirt, a wide shoulder-to-shoulder neckline, the whole cut simply. There have been a few at the club dances I coveted for you – one of silver in which you would be especially stunning. Then, with your hair piled high, you'll have all the graceful dignity of a Lady of the Empire. Get what you like, though, and I'll like it, too. I love you in anything, sweetheart, and I always shall.

Wanting you so,
K *

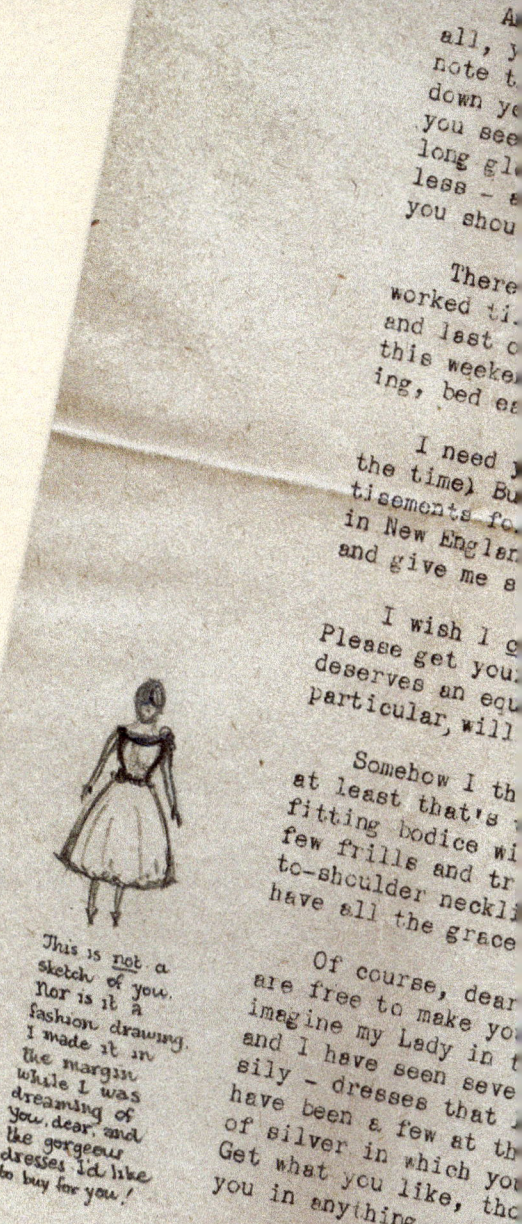

Friday afternoon, May 11, 1928
Philadelphia to Buffalo

Darling mine,

This morning Mr. Cecil returned from Scranton. He presented two advertisements I wrote for half pages in Collier's and Liberty, and brought them back "enthusiastically approved," without a single word having been changed!

About 9:30 Len left for Lewisburg, intending to pick up GG at the Penny Terminal. He was driving a flivver borrowed from one of the fellows in the office and took with him my suitcase, my tuxedo, my shoes, my collar buttons and studs, and some of my money! I hope he has his own girl when we see him tomorrow evening!

Al sez we'll leave at 1:30 tomorrow, taking Chick Carter and Parker Lambeth, a lad from the office who is a University of Richmond grad and a southern gentleman. He's rather lonely here in the North, away from his family. Len took him sometime ago, and he enjoyed it so, I thought I'd invite him for a dance this time.

The Central Pennsylvania Conference track meet is held in the Stadium tomorrow. If we make good time, we may see the end of it. I hope so, for our "son" Geddes is burning up the cinders this year.

I'm waiting impatiently for the joyous day when I may be forever your very own
Ken *

Saturday morning, May 12, 1928
Philadelphia to Buffalo

Sweetheart mine,

A wee bit of a note, dear, to tell you that I love you. For there is nothing else worth noting!

Last night I concocted a Treasure Chest and Treasure – Gold Dust, Bar Silver, Bags of Bullion – for the Treasure Hunt to end our "Y" program for the year Monday evening. The treasure is tracked down by notes, scattered all over town. The Chest is a squat cigar box. On top, the most gruesome skull I could devise, in black, blue, and green. Mother made the little Bags of Bullion. Marked with dollar and pound sterling signs & filled with 250 pennies, they constitute the only real treasure, for the Gold Dust is sand, and the Bar Silver shiny strips of type metal. When the notes are all in, the treasure dug up, we'll spend it on sundaes and sodas.

Bath and bed early last night, when work on the Treasure Trove was done. This morning is cool and clear – a glorious day for the drive to Lewisburg.

I nearly missed out on this note, because of a hurry-up order to think up names for a new series of Iron Skillets in colors, manufactured by Griswold. I thought hard and turned in my suggestions, but must call quits, for it's noon, and we want to get away promptly.

All my love to you, dear,
Ken *

Monday noon, May 14, 1928, Philadelphia to Buffalo

My own Sweetheart,

It was good to find your dear letter at the Demie house – next best to having you there. Bobby and Ken Van den Bree were waiting on the porch with it when we pulled in. Because Al didn't show up with the Cadillac until 1:55, it was 7:30 when we arrived. Fortunately, they were running two shifts because of the crowd, and we were in time for the second table. After supper, there was time for a quick stroll around campus with Parker and Chick before the dance began. Bobby had signed up Helen Bell for Parker and Betty Davis for Chick. She went with Ken, so I had no one at all. No sobs shook my frame, though, for it was rather fun.

I thought I'd cruise around and pick up dances where I wanted them, but I had a lot of request numbers and finally had to make out a program for myself in the orthodox way. Six of the ten dances, I took on the floor, and the others, I talked to the chaperones (the Drum-Warfel families). I had only one dance with Bobby. She was booked up solid by the time the dance began.

Almost everyone I met asked about you, honey girl – all my partners, the chaperones, several of the fellows, and the girls I met on the campus. Speaking of your friends, it may interest you to know that Helen Bell was fascinated by Parker Lambeth, the romantic Southern gentleman who went up with us. She suggested as much to me during our dance, and Bobby repeated the information emphatically next morning. I doubt whether her interest is returned, though Parker seemed to enjoy himself.

By the time the boys returned their girls to the Sem, it was well after midnight. Parker stayed at the house with Len, and Chick and I set out for Simpsons'. Geddes was still up, and we were all hungry, so off to Steininger's for ice cream and pretzels, slipping in just before it closed. It felt quite like old times, and it was 3:30 when we got to bed!

Four hours later, Chick and I crawled out to take a real tour of the campus. None of the Simpsons were up as we stole out the front door. No breakfast was ready at the house either, so we climbed the hill without it. By the time we'd done the campus, seen the Stadium, and bribed the East College janitor to let us into the observation tower above it, we were ravenous.

Back to the house and breakfast with Al Purks and Parker, who had just gotten up. Then a brief goodbye to Bobby, and we set out for home. All in all, there was so little time that I didn't see Aunt Jennie, or Vera, or some of the others you asked to be remembered to.

You'll hardly know the campus when you arrive in June. There's so much activity going on. The new dorm [Hunt Hall] is entirely finished; they're grading the lawn around it. New concrete walks have been laid all over the women's campus. The dining hall is going up rapidly, as is the Botany Building. The infirmary is being considerably enlarged and remodeled. Perhaps most interesting of all to you will be the magnificent living room in the new dormitory. It's breathtaking!

Oh, Caryl precious, come to me knowing that you have all my love,
Ken *

Hunt Hall, Harris Drive side, with a flivver parked in the driveway.[1]

Hunt Hall's formal living room.[1]

Wednesday, May 16, 1928, "Just before the battle, Sweetheart" Woodbury to Buffalo

One parting kiss I give thee, one parting note I leave thee – and all that sort of thing. Which means in 45 minutes I'll climb on the operating table to have my classic nose remodeled.

As an aftermath of my weekend (?), I picked up a wretched head cold. By 11:30 yesterday, my fifth & last handkerchief was approaching its saturation point; the barrage of sneezes showed no signs of ceasing. I knew it should be conquered before the operation, and everything was done at work that had to be, so I took the noon train home, poured pink pills into me, and stretched out on a blanket spread over the warm porch roof under a burning sun. All afternoon I baked there. Then a hot bath and bed right after supper. This morning I slept till 11, and I feel like a different person. The cold seems quite subdued, and I think I'm fit for the ordeal ahead.

If I'm not to keep the doctors waiting, I must run now, dear. I'll have Mother write you a note from my bedside this evening. I don't expect to feel in a writing mood myself! But don't worry about me, dear. It's just a simple operation, to better fit me to be your very own

Ken *

Friday afternoon, May 18, 1928, Woodbury to Buffalo

My Precious Lady,

It was a simple operation, and it's all over now. The actual operation was brief, interesting, and practically painless. I'd never had a local anaesthetic, and I found the sensation novel. I sat erect in an operating chair with a nurse beside me, watched everything, asked questions, and enjoyed it all as much as one can anything of the sort.

The doctor worked quickly, efficiently, and in less than half an hour had removed an incredible amount of bone. In the brief moment after he finished cutting, and before the packing began, I breathed deeply and freely as I never have before, and I felt as if twice as much air were reaching my lungs. Then each nostril was packed with yards and yards of narrow gauze, saturated with iodoform.

That night was the only unpleasant part of the whole process. As the effects of the cocaine wore off, my head throbbed and my teeth ached horribly. And because of the packing in my nose, I could hardly eat or talk, needing my mouth for air. I had to hold iced compresses across my nose to keep down swelling and retard bleeding. Mother came for a visit about nine, bringing some flowers and a letter from you. After she left, the doctor said stop the compresses and try for some sleep. But as soon as I turned my head to either side the blood came spurting out, and I had to give up all idea of sleep. I lay all night staring at the ceiling, rigid, gasping heavily through my mouth, moving only to change the compresses or ring for fresh gauze and ice. I got fearfully cramped in that one position, and it seemed years between each hour till daylight, another century till the doctor came at nine o'clock.

With all my heart, I threw myself into dreaming of you. I thought my throbbing head had found the pillow only you can give, that your cool, fresh lips were pressed against my flushed face and forehead. I seemed to feel your smooth, soft hand caressing my body beneath its warm, binding pile of blankets, soothing, cooling, quieting – questing for me. I half-felt the fragrant loveliness of you close beside me. It was so real, so sweet, and while the vision lasted, I could dream of such days and nights ahead.

Next morning, the doctor unwound the same miles of gauze, to give me back a bit of breath. My nose bled a little, stopped soon, and has given no trouble since. I stayed in bed all day Thursday, dozing & reading The Atlantic. After supper, the doctor released me. Bed as soon as I reached home. I slept till nearly noon today. I'm quite O.K. now, just weak, but I have to move slowly, to avoid starting bleeding again. Your Ken will soon be altogether himself again, honey.

All my love,
K *

Saturday afternoon, May 19, 1928, Woodbury to Buffalo

Sweetheart of mine,

What a dear, funny card came for me yesterday! I can't monopolize artistic laurels in our family any longer! And your wish was gratified, for the card found me out of bed & able to take a great deal of nourishment! After 12 hours' sleep, I crawled from bed with a splitting headache, but a big breakfast and some fresh air sent it flying – and I feel fine now. I drove to the specialist's office in Camden for an examination. He said the wound was healing splendidly.

I don't believe I told you anything about my accommodations at the hospital – or how generous both doctors were to me – to us. The hospital staff is a marvelous institution for a city the size of Woodbury, and it's renowned all over this end of the state. It has some 35 beds, 15 nurses, and 4 physicians, besides the usual staff of cooks, clerks, and chambermaids. I had a pleasant room on the side of the building overlooking the nurses' tennis court. Equipment & service were splendid. At least 8 nurses looked after me in the day and night I was there. The 4 meals were delicious, piping hot, and served nicely. China, linen, & silver were monogrammed with the hospital initial, and each tray had an attractive place card, with my name & room number in a silver holder.

The nicest part was the figure on my bill. Dr. Underwood, who heads the hospital & owns it, has been our family physician since I was a child. He knows I'm planning to be married. Though I had one of the nicest rooms from 2 P.M. one day to the next evening, with 4 meals, an operating room and all sorts of nursing, my bill was only $5! I protested mildly at the office when I left, but the girl said those were doctor's orders. I had expected at least $15. And the specialist, Dr. Klein, absorbed his preliminary examination, 3 hospital visits, and 2 subsequent treatments into his $50 fee. I think that is well under his usual rate. Everyone has surely been kind to me.

Oh, darling mine, I love you with my very soul. And I'm desperately eager to be your very own

Ken *

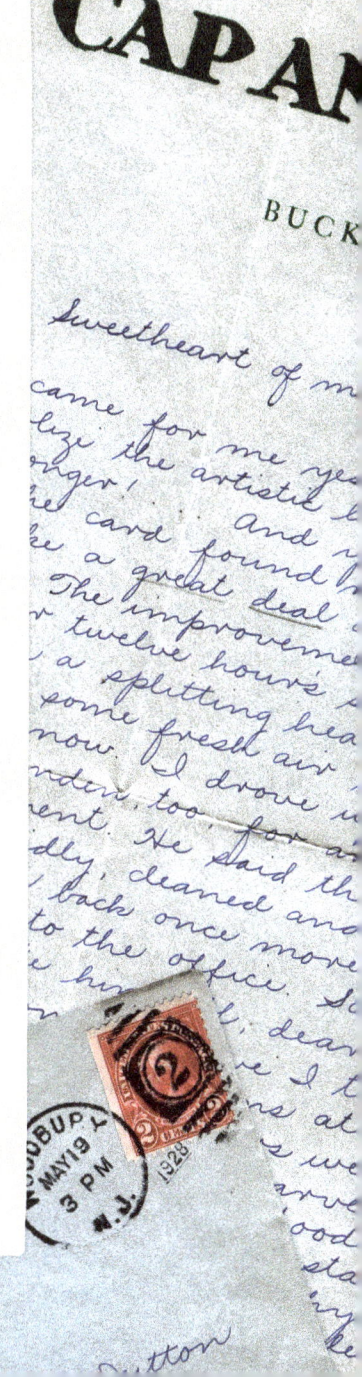

Sunday evening, May 20, 1928, Woodbury to Buffalo

"The Spirit of '49" Ken mentions in this letter refers to the 1849 California Gold Rush. Robert B. Green, a Slifer ancestor from Lewisburg for whom Ken's father Robert Green Slifer was named, died in California as a young man. His journey from Pennsylvania was harrowing; supplies, money, companions, and pack animals were lost along the way. The cause of his death, shortly after he arrived in California, is unknown. His journal, edited by Bucknell history professor Dr. J. Orin Oliphant, under the title "On the Arkansas Route to California in 1849," was published in 1955 by the Bucknell University Press. Although Green's journal "abounds in misspelled words, in erratic punctuation, and in odd constructions," Dr. Oliphant said he preserved "all such idiosyncrasies … because Green's deviations from precise English are of such character as to give his journal a peculiar charm." Of course – though my computer's spellcheck disagreed – I feel the same way about Ken and Caryl's courtship letters.

Darling mine,

I've spent the afternoon writing thank-you notes in return for the flowers 'n cake 'n ice cream that have come to me the last few days. The most appealing offering came from little Billy Storrie next door. He went off to the woods and picked me the most mammoth bunch of buttercups I ever saw! The house is full of flowers, and I am full of cake!

I am myself again, but the doctor wants to see me Tuesday, so I'll not get back to the office until Wed. I'm still hiding in my beard at home. I look like a Russian serf, or the Spirit of '49. Mother says it gives me an uncanny resemblance to my father some 28 years ago. It's been a glorious vacation from the razor – than which I loathe nothing more! Haircut AND shave tomorrow.

Oh, my dear, if you write many more letters, I'll have to buy a Rem. Rand cabinet to hold them all. I'm never tired of receiving and reading them, but they do accumulate amazingly. Much as I love your letters, I'm glad you are going soon to stop writing them and begin living them!

I'm sure I shall like the dress you bought, for I usually like everything about you. And I think buying your white shoes now is a good idea. What a tremendous thrill there is to plan even the smallest things for our wedding and the start of our life's companionship.

We'll all be glad to see you whenever you can come – glad to have you as long as you can stay. It seems only fair to your employer to stay another week if he asks it, and if the extra week of school runs till the 16th, I can expect you here about the 20th. One more week's separation, after eight months of it won't be so hard.

The weather is comfortable, & there are no mosquitoes yet! Our 3 big bushes of bridal wreath are solid masses of white blooms. Lilies-of-the-valley are thick along the north side of the house, the tulips still gay. I can only wait and hope – roses and moon – in June. Come flying to your

Ken – please! * ------- *

Wednesday P.M., May 23, 1928, Philadelphia to Buffalo

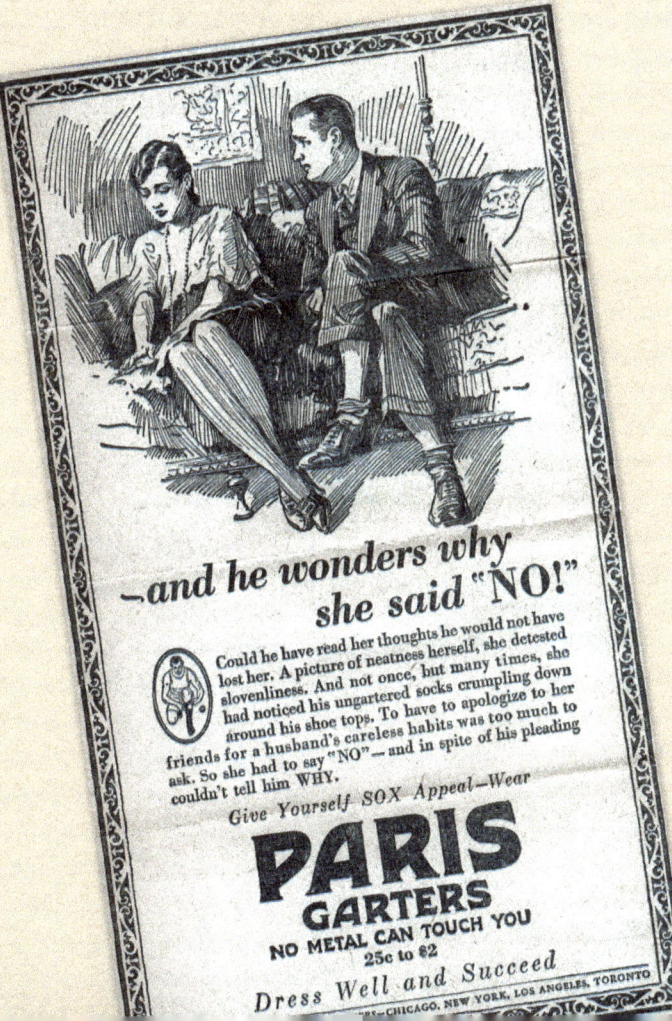

Sweetheart mine,

Monday I put in a strenuous day housecleaning.

Yesterday, I had my last appointment with the doctor. By the time I'd driven to the city and back, with treatment in between, it was noon.

"Count that day lost whose low, descending sun
Sees not one letter for my Lady done!"

I'm enclosing a significant advertisement that may change the course of our lives! It brought home to me most vividly the gross, repellent side of my slovenly self. For the first time I realized how uncouth and boorish I must seem to my fastidious Lady at times. I began to appreciate all that your delicate sensibilities must have suffered on my account. Since I'm incorrigible in the matter of garters, the only gentlemanly thing to do is to offer to release you from the bonds between us. If you take advantage of my offer, I'll understand. Unlike the dumbbell in the picture, I'll not wonder why. This is a desperate measure, but I cannot bear to think our love is merely a matter of "sox appeal"!!! But seriously, isn't this thing amusing, absurd (and appropriate)? It is the type of stuff a reputable agency will not touch or attempt.

Tonight I expect to resume tennis. The doctor said my nose has healed splendidly, and I need not see him again unless unforeseen complications develop. He noted I must be in fine physical condition for it to bleed so little and heal so quickly.

I had rather a reception in the office this morning and had to describe the operation at least a dozen times. Best of all, Mr. Lewis came in and talked to me for five minutes or more!

Oh, darling dear, I'm eager to begin living my life for you, with you, as

Your very own Ken   *

Thursday afternoon, May 24, 1928
Philadelphia to Buffalo

Precious mine,

I'm still excited three hours after reading the letter you mailed Tuesday. I think it would be best to follow our original schedule for your coming. After the church play on June 14 or 15 would be better than before. The later visit gives us more time to get ready, and will be more calm, unhurried, and pleasant. Too, we'll be decreasing the interval between the joyous ecstasy June will give and its climax in full companionship. Your 2 weeks' added salary is not a negligible factor, either. And I can hunt up more desirable apartments to show you.

While I was in the hospital, Mr. Cecil asked Len how I was getting along, then volunteered he considers me the best of the young writers, both in natural writing ability and in "dependability." Since there are about ten of us who might be classed as the Younger Generation, and since Mr. Cecil is almost the dean of the Old-Timers, his tribute means something to me.

I played two sets of tennis last evening, winning over a new club member, 6-4, 6-4. My game was poor after the layoff, but I felt fine physically, and the play produced no ill effects.

Tonight I must attend a meeting of the high school alumni executive committee. I don't usually go, but tonight is election of officers for next year, and there's a bit of politics in the air. Since Chick Carter is President, I must turn out to support the Administration policies!

Oh, darling mine, I've a limitless lot of love in my heart, all for you,

Always,
Ken   *

Friday morning, May 25, 1928
Woodbury to Buffalo

My precious Lady,

This morning, Mother woke up with the mumps! So, though I've been back at the office only two days, I must miss more time from my desk to act as nurse and cook. With these developments, I feel more strongly than ever that it would be best for you to wait until after the 16th. Dr. Underwood says the incubation period is 2–3 weeks. Coming within that period would be dangerous, unless you've had the mumps. Fortunately, Bobby and I are immune.

I'm eager to have you in my arms again, precious mine, and it will be hard, desperately so, yet our days and nights together will be all the sweeter for the sacrifice. I love you so!

Your own
Ken   *

Sunday evening, May 27, 1928, Woodbury to Buffalo

My precious Caryl,

I ache for word of you. At night my arms go out in quest of you, and I almost cry aloud in the agony of longing. But there is only emptiness beside me, darkness and silence all about.

Friday Mother grew increasingly worse, had a wretched night, and didn't sleep at all. Saturday, the doctor gave her pills to kill the pain, and suggested hot compresses of camphorated oil. That afternoon, a neighbor stayed with her, while I took my group team to Wenonah (3 miles) for a YMCA track meet. That evening, improvement began. Today, she's been much better.

It's kept me hustling, honey, cooking, nursing, keeping track of medicine times. Cooking is just for myself; I've made bouillon and Jell-O for Mother, while the neighbors have brought junket, broth, and custard. They've been in too, to help as they could. Mother will soon be well, if weak.

My dear, my head thinks it would still be best to delay your visit as we'd planned – but my heart rebels most awfully! I love you, want you so!

Your very own
Ken *

P. S. Thos. Cook's radio hour has just been picturing the glories of Bermuda. My sweet, we just must see it together, sometime!

Tuesday morning, May 29, 1928, Woodbury to Buffalo

My dear,

I'm a hurried, worried animal these days – and I know my letters reflect it all too accurately! When I go back to the office again, I hope my missives may be more satisfactory.

Yesterday I got up early to get a good breakfast for Len – orange juice, oatmeal, toast, omelet. When the dishes were done, beds made, and Mother had her tray, I hopped into the flivver and drove to the office. An hour and a half there to get the important things done, then hurried home to get dinner. (Hurried so, I forgot to mail your Sunday letter in the city.)

Grocery buying was one feature of a busy afternoon. At 4 P.M., I set at preparing a big supper for Len and myself. I washed lettuce, tomatoes, radishes, and assorted vegetables, hulled a quart of strawberries, made a salad, fixed two huge bowls of strawberry shortcake, and completed my menu with hamburger steak, peas, and fried potatoes. It was piping hot and ready to eat a little before six – but Len never came – the sap! I waited till 6:30, then ate alone. He has often played the same trick on Mother, but it was the first time I'd bumped against it. Though he has a phone right on his desk, he never thinks of using it! In that, he's the world's worst boarder! The kids liked our Treasure Hunt so much that we had another last evening, as the absolute end of our year's program. The hunt and a high school alumni committee meeting kept me busy till 10:30. By the time I'd done the dishes and stowed away the uneaten food, it was 11:30. And just then Len came breezing blithely in! Fireworks!

Honey mine, I'm coming to have a healthy respect for the profession of housekeeping. I know how much thought and energy it requires, and you may be sure I shall never decry your half of our partnership. Mother thinks I'm doing her job well, and the neighbors who come in to see her are amazed at the way the house looks and the meals we've had. Most of them had been frankly skeptical of my ability – or any man's. Now they concede I'll make you a good wife!

Oh, darling mine, this wearying recital isn't at all the sort of thing that's in my heart. There's a vast world of love there that got overlooked in the rush!

Your own adoring
Ken *

Sunday afternoon, June 3, 1928, Lewisburg to Woodbury

Caryl and Rolland's girlfriend, Gladys Jones, attended Bucknell's 1928 commencement exercises in Lewisburg. Caryl's dear friend Vera Herrick, from Buffalo, was graduating, and Caryl stayed with Aunt Jennie. Caryl gave this letter to Bobby to deliver to Ken in Woodbury the following day.

My own Dearest,

Gladys called for the Herricks and me at 7:30 this morning, and we were off to Lewisburg at 8:05. It was a beautiful day for driving. We stopped a couple of times for gas, & had lunch by a creek about 1:30. Gladys's Nash is a splendid car & just hummed along the road. I drove about 100 miles, & Gladys took the rest. The road is great all the way (mostly cement), no detours, & the mileage only 230 in all. A new road cuts off 40 miles, and the route is direct as can be.

We arrived about 4:30 & had a chance to cool off and clean up before dinner. I left the Herricks with Vera and was all cleaned up and dressed when Aunt Jennie returned from a ride. After dinner we visited the new dormitory, and it surely is beautiful. I can hardly realize I'm at Bucknell when I see that building. Then a trip to the Purity for ice cream before bed.

Yes, my dearest, I wish you could be here with me. Bucknell is never complete without you. A glorious moon last night was just wasted, 'cause we couldn't enjoy it together.

Loving you, wanting you so (I'll send my kiss by Bobby).
Your own Lady

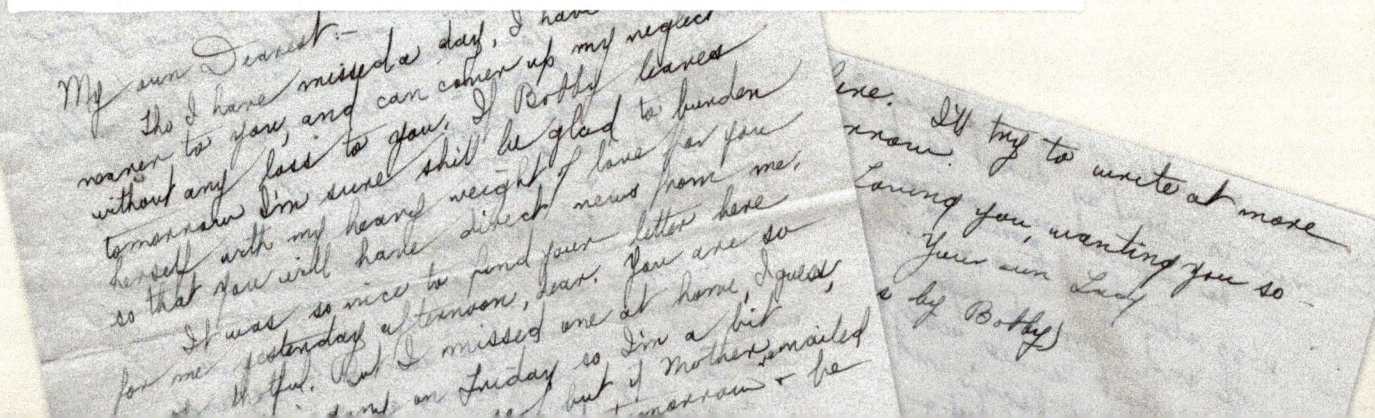

Tuesday noon, June 5, 1928, Philadelphia to Buffalo

My own Sweetheart,

Yesterday was dreary and rainy, but Bobby made the journey home to Woodbury safely. She was just running into the house as I swung 'round our corner. We're surely glad to see her! Mother and I think she's a pretty good kid, and we'd been increasingly lonely for her. For me there was the added thrill that she'd just come from you. How I envied her the glimpse of you she'd had – and her night with you – though that is one wish I didn't express audibly! Bobby's first words were to announce that she had a letter for me. How thoughtful of you to send it with her to save missing a day. It's so good to think, as I do more each day, that soon we'll not need to depend on letters and worry about their receipt. Oh, darling mine, only ten more days!

Last evening, I went up to church where the men of the play cast gathered to put up the scenery. So many doors enter into the action, that we want everything in place sometime before the play. It will be good advertising, too, to have the stage set so for Sunday School. We worked till 10:30, and when we left, everything was in place except portières, window curtains, etc. The result is much better than anything I had hoped for.

Oh, my Ladysweet, my love and longing are increasing beyond all expression, but I can endure it with the thought that you're coming all the way to my arms soon, to stay awhile. Don't forget to specify standard or daylight saving time, in advising me of your arrival! We mustn't have any last-minute tragedies!

Adoring you,
Your Ken *

Wednesday evening, June 6, 1928, Buffalo to Woodbury

Caryl responds to Ken's enclosure, "The Ten-Point Wife." It is a newspaper column by Helen Rowland, who writes like a cross between Erma Bombeck and Dear Abby: "Far too much is said about 'How to choose a husband,' and far too little about 'How to choose a wife.' If you ask the average man to name ten essential qualifications of the ideal wife, he would probably begin with 'beauty,' and finish with 'a talent for cooking,' or 'blonde hair.' Which shows how little intelligence he uses in the most vital decision of his life. There is a Ten-Point Wife somewhere for every normal man – but you can't recognize her by her permanent wave, or the dimples in her knees."

Rowland asks penetrating questions such as: "Is she the girl you want to go to when your head aches or your heart aches? Is she the girl who puts meaning into your work, and significance into your job? The girl who has tenderness enough to sympathize with you, brains enough to understand and inspire you, heart enough to be loyal to you – and love enough to stretch out over a multitude of your sins?" Ken underlines that final phrase, pencils in "Yes" replies throughout (once "Yes, emphatically"), but after the question "Is she the woman who understands you?" he writes, "I hope so."

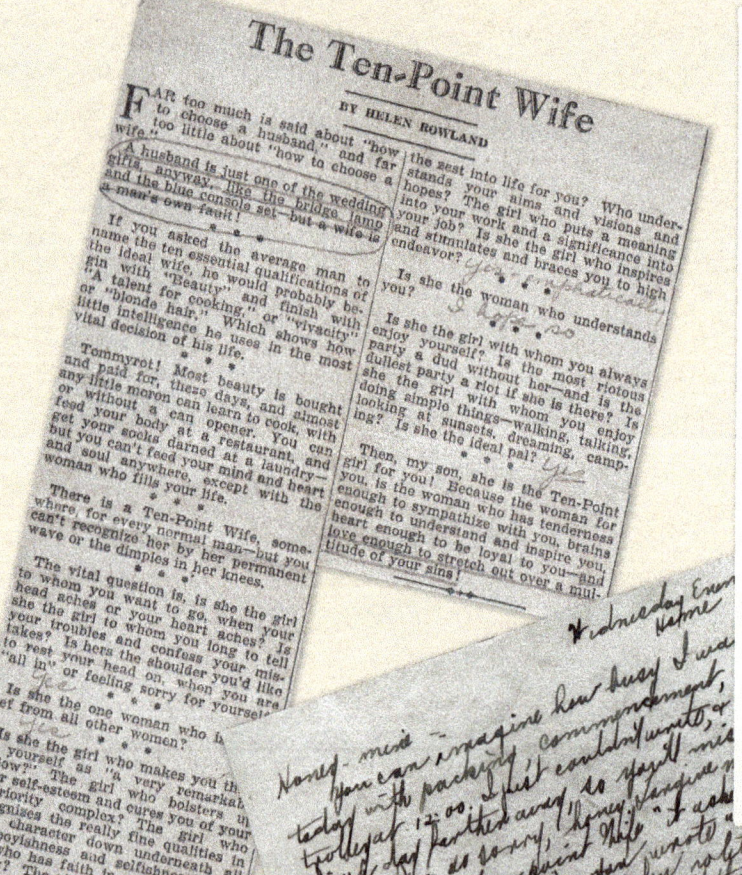

Honey mine,

In the "Ten-Point Wife," it asked, "Does she understand you?" & you wrote, "I hope so." I think I do, dear, for when no letter came for me this morning, I felt that you thot I would appreciate finding a letter awaiting me at home.

I was awfully late arriving home from Lewisburg tonight, so this is hurried. A longer note tomorrow.

I await your specific date for my coming, honey. If I should come by night, I s'pose Sunday would be the only morning you could not meet me, but if I came by day, you could meet me any evening.

Goodnight, Sweetheart. *

Judge Kenesaw Mountain Landis, first Commissioner of Major League Baseball (standing, speech in hand, left side of stage) is about to address the crowd at the dedication of the Christy Mathewson Memorial Gates, June 5, 1928. Caryl attended the dedication and wrote to Ken about the ceremony two days later.[1]

Thursday evening, June 7, 1928, Buffalo to Woodbury

My own dear Ken,

My successor is at the office this week. In the midst of closing the school session, I must train her. She's nice to work with, but it's a strain to explain the whys & wherefores of everything I do. All is over in a day & a half, and when you get this I'll be saying "Goodbye Forever" to my labors with Remington Rand.

Tues. in Lewisburg, the sunshine lasted for the dedication of the Christy Mathewson Memorial Gateway [built with contributions from every Major League Baseball team]. Baseball Commissioner Kenesaw Mountain Landis was the main speaker. Then another deluge; only one inning was played by each side.

Tues. eve. the clouds held their moisture long enuf to start the band concert; there was a fair crowd. The rain held off until the last number, then we returned in haste to avoid getting too wet. Prexy's reception was held in the living room of the new Dorm – so large that with 150 people in it, you think hardly anyone is there. From the reception, Ethel West-Knapp went with me to the Alumni Ball, but we were tired and left early.

Real sunshine at last Wed. morning for the exercises. I stayed to watch the procession, then went up to Commencement Hall. It surely did seem queer to realize that I am an alumna. Helen Bell was coming home at the same time, and I was grateful for her company. The R.R. car was empty enuf so we could spread ourselves and rest.

Tomorrow is the last day of school. The men pasted pictures in the classbook yesterday – and most of them did a characteristically messy job. But they saved me some labor, and the books are to be ready for distribution tomorrow morning. Then much autographing and mailing must be done.

Oh, honey, I have longed so to see you, that when I have you again, my heart will be just too full of gladness and love for mere words. I'll just hold you tight a long, long time. Oh, my dearest, I'm loving you so and ever so happy that soon I shall be your very own

Lady *

Friday evening, June 8, 1928, Buffalo to Woodbury

Dearest Ken,

School is all over at last, & I have but an interesting morning tomorrow to clear up last-minute things before I can leave for good. About 10:00, our classbooks came from the printer, & there was much autographing. At 12:15, they called me to the classroom in pretense of giving me a message, & when I got to the front, they nearly deafened me with cheers. When I tried to make a hasty retreat, they asked me to wait & presented me with a big box! When I got back to the office, I opened it & found another luncheon set, a real beauty. Mrs. Hemphill got the set – of a lovely ecru linen – in Canada. In these days when bridge tables are used so much for entertaining, you can use as many sets as you have.

I see you expect me to come by Saturday the 16th – a 12-hour trip. If you want me for the play, I could take the 5:10 A.M. (standard) and get there at 6:03 P.M. (daylight), but would you have time to bother with me that night, when you have to engineer the play? I'd love to see it, but I can wait another week & find loads to do in the interval. Loving you so –

Your Lady *

Sunday evening, June 10, 1928, Buffalo to Woodbury

My own Ken,

I had a lovely shower Saturday. Mother, Attie, and I got there at 2:30, tho the guests didn't come till 3. The table was pretty with a blue oilcloth on it, white candles, white flowers in a blue bow, a cunning little bride & groom, & all sorts of other pretty things. Even the little cakes were iced in blue & white.

When most everyone had come, they sent me out of the room, & each wrote an "ideal husband recipe," which I had to read when I came back. And I still think you're pretty ideal! Then I was taken into a room, & a wedding veil & shower bouquet were laid out on the bed. The veil was a curtain, all draped & ready, & the bouquet a big funnel filled with artificial white flowers and twelve kitchen utensils hanging from as many white ribbons: a paring knife; tablespoon; salt shaker; measuring cup; cookie cutter; aluminum strainer; vegetable brush; measuring spoon set; 2 kinds of can openers; a cloth holder; & a sprinkler top for a bottle. It surely was a clever article!

When I was all fixed up, I had to parade in to the wedding march & open my gifts. My, what a shower of bounty for our kitchen, honey! There were 2 small tablecloths in blue & white; 2 hand towels; 3 dish towels; 1 rubber apron & 1 cloth one; 2 custard glasses; a long-handled blue duster; a set of stainless kitchen silver (3 forks, 3 knives, & a paring knife); a blue sink drain; a dainty cake dish; a nest of 6 bowls; a small and a large frying pan; 2 egg beaters, one of which I will exchange; a handled blue dustpan; a blue mixing bowl; a blue china teapot; a blue saucepan; a covered blue baking dish; a fully equipped steam cooker; and 2 wire strainers. Wasn't that a lovely donation, dear? And such a help, for there are hundreds of things you have to have in a kitchen.

But now, honey, about my visit. I can't come this week, for Friday there is to be some sort of a shower for me. Get the play & house-hunting off your shoulders & a good rest, dear, & then I'll come to you, & you'll really be able to enjoy my visit. Besides the shower, I have a picnic of our C. E. & choir to engineer Saturday & a quartet number on Sunday.

Father is purchasing a small Buick tomorrow, & in it, Mother, Attie & I might drive down June 28 or 29, taking Attie to Salem, & Mother to various & sundry relations about Philly, & me to you! I know that means two whole weeks later, but if you wanted me earlier for a special reason, or later, I could arrange one trip by train, or we could disregard this whole plan. You help me decide, dear, and let reason, not love alone, be your guide. You know I want you, love you so.

Your own
Lady

Monday evening, June 11, 1928, Buffalo to Woodbury

Precious Honey mine,

I could have just sat down & cried this morning, when two letters came from you filled with joyous expectation of my visit this weekend. I knew just how disappointed you would be when you received my letter saying I could not come. I feel as badly as you do, but it couldn't be helped. After the girls had planned the party, I couldn't say I wouldn't be there, much as I wanted to see you.

Dear O dear, it's too bad, but I don't have to wait till the end of the month, to come with the folks. I could come early next week, tho coming with the folks will delay me only a week, & by that time I should be rid of my cold & more rested than now. Oh honey, it is hard to be so far apart, & to have to struggle so to get together.

Your vacation notice was an awesome surprise, announcing that your request is now on record.

Oh, I hope it can be changed, tho, without embarrassing you too much, dear. I know you, too, will realize how much better any time would be than Labor Day, tho I'm sorry I didn't realize the holiday date in time for your interview. And when I did, I thot you wouldn't want to make any more requests while you were out for the operation & your Mother's sickness. Then too, I've been trying to reconcile myself to that date, but it doesn't seem to suit anyone. What'll we do, honey? You see, your wife is already causing you much inconvenience & trouble! Beware of worse!

This afternoon I thot some air would do me good, so I tried out the new car. It's a great change. Father was offered a good exchange with our Willy, & we are glad to be rid of it. The new one runs like a charm.

Oh Sweetheart, I thot I'd see you in a few days, & you seem to be receding instead of approaching. If the joy of our visit should be increased by the waiting, we surely shall reach heights never before attained, for we shall have waited more than we ever did before – and never have we wanted each other so much. I'm trying to be brave, honey, but I want you so that it's tremendously hard.

Loving you so, dear
Your Lady

Mr. Slifer:
Your vacation will be the two weeks beginning Sept. 3rd. !
M. C. Roberts.

Tuesday afternoon, June 12, 1928, Buffalo to Woodbury

Dearest Ken,

This morning, Attie, Mother, & I went to Williamsville, just outside Buffalo, to attend the Women's Association. There was a short morning meeting, then lunch and an afternoon session – all very interesting and not long enuf to be tiresome. We stopped at the house on the way to the Doctor's office, & I found your letter, so thot I'd answer it while waiting. It's 6:30 and two still ahead of us.

You surely have been busier than any human being should be, & it is better for us both that my visit is delayed, much as we long to see each other. I hope you really will rest when this play is over.

What a thrill to hear you found the apartment! What is your plan to keep it till September? I'll leave the whole thing to your judgment; you & your mother have such good taste & can pick a satisfacatory place.

Yesterday Mother bought for us the other three pieces for OUR bureau set, & it is now complete. Now if I only had our silver, I would feel more satisfied. Busy day tomorrow with the dressmaker. With fewer people to look over my shoulder, I can write you more fully and lovingly.

Your Lady *

Wednesday morning, June 13, 1928, Philadelphia to Buffalo

My precious Caryl,

Your last evening's letter was a disturbing one, dear. My reactions & emotions are so tangled I doubt I can separate them clearly. Nor is the office atmosphere conducive to coherent, analytical thought. But when Monday's letter asks for a quick decision on train schedules, and Tuesday's tells me you don't expect to come for a couple of weeks yet, I hardly know what to say or think. We've planned on the 16th so long – and I've pinned all my hopes on seeing you then. I set the play date for the 15th for I knew we'd need all possible time, without conflicting with your visit.

I suppose it would be more sensible to wait awhile – but I don't want to be too sensible in love! Indeed, if we were to be strictly "sensible," we'd wait another year to be married. But neither of us wants to do that, do we, honey?

I've been living for this week, Lady mine, counting the days and hours. I had thought today would be the last letter I'd need to write. And the hope of seeing you has buoyed me through the maze of rehearsals and sign painting. I kept thinking, "A few days more of intensive effort, and then a glorious, glorious visit with my sweetheart!" Now everything seems empty, dull. Most of the fun has gone, and another unbearable wait stretches ahead. Oh, well.

I've told so many people you were coming! It's going to be rather difficult explaining, but it can be done. Gert Hunter is to take us riding in his Lincoln & his new Ford roadster with the rumble seat. The play is going so nicely now I hoped to have you see it. The Blackwoods & others want to entertain us. I hoped to take you to the reunion at the Club next Thursday, with buffet supper, bridge, and dancing. All but that can be postponed. Oh Caryl mine, why did you accept so many engagements for the weekend when you knew I wanted you so?

But amid all the gloom I have one piece of great good news. "Our" apartment owner told me the smaller of his 2 vacant apartments hadn't been rented, and he'd be glad to discuss it with me this evening. If I must decide, I'll make the best possible financial arrangement to hold it for us until September. I'd rather have you see it first, but at $40 a month it is too good an opportunity to let pass, & I can hardly ask him to hold off 2 more weeks against other offers.

So, Lady mine, I'm likely to decide our destinies this evening, unless I get word you've changed your mind again, and are coming this week after all. Please don't think that after waiting nine months for you, I'll let you go again in a week! Your father will have to allow you longer than that! I expected to put all my love into this letter, but now I must save out enough to stretch over a dozen more or so. It's well that love is elastic. For I do love you, Ladysweet!

Your very own
Ken *

Thursday morning, June 14, 1928, Philadelphia to Buffalo

Lady o' mine,

Your letters still are puzzling, dear, & I'm not a little concerned. I've tried to think them through. Perhaps I'm stupid. Perhaps selfish and jealous. But I simply can't understand the air of finality with which you say you cannot come to me. We've planned since the middle of May to have you come on June 16. Then as late as Friday evening, June 8, you wrote, anticipating your coming, asking immediate advice about train schedules, and speaking of arriving in time for the play.

The next letter told me a class meeting and party would keep you from coming Friday, and that you'd agreed to organize a picnic on Saturday, our original date. It was nice of the girls to plan an affair in your honor, but when you knew a week in advance that I wanted you, I should think it could be postponed for my sake. And why you accepted the picnic responsibility for Saturday, I don't know, dear! I do realize it would be most sane and sensible to let me store up sleep first. But I don't want to be sane and sensible! I don't want sleep, I want you! I've been counting the days, waiting, hoping, longing, and now that you're not coming, everything's upsidedown.

Yesterday came the queerest copy order I have yet received. It simply quoted a letter from the client – Tetley Tea. "Please prepare a special article about tea, to be recited from the platform of a special cooking school in Gardner, Mass." No other instructions or material offered. My essay on tea, for housewifely consumption, is going to be a masterpiece of fiction and fancy!

Let's leave the matter of the wedding date until you come, honey, if you ever do. I don't fancy the job of changing my vacation after the special dispensation already granted me. It can be done, though, if the need is acute. Looking over my letters, you'll find I suggested some time ago that Labor Day was a poor wedding day. Couldn't it be set for the day after – Tuesday? I'll need almost all that time to get to Buffalo. It's a two-day trip from here, and since I have to be at the office till noon Saturday, the day will be well gone before I can get started.

Perhaps our friends could be back by Tues. evening. But we're getting married for each other's sake, not theirs, Caryl mine. And the less fuss, the better. You're planning an ambitious church wedding, I s'pose, tho' you never asked me about it. At least you mentioned a soloist & organist. I'll go through with it to please you, honey, but I'd prefer a quiet affair. Women like ceremony; it does make marriage more impressive and awesome. But it costs us all considerably more, too.

Practice went splendidly last evening. We just did scenes that had been troublesome. I got to bed at 11:30 with a most annoying headache & couldn't sleep for more than an hour, thinking of you, Caryl mine. I wanted to feel your cool fingers caress my aching head, the soft touch of your lips that sweeps away pain like magic. I longed for the pillow only you can give. Dreaming of it, I finally fell asleep. Oh, my dear, I can hardly endure the wait for you. But I must, I love you so.

Hurriedly

Flustered, discouraged, and in a hurry, Ken doesn't sign his letter. During the next week, a flurry of now vanished letters between Ken and Caryl – some marked Air Mail, some Special Delivery – seems to have smoothed over misunderstandings.

Monday noon, June 18, 1928, Philadelphia to Buffalo

My own Caryl,

Saturday, I won my individual tennis match, 6-0, 6-4, and Woodbury won the team match, 6 matches to 3. My game was going well, and I had my opponent 5-0 in the 2nd set before he got a game. Then I eased up a little, and dropped four games before I could bear down again.

Come evening, we toiled at church, taking down scenery, curtains, etc., and restoring properties and incidentals to their owners. I didn't make up much sleep that night. Our capacity audience Friday night assures ample funds for the delegation to summer assembly. Comment on the play has been flattering, so whatever I think of it, the audience was pleased, and that is all that matters. Because everything did go so much more smoothly than I dared hope, I should be satisfied, too.

The more I think about your coming, honey, the less I care about the blamed reunion at the country club. I want my first evening with you alone. I won't feel like exchanging the social amenities with comparative strangers, when I'm aching so to talk to you and no one else. I don't think it would be so much fun for you, either – and it costs $3 a couple.

The rumor persists we are to be given a full holiday on Saturday for the rest of the summer. If it's correct, Len would leave for vacation Friday evening, and his room would be free for you for more than a week. So come whenever the best train leaves Williamsport, Lady mine, and if you were to arrive about dark, I might steal a kiss on the way home without anyone being the wiser!

Oh, precious mine, I think of nothing except that I'm to see you soon. "Caryl's coming, Caryl's coming!" weaves itself like a refrain through everything I write or think or do. If I were only musical, I'd set it to music, and whistle it, too! It's a most delightful, upsetting thought, turning all my mental pigeon-holes topsy-turvy. I'm afraid I shan't be good for much for the rest of this week. Forget my incoherencies, and remember my love. There's so much of it for you.

Always,
Ken *

Monday evening, June 18, 1928, Buffalo to Woodbury

My precious Ken,

I got two letters today, but I read the second one first, 'cause I wanted to see what you said after receiving my Air Mail. I'm relieved that you begin to feel the delay will work for the good of us both. Besides, now many days will be added on to the end of my visit. Ray! Pollyanna!

So we have a toaster! That's grand. I was hoping someone would give us one. I'm eager to see into your "Hope Chest." By the way, when we got the extra pieces of the bureau set home the other night, they didn't match. The set we have is between cream & white, and the pieces made now are white only. I hope I'll be in time to pick wallpaper. That will be fun, with you to help choose. If we can only keep the place without too much financial output, it will surely make planning and home-settling twice as easy.

I'm glad the play was so successful, and I'm sure you deserved the nice bouquets they threw.

Rolland came home this morning – early – and reported both a successful tying of the knot between Elliot (his roommate) and his girl, and their equally unfailing trip to our camp near Glens Falls, where they are going to spend a month's honeymoon. Today Rolland looks like a coal miner after an explosion, for he has been working in the rain, taking his car apart – engine, wheels, and even body, I guess.

This will reach you Wednesday, and within 24 hours I will be in your arms once more. Oh, my dear, I wonder if I will be able to collect myself to really talk to you for two or three days. I think I'll be too happy to talk, and I'll just look and look. And it'll be really you, and not your picture that I can look at. In joyous anticipation – till Thursday – your very own

Lady

Tuesday, June 19, 1928, Philadelphia to Williamsport, Pennsylvania
c/o Miss Phoebe Bloomfield

My Own,

Last week I entered a noon-hour class on "The Theory of Advertising." Seven or eight of us, cub copywriters all, comprise the class; our instructor is a veteran member of our Department who used to lecture on advertising at Leland Stanford and the University of Oregon. We meet on Tuesdays and Thursdays, with a roundtable discussion following the short impromptu "lecture." The class will fill a need I have felt for some time. Certainly, we'll have a clearer idea of what we're trying to do, and the most effective ways of doing it, when we've finished.

With class today, I could not use my lunch hour for the usual letter to you. I'll have to pound it out quickly now – on Ayer time! Not a new offense on my part, but I never like to do it. And I'm too excited to think clearly, because your coming is so close. Only two more days! Oh, Lady mine, it seems incredible that I'm going to have you again, after nine unending months of separation! Nine months of living on letters and memories and dreams!

It was good of you, and characteristic too, to so completely overlook my two boorish, unkind letters. I don't know what made me write you so, sweetheart. It must have been mingled disappointment, exhaustion, and sleeplessness. You might easily have answered in kind – but you didn't! I was so glad and happy when I read your gentle, generous letter last evening. God willing, you'll not be tested so again, honey.

This morning, as Chairman of the Tennis Committee, I boldly invaded Mr. Fry's big office to ask if the firm would appropriate money for the tournament again this year. He was very cordial, promised everything we needed, and talked about Mr. Black, Doctor Hunt, and other topics of mutual interest. He acceded also to another request that came to me as an inspiration. I asked if he would issue a memorandum over his own signature, sponsoring the tournament, saying that members of the firm are always glad to see organized recreation among the Ayer Family, and suggesting everyone avail themselves of the opportunity presented by the tournament. Such a proclamation will help swell our entry list amazingly.

"Certainly, Kenneth," sez he, "write whatever you think I ought to say, and I'll sign it for you!" You'd appreciate the episode if you knew how distant and remote most of our organization consider Mr. Fry. It helped give me just a little more confidence in myself, too.

Unless something urgent arises, this may be my last letter to you. I'm not sure either of Phoebe's address. Bobby remembered that she lived on Greenwood Avenue, so I'm sending this there. Here's hoping for its safe arrival – and yours.

Lovingly, longingly,
Ken *

Wednesday morning, June 20, 1928
Philadelphia to Williamsport

Special Delivery – 12¢. Ken has acquired the correct street address for Caryl's friend Phoebe – 407 Glenwood Avenue – so he writes again.

My precious Caryl,

The briefest bit of a note to assure you as to train times & wish you a pleasant journey. Oh, honey, it's glorious to think you're starting on your way to me. The Reading 4:40 will give me time to reach the Terminal from the office. Or, if easier, the Pennsy Buffalo Flier at 7:55 will be satisfactory. Suit yourself, and we'll let our attendance at the Country Club be decided by your wishes and your arrival time. Remember, all my love is guiding you, protecting you.

Happily, hastily,
Ken *

Wednesday evening, June 20, 1928
Williamsport to Philadelphia

My dearest,

Your Special awaiting my arrival here. Such a dear as you are! Other letter here, too. No time now, or this will not reach you tomorrow. But coming on the 4:40 Reading. Oh, Honey! See you then.

Your very own Lady

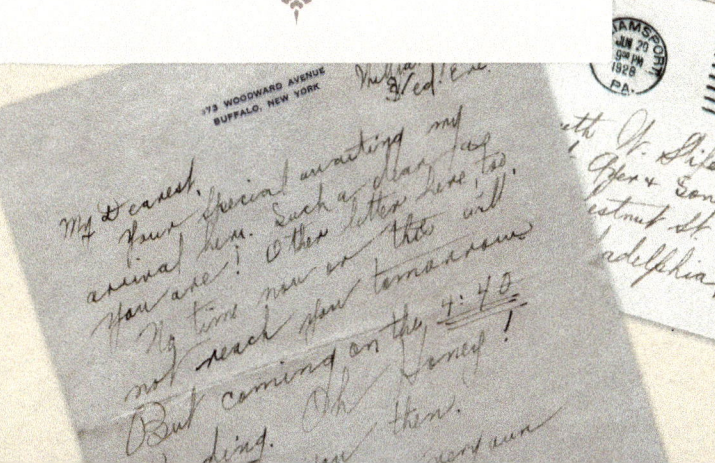

Caryl stayed at the Slifers' home in Woodbury from Thursday, June 21, to Tuesday, July 10, 1928.

Thursday afternoon, July 12, 1928, Philadelphia to Buffalo

My precious Caryl,

When I left you Tuesday, I hurried to the office and set right to work on my American Magazine page. I labored manfully most of the day, and by 4 P.M. it was ready to send off to Mr. Cecil. I'm afraid it wasn't quite up to standard, for I wrote mechanically, in a sort of half-daze, dreaming of your dear, lovely self and the joyous hours we had together. There are nine New Haven Clocks ticking away on my desk. I must dig in and write 3 half-pages, Saturday Evening Post. Rush job. Wish me luck. Entirely new series of clocks.

Yesterday I worked all day to complete six "Canada Dry" advertisements. In the evening, Len wanted some coaching for the tennis tournament, so we played singles & doubles together. When we reached home, Jean Mathews was there with Bobby. Ice cream and bridge till bedtime. We brought "our" mattress down, so the girls can sleep on the porch.

The savings fund possibilities are as follows. I can withdraw $203.64 (my balance Jan. 1), and retain my membership in good standing, losing however ½ the profits for 1928 (about $50). Or I can withdraw everything and begin as a new member, losing all profits for 1928. In that event, I'd receive on Sept. 1 approximately $302.84. The first possibility seems best, if we can make it reach. The perfect way would be to wait (if we only could) till Jan. 1, when we'd have about $500, and could withdraw it without penalty. Time yet to think it over.

It seems strange to start writing letters again. So easily did I slip into the habit of coming home to you in the evening that I still think of you as waiting for me with a happy smile and a kiss – I half-expect to see you even yet. It was the most natural thing in the world to me, while you were with us, honey. Now the act of writing destroys those precious illusions. I'll have to concur with your suggestion that we write less frequently. Since we have so much to do, and since there's so little time left, I suppose it's the most sensible course. If only the silences don't get too unendurable! But only two months more, and dreams shall become realities! *

All my love to you, Ladysweet

Ken *

Around July 12, 1928, Buffalo to Buffalo

Caryl sent the following undated note to her close friend Vera Herrick, also from Buffalo, who had just graduated from Bucknell.

> Our wedding date is set at last, in fair or rainy weather,
>
> When Ken and I shall plight our troth, and start life's way together.
>
> At Central Park* we hope 'twill be, in early evening time.
>
> And this is just a special note to ask you thus, in rime,
>
> If you will Maid of Honor be, in tuck or flounce or frill –
>
> Just so you're there to stand with me. Please say you can and will.
>
> Caryl
>
> [*Central Park Baptist Church in Buffalo]

July 15, 1928, Buffalo to Buffalo

A card bearing Vera's Herrick's response to Caryl is dated July 15, 1928.

> Dearest Caryl,
>
> Your little note, so sweetly writ, has given me great pleasure.
>
> And this is just to wish for you gladness and joy without measure.
>
> I know the day of which you speak will be both fair and clear;
>
> For with such two as bride and groom, no clouds would dare draw near.
>
> To stand with you, I'd love it, and Maid of Honor be,
>
> In flounce or frill, just as you wish – I'll do it with great glee.
>
> Vera

Friday afternoon, July 13, 1928
Philadelphia to Buffalo

My own Caryl,

Little but love to send this afternoon. It seems incredible you've been gone only four days, dear. It's hard to realize we've laid our wedding plans and paid for part of our furniture. Is it possible we're to be each other's for always – less than eight weeks hence? The joy I've had so recently – holding you close, caressing you, feeling your life almost fused with mine, learning the depth and wonder of your love – all this has made me eager for the still fuller companionship marriage is to bring us. Oh, Ladysweet, I do love you – deeply, unutterably, infinitely!

Last evening Len played tennis against Bobby, while I played with Mr. Holmes. My game was going well, and I took a hard-fought set 6-3, and two more games of another, when he had to stop to go to a meeting of the Board of Education. If I could have held the pace and beaten him, I'd have been much closer to the top of the ladder than I've ever been. But I s'pose my chance will come again. A bit of reading, and bed in good time.

Loving you always,
Ken!

Sunday evening, July 15, 1928, Woodbury to Buffalo

Sweetheart,

It was good to hear of your safe and uneventful trip home. I shall be happy when "coming home" for you will mean coming to me – and these long train rides alone are ended for all time! Now that you are home, honey, I'm hoping you'll take the finest sort of care of yourself. Never until this visit did I appreciate how little reserve strength and energy you had to spare. Now I'm honestly alarmed, precious mine. We've dreamed of our Someday so long that we just can't let anything spoil it. You must be well and fit for it, dear heart!

If the apartment at Kokos's is still empty, I'll snap it up about August 15th and start getting it ready for occupancy. It's such fun planning and dreaming

I've made out a tentative list for invitations and announcements. I'll just ask for announcements, for very few of the people I invite will be able to come all the way to Buffalo, and an invitation is little more than a request for a present. There is a large group that should receive some notice, but upon whom I have no claim. Men like Mr. Batten, Mr. Cecil, Mr. Lewis, with whom my contact is friendly, but purely business. I can hardly think of asking them for presents. As my list stands now, there are 24 invitations and 52 announcements; it includes perhaps eight that may appear in yours. I included the Bucknell Alumni Monthly, and Delta Sigma, which you may have thought of. In a few days, when everything is complete, I'll dig out the names and addresses, and send them to you. [Both Ken's and Caryl's invitation/announcement lists are preserved.]

It's getting late, honey, and I must to get to bed if I'm to be ready for Sept. Mother and Bobby send their love. Added to all that I send, it's likely to overwhelm you!

Ken   *———*

Monday, July 30, 1928, Stanley House, Lake Joseph, Ontario, Canada to Woodbury

An envelope (letter missing), addressed to Ken, is postmarked July 30, 1928, Stanley House, Ontario. Caryl was in Canada vacationing with her parents at Stanley House on Lake Joseph, Muskoka.

Tuesday, July 31, 1928, Philadelphia to Lake Joseph, Muskoka, Ontario, Canada

Precious mine,

Perhaps the gods of Advertising will forgive me for neglecting them and taking time I can ill afford from my work to write to such a lovely Lady. I'm sure they'd understand if they could see you, know you. I do love you so!

My biggest news is sure to please you. On our way back from the Club last night, Bobby wanted a lemon Coke – so naturally we went to Kokos's for Cokes! When the older brother brought our orders, I reminded him that if the apartment were still empty by the middle of August, I'd be around to do business. Just as we were ready to leave, he came over to say three couples wanted the apartment for September, but that the others had children, and he preferred to rent it to us.

Since I'm willing to take it August 15, only two weeks away, he'll waive that time & let us have it the whole month for half rent. That way, he can tell the other prospects the apartment is taken, and we can start moving in our furniture & fixing up at any time. It seemed a decent compromise to end our uncertainty, and I snapped him up on it. I'll take him a check for $22.50 tonight and start measuring for curtains, cupboards, etc., as soon as possible.

Your printer's proofs arrived yesterday morning. I returned them in the afternoon. They're unlike any I've ever seen but were tasteful, and I'm sure will be altogether satisfactory. I ventured to change the announcement slightly, in the manner indicated, having verified my first opinion by reference to two social handbooks.

FROM (Awkward, uneven)

>have the honor of
>announcing the mariage of their daughter
>Caryl Rushton

TO (Smoother, balanced)

>have the honor to announce
>the marriage of their daughter
>Caryl Rushton

Perhaps he won't make a correction at <u>my</u> suggestion, but it is simplified by the fact that he has to respace for the omitted "r" in marriage.

I'm playing tennis tonight with the fellow who trounced me at Haddonfield two weeks ago. He's just enough better than I to make for interesting tennis.

That's all I have time or paper to tell you 'ceptin' I love you, adore you, want you always,

K *

Many letters from Ken to his "Precious Caryl" during the month of August bear no salutation. Since most of them were typed in his Philadelphia office, it is likely Ken ceased beginning with terms of endearment because, with a messenger standing at his desk, he frequently had to yank the paper from his typewriter in order to start or finish a "rush order" assignment.

This letter conveys the news that Ken and Caryl have their own apartment at last! Great exhuberance and not a little angst surround the month-long preparations in what is to become their first home together. They have decided this larger apartment will be worth $45 a month. It is conveniently located at #5 Curtis Avenue, a one-block-long street connecting Broad Street – Woodbury's main north-south thoroughfare – with the town's railroad station. This apartment, over Kokos Bros.' store in the town center, has no available yard. However, everything the newlyweds will need is within walking distance – shopping, Ken's commuter train, his mother's house (about seven blocks in the opposite direction), and their church, only one block away.

Wednesday, August 1, 1928, Philadelphia to Stanley House Muskoka, Ontario, Canada

First and foremost, at last our apartment is ours! No more advertising for "Kokos Bros." No more anxious watching for us. I turned over a check to the elder brother last evening, and he surrendered the key to me! Whee! Whoops! Oh, honey-girl, it gave me a tremendous thrill to stalk through the bare and empty rooms with a feeling of pride and possession. Everything is fresh and clean, the bathroom sparkling white! The place has its limitations, but it does seem made to order for us – to start our new life together.

Len accompanied me on an inspection tour, the first he'd seen the place, and liked it very much. The lights had been turned off while the apartment was empty, but we borrowed a flashlight from Mr. Kokos and measured for curtains. There are double windows in each of the four rooms, an extra one in the living room, and one in the bedroom closet, making ten in all. Each is exactly 32" wide and 54" deep – inside measurement. Our 9' x 12' rug is just the right size. It will fit nicely and leave a clear floor space of 2½' or 3' all around the edge. In all the rooms, the floor is stained and finished only four feet from the wall. We'll have to get a full-sized rug for the bedroom, or else finish the rest of the floor.

I think we ought to pay cash to Mr. Focer when the furniture is delivered. Then he'll be all the more ready to get us anything else we need. At your convenience, plan to send more money.

Last evening I played the chap who trounced me in the Haddonfield tournament, and managed to win a fast, exciting match from him 8-6, 7-5. It was as good tennis as I ever produced, and compensated somewhat for the previous defeat.

A note from Gert is enclosed. Now all our wedding party have accepted – except Rolland. Oh, Ladysweet, I'm loving you so, hungering with all my heart to be your very own

Ken *

Friday afternoon, August 3, 1928, Philadelphia to Stanley House Ontario, Canada

I'm laboring diligently on ten advertisements for a prepared pancake flour and maple syrup, marketed in the Middle West by Robb-Ross Company, and on five advertisements for Frute-Gel, a fruit-flavored gelatin dessert made by the same company. I will be quite a domestic science expert before I'm through, what with this stuff, tea, seasoning, and spices!

Last evening I ran a Treasure Hunt for my Sunday School class, finishing off with games, ice cream, and cake. This is the last time for the present outfit, and I'm glad of it. I wish there were no more to come, for I'm tired of trying to teach the undisciplined kids one has to handle in this generation. I wanted to quit at the end of the first year, & I'm even more disgusted now. I s'pose I'll hang on, but if it weren't for you and Mother, I'd never be doing anything of the sort.

Mother has some assorted covers for us, and I can get splendid new ones through the house here, from our client, the Old Town Woolen Mills of Guilford, Maine. It takes only two weeks for them to come from the factory, and we can make our selections together at leisure.

Tonight the House of David baseball team plays at Woodbury. They are good ball players and sideshow curiosities as well, with their long matted hair and beards. Several of their players have been offered big league contracts, which they refused because of religious vows.

Can you feel my love across the miles, Sweetheart? There's so much of it for you. I'm adoring you always,

Ken *

Monday evening, August 6, 1928
Stanley House, Ontario, Canada
to Woodbury

This postcard pictures Stanley House, a two-story lakefront inn on a wooded hillside.

Just a card this time, 'cause it's almost mail time, & I'll tell you all about it in a letter tomorrow.

X = M & F's room; XX = My room.

Summer house is just at left of flagpole.

May go home Sat. or wait till Mon.

Anyway, write no more here. Till next time –

Love

C.

Tuesday P.M., August 14, 1928, Philadelphia to Buffalo

Today started off all wrong, and I've been behind ever since. Yesterday afternoon, the assistant production manager gave me a rush order on "Canada Dry" – for The Wall Street Journal. Copy absolutely had to be in New York this morning, which meant I was to write it at home last night so I could phone it over today. I was glad to do it, for the advertisement needed wasn't over long, and I'm glad to keep up connections with an account as large as "Canada Dry."

As the express roared out of Woodbury this morning, I realized the copy I'd painfully prepared and carefully packed in my satchel was still at home. I hopped off the train in Camden, boarded another back to Woodbury, and rushed out to the house. Caught a bus to Phila., hurried to the office, and phoned the copy to New York. Fortunately, it was on time and got an immediate approval. But wasn't it a stupid stunt start to finish? I'm irritated and disgusted with myself.

Last night Mother and I drove to Pitman to see Mr. Focer and to make two appointments for Haydn White and an artist at Ayer who was married recently. (With all the customers I'm taking him, we ought to get a discount on our furniture!) I told Mother about the four chairs and table set in walnut we'd seen, and she said she'd like to give us something like that, or anything we want of the sort. With a new rug given us, we could afford something like our $29 set of table and chairs, and have our dining room more nearly on the plane of our living room and bedroom. The dining-room-of-all-work will be the first a visitor sees, the one where we'll spend a great deal of our own time. Then, with your one overstuffed chair, my desk chair, four new ones, and the suits we already have, we ought to get along nicely. Not to mention stools in the kitchen and bath!

I made arrangements with Mr. Focer, too, to have our own furniture delivered next Monday. I would have planned it for the latter part of this week, but we're going down to the shore (Stone Harbor) for the whole weekend (our last vacation as one family). Besides, if we are to have small rugs in the bedroom, I'll have to finish the floor all over with stain and varnish before the furniture is moved in.

Oh sweetheart mine, it's been a hectic day – and then I'm stirred further by the thought that our Someday is only three weeks off! Perhaps you can understand the excitement and the tension I'm working under. My Lady, I love you, and I'm so very eager to be your own

Ken *

Thursday afternoon, August 16, 1928, Philadelphia to Buffalo

I'm sorry I had no time to write yesterday. I was busy, and I'm likely to be even more so during the next two weeks. Besides several New Haven advertisements, I must get out the entire Dixon campaign for 1929! The copy order came through with a finish date of September 15, allowing a month for it. But when I explained I'd be away for two of those weeks, the powers decided I must finish it before I leave! So now the order is dated September 1 – only two weeks away. It's going to keep me humping hard – particularly with all the outside distractions. Even when I'm busiest, tho, I'll get letters to you somehow. There's so much we must talk over.

Even before your letter, I had decided to stain the bedroom floor myself, so I bought a pint of Golden Oak varnish/stain. I intend to apply one coat this evening and another tomorrow night. This way it will have the whole weekend to dry before any furniture is put on it.

Your suggestion about the hooks in the hall is good. I'll get a long board, paint it white to match the woodwork, then screw it to the wall to set hooks in. Another thing: I'd feel much safer with a good tumbler lock guarding our goods while we're roaming around the Adirondacks; the smaller key is much handier in the pocket, and the self-closing latch is a convenience. I think a small refrigerator can be put in the corner of the kitchen. We'll not need more than a 50-pound ice capacity. That leaves room for a table and closet space above.

"Refrigerator" here means a non-electric icebox. The one Ken and Caryl chose is listed at $11.75 on the September 27 receipt from W. F. Focer Furniture, showing nine items and a 10% cash discount.

When your Father sees our new bus, and understands the difference in the local service, he'll appreciate Mother's choice. The Chevrolet is roomier than a Ford, much better looking, and will go altogether far enough and fast enough for her purposes. One of the chiefest factors in the decision: We couldn't have gotten a Ford delivered in time for us to come to Buffalo.

I hope you're getting the invitations out, honey. Three weeks ahead is the conventional time, and we're well inside that now. (I've been studying "Weddings" in 2 social handbooks!)

Now I can only say that I love you – and then stop short. But I'll never stop adoring you.

Ken *

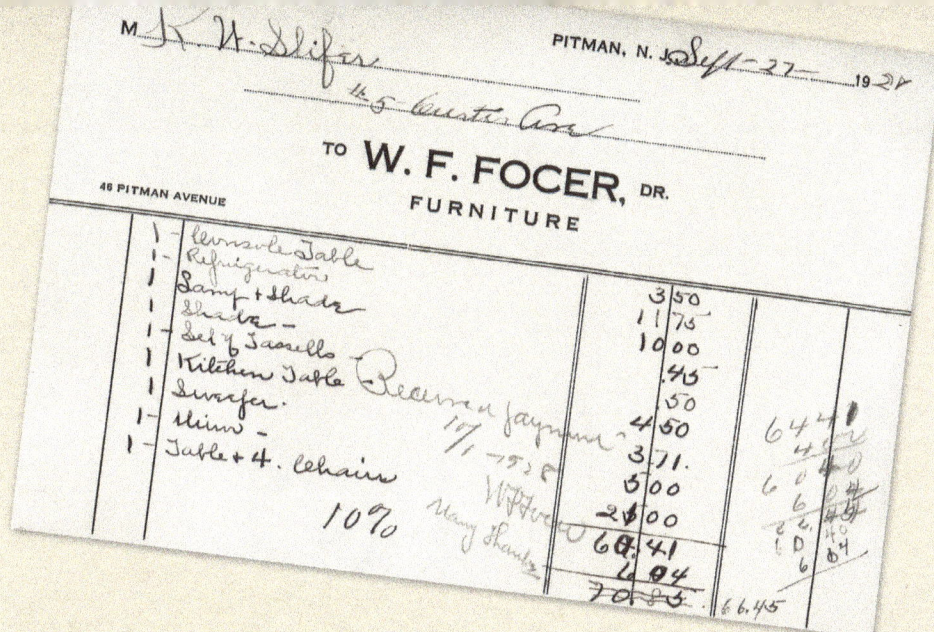

Friday afternoon, August 17, 1928, Philadelphia to Buffalo

How splendid of the Duttons [Caryl's Pennsylvania relatives] to send us a complete silver service! Perhaps you can have your own order cancelled. But if we do get two sets of silver, we won't need to buy any for everyday use, and we can be stylish all the time!

After atrocious tennis last evening, I donned old clothes, and took the necessary tools up to Our Apartment, to stain the floor. When I opened the can of finish, I found that the stupid clerk had given me Dark Oak, instead of the Golden Oak I asked for. We decided Mother would buy the proper stuff today, and Bobby would put on one coat for me this morning. Then I may be able to add another coat late tonight, or early tomorrow morning. That's the only way we can apply two coats before the furniture is moved in on Monday.

I had to pull this out of the machine to write some copy, and there's no use starting another sheet. Remember only that I'm thinking of you, loving you so!

Ken *
P.S. 4:49 P. M. CAME THE RAISE!

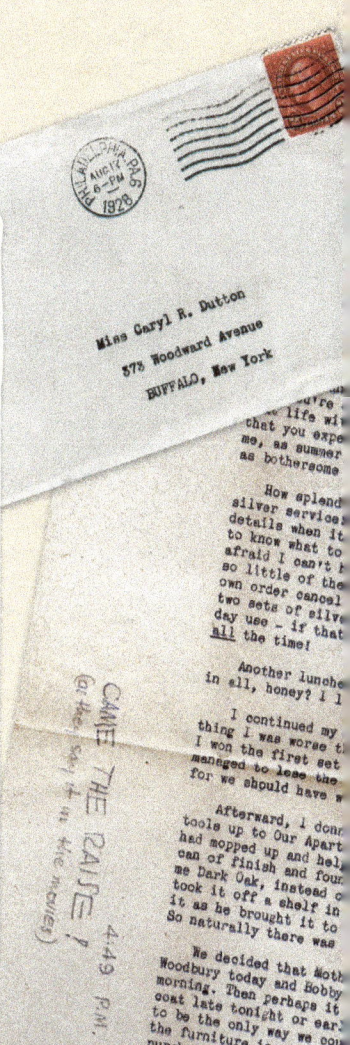

Monday afternoon, August 20, 1928, Philadelphia to Buffalo

These are fearfully busy days. Friday, in a business way, was about the most encouraging day I've ever had. Three reports came to my desk. One on Pancake Flour and Syrup, five advertisements, "Okay without change, client very much pleased"; one on Frute-Gel, same story, five ads okay, client pleased; AND a report on the 21 advertisements I wrote in such a hurry for Southern Baking Company, saying that the client was delighted! Nor was there a single change in all the copy – the biggest campaign I've prepared yet. Then, the raise!

I opened my envelope a week ago and found $35. I was expecting $40 and didn't want to say anything until I'd had time to investigate. Mr. Lewis was occupied all week with conferences, and it wasn't until late Friday that I was able to see him. He was hurrying to leave on vacation and signing checks all the time I talked to him. He'd forgotten the details of our conference last spring but said that if he had promised me $40, of course I'd get it, that he had a taxi waiting, and that I should come see him as soon as I got back to the office after vacation. I'd like to have $40 now, but so long as it is coming, we can get along for a few more weeks. It is a delicate matter for me to press. I was almost afraid to go to him, though I'm very glad I did.

My ushers' presents arrived on Friday, also. They were discounted 45%, much more than I dared hope. Incidentally, Rolland has never accepted my invitation to serve as best man.

On Friday, Mother bought shellac for the bedroom floor. Bobby put on the first coat, and since it dried quickly, I applied the second that evening. The result will be quite satisfactory.

The furniture is to be delivered today. What a thrill that will be! Mother was going to deposit your check for me this morning, so I can pay Mr. Focer in full tonight. Thank you for the money, dear. I think it will cover everything, and I'll render a strict accounting.

We had a pleasant weekend at the shore. I'm pink today, and the back of my neck is pretty tender, but I'm not badly burned – as I was last year.

John Frazer's invitation arrived this morning, and we admired it together. I still find it hard to believe that my name is on it. Just before lunch, Al Purks called to thank me for his and offer congratulations.

Tomorrow I'm going to get your wedding ring! Thank you for the sample you sent for your engagement ring size. This little brass ring will do nicely.

Yes'm, it is customary for the bride and groom to exchange gifts, but since we are giving ourselves, each to the other, and since that gift is priceless, anything else would seem unnecessary. Let's hope no one asks to see the "bride's gift," or the "groom's gift"!

I think this is about the wildest missive I've ever sent. I can't remember when I have typed so fast or taken so little time for thought. But there are so many things to do before I can even think of starting to Buffalo, that I'm appalled, dismayed. Only by working at top speed can I hope to finish them. And your letters are bound to suffer. But I'll try to make it all up to you, when at last I'm your very own

Ken *

Tuesday afternoon, August 21, 1928, Philadelphia to Buffalo

Of necessity, dear, this must be another matter-of-fact, business note. Someday, when we're going over our collective letters, we'll have to delete the last chapter. It's too bad that rosy Romance has to yield to prosy Reality.

Of course it will be all right to freight things. I'll have one of our local expressmen collect everything from the freight office and move my own things at the same time – desk, table, bookcase, trunk, etc. That way it can all be done in one grand orgy of moving.

Mother bought 4 baskets of potatoes yesterday, 2 of them for us. The season is at its height, prices are low, and they are the best kind for winter storage. She'll keep them in our cellar, and you can get small quantities as you want them. She arranged, too, to have Marguerite clean the whole apartment before we come back, and will buy us a mop, dustpan, & brush for the purpose.

The prices you quoted for wedding pictures are a bit staggering, honey. I'd like to have a picture of my lovely Lady in her bridal veil, but if you decide against it I shall try to be content. I know that expenses have been fearfully heavy.

The furniture was delivered yesterday. Mr. Focer was sitting on the steps waiting for me as I came up Curtis Avenue from the train. He had put everything in place, and it seemed to be in good condition. I paid him in full and had a remaining bank balance of $8.64, so you can see that your check was just about the right amount.

I had paid for the ushers' presents earlier in the day, and had about $25 in my pocket. Most of that went today for The Ring that is to make you mine! I picked a pattern I think you'll like, and it will harmonize with the other. It's being engraved, and I'm to get it at the end of the week.

Though I'm almost broke, I have the comfortable feeling that I'm free of debt, and most of the things we need are paid for. This week's salary will go for the hat, shoes, & socks. And I bought new pajamas for our honeymoon today! Next Friday, I'll receive 3 weeks' salary all at once, and that will cover rent for a month and our honeymoon, with the Penny Fund added. I still have a tidy sum in the House Fund that is increased each week, and that, added to your reserve (which I hope we'll not need to touch again), should fortify us against any likely emergency. Incidentally, I have five dollars in pennies that should be credited to the Penny Fund. How much does that make us in all? It will be interesting to see how much of our honeymoon it will cover.

There are so many things to talk over that I must have overlooked something. Perhaps you think I've overlooked my love, but I haven't, honey. I hope I can make you understand its depth and strength when I have you in my arms again. Then I shall begin to live it – for you alone.

Wanting you so,
Your Ken *

Wednesday afternoon, August 22, 1928, Philadelphia to Buffalo

I gave Bobby a brief driving lesson last evening (she picks it up very quickly), and then spent the rest of my time sorting out books and getting my bookcase ready to move. Books! Books! I never realized before that I had so many. How many books will you be bringing, honey?

I've had a marked acquisitive instinct all my life, and many things bring memories that make them hard to throw away. But wholesale housecleaning is the best possible thing. I'd never get at it without some such provocation. (Just as Rolland and I used to make a frenzied effort to clean 10 East Wing, with special company coming.)

John Frazer may be my traveling companion. If he is, we must start Friday, for his inflexible conscience won't let him travel on Sunday. [John, a Quaker, and his brother Grant would become conscientious objectors during World War II.] He'd pay full fare and go by train, rather than waver from his convictions. His constancy is admirable, but it makes things more difficult. I'm not sure I can have Clem's flivver on Friday. And I'm going to be busy almost every minute here at the office, until time to start. Losing a good part of Friday would only add to my burdens. I don't care to drive 500 miles alone, tho. I'm a gregarious soul and prefer congenial company.

I play my semi-final match in the Ayer tournament tomorrow evening. Wish me luck.

Oh, darling mine, I'll be so glad when all the worry and excitement is over and we can settle down just to enjoy each other! I do love you so, my Ladysweet, and I'm wanting you, hungering more for you every day. Less than two weeks now until I am forever your own adoring

Ken *

Sunday evening, August 26, 1928, Woodbury to Buffalo

Precious Lady mine,

On my way home Friday, I bought a Yale lock ($4.25) for our door. Next morning I took Mr. Kircher (carpenter friend from church) to help me attach it. Not till we had the hole bored in the door did we notice the lock parts weren't complete. The things I thought weren't printable! Nothing to do but hop in the car and drive to the city for the rest of it. I justified the trip by stopping at Sears-Roebuck in Camden for a bathroom cabinet. I hope the one I chose ($3.65) will suit you. It will fit in the available space, has 3 shelves, a small drawer, and a largish mirror.

In the afternoon, we finished up with the lock. Then I put the cabinet together, hung it, planned the fixture for the hall coat hooks, and gave the bedroom floor a third coat. (I managed to push everything but the bed against the wall and stained half the floor at a time.)

Shellac and stain cost in all $1.90. I had to spend $1.27 for light bulbs too. With all these items and a couple others, my week's salary looks sick. I'll not be able to get the hat and shoes I need. Guess I'll just have the old ones done over. Had to get a new dress shirt and tie. My full dress is being freshened up and altered slightly ($5.00). Just discovered today that my white vest is tighter and more worn and soiled than I remembered. New vest ($7–$8). And so it goes.

Next week there'll be $105 in the envelope. $45 goes for rent. $10.50 goes into savings fund. I have to put new brake bands in Clem's car and have it overhauled – at least $10. Then $5 to Mother for board, and $3 in church envelopes for the weeks I'll be away. In all, I'll be lucky to have $30 and your ring when I leave here. You'd better draw out all our Honeymoon Fund, and deposit some more money in a checking account, where it will be available if we need it!

It looks now as if I'll arrive Sunday evening, as originally planned. Probably I'll be alone too, for John is stubborn enough in his convictions to go all the way by train – Saturday. I don't relish the prospect of 500 miles by myself.

The receipt for your shipment is carefully tucked away, and I'll handle it promptly when it comes. I don't know about the curtains and rods, but I'll try to get them up. It was good of Rolland to work so hard for us. I appreciate it, and will try to write him tomorrow.

My room is beginning to look bare. I spent the whole afternoon in it, and now my trunk, table, and desk are about ready to be moved.

A great world of love and longing to you, dear,
Ken *

P. S. Sholls were here this afternoon. Their invitation hasn't arrived yet. They came home from vacation and found a "2¢ postage due" notice from Buffalo. They sent a stamp last Tuesday, but have heard nothing since. Mr. Sholl, as a brother Demie, rode me for our Scotch tactics!

Incidentally, he took your picture and a detailed story for his two Camden papers.

Wednesday, August 29, 1928, Philadelphia to Buffalo

Just a hasty note of odds and ends, with a lot of love tucked into it, too.

Lost my finals match last night, 6-2, 6-3, 4-6, 8-6. "Bo" Wood played brilliant tennis. I was lucky enough to catch him on an off day last year. Last night he had everything, and I was on the defensive start to finish. Oh well, I get my name on the cup as runner-up anyway.

I'm sorry you feel so tired, honey. I wish we hadn't attempted all this "pomp and circumstance." It seems an empty pleasure, for the energy it extracts. Mother is tired as well, & she has a double responsibility, what with getting Bobby ready for college, and getting me ready for marriage!

I warned Clem that use of the flivver for the trip to Buffalo and for the honeymoon was the only present we'd accept from him. It seemed the decent thing to do, especially since we'd said the same thing to the Sweets who are providing their Lake George cottage for the honeymoon.

Mr. Kircher has trimmed and beaded a nice piece of board for our row of coat hooks in the hall. I'll get it painted and perhaps put up tonight. Time for the bell, sweetheart, and I must hurry home. Forget my hurried, hectic letters, and remember only that I love you dearly.

Wanting you so,
Ken *

Rev. and Mrs. Elwood Herbert Dutton
request the honor of your presence
at the marriage of their daughter
Caryl Rushton
to
Mr. Kenneth Wilson Slifer
on Tuesday, the fourth of September
One thousand nine hundred twenty-eight
at seven-thirty o'clock
Central Park Baptist Church
Buffalo, New York

At Home
after October first
Woodbury, New Jersey

Reception
immediately after the ceremony
at three-seventy-three Woodward Avenue

Please respond

Thursday evening, August 30, 1928, Woodbury to Buffalo

My precious Caryl,

Though it's hard to realize, this is probably the last letter I'll write you for a long, long time. I wish I could make it so loving and eloquent that you'd treasure it always! You deserve such a letter for the dear that you've been.

A terrific thunderstorm tonight blew out the lights, keeping us inactive awhile, and preventing me from doing many of the errands I'd planned. When the rain slackened, I sallied forth anyway.

The freight consignment you started long ago has not arrived. I left the receipt, apartment key, and money for the expressman with Mr. Pierpont. He'll take care of it promptly. Our rent is paid for Sept. (!), and I also paid for having the flivver overhauled. With new brake bands, oil change, wash, and going over, charges were only $6.85. I gave our coat rack a second coat of white paint, and hope to put it up tomorrow. Touched up some spots on the bathroom cabinet.

Geddes says he invited Aunt Jennie to ride up with him on Monday! John still refuses to see the light. He doesn't want to bother you and will go to a hotel. Chick is coming by train with Clem & Bec and will stay with them at a hotel. Gert is touring in Canada and will be in Buffalo for the wedding. He won't expect entertainment. Can you substitute Geddes for John and Chick? He has entertained me so often.

Don't expect me Sunday evening until you see me. I have no idea when I'll arrive, though I'll push the flivver hard to get to you! Loads of love from

Your adoring, sleepy
Ken *

P. S. Have you told your Father that I'll need instruction in contraceptive methods? Please do.

Epilogue

On Tuesday, September 4, 1928, Caryl Rushton Dutton and Kenneth Wilson Slifer were wed at Central Park Baptist Church in Buffalo, New York, at 7:30 p.m., with a reception afterward at the Duttons' home at 373 Woodward Avenue. Caryl's sole attendant was her good friend Vera Herrick. The next day's chatty story in the *Buffalo Times* was crammed with more than a dozen mistakes, among them misspellings of names and hometowns of family and friends, like "Roland" for Rolland, and "Louisburg" for Lewisburg. This coverage must have distressed the families. Some quotations are included here, but in order not to confuse readers, I've corrected errors. I have found just two wedding photos, both showing only the bride.

> The ceremony was performed by the Reverend E. Herbert Dutton, father of the bride, assisted by the pastor of the church, the Reverend S. G. Reynolds. The bride was given in marriage by Mr. Lewis R. Dutton of Philadelphia [Herbert's cousin], who was best man at the wedding of her father and mother. The bride looked very lovely, in the ivory satin gown worn by her mother. She carried an immense armful of white roses, and was preceded down the aisle by Pauline Dutton, in the daintiest canary frock smocked in blue. Pauline carried a basket of garden flowers, which she scattered in the bride's pathway. Miss Vera Herrick attended as maid of honor, wearing a bouffant gown of orchid taffeta.
>
> Rolland Nelson Dutton, brother of the bride, was best man, and the ushers were T. Burns Drum of Lewisburg, Pa.; Edward W. Carter, Pitman, N. J.; Walter G. Reiman, Buffalo; and Roy K. Clement, Woodbury, N. J.

> The church was effectively decorated with masses of roses, delphinium, and palms; the center of the church was reserved for the families of the bride and bridegroom, and the entire auditorium was filled with her many friends and well-wishers.
>
> After the ceremony, Dr. and Mrs. Dutton held a reception at their home in Woodward Ave. The bride's table was done in white, centered with a white bell under which her parents had stood for their wedding ceremony. Mrs. Dutton wore an attractive gown of peach georgette, embroidered; and Mrs. Robert Slifer was gowned in floral georgette over satin.
>
> Mr. and Mrs. Slifer will reside in Woodbury, N. J.

The marriage of Ken Slifer and Caryl Dutton lasted sixty-three years, all of them in one location or another in Woodbury, New Jersey. To chronicle the many significant events the Slifers shared during those years is impossible, so I've simply chosen some that are especially memorable for me.

Ken held on to his job with the N. W. Ayer & Son advertising agency in Philadelphia through the Great Depression, which began the year after their wedding. However, he once told me with a smile, "In 1933, I took my third pay cut – the same day we learned you were on the way." Since reading their letters, I've wondered how much those pay cuts might have been.

Ken kept his promise to himself never to make his home far from his mother, Edna. She lived independently in her house, just blocks from Ken and Caryl, until she suffered a stroke in 1964; she died shortly thereafter, at 85. And during her father's retirement, Caryl was pleased to welcome her parents to Woodbury, where they lived out their lives among family. Herbert died in 1944, at 72. Mabel spent the rest of her life ministering as a Church Visitor for Central Baptist; she lived to be 88 and died in 1967. As for Attie (Eliza Harris), I remember an aura of kindness about that sweet woman who became a beloved part of the Dutton household in 1901, when she was only 12. She survived a stroke in 1928 and lived on into the 1940s.

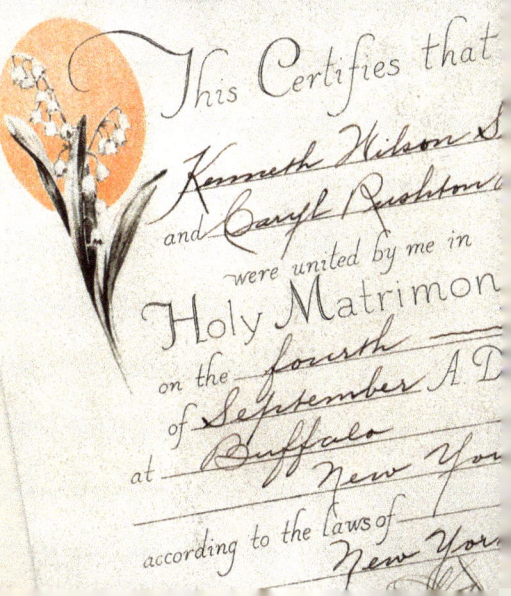

Caryl's brother Rolland, following in his father's footsteps as a Baptist minister, continued preaching and teaching into his 80s. Ken's sister Bobby, in later life, was active in volunteering, particularly in hospitals, and was a renowned advocate for stroke victims and their families. Both Rolland and Bobby married, had three children each, survived their spouses, and lived into their 90s.

Ken and Caryl's love also produced three children. To the Slifers' great sadness, they could raise only two. Their first son – born between me (1933) and my younger brother, David Kenneth (1938) – died in the hospital shortly after his birth.

As a child, I gradually became aware that not everyone's parents were as terrific as mine. In elementary school in the 1940s, I was a determined tomboy – after all, boys had all the real fun. I insisted on wearing plaid shirts and denim bib overalls every day (except the days I wore my Girl Scout uniform), in an era when girls never wore anything but skirts or dresses. Once, our school principal called my father to alert him that Diane was playing football with the boys during recess. Dad's unfazed reply: "Yes, she does that all the time in our yard, too." Later, as my tomboy phase faded, a close high school friend was warned by her father: "Never – ever – dance with Negro boys." I found such a parental proscription unimaginable.

In the 1940s, when the word "pregnant" could not be uttered in polite company (women were "expecting" or "in a family way"), my friends felt comfortable quizzing my mother about sex, and babies, and what labor pains were like. Thus it seemed only natural that when some of my teenage girlfriends rented a summer cottage at the New Jersey shore for a week, they requested Caryl Slifer as chaperone.

When one friend in my high school did become pregnant, her parents tossed her out of their home. I did not plan to follow her example. But I had to ask my mother how my own parents would react in that situation. I'll never forget her quick response: "Oh, honey – that's when you'd need your family the most!"

Slifer Christmas Letters 1950(top), 1957(middle) & 1967(bottom)

On many occasions, Caryl and Ken provided a home for others' children. Students from India, El Salvador, and Cameroon lived with them for extended periods. Other foreign students were regularly welcomed for shorter visits. Once, a student boarded a bus in Philadelphia with his battered suitcase and, in a thick accent, asked for a ticket to Woodbury. He later reported that the driver, his identity unknown to any of us, responded, "You going to Slifers'?"

Another time a Chinese woman, fleeing her country's Communist régime, was referred to the Slifers by a church agency. Of course they took her in; I'm not sure how many weeks she stayed.

In 1950, Caryl and Ken acquired an entire new family. Six years after the end of World War II, Church World Service was still searching for a sponsor for Jadwiga Motorna, a widow, and her four children – Polish refugees in a European Displaced Persons camp. No one had wanted to take on a non-English-speaking family of five – with no wage earner. By that time, I had started college. But Dave was in junior high, and he had just begun to enjoy being The Only Child, instead of The Kid Brother. Suddenly he had to share his home and his parents with Zofia (14), Gregory (11), Tamara (10), Edmund (4), and their mother Jadwiga. The years of the Motornas' struggles to learn English, to survive, and, for the most part, thrive in this new culture were amazing, as were the Slifers' constant efforts to encourage and support the family. Occasionally, someone joshed that Ken and Caryl just wanted more deductions for their tax return. Actually, the Motornas never qualified as Slifers' dependents.

When Ken died 46 years later, at the age of 92, Zofia sat with our family at his memorial service. Suddenly she handed me two typed pages – a tribute she had written to him. Composed in beautiful English, it began with the Thanksgiving Day four Slifers had driven to Ellis Island in a Plymouth station wagon, meeting and taking home five strangers – with their few worldly goods – who spoke only Polish. Zofia insisted that I read the essay for her, because she couldn't, without breaking down. I complied. But it was tough.

The Slifers were tireless volunteers in Woodbury's Central Baptist Church, and beyond. Caryl served two years as president of the American Baptist Churches of New Jersey and worked on national American Baptist boards. She also spent years fundraising for Ellen Cushing Junior College, a small Baptist school in Pennsylvania that has since folded. Ken taught his Sunday School class, the "CHAIN GANG," until the junior high boys he started with in 1926 were becoming grandfathers. Meanwhile, Caryl taught a women's "Tri-Sigma" class ("Stewards of Sunshine and Service") almost as long.

Ken (back row, center) and the CHAIN GANG in their 12th year, April 17, 1938

In the 1950s, Ken and Caryl temporarily combined their Sunday School classes for a series on religions of the world. They invited representatives of different faith communities – Buddhist, Muslim, Hebrew, Mormon, Quaker, and others – to speak at these sessions. When a layman from a nearby Roman Catholic church was forbidden by his priest to enter a Baptist church, the Slifers moved the class to a friend's home next door for that Sunday, and the interfaith discussions continued as planned.

When Ken organized a fifty-year Chain Gang reunion, in 1976, former class members returned to Woodbury from all over the country. The class, their name explained as CHRIST HAS ALL I NEED – GOD ALWAYS NEEDS GENTLEMEN, also included two brothers whose last name was Link (front row: John Link, second from left; Joe Link, second from right). Their name had been shortened when the family immigrated from Hungary after World War I, and Caryl met them when she volunteered through a church program to tutor newcomers in English.

In 1998, Joe Link unexpectedly appeared at Ken's memorial service in Woodbury. I was amazed. Joe had long since retired to Florida. But when I thanked him for making such a journey, he replied simply, "Diane, I couldn't NOT come." Soon thereafter, Joe, a graduate of Bucknell University, endowed a permanent Kenneth W. Slifer Memorial Scholarship there.

After Ken and Caryl both relinquished regular teaching responsibilities, there came a time when Central Baptist couldn't find leaders for the high school fellowship — so a poll of the youth themselves was taken for suggestions of possible names. The young people asked for the Slifers, who were then in their seventies.

Ken and Caryl cared about the whole world. They were always working to improve interracial and interfaith understanding, when few others were doing so in our small town.

Caryl regularly moderated a "Panel of American Women," which included one Protestant, one Catholic, one Jewish, and one African-American representative. They presented their program to civic and church groups and women's clubs by telling their personal stories, and then answering audience questions. Once when I was in attendance, a panelist rose to introduce herself. She opened to a roar of laughter simply by giving her name and then adding, "I have nine children, so you know which church I represent."

Caryl introduced The Green Circle Program to Woodbury elementary schools. This program, originated by Quakers in Philadelphia, eventually spread across the country. Volunteers — who might be adults, or church youth groups, or Girl Scout troops — are recruited and trained to visit classrooms armed with a flannelboard, a story, and a variety of colorful felt figures. The figures represent people with religious or ethnic differences, or physical disabilities, who often get shut out of our circles. (You — the child — are the person at the center of the circle.) As listeners identify with the unfolding story and begin to decide they need to include those people inside their circle, the green (the color of growth) circle on the board starts to expand. And it keeps growing. By the time the program ends, the circle, full of people, covers the whole flannelboard, and class

members are all wearing their own green circles, which are made by twisting and pinning on a green pipe cleaner. Each child is encouraged to wear the green circle home and to share the story of its origin. The Slifers faithfully supported Fellowship House in Philadelphia. A couple of their dogeared books I especially prize today were bought at Fellowship House dinners, when the author, a young preacher, had been the speaker. One flyleaf reads, "Best Regards – Martin Luther King, Jr."

The Gloucester County Good Will Council – an interracial, interfaith group, including some mixed-race couples, who met regularly for a fellowship supper and work on whatever areas of discrimination they could tackle – was launched in Woodbury by the Slifers and friends from other churches, both white and African-American. Ken often spoke to Rotary, Kiwanis, and other service clubs, stressing equal opportunities in jobs and education and housing. Not every group was particularly welcoming. But at least they listened.

Sometime during the 1950s, the Slifers rented the apartment over their garage to a young African-American chemist from a nearby oil refinery and his wife who had not been able to find suitable housing in the area. Not until years later did I learn that some folks on our block began referring to our street as "The N——r Neighborhood."

Ken, David, and Diane, 1939

Always concerned for education, the Slifers quietly mailed personal checks, helping at least eighteen youth to attend college. Most of them were the first in their families to do so.

The Slifers were constantly raising funds for good causes. During my growing-up years, our screened-in porch always was piled with army-surplus duffle bags, in which Caryl packed good used clothing she collected from friends. Periodically, she mailed the duffle bags to Mather School in South Carolina, run by Northern Baptists for poor African-American girls. The school sold the garments inexpensively in their thrift store to students and nearby residents.

Ken's advertising skills were much in demand. For years, he solicited friends and neighbors for countless causes, and he headed fund drives for:

- A home built for Woodbury's only double amputee of World War II and his family.
- Radio Free Europe (in the 1960s broadcasting to 80 million people behind the Iron Curtain).
- Central Baptist Church (a new building at a new location, and later an addition).

- Gloucester County (N.J.) YMCA (a new and larger facility that would include the county's first integrated public pool).
- The Gloucester County (N.J.) United Way (inaugurated by Ken).
- Bucknell University (many campaigns).
- Delta Sigma fraternity at Bucknell University (now Delta Upsilon).
- Peddie School in Hightstown, N.J. (the Baptist-related prep school that ran Camp Kanuka and where Ken was later a board member).
- Habitat for Humanity International (builds and repairs houses with people in need all over the world, using volunteer labor and donations. Ken provided the organization's first logo and letterhead [below] following its founding in 1975.)

I took a snapshot of both Slifers, then near 80, working on renovating an old house with our Salem County, N.J., Habitat for Humanity affiliate. At the same time, they were meeting with Woodbury officials to help launch a Gloucester County Habitat affiliate.

In 1979, I received an unforgettable Christmas gift from my parents: a check for a Habitat house, to be constructed in the jungle village of Ntondo, Zaire (now the Democratic Republic of Congo). The cost of one house in Zaire at that time was $2,000. I've never seen it, but I know it's there, built by our friend, volunteer Patricia Clark.

Ken and Caryl always shared an enjoyment of sports, although she never had Ken's boundless energy. Their first love was tennis. For their 50th wedding anniversary, in 1978, we surprised them by gathering relatives from everywhere for an all-day, intergenerational tennis party on our farm's tennis court. Two years later, when they were both 75, Caryl and Ken won a match against a couple of their younger friends, and he announced gleefully, "You've just lost to a 150-year-old doubles team!"

Until 1947, the vacant lot behind the Slifers' Woodbury home had been our World War II "Victory Garden." However, it was just wide enough to build a standard tennis court, and in 1947, Ken achieved his long-held wish. Years of matches with family and friends followed. Some were casual, others serious. One summer evening, walking home from his train as usual, Ken headed for our back door.

Slifers on the tennis court behind their home, 1947

Slifer Christmas card, 1967

Passing four total strangers playing on the court, he called out politely, "I have a tennis date here at 6:30." He got a startled reply: "But – this is The Texaco Tournament!"

Ken decided to retire at age 60 in 1966, exactly 40 years after his first day at N. W. Ayer & Son. He planned to do two things he'd long dreamed about: 1) attend art school, and 2) launch a year-round indoor tennis center. Tennis indoors was a fairly new concept at the time. He had to give up his first dream, the Philadelphia College of Art, after one semester. He loved it, but starting Haddonwood Indoor Tennis, located between Haddonfield and Woodbury, was turning out to be a full-time job for him and Caryl alike. There were frequent midnight wake-up calls too, if something set off the burglar alarm, or if there was a plumbing emergency. The Slifers also organized "Haddonwood Tennis Tours" – long-weekend trips to resorts in places like Spain, Portugal, and Bermuda. Ken's courtship letter of May 27, 1928, describes a radio commercial for the "glories of Bermuda." He writes, "My sweet, we just must see it together sometime!" – and more than forty years later, they made it.

Once our whole family – three generations, including Vic's mother, Betty Scott – was able to join the group on one of the winter tennis trips. En route home on the plane, my son – five-year-old Kevin – announced, "When I die, I'm going to Bermuda!"

Their tennis business expanded. But so did the headaches that management entailed. On more than one Thanksgiving, we carried the entire family's dinner 24 miles, from our farm to Haddonwood. The Slifers always gave most of their staff that day off – but lots of players still wanted to come for a tennis workout after their feast. Nearly 20 years after Haddonwood opened, Ken and Caryl finally relinquished that enterprise, and we all heaved a sigh of relief.

Whether or not they were physically together, the Slifers' love affected everything they did. When Caryl was away at a conference or meeting, Ken sometimes tucked tiny, precisely lettered love notes in drawers around the house, for her to find on her return. And once, hugging her on the tarmac as Caryl exited an airplane in Philadelphia, Ken famously cracked one of her ribs with an exhuberant hug.

Caryl died in our Salem, New Jersey, farmhouse on September 12, 1991, with Ken holding tightly to her hand. True to their spirit of generosity and selflessness, she and Ken, who died on December 20, 1997, willed their bodies to the National Institutes of Health's Baltimore Longitudinal Study of Aging at Johns Hopkins medical center, a program in which they had been longtime volunteers.

Ken's irrepressible sense of humor leads me to conclude their story with a smile. In 1930, two years after their wedding, Caryl was in Buffalo visiting her parents. Ken painted her another envelope, enclosed a letter, and even spent 12 cents for Special Delivery.

Loss

A sudden stillness settled on the house.
Upstairs in the back room, the family,
Three generations, gathered by the bed
In farewell to a grandmother much loved.
Fall sunlight in a stream illumined there
The grandfather, who stiffly sat and stared.
Refusing to encompass such a grief,
He gripped more tightly the familiar hand,
Joyfully joined with his own, six decades past.
Each person present breathed each labored breath;
Each struggled to pull in more air, until
No more breaths came. Still no one moved at all.
The nurse sat quietly in the next room.

A moment later, startled eyes looked up
To see their pastor, shepherd to a flock
Spread over many miles, walk through the door.
"How did you know?" There was no time to call.
At first they wondered. Then, of course, they knew.

— Diane C. Slifer Scott

In loving memory of
Caryl Dutton Slifer
(June 26, 1905 – September 12, 1991)
& Kenneth Wilson Slifer
(September 19, 1905 – December 20, 1997)

Diane Caryl Slifer Scott has been
writing since childhood — initially for school publications, then as editor of her high school yearbook, and later for the Bucknell University literary magazine, *Et Cetera*, edited by her classmate Philip Roth. As a freelance writer, she has published articles in a variety of newspapers and magazines, and she edits a newsletter for the accounting firm Warner & Company, CPAs in New Jersey. Diane co-authored three books — with Habitat for Humanity founders Linda and Millard Fuller — to help launch that international affordable-housing organization. And friends enjoy receiving poems written for their special occasions.

A native of New Jersey, Diane and her husband, Victor Scott, both Bucknell graduates with degrees in English literature, spent 45 years raising trees, shrubs, evergreens, dozens of dogs, and three children on their 300-acre farm in the Garden State. The farm, which they sold to The Nature Conservancy, has become a New Jersey Wildlife Management Area and a destination for hikers, hunters, and birdwatchers. Diane and Vic are now retired in Asheville, North Carolina.

• • • • • • • •

Acknowledgments

Flivverin' With You is a book about love. And the lovingkindness of many people has made it possible.

The folks at Blue Blaze Books handled every publishing detail required by the complicated manuscript. Sandy Taccone led a stellar team that included Beth Roth, Becky Taccone, Ed Gifford, and my daughter, Wendy Scott.

Another invaluable member of the Blue Blaze team was my talented and tireless editor Katherine Ward, who provided wisdom, expertise, and another Bucknell connection. She also guided me gently through lengthy phone conferences. Space requirements meant we had to carefully cut, often more than once, from each of the nearly 400 surviving letters, to preserve the integrity of the narrative of my parents' five-year courtship.

The Alumni Office at Bucknell University and especially Isabella O'Neill, Curator of Special Collections/University Archives, dug out photographs and arcane but useful information about Bucknell during the 1920s.

Special thanks go to my ever-lovin' husband Vic, for his faithful encouragement and support through fifty-nine years of marriage, and, particularly during my thirteen years on this project, for his patient acceptance of a mostly cockeyed meal schedule.

I'm enormously grateful to you all.

Colophon

This publication is a production of Blue Blaze Books.

All original illustrations © Kenneth W. Slifer
Author: Diane C. Slifer Scott
Editor: Katherine S. Ward
Creative Director: Sandra L. Taccone
Principal Designer: Beth Ann Roth
Principal Researcher: Rebecca L. Taccone

The body text is set in Berthold Akzidenz Grotesk, with the date headers set in Flirt, a typeface designed by Patrick Griffin. Page folios and letter text is set in Goudy Old Style, with cover and chapter titles set in Odette, a typeface designed by Morris Fuller Benton and Rebecca Alaccari. And finally, Tupelo by Philip Bouwsma is used on the cover art, in the phrase "in Letters" and for the lead-in text on the back cover book synopsis.

Cover and page layouts were created using Adobe InDesign® and Adobe Photoshop®.

Printed by Lightning Source Inc., an Ingram Content Group company

Endnote
[1] Selected photos are reproduced with permission from the Special Collections/University Archives, Bertrand Library, Bucknell University

www.ingramcontent.com/pod-product-compliance
Lightning Source LLC
Chambersburg PA
CBHW061819290426
44110CB00027B/2916